THE FLETCHER JONES FOUNDATION

HUMANITIES IMPRINT

The Fletcher Jones Foundation has endowed this imprint to foster innovative and enduring scholarship in the humanities.

The publisher and the University of California Press
Foundation gratefully acknowledge the generous support
of the Fletcher Jones Foundation Imprint in Humanities.

God Rock, Inc.

God Rock, Inc.

The Business of Niche Music

Andrew Mall

UNIVERSITY OF CALIFORNIA PRESS

University of California Press
Oakland, California

© 2021 by Andrew Mall

Library of Congress Cataloging-in-Publication Data

Names: Mall, Andrew, 1978– author.
Title: God Rock, Inc. : the business of niche music /
   Andrew Mall.
Description: Oakland, California : University of California
   Press, [2021] | Includes bibliographical references and index.
Identifiers: LCCN 2020021309 (print) | LCCN 2020021310
   (ebook) | ISBN 9780520343412 (cloth) | ISBN
   9780520343429 (paperback) | ISBN 9780520974784 (epub)
Subjects: LCSH: Contemporary Christian music—United
   States—History and criticism. | Contemporary Christian
   music—United States—Marketing. | Sound recording
   industry—United States—History. | Market segmentation—
   United States. | Rock music—Religious aspects—
   Christianity.
Classification: LCC ML3187.5 M37 2021 (print) |
   LCC ML3187.5 (ebook) | DDC 782.42/171—dc23
LC record available at https://lccn.loc.gov/2020021309
LC ebook record available at https://lccn.loc.gov/2020021310

28 27 26 25 24 23 22 21
10 9 8 7 6 5 4 3 2 1

This book is dedicated to the memory of Melody Percoco, whose love for music carried us through the brightest and the darkest times.

Contents

List of Illustrations ... ix
Acknowledgments ... xi
Playlists ... xvii

Introduction: Popular Music, Markets, Margins,
and the Curious Case of Christian Music ... 1

PART ONE. CHRISTIAN MUSIC: AN INDUSTRY AND ITS HISTORY

1 "Why Should the Devil Have All the Good Music?"
The Christian Market's Origins ... 31
2 *The Great Adventure*: Commercial Success in the
Christian Record Industry and the Price of Profit ... 67
3 *A Wolf in Sheep's Clothing*? Christian Ethics
Encounter Rock ... 94
4 "Find a Way": Amy Grant and the Christian
Market's Mainstream ... 115

PART TWO. NICHE MUSIC MARKETS: ETHICS, PROFITS, AND RISK

5 *Music to Raise the Dead*: Christian Music and
the Ethics of Style ... 137

6 *Lost in the Sound of Separation*: Resistance at Christian
  Music Festivals 166
7 From Margins to Mainstreams and Back:
  Crossover Cases and Their Markets 194
Conclusion: The Stability of Risk and the Risk of Stability 214

Appendix 1. Discographies 227
Appendix 2. Pop Singles with Christian References (1957–70) 237
Appendix 3. Major Christian Record Labels and Subsidiaries 239
Appendix 4. Successful 1990s-Era Pop Singers' Albums 241
Notes 243
Bibliography 265
Index 277

Illustrations

1. Album cover for Larry Norman's *So Long Ago the Garden* (1973) / *43*
2. "The Jesus Revolution," cover of *Time* magazine, June 21, 1971 / *47*
3. "The Great Jesus Rally in Dallas," cover of *Life* magazine, June 30, 1972 / *50*
4. *CCM* magazine, March 1983, April 1986, and June 1988 / *71*
5. Rez Band performing live in 1987 / *101*
6. Album cover for Amy Grant's *Unguarded* (1985) / *120*
7. Album cover for Amy Grant's *Heart in Motion* (1991) / *125*
8. David Marshall of The Burial performing at Cornerstone Festival 2009 / *143*
9. Demon Hunter / *150*
10. Fanzine ads for Cornerstone festivals in 1989, 1991, and 1994 / *160*
11. Josh Scogin of The Chariot performing at Cornerstone Festival 2010 / *183*
12. Timbre performing at Cornerstone Festival 2010 / *185*
13. David Bazan performing at AudioFeed Festival 2017 / *190*

Illustrations

Acknowledgments

I have been working on this project, in one form or another, for over a decade. There are many friends, colleagues, acquaintances, and loved ones who have been instrumental in supporting and inspiring my research during that time.

First and foremost, Timothy Rommen has consistently encouraged me and this project from its earliest moments through the present day. He was a sounding board for a prospective graduate student considering a conference paper on Christian punk; he later served as the external reader for my dissertation on underground Christian rock. Over beers at the Lamb and Flag in Oxford, we sketched out this book's structure and organization on a napkin together; he later advised me on finding the best press for the project. I could not ask for a better advocate and mentor, and I am proud to know him as a friend and colleague. *God Rock, Inc.* started as a seminar paper and, later, a PhD dissertation at the University of Chicago. My advisor, Travis Jackson, was a key source of critical clarity during my ethnomusicology program. My other committee members, Philip Bohlman and Kaley Mason, also provided timely advice and mentorship. In addition to faculty mentors, my fellow graduate students and our postdocs inspired and pushed me to do my best and most rigorous work; many remain trusted friends and colleagues today: Rachel Adelstein, Nate Bakkum, Jayson Beaster-Jones, Melissa Bilal, Vicki Brennan, Majel Connery, Genevieve Dempsey, Byron Dueck, Jeffers Engelhardt, Cesar Favila, Michael Figueroa, Luis

Manuel Garcia, Danny Gough, Andy Greenwood, Erika Honisch, D.J. James, Alisha Lola Jones, Jaime Jones, Andrea Harris Jordan, Rehanna Kheshgi, Wayne Marshall, Monica Mays, Kristin McGee, Roger Moseley, Michael O'Toole, Joshua Pilzer, Rumya Putcha, August Sheehy, Shayna Silverstein, Jim Sykes, Joshua Tucker, Greg Weinstein, Suzanne Wint, and Lillian Wohl. The University of Chicago also supported this project materially in the form of several research and travel grants, as well as a Mellon Foundation fellowship to support a dissertation writing year. At DePaul University, Kate Brucher, Judy Bundra, Allen Salzenstein, and many others welcomed me as a colleague and trusted me to lead a large teaching team responsible for all first-year music majors as we immersed ourselves in Chicago's music scene. Many of the ideas in this book originated in the courses I took at Chicago and taught at DePaul.

Northeastern University has been my institutional home while writing *God Rock, Inc.* Our chair, Dan Godfrey, has been encouraging and supportive. Matthew McDonald and Hilary Poriss have provided timely advice as I have learned and navigated our institutional politics; all three have helped me protect my time from the other demands of faculty life. Tony De Ritis saw potential in a newly-minted PhD when he hired me at Northeastern. Deirdre Loughridge has been a valuable coconspirator, friend, and neighbor in addition to the more mundane (but welcomed) help of reading and commenting on an early chapter draft. Murray Forman has dragged me off-campus for drinks and perspective at the most opportune moments. Kelli Alvarez, Jim Anderson, Susan Asai, Doug Bielmeier, Katherine Chan, Melissa Ferrick, David Herlihy, Hubert Ho, Francesca Inglese, Leon Janikian, Mark Lomanno, Psyche Loui, Rebekah Moore, Brian Robison, and Ron Smith have all been instrumental in making our corner of Ryder Hall a pleasure to work in year after year. The College of Arts, Media and Design has supported this project materially with teaching releases and several grants to fund fieldwork, conference travel, and interview transcriptions. I have learned more from my students in the music industry and popular music courses I teach at Northeastern than they probably realize.

I consider myself fortunate indeed to participate in strong networks of scholars. I have learned much from and with friends who research and perform a wide variety of Christian musics: Ibrahim Abraham, Sarah Bereza, Joshua Busman, Florian Carl, Jonathan Dueck, Sarah Eyerly, Tripp Hudgins, Bo kyung Blenda Im, Birgitta Johnson, Deb Justice, Heather MacLachlan, Maren Haynes Marchesini, Marissa Moore,

Nate Myrick, Anna Nekola, Adam Perez, Mark Porter, Tanya Riches, Lester Ruth, Stephen Shearon, Marcell Steuernagel, Tom Wagner, and Dustin Wiebe. Many of us are early-career scholars for whom this network has been an invaluable resource while navigating graduate school, searching for jobs, and establishing careers. It is difficult to overstate how valuable Monique Ingalls has been as a fulcrum for this network: her editorial work on several religious music volumes and establishing a series at Routledge, as well as her organizational work cofounding the interdisciplinary Christian congregational music studies network and what became the SEM's Religion, Music, and Sound Section, have been instrumental in establishing a supportive structure for my work and that of dozens of other scholars around the world. Working with her as a friend and colleague in the years since I met her before even starting graduate school has been one of the great pleasures of my professional life. Christian music scholars otherwise disconnected from this network have responded to my emails and inquiries with grace and patience: Larry Eskridge, Stephen Marini, David Stowe, and Shawn David Young. *God Rock, Inc.* is centered in popular music studies as much as it is about Christian music, and my thinking and writing have been influenced by friends and colleagues active in the AMS's Popular Music Study Group, IASPM-US, and the SEM's Popular Music Section: Christa Bentley, Mark Butler, Amy Coddington, Mike D'Errico, Lauren Flood, Daniel Goldmark, K. E. Goldschmitt, Kwame Harrison, Eric Hung, Robin James, Brian Jones, Kathryn Metz, Karl Hagstrom Miller, Justin Patch, Chris Reali, Victor Szabo, David VanderHamm, Steve Waksman, Elijah Wald, Aleysia Whitmore, and Brian Wright.

During my fieldwork, Glen and Sara van Alkemade became true friends and asked perceptive (and timely) questions of my research; they also opened doors at JPUSA and Cornerstone from which I continue to benefit. Thanks to all at JPUSA who have shared with me your community and ministries: Ed Bialach, John Herrin, Ted Jindrich, Glenn Kaiser, Andrea Spicer, Rich Troche, Genesis Winter, and many others. The staff of the Center for Popular Music at Middle Tennessee State University provided invaluable research and logistical assistance during and following several archival trips: Grover Baker, Stephanie Bandel-Koroll, Dale Cockrell, Lucinda Cockrell, Greg Reish, and their colleagues. During my fieldwork visits to middle Tennessee I enjoyed the hospitality and fellowship of Brian Ban, Michael Barger, David Lim, Mark and Brandy Nicks, Adam Riggs, Joshua Stump, and Jerianne Thompson. Thanks to all of the artists, musicians, and music industry professionals who took time out of your busy lives to chat with me about your work, music, and industries. I quote many of you by name in *God Rock, Inc.*: Nick Barre, Jeff Carver, John Dunn, the late Billy Ray Hearn, Chad Johnson, David Marshall, John Mays, Andy Peterson, Billy Power, John Styll, John J. Thompson, and Luke Welchel. Although I don't quote everyone I interviewed during my fieldwork, this project reflects what I learned from all of you.

I test-drove portions of this material in many forums over the last decade, including presentations at AAR, AMS, the Christian Congregational Music Conference, the Embracing the Margins symposium, IASPM (international), IASPM-US, MEIEA (which also provided a research travel grant), MIDSEM, SCSM, SEM, the Sound and Secularity symposium, and guest talks at Brown, Columbia College Chicago, DePaul, Northeastern, the University of Birmingham, the University of Chicago's ethnomusicology workshop, the University of St. Francis, and the Yale Institute of Sacred Music. Thank you to all who have worked to organize and coordinate these events and visits. At the University of California Press, Raina Polivka's enthusiasm for this project was apparent from her first response to my initial email inquiry, and I welcomed her editorial guidance and insight throughout the revision process. Thank you to Dore Brown, Jessica Moll, and Madison Wetzell for your diligent attention to this book during production. I am lucky to have benefitted from Theo Cateforis's and Eric Weisbard's keen feedback, both of whom read the full manuscript as (anonymous) reviewers and helped me shape and hone my ideas and arguments. Any remaining faults or inaccuracies are mine alone. Several people assisted with securing permissions for this book: Bob Andrews for David Bazan, Ross Cluver at *CCM* magazine, Carl Severson for The Chariot, Ryan J. Downey for Demon Hunter, Hilde Bialach and Terry Wheeler at Grrr Records (for Rez Band), Sara van Alkemade at JPUSA (for Cornerstone), and Timbre.

Finally, my family: I would not be writing about Christian music at all if my parents, Ted and Claudia Mall, hadn't taken me to church every Sunday during my childhood, and if my sister, Esther Langguth, hadn't introduced me to Christian punk and metalcore right before I started graduate school. My other siblings and in-laws have been supportive during what must have appeared to them as a never-ending process of research and writing: Aaron Langguth, Peter Mall, and Brad and Lydia Zopf. I met Liana Percoco immediately upon moving to Chicago; she has been my constant companion and cheerleader for over eighteen years.

Thank you for giving me the time and space to work when I needed it, and a reason to close the laptop and leave the office when I needed that too. Our daughter Michaela has inherited her mother's gift of movement and my inquisitiveness; teaching and learning from her has been a lesson in humility and love. Melody Percoco was taken too early to witness this project's final stages, but I see her spirit in her daughter and granddaughter every day and am lucky to have had her in my life. She would have been so excited to finally read my book.

Playlists

To help you follow my comparative, critical, and descriptive analyses of musical performances and recordings, I have created individual Spotify playlists for every chapter. Links to the playlists are provided at www.ucpress.edu/9780520343429 and on my companion website andrewmallphd.com. The availability of songs on Spotify (and other streaming services) changes as license terms expire or are modified. Songs marked with an asterisk were not available on Spotify at the time of publication, but they may be found on other streaming services, such as YouTube.

Songs are listed on the playlists below in the order that they appear in the text; many are mentioned only in the endnotes or appendix 2, which documents many popular songs that explicitly refer to Christian belief released in the late 1950s and '60s. I describe many songs in analytical and critical detail, but others simply serve as musical examples of an album or artist I refer to without discussing the specific song itself. The songs and artists listed below are flagged throughout the book with the icon 🎧.

I have also assembled discographies for many of the artists I discuss, which are included in appendix 1. These are indicated in the text with the icon 💿.

INTRODUCTION

1. Petra, "I Am on the Rock" (*Beyond Belief*, 1990)

2. Michael W. Smith, "Place in This World" (*Go West Young Man*, 1990)
3. Michael W. Smith, "Friends" (*Michael W. Smith Project*, 1983)
4. Jars of Clay, "Flood" (*Jars of Clay*, 1995)
5. As I Lay Dying, "Forever" (*Frail Worlds Collapse*, 2003)
6. Haste the Day, "American Love" (*Burning Bridges*, 2004)
7. UnderOath, "Reinventing Your Exit" (*They're Only Chasing Safety*, 2004)
8. Lauren Daigle, "You Say" (*Look Up Child*, 2018)
9. Sleeping Giant, "The Army of the Chosen One" (*Sons of Thunder*, 2009)
10. Lecrae, "All I Need Is You" (*Anomaly*, 2015)

CHAPTER 1

1. People!, "I Love You" (*I Love You*, 1968)
2. People!, "We Need a Whole Lot More of Jesus (And a Lot Less Rock and Roll)" (*I Love You*, 1968)*
3. Wayne Raney, "We Need a Whole Lot More of Jesus (And a Lot Less Rock and Roll)" (backed with "Don't You Think It's Time," 1958)
4. Larry Norman, "Sweet Sweet Song of Salvation" (*Upon this Rock*, 1970)
5. Larry Norman, "I Wish We'd All Been Ready" (*Upon this Rock*, 1970)
6. Barry McGuire, "Eve of Destruction" (*Eve of Destruction*, 1965)
7. Larry Norman, "I've Got to Learn to Live without You" (*Only Visiting This Planet*, 1972)
8. Larry Norman, "Why Should the Devil Have All the Good Music" (*Only Visiting This Planet*, 1972)
9. Larry Norman, "The Same Old Story" (*So Long Ago the Garden*, 1973)
10. Larry Norman, "Nightmare #71" (*So Long Ago the Garden*, 1973)
11. Elvis Presley, "Peace in the Valley" (*Peace in the Valley* EP, 1957)

12. Pat Boone, "A Wonderful Time Up There" (backed with "It's Too Soon to Know," 1958)
13. Peter, Paul and Mary, "Tell It on the Mountain" (*In the Wind*, 1963/64)
14. The Impressions, "People Get Ready" (*People Get Ready*, 1965)
15. The Byrds, "Turn! Turn! Turn!" (*Turn! Turn! Turn!*, 1965)
16. Simon and Garfunkel, "Mrs. Robinson" (*Bookends*, 1968)
17. The Edwin Hawkins Singers, "Oh Happy Day" (*Let Us Go into the House of the Lord*, 1968/69)
18. Norman Greenbaum, "Spirit in the Sky" (*Spirit in the Sky*, 1969/70)
19. Judy Collins, "Amazing Grace" (*Whales & Nightingales*, 1970)
20. Murray Head, "Superstar" (*Jesus Christ Superstar*, 1970)
21. Johnny Cash, "I See Men as Trees Walking" (*The Gospel Road*, 1973)
22. Ocean, "Put Your Hand in the Hand" (*Put Your Hand in the Hand*, 1971)
23. Honeytree, "Clean before My Lord" (*Honeytree*, 1973)
24. Second Chapter of Acts, "Easter Song" (*With Footnotes*, 1974)
25. Bill Gaither Trio, "Let's Just Praise the Lord" (*He Touched Me*, 1969)
26. Bill Gaither Trio, "He Touched Me" (*He Touched Me*, 1969)
27. The Imperials, "He Touched Me" (*Love Is the Thing*, 1969)
28. Elvis Presley, "He Touched Me" (*He Touched Me*, 1972)
29. Keith Green, "Your Love Broke Through" (*For Him Who Has Ears to Hear*, 1977)
30. Keith Green, "Your Love Broke Through (live)" (*The Live Experience*, 2008)
31. Keith Green, "You Put This Love in My Heart" (*For Him Who Has Ears to Hear*, 1977)
32. Keith Green, "Soften Your Heart" (*No Compromise*, 1978)
33. Keith Green, "Pledge My Head to Heaven" (*So You Wanna Go Back to Egypt*, 1980)

CHAPTER 2

1. Steven Curtis Chapman, "The Great Adventure" (*The Great Adventure*, 1992)
2. Steven Curtis Chapman, "Heaven in the Real World" (*Heaven in the Real World*, 1994)
3. Steven Curtis Chapman, "The Great Adventure—re:created" (*re:creation*, 2011)
4. Steven Curtis Chapman, "Heaven in the Real World—re:created" (*re:creation*, 2011)

CHAPTER 3

1. Sandi Patty, "How Majestic Is Your Name" (*Lift Up the Lord*, 1982)
2. Sandi Patty, "Sing to the Lord" (*Songs from the Heart*, 1990)
3. Michael English, "Holding Out Hope to You" (*Hope*, 1993)
4. Children of the Day, "For Those Tears I Died" (*Come to the Waters*, 1971)*
5. Ray Boltz, "Thank You" (*Thank You*, 1988)
6. Ray Boltz, "I Pledge Allegiance to the Lamb" (*Allegiance*, 1994)
7. Jennifer Knapp, "Undo Me" (*Kansas*, 1998)
8. Everyday Sunday, "Breathing for Me" (*Best Night of Our Lives*, 2009)

CHAPTER 4

1. Amy Grant, "Baby, Baby" (*Heart in Motion*, 1991)
2. Amy Grant, "Father's Eyes" (*My Father's Eyes*, 1979)
3. Amy Grant, "Look What Has Happened to Me" (*Never Alone*, 1980)
4. Amy Grant, "El Shaddai" (*Age to Age*, 1982)
5. Amy Grant, "Find a Way" (*Unguarded*, 1985)
6. Peter Cetera and Amy Grant, "The Next Time I Fall" (*Solitude/Solitaire*, 1986)
7. Amy Grant, "Saved by Love" (*Lead Me On*, 1988)

8. Amy Grant, "Every Heartbeat" (*Heart in Motion*, 1991)
9. Amy Grant, "That's What Love Is For" (*Heart in Motion*, 1991)
10. Amy Grant, "Good for Me" (*Heart in Motion*, 1991)
11. Amy Grant, "I Will Remember You" (*Heart in Motion*, 1991)
12. Amy Grant, "Lucky One" (*House of Love*, 1994)
13. Amy Grant, "Big Yellow Taxi" (*House of Love*, 1994)
14. Amy Grant, "Takes a Little Time" (*Behind the Eyes*, 1997)

CHAPTER 5

1. Rez, "I Think You Know" (*Between Heaven 'N Hell*, 1985)
2. Resurrection Band, "Midnight Son" (*Rainbow's End*, 1979)
3. The Burial, "Demons Never Sleep" (*The Winepress*, 2010)
4. The Burial, "Reconciliation" (*The Winepress*, 2010)
5. Stryper, "Calling on You" (*To Hell with the Devil*, 1986)
6. Stryper, "Honestly" (*To Hell with the Devil*, 1986)
7. Demon Hunter, "I Am a Stone" (*True Defiance*, 2012)
8. Demon Hunter, "Not Ready to Die" (*Summer of Darkness*, 2004)
9. Demon Hunter, "The Last One Alive" (*Extremist*, 2014)
10. Casting Crowns, "If We've Ever Needed You" (*Until the Whole World Hears*, 2009)
11. Casting Crowns, "If We've Ever Needed You (live)" (*Until the Whole World Hears . . . Live*, 2010)
12. Casting Crowns, "Oh My Soul" (*The Very Next Thing*, 2016)
13. Adam Again, "This Band Is Our House" (*Homeboys*, 1990)
14. The Choir, "If I Had a Yard" (*Circle Slide*, 1990)
15. 77s, "The Lust, the Flesh, the Eyes and the Pride of Life" (*77s*, 1987)

CHAPTER 6

1. Altar Boys, "Jesus Is Number One" (*When You're a Rebel*, 1985)
2. Undercover, "I'm Just a Man" (*Branded*, 1986)
3. One Bad Pig, "Smash the Guitar" (*Smash*, 1989)

4. Living Sacrifice, "Sudden" (*Ghost Thief*, 2013)
5. The Chariot, "Dialogue with a Question Mark" (*Everything Is Alive, Everything Is Breathing, Nothing Is Dead, and Nothing Is Bleeding*, 2004)
6. The Chariot, "Abandon." (*Wars and Rumors of Wars*, 2009)
7. The Chariot (featuring Timbre and Dan Smith of Listener), "David De La Hoz" (*Long Live*, 2010)
8. Timbre, "Like Spinning Plates" (*Little Flowers*, 2010)
9. Timbre, "I Will Go Plant Little Flowers" (*Little Flowers*, 2010)
10. Pedro the Lion, "Lullaby" (*Whole* EP, 1997)
11. Pedro the Lion, "Diamond Ring" (*The Only Reason I Feel Secure*, 1999)
12. Pedro the Lion, "Promise" (*It's Hard to Find a Friend*, 1998)
13. Pedro the Lion, "The Secret of the Easy Yoke" (*It's Hard to Find a Friend*, 1998)
14. Pedro the Lion, "Foregone Conclusions" (*Achilles Heal*, 2004)
15. David Bazan, "In Stitches" (*Curse Your Branches*, 2009)
16. David Bazan, "Hard to Be" (*Curse Your Branches*, 2009)
17. David Bazan, "Curse Your Branches" (*Curse Your Branches*, 2009)
18. David Bazan, "When We Fell" (*Curse Your Branches*, 2009)

CHAPTER 7

1. Mutemath, "Control" (*Reset* EP, 2004)
2. Sixpence None the Richer, "Kiss Me" (*Sixpence None the Richer*, 1997)
3. Chevelle, "The Red" (*Wonder What's Next*, 2002)
4. P.O.D., "Alive" (*Satellite*, 2001)
5. Sufjan Stevens, "We Wish You a Merry Christmas" (*Silver & Gold* Vol. VII, 2012)
6. Sufjan Stevens, "Come Thou Fount of Every Blessing" (*Songs for Christmas* Vol. II, 2006)
7. Sufjan Stevens, "The Transfiguration" (*Seven Swans*, 2004)
8. Sufjan Stevens, "The Only Thing" (*Carrie & Lowell*, 2015)

9. MxPx, "Responsibility" (*The Ever Passing Moment*, 2000)
10. UnderOath, "Writing on the Walls" (*Define the Great Line*, 2006)
11. mewithoutYou, "C-Minor" (*Brother, Sister*, 2006)

CONCLUSION
1. Switchfoot, "Meant to Live" (*The Beautiful Letdown*, 2003)
2. Bob Dylan, "Gotta Serve Somebody" (*Slow Train Coming*, 1979)
3. Jeremy Enigk, "Explain" (*Return of the Frog Queen*, 1996)
4. Duvall, "All in Your Hands" (*Volume & Density*, 2003)
5. Amy Grant and Tori Kelly, "Baby, Baby" (2016)

Introduction

Popular Music, Markets, Margins,
and the Curious Case of Christian Music

I was first introduced to Christian music in the early 1990s. My parents are devout Christians, themselves the children of ministers, and met while students at a small Bible college in central Texas. My father later attended Southwestern Baptist Theological Seminary in Fort Worth. After he was ordained, he worked for the Southern Baptist Convention's Home Mission Board (now the North American Mission Board) directing an office that ministered to the diplomatic community in New York City. During my childhood, we attended a white Southern Baptist church in suburban northern New Jersey, usually going three times a week. Our family's social life revolved around the church and my dad's work: Bible studies, hosting international diplomats for holidays, monthly potlucks, regular Saturday drives into New York to feed the homeless in the East Village's Tompkins Square Park, Vacation Bible School (a weeklong summer camp held at church), weekend retreats, worship services, and even a few Christian concerts.

It was during middle school that I discovered pop music through Top 40 radio (mostly New York's Z100). As the oldest of four children I had no big brother or sister to introduce me to cooler music, and neither of my parents listened to music very much. But they humored my interest in music, tuning into the Top 40 countdown radio shows hosted by Shadoe Stevens and Rick Dees on our drives to and from church every Sunday. Some of the music to which I was listening made them uneasy, and the youth ministers at church taught us that it was sinful to idolize and listen to musicians who, judging by their lyrics and lifestyle choices (drug and alcohol abuse, extramarital sex, rebelling against authority), so clearly held God and Christianity in contempt. For several of my teen years, a highlight of the summer was our church youth group's weeklong trip to Centrifuge, a Southern Baptist summer camp. One year I returned from Centrifuge so convicted about the wrongness of listening to secular music that the following Sunday I made a tearful public commitment in front of our entire church congregation to listen only to Christian music.

Where did a middle schooler find Christian music in North Jersey? The Sam Goody in our local mall carried some gospel CDs but nothing that sounded like the rock music I heard on the radio. Instead, my parents took me to the local Christian bookstore, a franchise of the Family Bookstores chain. Christian bookstores carry more than books and Bibles; they are essentially small department stores, also selling clothes, gifts, home décor, jewelry, music, and stationery. The music section had a "recommended if you like" sign that suggested Christian artists who purportedly sounded similar to specific contemporary Top 40 artists. Among others, I bought cassettes by DeGarmo & Key, Recon, White Heart, and Petra, whose 1990 album *Beyond Belief* quickly became a favorite, especially the song "I Am on the Rock" (🎧).* I got my first CD player as a birthday present in July 1992 and bought several Christian CDs in the coming months: DC Talk's *Nu Thang* and *Free at Last*, Amy Grant's *Heart in Motion*, Michael W. Smith's *Change Your World*, and Petra's two-disc career retrospective *War & Remembrance*. Our church sometimes hosted concerts, such as Steven Curtis Chapman touring in support of his 1992 album *The Great Adventure*. And in 1993, my mom took me to my first major concert when we went with a group of other church members to see Michael W. Smith's *Change Your World* tour, with Christian hip hop group DC Talk as the opening act. Smith's single "Place in This World" (🎧) and his earlier song "Friends" (🎧), which has soundtracked countless high school graduation videos, were crowd favorites that prompted a theater-wide sing-along. It was heavenly.

---

* I have compiled Spotify playlists for every chapter; you will find these in the Playlists section at the front of the book. The songs and artists that appear on those playlists are indicated in the text, endnotes, and appendix 2 with the icon 🎧. I have also created discographies for many of the artists I discuss; these artists are flagged in the text with the icon ●, and the discographies can be found in appendix 1.

. . .

God Rock, Inc. addresses the roles of markets in the production, distribution, intermediation, and consumption of niche popular music in the United States. I have defined *markets* as "realms in which popular music is commodified, produced and distributed, bought and sold, or imagined to be."[1] In other words, popular music markets are spaces in which the interactions of musicians, listeners, and cultural intermediaries (those professionals who connect musicians to listeners and vice versa) are grounded in the production and consumption of music. Individual markets might be defined by their constituent musical genres or styles, audience demographics (age, class, gender, race/ethnicity, religion, sexuality), geographic regions, participants' ideologies, important infrastructural components (such as performance venues, radio stations, or record labels), or some combination of these. Markets are real, populated by actual people, institutions, and musics. But markets are also imagined and idealized, with both artists and audiences often described in homogenous terms that generalize about a market's typical sound and "average" listener.

Mass markets are the biggest markets, with the largest numbers of consumers and the greatest potential for making the most money: mainstream pop, Top 40, celebrity artists, and contemporary hit radio. Niche markets, on the other hand, are smaller, more discriminating, with specialized audiences: the subgenres and substyles of popular music that attract passionate music connoisseurs. As Eric Weisbard shows in his study of radio formatting in the 1970s and later, markets coexist alongside each other (sometimes literally so, on the radio dial); pop music is not defined by a single mainstream, he demonstrates, but rather by multiple, concurrent mainstreams.[2] Markets are not mutually exclusive but overlap and intersect like complicated, multidimensional Venn diagrams, often sharing artists, audiences, industry professionals, and infrastructures. They are not static and have evolved from identifiable (if not uncontroversial) origins; over time they change, splitting and merging, growing and contracting.

This book is specifically about the market for Christian popular music, which I trace back to the Jesus People movement in the late 1960s. Hymn writers had been influenced by popular music since at least the nineteenth century, and in the twentieth century, Christian record labels emphasized Black gospel and white Southern gospel, genres that are largely indigenous to the United States.[3] But the Christian music that accompanied the Jesus People movement represented the first collective effort to produce, perform, and circulate music that addressed Christian themes using youth-oriented, contemporaneous styles of commercial popular music: folk, pop, rock and roll, and others. As a category, Christian music can include subcategories such as Jesus music, Christian rock, contemporary Christian music (CCM), and contemporary worship music (CWM), among others. These subcategories are neither unchanging nor immutable; like the secular categories of "rock" and "pop," over time they have frequently overlapped and converged. As David Brackett observes, although musical characteristics might not change, their categories do: "music that was once 'pop' (and before that 'rock') is now classified as 'easy listening.'"[4] Rather than tease out the specific musical differences between any of these categories, in *God Rock, Inc.* I am more interested in how this market emerged and has transformed over four decades. I use the term *Christian music* (or sometimes *Christian popular music*) to refer to this category in general, only discussing more specific subcategories when the distinction is important. In the pages and chapters that follow, I discuss Christian artists and bands, Christian festivals, Christian music magazines, and Christian record labels to examine how Christian music industry executives and festival directors make business decisions, what Christian artists' music and performances reveal about their beliefs, and how the reactions of Christian fans and music writers contribute to the market's overall discourse.

This book is also about popular music markets in general—about understanding the various forces that construct, police, alter, and enable the transgression of their aesthetic and social boundaries. Popular music studies does not lack for conceptual frameworks or hermeneutic categories. Scholars and music critics talk about genres and subgenres, tracing musical developments, influences, and intersections. We address the sociology of scenes, subcultures, and tribes as important elements that inevitably impact those genres. We consider how these constituent social and aesthetic components function in local, trans-local, regional, and global contexts, increasingly paying attention to the impacts of migration and movement on popular music. And we necessarily examine the commercial industries that promote and profit from music, often in ways that are inequitable, mirroring long-standing social hierarchies and other disparities of power and representation. The problem, however, is that scholarship situated within any one of these analytical frames—genre, subculture, scene, geographic region, industry—often has little to contribute of theoretical importance to scholarship situated within a different analytical frame. As a result, popular music scholars frequently talk past each other, focused on their topics contextualized within a (relatively) small body of specialized literature but paying less attention to how their arguments advance discourse in the field as a whole, or even society in general.

One solution is to broaden the analytical frame as wide as possible, as Brackett does by redefining popular music genres as expansive categories in which musical characteristics are but one of many defining features.[5] The solution I propose and model differs by using an expansive category (markets) within which other taxonomies remain valid and useful. Studying popular music markets can unify an otherwise diffuse body of literature and enable broad comparisons. It might be difficult, for example, to explain how genre studies might inform the sociology of popular music, or to draw larger conclusions from individual case studies of music subcultures, technologies, and record labels. But consider, instead, asking what we might learn about *markets* from studying genres, audiences, subcultures, technologies, or industries, either separately or together, as does Richard Peterson when parsing the various explanations for the popularization of rock and roll in the mid-1950s, or Keir Keightley when considering the broader effects of the competing microgroove record formats (the 33⅓ LP and the 45) on popular music during a similar period.[6] Ultimately, because markets contain all of these constituent components without negating the importance of any single one, they better enable comparisons and avoid essentializing and imposing incompatible theoretical frameworks.

Studying markets also enables popular music scholars to take seriously the same taxonomies and categories that music industries use. Throughout my fieldwork and research for this project I encountered cultural intermediaries (usually record label executives) and published discourse (often in *CCM* magazine) discussing the "Christian market" and the "general market," by which they meant the larger market for commercial popular music that did not presume or promote Christian identity as a core characteristic. (Sometimes they referred to the general market as "the mainstream" or as "the secular.") But they rarely talked about Christian music as a genre or framed it as a scene or a subculture. Cultural intermediaries outside of Christian music think and talk about their work in terms of markets also, as I have learned while researching music festivals, radio stations, and record labels. In part, this reflects the influence of capitalism, the commodification of music, and the importance of knowing who your consumers are—that is, who you anticipate will attend your festival, tune into your station, or stream or buy your recordings—so that you can better meet their needs and expectations, thus securing a larger market share and your own financial health. I am not an apologist for capitalism and the inequities it perpetuates, but I do think it is important both to acknowledge that contemporary popular music is always already immersed in capitalist systems and to develop theoretical frameworks for popular music scholarship that explicitly address the material conditions of capitalism. Grounding our analyses of popular music in the same categories that its industries use situates our criticisms and interventions within actually existing practices.

One way to do this is to research cultural intermediaries and the work of cultural intermediation. Ethnographers of popular music have long focused on audience and reception studies: researching concerts, fandom, festivals, local scenes, music listening, nightlife, and other topics as participant-observers from the perspective of audiences. Daniel Cavicchi's study of Bruce Springsteen fans is exemplary in this regard.[7] The ethnomusicologist David Pruett argues that "mainstream popular music" scholarship would benefit from more ethnographic studies that explicitly engage artists' perspectives, describing as a model his own methodologies in conducting fieldwork with the MuzikMafia, a group of commercial pop-country artists including the duo Big & Rich and others.[8] But I think this call is unproductive: traditional ethnographic research methodologies value building sustained, informal relationships with interlocutors, yet gaining ethnographic access to mainstream pop artists is difficult if not impossible for most academic scholars. What little access we might have is often constrained by an artist's need to maintain their celebrity persona, promote a project or agenda, or shield their private lives from public view. Without the opportunity to build rapport over extended periods of time, formal interviews and other interactions yield the same scripted, sanitized information that artists and their publicists make available to journalists and talk show hosts.

Cultural intermediaries, on the other hand, are often more accessible than artists (aside from those who are themselves celebrities) and can be more willing and able to speak about their work without resorting to press-friendly talking points, even when they are likewise engaged in promoting projects or agendas. The sociologist Pierre Bourdieu has given as examples of cultural intermediaries "the producers of cultural programmes on TV and radio or the critics of 'quality' newspapers and magazines and all the writer-journalists and journalist-writers," distinguishing this group from the decision-making "gatekeepers" who control access to the means of production.[9] In the music industries, cultural intermediaries may not create the music, but they are central to its dissemination. The work that they do—what Devon Powers describes as processes "by which art, music, and other forms of cultural production circulate, assume meaning, and gain value"[10]—establishes the material conditions in which musicians write, record, and perform music, and audiences listen to music. In doing so, the cultural intermediation of popular music is a constituent component of "musicking," which Christopher Small defines as "tak[ing] part, in any capacity, in a musical performance."[11] Insight into the decision-making processes and practices of cultural intermediaries can help us understand broader trends in music markets.

Much of this work has already been done in music industry studies, an interdisciplinary field of study that attempts to understand the processes of music production and distribution. One strand of this field has emphasized the roles of record labels, exemplified by the work of R. Serge Denisoff in the 1970s and '80s, David Hesmondhalgh and Keith Negus in the 1990s, and Alex Ogg in the 2000s, among many others.[12] Reflecting John Williamson and Martin Cloonan's reminder that music industry analysis need not be conflated with studying only record labels, many others have addressed the economies, histories, politics, and regulatory environments of the business of music more broadly, including David Bruenger, Simon Frith, Reebee Garofalo, Fabian Holt, and Richard Peterson.[13] Recent scholarship by Eric Drott, Lee Marshall, Jeremy Wade Morris, and others has examined the impact of online streaming on the music industries.[14] With few exceptions, however (Negus and Holt being the most obvious), relatively little music industry scholarship incorporates ethnographic research methods. Ethnomusicologists studying cultural intermediaries and their work are poised to make significant contributions to our understanding of the production, circulation, meaning, and value of popular music: *God Rock, Inc.* thus joins Shannon Garland's analysis of Fora do Eixo (a Brazilian network of cultural collectives), Timothy Taylor's study of Burger Records, and Aleysia Whitmore's research into the label World Vision, among others, as modeling a crucial approach to the ethnography of popular music and music industries.[15]

Christian music is a fascinating lens for this work because it is both niche and mass, marginal and mainstream, related to but in many ways distinct from its general market counterparts; understanding its boundaries can help us understand the boundaries of other music markets and their relationships to each other. A market's boundaries are important because they reflect and perpetuate its conditions of inclusion and exclusion, conditions that comprise the accumulated actions, beliefs, decisions, and values of everyone who participates and has invested in that market. By everyone I mean *everyone*—not just the C-level executives in record label corner offices in New York, Los Angeles, and Nashville, but their artists, musicians, and songwriters, their audiences and fans, and every entertainment industry professional in between. Markets are not just top-down constructions, prescriptive categories of consumption imposed by music industries. Nor are they only bottom-up, reactionary grassroots movements uninfluenced by the needs and forces of capitalism. Rather, markets represent negotiations between acts of production and reception, prescription and reaction, creation and consumption, with every interaction confirming and altering boundaries. Participants involved in the work of cultural intermediation rely on boundaries—both implicitly and explicitly—to justify business decisions that have real-world consequences for the music and artists to which listeners and audiences have access. Boundaries teach participants what is welcome and what is forbidden in any given market—both what music *sounds* good (the market's aesthetics) and what acts and behaviors *are* good (the market's ethics). And because markets change over time, their boundaries are inherently flexible, responding to changes in the aesthetics and ethics that participants value.

Ethics and aesthetics are mutually co-constitutive in music markets, at times explicitly, but more often implicitly so.[16] Ethics of production, distribution, mediation, and reception both define and limit markets' accessibility. Because a market's ethics can impact its material and ideological conditions, they can prescribe both acceptable and inappropriate musical elements. But they can also set preconditions for participation that have seemingly little to do with the music itself. Christian cultural intermediaries, for example, have long negotiated a tension between circumscribing their market by their target consumers' faith identity on one hand while promoting accessible, derivative popular music largely indistinguishable from contemporaneous mainstream pop on the other hand. Consider indie rock as another example: while constituting little more than an aesthetic category by the second decade of the twenty-first century, it is rooted in the do-it-yourself (or "DIY") anti-corporate ethic of U.S. punk and hardcore in the 1970s and '80s.[17] Shadow infrastructures, parallel to and yet distinct from those of the general market, developed around both of these markets, further inscribing their marginality. Their ethics became aesthetic mappings that sounded something meaningful to listeners and cultural intermediaries, even if those aesthetics did not explicitly articulate or index the market's ethical values. In other words, while we may not be able to define what Christian or DIY ethics sound like, we can interrogate their relationships to the sounds of their markets in particular contexts.

At the heart of contestations over Christian music's boundaries are contestations over its meaning and purpose. For example, the long-running contestation between commerce and ministry as competing objectives illustrates the central question of all conflicts within the Christian market: what is Christian music *for*? No other popular music market that I know of has to navigate between these two specific goals; thus, explaining the history, nuances, and repercussions of this conflict clearly distinguishes Christian music from other popular musics. I do so by exploring commerce, ethics, resistance, and crossover in the context of the U.S. Christian market, grounded in case studies and illustrative examples between the 1960s and 2010s. But although Christian music may be novel to many readers, it is not irrelevant to broader discourses in and about popular music. Echoing Simon Frith, who notes that the boundaries of popular music genres often rely on "a basic (if unstated) agreement within a genre about what their music is for," I challenge you to think of a defining conflict in a popular music niche market or subgenre that you know well and boil it down to a central question that does not resemble this one.[18] What is indie rock for? What is Chicago blues or Italo disco for? What is Detroit house, mumble rap, or third wave emo for?

Jay Howard and John Streck address these differences of opinion over the purposes and objectives of Christian music and Christian artists in their book *Apostles of Rock*. They divide the Christian market into three categories: separational, integrational, and transformational. Separational Christian artists, they write, "maintain a stark distinction between Christian and secular culture while at the same time remaining committed to reaching non-Christians and making converts."[19] Integrational artists, on the other hand, are "opposed to the idea of withdrawing into an isolated Christian subculture [and] developed new rationales for their music that would allow them to integrate themselves, as well as their Christian beliefs, into mainstream culture."[20] These two positions reveal competing approaches to ministry: the first suggests that evangelism works best if Christianity (and, by extension, Christian culture) provides a true alternative to the secular world; the second understands effective ministry as taking place within the (non-Christian) culture it hopes to change. Crudely put, this is perhaps the difference between *drawing people in* to Christianity or *bringing it to* them. Transformational artists adopt something of a mediating position, in which music is valued for its aesthetic qualities and not for its religious or commercial utility; their goal is "not to enter or to withdraw from mainstream culture but to enable its transformation."[21]

These different positions reflect distinct perspectives on the appropriate degree of intersection and interaction between the Christian and general markets, perspectives that are grounded in theological arguments about the appropriate degree to which Christians should engage with secular culture—the degree, for example, to which Christians can safely be *in* the world but not *of* it (that is, not adhering to secular values despite living in a secular society). Crucially, they also indicate different opinions on the proper role of capital. Transformational artists—for whom "the choice to pursue artistic purity has often meant commercial obscurity"[22]—must choose between their aesthetic goals and those prescribed by market pressures. Stories of critically lauded artists who never achieved significant commercial success anecdotally reinforce this perception, as do those of artists who became successful after following the aesthetic and stylistic suggestions of their record labels. Integrational artists emphasize entertainment over the pursuit of aesthetic and ministerial goals. From a transformational perspective, integrational artists abandon their artistic visions; from a separational perspective, they water down Christianity's message for commercial gain. From an integrational perspective, however, commercial success is legitimizing: it proves that popular music from a Christian perspective can connect with listeners and consumers on a mass scale and provides worldly evidence of God's influence and validation. In other words, according to Howard and Streck, "integrational artists argue that because the music sells it must speak to the hearts and minds of Christians and non-Christians alike; therefore, it must be authentic."[23] Separational music is explicitly theological, charged with "reaching the non-Christian with the gospel message, encouraging Christians in the daily exercise of their faith, and/or offering praise and worship to God."[24] But some critics charge that it commodifies religious beliefs and practices and can even negatively impact the faith of artists who must balance commercial viability against their religious beliefs. The results are often oriented less toward listeners who want to be challenged in their faith and more toward those who prefer to have their faith (re)affirmed. This focus on affirmation recasts the business of music itself as ministry and "simply define[s] consumption as religion," a self-perpetuating situation that ensures that separational Christian music will remain irrelevant to people who care little about its ministerial potential or theological import.[25]

The objectives that Howard and Streck define are not unique to Christian music: every niche market vacillates among separational, integrational, and transformational perspectives and debates the appropriate relationships between commerce, aesthetics, and ideology. In Christian music, these discourses are transparent and often foregrounded; thus, the lessons they have to offer about markets' boundaries are more readily accessible. From an outsider's perspective, the Christian market often appears to be relatively homogenous. From an insider's perspective, however, it is incredibly diverse and nuanced along many dimensions, like Christianity itself. For these reasons and many others, the Christian market has much in common with many other markets, both mass and niche. My hope is that the lessons I draw from Christian music will be useful to studies of other music markets further afield. While you will learn a lot about Christian music in *God Rock, Inc.*, you will also walk away from this book with ideas about any number of popular music markets I do not address.

CHRISTIAN MUSIC AND ITS DISCONTENTS

I never used to tell people that my first concert was DC Talk and Michael W. Smith. Instead, throughout my adolescence and much of my adulthood, I almost always singled out Lollapalooza 1994 as my first concert: the summer after ninth grade, my mom drove me and three church friends to the old Downing Stadium on Randalls Island in New York City. Despite my earlier commitment to stop listening to secular music, in high school I listened to less and less Christian music. I became quite a passionate fan of "alternative rock," and I also started digging into classic rock, buying LPs that my youth ministers had explicitly warned me against at garage sales. I went to arena concerts at the Garden State Arts Center (now the PNC Bank Arts Center), Madison Square Garden, the Meadowlands, and elsewhere. Perhaps most significantly, I discovered Jersey's local DIY punk and hardcore scene and went to shows almost weekly at American Legion, Knights of Columbus, and VFW halls, a local teen club named Obsessions, and punk houses to see bands like Bigwig, the Bouncing Souls, Lifetime, and 25 Ta Life.

I knew about Christian punk bands like Audio Adrenaline, MxPx, and One Bad Pig from our youth ministers' and the Christian bookstore's recommendations, but it was too little, too late. One year, on New Years' Eve, I took my girlfriend (who was not a churchgoer) to see Jars of Clay play at a local church. They are an acoustic rock group whose crossover single "Flood" (🎧) climbed the *Billboard* Hot 100 chart in 1996, peaking at #37. But we were not impressed—Jars of Clay could never really measure up to the arena concerts we attended together, nor the local punk and hardcore shows we went to regularly. After I moved to Bethlehem, Pennsylvania, to attend college at Lehigh University, I stopped attending church entirely. In college I regularly drove to shows with friends and worked at a local CD and record store. I told anyone who asked that I was agnostic, but in truth I was ambivalent: church and the Christian faith no longer held important places in my life.

We tell stories about our pasts, in part, to construct more-or-less linear narratives that explain our present selves to each other. I had long written the DC Talk and Michael W. Smith concert out of my personal history not (only) because I was embarrassed by it but because it never illustrated the ways in which music has been significant in my personal life. Lollapalooza, on the other hand, totally did: by positioning my musical coming-of-age within the alternative rock explosion of the early 1990s, it rooted my later love for DIY scenes in the commercial success and popularity of artists and subgenres that had long been marginal to mainstream popular musics. Perhaps another way to explain this is that going to see DC Talk and Michael W. Smith with a church group was less a concert experience than it was yet another church activity to which I was taken; attending Lollapalooza to see Green Day and The Breeders and The Smashing Pumpkins with a group of friends, on the other hand, was the first time I went to a concert because I wanted to see these bands perform, spent months looking forward to it, and talked about it in the following weeks and months. Recently I have been outing myself as a lapsed Christian music fan, but doing so has a strategic purpose: it authenticates me as someone with a decades-long connection to these artists and their market, enabling me to connect with others who have similar memories and backgrounds, and it provides a convenient point of origin for the book you are now reading. Even though I still do not attend church regularly nor identify as a Christian, Christianity itself is again important in my life, albeit primarily in a professional capacity. I have rescued Michael W. Smith from the dustbin of memory because that early concert helps explain my interest in Christian music; with apologies, his music has finally found a place in my world.

. . .

The Christian music I discuss in *God Rock, Inc.* originated during the countercultural revivalist Jesus People movement in the late 1960s and early '70s, which historian Larry Eskridge argues was one of the most important religious events in the United States in the latter half of the twentieth century.[26] Its successful spread among countercultural youth in California and elsewhere was largely due to its preachers', ministers', and converts' willingness to use contemporary cultural practices to discuss and promote their faith. Traditional Christian hymns did not suit this movement well; instead, the Jesus People celebrated their faith and sang its praises in music influenced by folk, pop, and rock. Other cultural practices were similarly recast as Christian by the Jesus People, including coffeeshops, drama, music festivals, visual art, writing (including alternative newspapers, literature, New Journalism, poetry, and self-published zines), and communal living. Eskridge explains that this was a marked change from earlier generations of evangelical Christians: "It was all right for evangelical kids to occupy their own cultural space distinct from that of their older evangelical brethren. In fact, the Jesus People movement marked the first time that American evangelical youth received a go-ahead to replicate the larger youth culture, albeit with proper evangelical respect for moral probity."[27] This "first time" had been a long time coming: the distinction between secular public culture and evangelical Christianity in the United States dates at least to the early twentieth century, when Christian fundamentalism gained steam as a movement criticizing the spread of relatively modern cultural, social, and theological positions within mainline Protestant dominations.

This split was made visible by the Scopes Trial in 1925, in which William Jennings Bryan prosecuted high school biology teacher John T. Scopes for breaking a Tennessee state law that prohibited teaching Charles Darwin's theories of evolution in public schools. Bryan had turned to fundamentalist Christianity in 1920 after an earlier career as a politician: two terms as a U.S. representative from Nebraska (1891–95), three campaigns as the Democratic nominee for president (1896, 1900, and 1908), and an appointment as Woodrow Wilson's secretary of state

(1913–15). The Scopes Trial attracted nationwide attention both to the east Tennessee town of Dayton and to the theological conflict between Christian fundamentalism and modernism. Fundamentalist Christians follow a strict, conservative, and literal interpretation of the Bible. From the fundamentalist perspective, Darwinian evolution is antithetical to the biblical creation story in Genesis. The historian Preston Shires notes that fundamentalists in the early twentieth century oriented their daily lives exclusively to the teachings of the Bible and practiced a morality informed "by the standards of Victorian evangelicalism": prohibiting dancing, drinking, popular music, smoking, and theater, and largely withdrawing from secular culture.[28] Although Bryan secured a nominal victory in the Scopes Trial—a small win of fundamentalist over modernist evangelical theology—it was later overturned on a technicality. (The Tennessee law in question, the Butler Act, was not repealed until 1967.)

During the trial, however, the national media portrayed Bryan's arguments as culturally and intellectually regressive. This response further marked fundamentalist Christianity as a separate (and separatist) domain peripheral to U.S. public culture, including mainline Protestant denominations, which were more liberal and articulated what Howard and Streck might identify as an integrational approach in that they navigated between distinct religious and secular spheres more fluidly, opposing the sociocultural withdrawal that fundamentalists preached. For many non-Christians, fundamentalism's conservative theology and separatism marked it as an extreme form of Christianity. It was exotic—just as the Catholic Church's hierarchical organization, headquartered at the Vatican, was also exotic—and increasingly foreign to the everyday lives of non-Christians and mainline Protestants alike. That said, then as now, Christianity as a whole consisted of diverse theological orientations and biblical interpretations. Despite sharing basic articles of faith, twentieth-century U.S. Protestants were not monolithic in their theology or in their preferred degree of engagement with secular culture—for example, the charismatic practices of Pentecostalism and the ritual liturgies of the Episcopal Church, among others, represent significantly different approaches. Central to this narrative, however, are the relatively liberal mainline Protestant denominations, the peripheral (yet highly visible) fundamentalists, and—emerging during World War II—a "new evangelical" movement that mediated between these two positions.[29]

New evangelicalism explicitly endorsed the infallibility and authority of the Bible in everyday life (as did fundamentalism) yet shunned separatism, choosing instead to engage mainline denominations and secular culture in order to "make a political, social, and of course, spiritual impact"—that is, to enable their transformation.[30] Although new evangelicalism was more culturally accommodating than fundamentalism, it attracted theological conservatives who disapproved of the increasing liberalism and hierarchism within the mainline denominations. The lack of denominational oversight within new evangelicalism better enabled parachurch organizations and nondenominational churches—particularly those that fit Donald Miller's description of "new paradigm churches"[31]—to adapt their messages and objectives to changes in popular culture more quickly. Several youth and campus ministries flourished under new evangelicalism, including Inter-Varsity Christian Fellowship (founded in 1939), Youth for Christ International (founded in 1945), and Campus Crusade for Christ (founded in 1951, known as Cru since 2011), among others. By the late 1960s, new evangelicalism, once an "outsider rendition of reactionary Christianity," had become a legitimate theological orientation in U.S. Protestantism, responsive to the needs of both conservative adult and liberal youth Christians, effectively paving the way for the Jesus People movement.[32] Evangelical culture secured a strong presence in the U.S. public sphere by the late 1970s, exemplified by President Jimmy Carter's public Christian faith, the role of Jerry Falwell's Moral Majority during Ronald Reagan's successful presidential campaign in 1980, and the broader political and cultural influence of the Religious Right. In actively engaging U.S. public and political culture, Heather Hendershot writes, conservative U.S. Protestants effectively transformed themselves "from separatist fundamentalists into engaged evangelicals" over fifty years (1920s–'70s).[33]

This transition was facilitated by the simultaneous expansion of Christian commodities, media, and material culture, legitimizing Christianity from the perspective of a U.S. middle class increasingly defined by consumption and suburban affluence. The expansion of Christian consumer goods that accompanied the Jesus People movement indicated that Christianity was no longer only something you believed but was also something you wore, read, watched, listened to, hung on your walls, and stuck to your car's bumper. Although we might debate the degree to which the emergence and growth of Christian music and its infrastructures during and following the Jesus People movement played a significant role in this shift—did Christian music cause the commodification of faith or was it a victim?—it is clear that, although Christian music initially emerged as a tool for evangelism, conversion, and edification, over time it became yet another profit-generating lifestyle component of contemporary U.S.

evangelical culture. From the outset, Christian music was doubly marginalized: artists such as Keith Green, Barry McGuire, Larry Norman, and others were too religious for the general market but too aggressively rock and roll for the Christian market at the time, which preferred African American and white Southern gospel. In response, supporters developed a new infrastructure to promote Christian rock: labels such as Myrrh and Sparrow produced and distributed recordings, *CCM* magazine was the market's equivalent to both *Billboard* and *Rolling Stone*, and Christian bookstores were its main retailers. Taking a moniker from *CCM* magazine, contemporary Christian music (or CCM) matured into the market's stable mainstream in the 1980s, accompanied by flourishing labels, music publishers, radio stations, and touring networks.

By the 1990s, the Christian market was commercially successful enough to attract the attention of multinational entertainment conglomerates; following a period of corporate consolidation, three major Christian labels emerged as subsidiaries of the three largest record companies: EMI Christian Music Group (now Capitol CMG), Sony's Provident Label Group, and Warner's Word Entertainment (owned by Curb Records since 2016). Market growth followed corporate consolidation, and several Christian artists "crossed over" into the general market in the 1990s: DC Talk, Amy Grant, Jars of Clay, Sixpence None the Richer, Michael W. Smith, and others had Top 40 hit singles and acquired new general market fans. Christian music followed stylistic trends in general market contemporary pop music, partly to offer a Christian alternative to the general market (thus, the "recommended if you like" signs in the Christian bookstores of my youth). As Christian music's mainstream became increasingly proscribed and inflexible, other niche Christian musics emerged to serve the needs of artists and audiences with more diverse tastes: Christian goth, Christian hip hop, Christian metal, Christian punk, and others filled this unmet demand. Despite these clear strides, Christian music remained marginal to the general market: its artists' explicit faith identities endeared them to the Christian market but segregated them from the general market, establishing boundaries more clearly than did their music, which was often criticized for being blatantly derivative.

DEFINING CHRISTIAN MUSIC

I have a confession to make: I did not set out on this project because of some half-remembered Michael W. Smith concert from my adolescence.

The truth is that I wanted to study DIY underground rock, and I intended to include Christian punk only after my youngest sister, Esther, introduced me to some of the bands she had started listening to in the early aughts. During a family road trip to Michigan in the summer of 2003, she told me about a Christian youth club she had been going to for several years called Souled Out that frequently held emo, hardcore, metalcore, punk, and ska shows. She introduced me to As I Lay Dying (🎧), Haste the Day (🎧), Project 86, Still Remains, and UnderOath (🎧), and told me about Cornerstone Festival, the Christian festival in rural western Illinois that was practically a pilgrimage site for subcultural Christians.

I had never encountered indie or DIY Christian bands before, and Esther's interest piqued my interest. I initially set out to interrogate what, to me, seemed to be an obvious cognitive dissonance: how do these artists and fans reconcile the conformity that white U.S. evangelical Christianity demands—both as a faith and as a culture—with the resistance that hardcore, metal, and punk articulate? These bands' faith was an implicit (if expected) component of their identity inseparable from the music they made, which, more often than not, did not praise or preach or proselytize like the Christian music I had listened to as a younger teenager. They were usually signed to independent labels (such as Facedown, Pluto, Takehold, and Tooth & Nail) that were relatively unaffiliated with the major Christian record companies; they toured a network of underground and DIY coffeeshops, clubs (including Souled Out), and house venues. Before we carried our social networks in pocket-sized supercomputers, fans learned about these bands through word-of-mouth, online bulletin boards, and print fanzines like *Heavens Metal* (later *HM Magazine*), *Radically Saved*, and *White Throne*.[34]

The parallels between the Christian and non-Christian hardcore, indie, metal, and punk DIY scenes are unmistakable, and the shared affinities for DIY and anti-mainstream ethics often trump differences in faith identities to enable intersections and overlaps between the two.[35] That said, a common Christian faith was a given at Souled Out and in the larger networks of Christian music, and it was (and is) central to understanding these scenes and communities. A band's public claim to Christian identity functions as a seal of quality—not necessarily that their music is any good, or even that they sing about loving Jesus, but rather that it adheres to Christian morals and that they do not sing about loving hedonism or nihilism. You did not risk the eternal damnation of your soul, in other words, going to Souled Out or Cornerstone;

but who knew what messiness awaited you at secular clubs and festivals. Many evangelical teenagers experience their Christian identity as oppositional and marginal to the dominant culture.[36] Esther and her friends might not have driven to Chicago for DIY punk shows at the storied Fireside Bowl (which I did almost immediately upon moving to the area after graduating college), but their community at Souled Out and later house venues was no less subcultural. Venues such as Souled Out, much like the Fireside and the Knights of Columbus halls of my youth, provide physical places for these music communities to flourish far from the expectations and values of the mainstream.

. . .

As I started learning more about underground Christian punk, I realized that the Christian hardcore and metal bands my sister was listening to were just one chapter of a much longer history of Christian music—a musical category whose stylistic variety is often subordinated to its artists' faith identity. For example, in the 1970s there were bluesy and hard rock artists (such as Larry Norman and Resurrection Band) and others who played more of a soft-rock style, rooted in piano accompaniment and tight vocal harmonies (including Children of the Day, Keith Green, and Second Chapter of Acts, three of the most popular '70s Christian artists). These artists contrasted sharply against the white Southern gospel vocal groups and adult-oriented balladeers that populated most existing Christian labels' rosters at the time. "Contemporary Christian music," an explicitly genre-neutral term, describes the market's mainstream category so well precisely because it is so neutral. CCM manifests a big-tent approach to categorizing sound, defined less by its musical characteristics (roughly defined as pop music for adults aged twenty-five to fifty-four) than by its lyrical content, representing a biblically grounded Christian worldview.

As the Christian market's mainstream became oriented toward adult listeners in the 1980s and '90s, its margins were increasingly populated by youth-oriented Christian artists. Christian radio programmers, who have occupied significant roles in enforcing the market's sonic boundaries, typically ignored Christian bands that played heavy metal, punk, and other aggressive rock styles, which meant that the major Christian record labels also often ignored them. Something curious happened in the 2000s, however: hard rock bands like MercyMe, Red, Skillet, and others performed for larger and larger audiences on tour and at Christian music festivals, and radio programmers welcomed them onto previously inaccessible playlists at commercial Christian radio stations. Now you can hear Michael W. Smith, Skillet, and Lauren Daigle (🎧)—a Grammy Award-winning CCM singer-songwriter with a very strong growth trajectory in late 2018 and early '19—on the same radio stations that would have ignored any singles with distorted guitar twenty or twenty-five years earlier.

Christian listeners today are increasingly likely to hear contemporary worship music (or CWM) on the airwaves or on playlists curated by the major music-streaming services (such as Spotify's "Top Christian" and "Christian Mix" playlists). CWM's origin story is also rooted in the Jesus People movement, when young evangelicals began to incorporate popular music styles into the music they sang during worship services. Stylistically, CWM has followed the same trends as CCM in the intervening decades, and the two markets' aesthetics are virtually indistinguishable. Instead of style, Christian music scholars and observers have tended to distinguish between CWM and CCM by their functions, describing CWM as music that enables you to connect to God both in public moments (at a church's worship service) and in private ones (a solo devotional at home with your morning coffee), reveals theological lessons and truths, and enables religious reflection; and CCM as music that entertains you, gets you to dance, or distracts you from banal daily chores and activities. The Christian market's industries and infrastructures have reflected and perpetuated this distinction in the past, with separate awards, charts, labels, metrics, and publishing firms for CWM and CCM. There is no longer any meaningful infrastructural boundary between CWM and CCM, however. They are stylistically identical; artists move between both fluidly, writing and recording music for both worship and entertainment contexts; and Christian music companies (including record labels and publishing firms) have invested in CWM at greater rates, as worship music has proven to be good for business.

Although popular worship artists like David Crowder Band, Elevation Worship, Hillsong United, Chris Tomlin, and others have tended to focus on writing, recording, and performing music for worship, their music has increasingly circulated in multiple contexts. Thus, the utilitarian distinction is no longer useful either, at least not in terms of identifying an artist as either CWM or CCM: CCM artists release worship albums and lead worship; CWM artists play arena concerts, and worship music is increasingly a form of entertainment. The same song, in other words, could easily serve both as worship and as entertainment. Ari Kelman describes this blurring of boundaries as posing existential challenges to worship leaders and songwriters concerned with decentering themselves from their listeners' attention.[37] Some churches are still recovering from the "worship wars" that pitted CWM against traditional hymn singing, but progressive worship services are incorporating Christian metal, Christian hardcore—such as the band Sleeping Giant (🎧)—or even secular rock music, as April Stace documents.[38]

If we cannot usefully distinguish between CWM and CCM by their aesthetics, infrastructures, or uses, is there a meaningful reason and way to differentiate between the two? I do think it is worthwhile to do so: attending a worship service and attending a concert are two very distinct experiences with entirely separate sets of expectations and objectives. But it is not useful to reduce and constrain any single artist or song to a single market, in part because we do not have a similar expectation in the general market where artists move between markets (Taylor Swift shifting from country to pop) or even entire entertainment industries (every pop singer who has ever acted in a movie) with little backlash. Instead, I argue that we should consider the particular performance contexts to distinguish between CCM and CWM: when Monique Ingalls defines CWM as "a global Christian congregational song repertory modeled on mainstream Western popular music styles," she explicitly ties it to participatory contexts (in "congregational song," we sing *together*) in contrast to the presentational contexts of CCM (in which artists sing *to* us).[39]

Thomas Turino describes participatory performances as having "no artist-audience distinctions, only participants and potential participants performing different roles, and the primary goal is to involve the maximum number of people in some performance role." In presentational performances, however, "one group of people, the artists, prepare and provide music for another group, the audience, who do not participate in making the music."[40] I admit that, in the context of Christian music, this is an imperfect distinction—how might we describe a private moment in which an individual listens to music while entering a meditative, prayerful, or transcendent state, for example? or what about a joyful, communal rendition of "Amazing Grace" following a singer's religious testimony at the end of a Christian punk concert?—but this messiness is authentic to the overlapping and multivalent possibilities with which songwriters, artists, and cultural intermediaries grapple on a regular basis. CCM and CWM might be inextricably related and conflated as genres or sociocultural contexts (Ingalls describes CWM as a subgenre of CCM, while Kelman suggests that CWM is a distinct "scene" within CCM's broader evangelical subculture), but discussing CCM and CWM as relatively separate *markets* enables us to reconcile these intersections with distinct performance practices.[41] Thus, throughout *God Rock, Inc.* I focus more on music and artists in presentational contexts than I do on participatory ones.

The market for Black gospel music is also relatively separate from the Christian market I address in this book. There are at least two reasons for this. First, the U.S. music industries have long maintained separate infrastructures for Black and white markets, even while the latter profited by appropriating the former. Karl Hagstrom Miller writes about the stratification of music markets along the Black/white racial divide in the United States in the late nineteenth century and throughout the twentieth century.[42] Segregated dance halls and "race records" (the standard record industry term used to indicate music that was performed by and marketed to racial and ethnic minority consumers) in the first half of the twentieth century illustrate this; the latter half of the century saw little change, with separate record labels (or subsidiaries) for Black music that was then played on largely segregated commercial radio airwaves, with separate formats for Black and white listeners.[43] Even when Black music has become popular among white audiences, the music industries often reacted to preserve their de facto segregation: having white rock and roll artists cover Black artists' hit songs during the 1950s and '60s, for example, and privileging hip hop songs that incorporated white pop aesthetics at Top 40 radio stations in the 1980s and '90s, as Amy Coddington shows.[44] In other words, the fact that Black and white musics are separate in the Christian market is little different from their separateness in the general market.

The other reason Black and white Christian musics are relatively separate is that Black and white Christian congregations are relatively separate. U.S. evangelical Christians may live in increasingly integrated communities, but their churches have been slow to follow. To paraphrase Martin Luther King Jr., eleven o'clock on Sunday morning remains the most segregated hour of Christian America, even well into the twenty-first century. As in the general market, the Christian markets reflect that segregation and this country's long history of systemic racism, with separate record labels to distribute and promote gospel artists for distinct radio formats (and other channels for intermediation) that target Black listeners over white ones. Many of my interlocutors in the Christian industry acknowledged this segregation as a troubling fact: problematic, but impossible or impractical to change. This tacit acceptance among cultural intermediaries is itself troubling, because by failing to resist or challenge the status quo they reproduce and perpetuate it. There are nods to integration here and there: most major Christian labels do sign Black artists, either directly or through a gospel music subsidiary; the Gospel Music Association (or GMA, the Christian market's main trade organization) advocates for the entire industry and features diverse lineups on its annual awards show (the Dove Awards) and in its various workshops; and some Black artists have been successful among white listeners, including Andraé Crouch in the 1970s and '80s, BeBe and CeCe Winans in the 1980s and '90s, Kirk Franklin in the 1990s and 2000s, and Lecrae (🎧) in the 2010s, among others.[45] Nonetheless, Christian music remains overwhelmingly white, and examining gospel remains largely outside the scope of this book.

. . .

I do not really like listening to Christian music. I am continually surprised by how good many Christian hardcore and metal bands are, and had I discovered them under different circumstances, I might have become a fan. But I am not a fan: I do not listen to Christian music in my free time, attend Christian concerts for fun, subscribe to Christian playlists or podcasts, or follow Christian artists on Facebook or Twitter. Many scholars in ethnomusicology and popular music studies, my two disciplinary homes, choose to research musics that they already enjoy or are otherwise invested in as fans, teachers, or musicians themselves. The ethnomusicological scholarly and pedagogical canons reflect this, with an abundance of publications and courses on non-Western music that reveal the discipline's colonialist heritage, such as the music of Africa and the African diaspora, the Middle East, South Asia and Southeast Asia, and many other regions and cultures around the world. But there are comparatively fewer studies of, say, Nordic folk music, freely improvised music in Germany, Western art music, or even Western art music in non-Western cultural contexts. One result of ethnomusicologists reproducing the discipline's scholarly canons is that students of ethnomusicology are then mostly exposed to only those musics in their courses and ensembles. Another result is that, for topics where the discipline as a whole lacks expertise, its members are less suited to advise research projects, communicate with non-academic audiences, or evaluate new scholarship (necessary for career advancement within academia).[46] The canons of ethnomusicology are thus self-perpetuating.

In popular music studies the situation is different. Eclectic, niche popular music genres with a relative lack of commercial success attract music connoisseurs and superfans from whose ranks many popular music scholars have graduated. The result is that the margins of popular music are overrepresented in the academic press. This is a notable shift from early popular music scholarship in the 1970s and early '80s, much of which did indeed take massively popular music seriously as an object of study.[47] Pop is too popular, it turns out, for popular music studies. On its face, this is a noble pursuit: instead of adding to the piles of pages and listicles about Top 40 chartpop, scholars expose their readers to otherwise unknown or unheralded musics and musicians. But William Brooks argues for an objective approach to popular music studies, in which taste itself is absent, noting that "preserving the obscure is no justification for neglecting the commonplace."[48] When we do preserve the obscure at the expense of the commonplace, we fail to cast a critical lens on the most commercially successful and popular musics. We also fail to take seriously the musical tastes of the largest audiences, willfully courting obscurity. In a 2013 keynote lecture to the Society for Ethnomusicology's Popular Music Section, the music writer Elijah Wald noted an ageist and gendered effect as well, when he observed that, by not paying attention to mainstream pop artists like Katy Perry, scholars snub the fandom and tastes of teenage girls.[49] Elsewhere I argue that this self-selected subject bias distorts the field's overall contributions and limits its relevance to the broader culture.[50] In both ethnomusicology and popular music studies, a recursive, self-perpetuating system in which only certain areas of inquiry are suitable subjects of scholarship can feel unwelcoming to some members, particularly those from underprivileged backgrounds or who embody diverse and intersectional identities. In this way, the scholarly world remains largely cis-hetero, male, Western, and white.

One way to break this cycle is to set aside our personal tastes to research (and support and welcome research on) topics that are relatively unpopular in our academic disciplines, such as Christian music. The ethnographic study of congregational song and worship music has grown substantially in the early twenty-first century, anchored by the biennial Christian Congregational Music Conference at Ripon College Cuddesdon, a growing collection of edited volumes,[51] and recent monographs by Jeffers Engelhardt, Mark Porter, Jonathan Dueck, April Stace, Monique Ingalls, Ari Kelman, Tom Wagner, and several others.[52] Studies of Christian music's presentational contexts, however, are largely absent from ethnomusicology and popular music studies. The academic literature on Christian music tends to focus on its history,[53] sociology,[54] or subcultural niches.[55] But its market has been overlooked in popular music scholarship, in part precisely because it is so banal. If we are going to take scholarship on Katy Perry seriously (and I agree with Wald that we should, partly because her career started in the Christian market), then we also need to take seriously scholarship on mainstream, mass market pop and its derivatives, including Christian music. You do not have to be a fan of the music to say something critical and insightful about it; in fact, objectivity might strengthen your analyses and insights.

MUSIC ON THE MARGINS

I began researching this book in earnest in 2009, gathering data using a mixed-methods approach. Multi-sited ethnographic participant observation has been my primary research methodology, and I conducted primary fieldwork in 2009–12 at Cornerstone Festival, in Chicago, and in Nashville, which serves as the de facto center of the Christian music industries. In Chicago I attended church regularly as an ethnographer at Jesus People, U.S.A., the intentional community that organized Cornerstone for twenty-nine years, and attended concerts and other social events.[56] While in Nashville I attended church and participated in other events at the Anchor Fellowship, a church that caters to college students, subcultural Christians, and professionals in the Christian music industries.[57] I conducted follow-up fieldwork in 2017 in Chicago and at another Christian music festival, AudioFeed. During my trips to Nashville I also conducted archival research at the Center for Popular Music at Middle Tennessee State University (in Murfreesboro), including a follow-up trip in 2018. In addition to the informal chats and relationships with interlocutors throughout my fieldwork, I conducted many formal interviews with several current and former record label executives and recording artists in Chicago, Nashville, and Seattle (where Tooth & Nail Records is located). I supplemented these qualitative data with quantitative data, including publicly available industry metrics provided by the Recording Industry Association of America and the Gospel Music Association.

Although I no longer self-identify as a Christian, throughout my fieldwork I was able to draw upon my childhood experiences as a regular churchgoer to authenticate myself to Christians as a researcher already familiar with their beliefs and practices. When they asked me if I was a

Christian, I typically replied that I had grown up attending a Southern Baptist church, that my father was a pastor, but that I no longer considered myself a Christian. I found that this brief history was typically accepted and unchallenged by my interlocutors. In many instances, this led to a more in-depth conversation about spirituality, Christian beliefs, and personal faith (or my lack thereof). To some of the evangelicals I encountered in my fieldwork I was a "backslidden Christian," ripe for ministry and recovery. Others saw me as an agnostic, a liberal/elite academic, or a "searcher," and used Christian apologetics as a way to witness to me (that is, they attempted to use reasoning and logic to describe their own paths to faith in an attempt to convert me). Still others did not press me on matters of faith; they answered my questions and tolerated my observing worship without questioning my own beliefs. Sometimes this felt comfortable: we were learning about each other's worlds and worldviews, not in a transactional, quid pro quo kind of way, but collaboratively. At other times, however, my discomfort highlighted the boundaries between my world and that of my interlocutors, where I remained a religious outsider. Nevertheless, my background provided me with a degree of cultural insiderness, as did my experiences as an active participant in underground music scenes and my music industry expertise. This facilitated my interactions with record label executives and other cultural intermediaries, authenticating me as someone professionally invested in the field beyond the personal investment of a typical fan.

I draw from these experiences and data throughout *God Rock, Inc.* to examine the boundaries of the Christian market through the lenses of several themes: commerce, ethics, resistance, and crossover. The book is split into two parts. Part 1 addresses Christian music through its historical narrative, problematizing commerce and the market's boundaries chronologically through the market's commercial success, the consolidation of its record labels, and the success of its biggest star: Amy Grant. Chapter 1 turns to Christian popular music's origin in the Jesus People movement of the late 1960s and '70s. During this period, an infrastructure emerged to support Jesus music in the absence of significant investment on the part of the existing (secular) record industry. Several case studies from this period illustrate the interrelatedness of commerce, ethics, resistance, and crossover in establishing the market's boundaries as well as in enabling their transgression. In chapter 2, I address the practices and priorities of the largest Christian record labels and the reactions of fans and other cultural intermediaries to the accelerating growth and corporate consolidation of the Christian market during the 1980s and '90s. This dramatic infrastructural shift represented a significant investment in the Christian market on the part of secular, for-profit multinational entertainment conglomerates. Drawing from reporting and editorial writing in *CCM* magazine and its sister publications (*MusicLine* and *The CCM Update*) in the 1980s and '90s, I demonstrate a range of responses to the complicated debate about prioritizing commerce, aesthetic, or theological concerns among record label professionals and other Christian market participants.

In chapter 3, I consider the ethical objections to Christian popular music. These objections were first made by conservative evangelicals in the 1960s and '70s, who argued that the music was incompatible with Christian values and lifestyles. The televangelist Jimmy Swaggart emerged as a particularly vocal opponent in the 1980s, and in a 1985 interview for *CCM* magazine, editor John Styll and Swaggart laid out what appeared to be mutually exclusive views on the appropriateness of contemporary music (including both rock and pop) for Christians. As the Christian market's main periodical, *CCM* magazine provided a space where its ethics could be debated and also enacted. When several Christian artists faced professional repercussions for immoral behavior in the 1990s, Styll and his staff used their platform to advocate for those artists' rights to atone and account for their sins in private. To end Part 1, I turn to Amy Grant's career in chapter 4. For many years, she was the Christian market's most successful artist, and thus her attempts to cross over into pop music's general market in the late 1980s and early '90s was perhaps expected. The trajectory of her career maps onto transitions that the entire market experienced during the 1980s and '90s; one could describe Amy Grant's career as inflecting the ways in which issues of commerce, ethics, resistance, and crossover have complicated the contestations over the Christian market's meaning and purpose.

Following the largely chronological groundwork laid in these first four chapters, part 2 turns to a thematic organization to address ethics, resistance, and crossover. Each of these, together with commerce, are interrelated and codependent: resistance, for example, is partly a response to industry consolidation; ethics informs crossover strategies, as well as consumers' reactions to crossover. In chapter 5 I address ethics as a tool for establishing and policing markets' boundaries. The ethics of belonging can be used both to exclude participants from markets and to justify the inclusion of others. Christian artists frequently perform ethics—that is, they articulate their ethical appropriateness for the Christian market—and in this way ethics becomes yet another avenue through which participants define niche markets. This chapter builds on Timothy Rommen's "ethics of style" and Jeffers Engelhardt's "right way" singing in Christian contexts and applies them to the Christian market.[58]

In a seminal book, Dick Hebdige argues that subcultures are defined by their resistance, usually expressed via stylistic and ideological resignifications and transgressions.[59] At its emergence, Jesus music marked a particularly notable break, in that it resisted both dominant evangelical culture and the secular themes of contemporaneous popular music. As the Christian market matured in the 1980s and '90s, it increasingly promoted mainstream Christian popular music. The formerly marginal market spawned new substyles—the periphery's peripheries; niches of niches—and Christian hardcore, metal, and punk came to define the Christian market's margins. In chapter 6, I explore ways in which resistance is articulated, presented, and sold in the Christian market. Case studies illustrate resistance and oppositionality in lived experience at music festivals (Cornerstone and AudioFeed) and in the music and performances of several artists (The Chariot, Timbre, David Bazan).

In chapter 7, I turn to crossover, the process of an artist transitioning from one market to another. I define *crossover* not only as the transition from niche to mass markets but also from niche to niche or mass to mass. Building upon Amy Grant's paradigmatic example of crossover, in this chapter I illustrate the challenges and benefits of fringe crossover and reverse crossover through brief case studies of several bands, many of whom have been affiliated with Tooth & Nail Records. I examine how crossover itself is implicated in the forever-changing states of markets' boundaries. In the book's conclusion, I make the connections between commerce, ethics, resistance, and crossover explicit. One way of thinking about these issues, particularly when they are deployed to police boundaries and enforce expectations—is as providing a way to guarantee as much stability as possible in markets and industries marked by perpetual (and often unpredictable) change. Chad Johnson, a former Christian record label executive, chose the opposite path: abandoning a stable career and launching a new nonprofit organization to support and train Christian artists committed to ministry for the music industries' new models of finance and audience engagement. His example, maybe better than all of the others throughout this book, demonstrates that niche markets can indeed find relevance far from the peripheries where they began. Perhaps music on the margins is not so marginal after all.

PART ONE

Christian Music

An Industry and Its History

1

"Why Should the Devil Have All the Good Music?"

The Christian Market's Origins

The roots of the market for Christian popular music lie in the Jesus People movement, an evangelical youth revival that emerged in California during the late 1960s, in parallel with the countercultural movement. Street evangelists ministered to youth, students, and hippies, engaging them directly on college campuses, in coffeehouses and nightclubs, or even literally on the street instead of through church-based programs or parachurch ministries. In a traditional model of evangelism, these countercultural converts would in turn minister to their peers in coffee shops, on college campuses, at rock concerts, and other unconventional settings. Certainly this was the hope of Bill Bright, the founder of Campus Crusade for Christ, whom historian Larry Eskridge describes as wanting "to train an army of half a million local lay evangelists who would spread the gospel throughout America by the nation's bicentennial in 1976."[1] But young Christians first had to be secure and confident in their new faith in order to convert others, so street evangelists focused on making Christianity immediately meaningful and relevant to their daily lives. For these ministers and their many young converts, Jesus Christ was not some unapproachable, abstract deity but rather an accessible hippie whose teachings resonated with their daily concerns. Evangelism itself—converting someone to Christianity—became recast as a form of activism that addressed the kinds of issues that animated the counterculture.[2] It was effective for a variety of reasons: the Jesus People movement's form of Christianity broke both from previous generations' religious traditions and from the increasingly permissive morality of the 1960s, especially in terms of sex and drugs; it also benefitted from a growing popular interest in spirituality unattached to organized religion. Rejecting sectarian views, traditional worship practices, authoritarian leadership, and conventional sociocultural expectations, the Jesus People reframed Christianity as a set of beliefs opposed to middle-class norms, simultaneously speaking to youths' disenchantment with materialism and their distrust of mainline denominations. Finally, it incorporated popular culture into the Christian lifestyle: within the Jesus People movement, coffeehouses, alternative newspapers (Duane Pederson's *Hollywood Free Paper* was a popular resource), and rock and roll were not taboo; rather, they became important tools for evangelism and biblical teaching.

It might help to think of the Jesus People movement as "rebranding" Christianity for 1960s' countercultural youth whose concerns were distinct from, if not unrelated to, those of their parents.[3] Like most modern branding campaigns, a huge variety of goods and media promoted this newly culturally relevant version of Christianity: bumper stickers, buttons, jewelry, literature, movies, music, musicals, T-shirts, and so on. The Jesus People movement was not centralized—there was no official Jesus People marketing team strategy—so we have to find other explanations for the deluge of faith-based consumer goods that appeared during this time. One explanation is that the Jesus People, many of whom were converted hippies, simply translated the counterculture into Christianity. Thus, Christian coffeehouses, communes, newspapers, and rock music attest to the Jesus People movement's acceptance of contemporaneous popular culture. Entrepreneurs, including those invested in ministry and those invested in profit, designed and sold ready-made fashion, knickknacks, and other items, commodifying the Jesus People movement as readily as they did the counterculture. The popularity of the Jesus People—both as a movement that attracted new converts and as a newsworthy cultural phenomenon that sold newspapers and magazines—exposed a market for contemporary religious goods and media.

Another explanation, however, situates the consumer goods during this period within a longer history of material Christianity, or the physical stuff that constitutes religious practice and identity for many Christians in the United States. Colleen McDannell writes of the ebb and flow of these goods' popularity: in addition to the altars, Bibles, hymnbooks, icons, and other sacred objects long found in Christian homes and places of worship, Christian decorative and household products were a fashionable component of the Victorian aesthetic in the nineteenth century. These goods were commonly produced and sold by secular companies who found the religious market to be profitable. Middle-class consumer tastes changed in the early twentieth century, however, driven by mass culture, industrialization, and urbanization. By the end of World War I, religious themes were no longer in style, and secular producers and retailers that targeted middle-class consumers deemphasized unprofitable religious commodities. As these companies pulled out of the market for religious goods, Christian companies emerged to fill this niche, finding demand for Christian-themed household objects reduced from the broader U.S. middle class to primarily working-class Christian households.[4] From this perspective, the market for Christian goods follows fashion trends just as other consumer markets do: companies invest in the market when it is strong and divest when it is weak, leaving it to smaller producers as a comparatively small niche. By the 1970s, however, the market had rebounded dramatically: Christianity was fashionable again following the visibility of the Jesus People movement, and the demographics for Christian goods had expanded.

The growth of consumer culture following World War II had several effects. Lizabeth Cohen, for example, writes of mass consumption contributing to a shared sense of U.S. nationalism while simultaneously furthering social stratification along class, gender, and racial divides.[5] President Jimmy Carter diagnosed the United States' economic woes in 1979 as symptomatic of, in part, "self-indulgence and consumption" in his "crisis of confidence" speech on July 15, 1979.[6] Daniel Horowitz documents the critical trajectories that ultimately validated consumption as integral to meaning-making itself and not merely a poor substitute for elite culture.[7] Within white U.S. evangelicalism, consuming Christian goods became a way for Jesus People converts to celebrate their newly held religious beliefs. But, more significantly, it further cemented the idea among evangelicals that everyday acts, including acts of consumption, could and should be imbued with religious intent. As McDannell writes (echoing Cohen), in the United States, "being Christian means to have a Christian life style that includes purchasing goods from a fellow Christian. . . . Making, selling, marketing, and purchasing link Christians together."[8]

What both of these explanations have in common is the significant role that the commodification of religion plays. The buying and selling of salvation and praise have been central to Christianity for centuries; purchasing (and profiting from) religious goods was not a new feature of the Jesus People movement. Relationships between religious practice (or the promise of salvation) and the market for material goods and services have long been uncomfortable: the Roman Catholic Church's selling of indulgences was a target of Martin Luther and other Protestant reformers in the sixteenth century, and many Christians still disagree about the appropriate role of capital, capitalist markets, and wealth in religious contexts.[9] And yet, a major legacy of the Jesus People movement—including the record labels, artists, and executives who exploited its music—is that it normalized consumption practices within white U.S. evangelical culture. As McDannell shows, by the 1970s Christian products were no longer only associated with working-class identity but also with the increasing numbers of young, middle-class evangelicals. Media scholar Heather Hendershot argues that in embracing capitalism's conflation of consumption with social identity, evangelicals situated consumption as a central component of the Christian lifestyle: "To purchase Christian products is to declare one's *respectability* in a country in which people are most often addressed by mass culture not as citizens but as consumers. In America, to buy is to be."[10] As members of an identifiable and desirable market, evangelicals staked a claim for participation in public discourse.

The Jesus People privileged freedom of expression and embraced popular music styles relevant to their daily lives. Because Jesus People musicians such as Agape, Phil Keaggy and Glass Harp, Love Song, Larry Norman, and others wanted to sing about their faith, they faced resistance from the dominant (secular) record labels. In short, they were too Christian for rock and roll, but they were also too rock and roll for Christian record labels. Word Records, the largest Christian label at the time, primarily released recordings of hymns and white Southern gospel musicians. Although Word's owner, Jarrell McCracken, feared that Jesus music would dilute the label's core brand identity, in 1972 Word launched a new subsidiary: Myrrh Records would produce and release recordings of Christian popular music. Other Christian labels emerged in the 1970s, many with no previous experience in the record industry or Christian market: Lamb & Lion, Maranatha! Music, Sparrow, and Star Song, among others. These labels were part of a new infrastructure for Christian music's nascent niche market: Christian artists recorded for Christian record labels and wrote songs for Christian publishers; Christian consumers listened to Christian radio; and Christian records were reviewed in Christian magazines and sold by Christian retailers, who readily provided "safe" alternatives to secular artists.

One effect of this separation and insularity was that the diversity of aesthetic, ideological, and theological orientations within Christian music was rarely apparent to outsiders, who typically had a monolithic and undifferentiated assessment of Christian music (if they were aware of it at all). Much like Christianity itself in the United States, Christian music was (and still is) incredibly varied. Recording artists perform many musical styles and represent numerous ideological and theological orientations, ultimately pushing the boundaries of what constitutes Christian music—a question that Christian consumers and the companies marketing and selling Christian commodities both face. Despite the changing demographics and tastes of evangelical Christianity following the Jesus People movement, debates over the appropriateness of popular music within Christianity dominated discourse in the 1970s and into the '80s. Essentially, participants asked whether popular music could—or should—be employed in service to God. This argument, which I discuss further in chapter 3, harbored transparently racist perspectives (many of which were recycled from the moral panic over rock and roll in the 1950s), substituted individual tastes for theology, and ignored past debates about musical appropriateness throughout the history of Christianity.

Other debates, however, are rooted in differing opinions over the ideal objectives for Christian music. These differing opinions emerged regularly throughout my research, in primary and secondary sources, during formal interviews and informal conversations with interlocutors, and throughout the course of my ethnographic research. The following six sets of questions articulate their core concerns:

1. Is Christian music's primary purpose to serve as worship, as entertainment, as an evangelizing tool, or as something else? What should its lyrical and aesthetic priorities be to help fulfill this purpose?
2. What are the aesthetic boundaries of Christian music? Are any musical styles incompatible with Christianity, or are all styles appropriate for Christian expression?
3. Who is Christian music's target audience: Christians or non-Christians?
4. Should Christian recording artists pursue crossover success in the general market?
5. How should record labels and other companies in the Christian market balance commercial with theological concerns when articulating their goals and measuring success? What should be

the market's orientation to the broader missions and ministries of evangelical Christianity?

6. If Christian music is primarily identified by its lyrical content, what makes lyrics particularly Christian? Must Christian artists explicitly address their faith for their music to be Christian? How should we categorize music by general market artists who are Christians? Can instrumental music be Christian?

These questions' moralizing and prescriptive tone reflect absolutist positions that have been common in the Christian market for decades. Each participant's perspective is informed by personal faith; Christianity itself is positivist, grounded in the belief of an absolute truth. There is often little ambiguity or nuance in individuals' positions on these issues and little compromise within the debates themselves. Embedded within all these debates are theological arguments over Christianity's role in the world, its ideal degree of engagement with or resistance to secular culture, the objectives for Christian music and musicians, and ultimately the boundaries of Christian music. When conflated, these debates might be reframed as asking what constitutes "authentic" Christian music. Authenticity, in this context, is socially constructed and best understood as a process of authentication and not an inherent quality of the music itself.[11] Ultimately, this is a foundational question about Christian rock's ontology—what it *is*.

In the rest of this chapter, Jesus music case studies illustrate the complexities of this ontological question and the four themes of this book: commerce, ethics, resistance, and crossover. I highlight the challenges that emerge when capitalist markets for popular music, the business and ministerial objectives of the nascent Christian music industries, and the theologies of Jesus People evangelicals collide. The early career of Larry Norman, a central figure in origin stories frequently cited as the "father of Christian rock," demonstrated how a mythology of resistance can actually serve a strategic role in affirming belongingness. The Jesus People movement itself crossed over into mainstream popularity as local, regional, and nationwide news media paid increasing attention to its growth. In particular, Explo '72, a large Jesus People convention and festival in Dallas, Texas, marked the movement's peak in U.S. public discourse. General market record labels had released many songs that addressed Christianity and Christian beliefs through the early 1970s, but Christian music increasingly became the commercial domain of labels like Benson, Sparrow, and Word around this time. Although these labels invested heavily in establishing infrastructures to support Christian artists, they often faced decisions that pitted their ethics or theological priorities against the financial health of their institutions, such as the choice that Billy Ray Hearn faced when one of his best-selling artists, Keith Green, asked to be released from his recording contract with Sparrow Records. These conflicts revealed diverging opinions about the objectives and goals for Christian music.

THE ETHICS OF KEITH GREEN

In 1979, Billy Ray Hearn—founder, owner, and head of Sparrow Records—was anxiously waiting for Keith Green to record his third album. Founded in 1976 and independently owned and operated at the time, Sparrow was quickly becoming one of the Christian market's better-known record labels. A pianist and songwriter, Green was one of Sparrow's stable of core, top-selling artists. Keith Green's first two Sparrow albums—1977's *For Him Who Has Ears to Hear* and 1978's *No Compromise*—had been so strongly received that other labels had come calling with cash signing bonuses, expense accounts, and other perks. Hearn, of course, wanted Green to stay with Sparrow, both because the artist's focus on ministry aligned well with the label's mission and because Hearn had deliberately kept his artist roster and schedule of new releases small; thus, the financial consequences of losing a top-selling artist would be great. Green signed a new contract with Sparrow in part as a reaction against the offers from other labels: wary of the overlap between the business of music and his music ministry, he acted to remove the monetary temptation.[12] Keith Green chose what was likely a financially worse deal with Sparrow partly because it enabled him to cast his career as a ministry unconcerned with capital.

And yet, by the middle of 1979, Green was increasingly convinced that signing with Sparrow and remaining an artist in the for-profit market had been a mistake, no matter how little actual profit there was. As his widow, Melody Green, explains in her memoir, although Keith Green often performed for free, his records were not freely available: "Were they 'products' or 'ministry'? Keith could see where his recordings might be a bit of both, but his reason for doing them was definitely ministry."[13] Following a lot of prayer, Bible study, and discussion with his wife and other trusted advisors, Green concluded that selling records was inconsistent with his ministerial objectives. He met Hearn at his house in Northridge, California, to give him the bad news:

"I need to ask you to let me out of my contract.... I blew it. God just told me to start my own label and give my records away. I'm really sorry. I don't know what to do. I know I signed a contract and I'll honor it if I need to, but I'm asking you to release me from it." ... Finally, Billy Ray said, "If God doesn't want you at Sparrow and I try to keep you, then I'd be fighting against God. That means God will be standing against me and the whole company.... I'll let you go."[14]

Hearn recounted to me in an interview many years later, "Of course, I did it, because when God's telling somebody to do something, I'm not going to stand in the way."[15]

This entire conflict, culminating in Green's act of humility ("I blew it") and Hearn's sacrificial acquiescence ("I'll let you go," "I'm not going to stand in the way"), neatly illustrates the central question at the heart of all conflicts within the Christian market, that of objectives: in short, what is Christian music *for*? Uncovering and understanding objectives is an important step in comprehending the ways in which the Christian market is distinct from and similar to the general market. Keith Green was a convert of the Jesus People movement and, in 1979, still very much an ascending star in the world of Christian music. He had felt God's calling to move from Los Angeles to rural east Texas, where he would shift his focus from a full-time music career in which ministry played a secondary, albeit important, role to a full-time ministry centered in an intentional community supported, in part, by his music career. He was not turning his back on his career, but he was resisting what he understood to be the corrupting influence of commerce more firmly than when he had turned down other offers and re-signed with Sparrow Records. Green had already made the decision to upend his life and those of his family and community members (scattered around L.A.'s Woodland Hills neighborhood in several different houses and apartments) when he finally gathered the courage to ask Hearn to be released from his contract, knowing full well that Hearn—a fellow Christian, yes, but also a businessman—had every right to ask him to fulfill his responsibilities to Sparrow. Imagine Billy Ray Hearn himself, in his comfortable suburban living room, confronted by this request from Green—an artist whose success had helped keep Sparrow afloat and allowed Hearn to invest in other artists' careers, and whose potential as a crossover artist was evidenced by the serious interest from other record labels. Hearn, who had majored in church music and later attended seminary, landed in the Christian music industry through a somewhat organic process of searching for effective ways of using music to minister to youth and young adults. And yet, despite his training as a musician and a music minister, granting Green's request was not an automatic "Yes," because it endangered the welfare of his business and, thus, the welfare of his family, employees, artists, and their families. How did these two men get to this point? How do they move forward?

This episode clearly illustrates how the commercial realities of selling Christian music can come between two people who otherwise agree on so many other things and believe they love and serve the same God. But in Christian music, as in Christianity itself, there is no single accepted approach to interpreting biblical scriptures and Jesus's teachings and applying them to daily life. Green and Hearn did not arrive at this conflict through a fundamental disagreement over how separate their market should be from the general market, and in this instance the structural foregrounding we find in Howard and Streck fails. To understand the forces at play here and in other situations in music markets—those that define moments of disjuncture and disruption as well as those that are mundane and even banal—we need to dig deeper, to grapple with the aesthetic, commercial, and ideological (or theological) reasons behind the conflicts. No figure in the early history of Christian music personifies the conflict between these priorities better than Larry Norman, whose career was marked more by his resistance to existing norms than by his role in establishing new ones.

CHRISTIAN MUSIC AS RESISTANCE: THE CAREER OF LARRY NORMAN

Larry Norman's career in the music industry started as a member of the San Jose-based psychedelic rock band People![16] After a hit single on Capitol Records in 1968 with a cover of The Zombies song "I Love You" (🎧), Norman left the band. Following a short stint writing musicals for Capitol, he reemerged as a solo artist with the album *Upon This Rock* (1970, Capitol), a strong and unapologetic statement of his Christian faith. His next three studio records were marketed as a trilogy and further cemented his reputation as the Jesus People movement's best-known rock and roll artist. Norman released the last of these, 1976's *In Another Land*, on his own label: Solid Rock Records (🎧). Solid Rock was an artist-directed Christian record label, releasing albums by Norman, Mark Heard, Tom Howard, Randy Stonehill, and others between 1976 and 1981.[17] By 1980, however, Solid Rock had imploded and Norman's career was on the rocks. John J. Thompson suggests that Norman's overreliance on his waning celebrity in the late 1970s and his inability (or unwillingness) to sign artists with obvious commercial potential were partly to blame for Solid Rock's failures.[18] Fans turned elsewhere as new Larry Norman records were continuously delayed and performances grew increasingly sporadic. Norman became reclusive; when he did appear in public it was to feud with fellow Christian artists and others in the Christian market.

Larry Norman's reputation is as a brilliant but troubled artist—an outlaw musician, unwelcome in secular music industries because he was unapologetic about his Christian faith, but similarly unwelcome in Christian music because he unapologetically loved rock and roll. In Norman's hands, and in the mythology he cultivated around his own persona, Jesus music itself resisted both the prevailing norms of the 1960s' popular music market and the accepted standards for white U.S. evangelical Christian culture. This liminality is apparent early in his career: the song "We Need a Whole Lot More of Jesus (And a Lot Less Rock and Roll)" (🎧), which would have been the title track of People!'s 1968 debut LP had Norman gotten his way, is less a statement of faith than it is a parody of conservative Christians who preach against the dangers of rock and roll. People!'s version is a satirical, tongue-in-cheek cover of a sincere revival song, originally written by country and gospel artist Wayne Raney. A preacher calls a congregation to their feet (as if at a worship service) and a revivalist singer, accompanied by piano at a moderate (but loose) tempo, warns about increasing crime: "This world is about to go." Over several stanzas, we learn that the solution can be found in salvation, "old-fashioned preachers," a revival that would "keep the love of God in our souls," and (of course) Jesus; the congregation joins in on the refrain with a tambourine. Norman's history with organized religion was contentious throughout his career, and the parody we hear in "We Need a Whole Lot More of Jesus" is consistent with his persona as an outsider Christian constantly needling conservatives for shunning difficult theological questions in favor of easy platitudes. The song is true to Norman, in other words, but because it is not a sincere expression of faith, it also complicates the common origin story of his leaving the band. According to that story, he left because Capitol retitled the album *I Love You* after the band's million-selling single—a conflict that clearly places faith and commerce in opposition to each other and paints Norman as a martyr.[19]

While People! was largely a general market band with a few songs that addressed spiritual themes—not unusual in the world of psychedelic rock—on *Upon This Rock*, Larry Norman the solo artist was clearly writing from a Christian perspective. He shed People!'s Bay Area psychedelic rock for the sound of bluesy rock and roll and folk-influenced protest songs, equal parts Rolling Stones, Neil Young, and electric-era Bob Dylan. On this and his later records, Norman's tenor singing voice vacillated between gritty and clean timbres. While he often shelved the blues-rock for '70s-era balladry, complete with lush string accompaniment, he stopped short of the close vocal harmonies and far from the synths of other '70s artists, in both the Christian and general markets.

Norman wrote songs not just as a Christian but as one who clearly connected with the resistant ideals and theologies of the Jesus People movement. "Sweet Sweet Song of Salvation" (🎧) is a boogie blues that portrays evangelism and conversion as joyous, a rendering that aligned with the passion and excitement about religious beliefs common to Jesus People converts. "I Wish We'd All Been Ready" (🎧) is a ballad that imagines the world after the rapture in which Christians are taken to heaven (as promised in the Bible), leaving nonbelievers behind: a husband disappears from bed, a man disappears while walking with his friend. "Children died, the days grew cold / A piece of bread could buy a bag of gold / I wish we'd all been ready," Norman sings plaintively, in an upper register, accompanied by acoustic guitar, piano, and strings. This apocalyptic song has proven to be the most resilient in Norman's catalog and perhaps the piece that best identifies him as a Jesus People musician. As Eskridge notes, Jesus People movement ministers and converts anticipated that the biblically prophesied end-times were arriving in short order: "This expectation affected the urgency of their evangelistic efforts and served as a filter through which they perceived the cultural, social, and political world around them."[20] Hal Lindsey's bestselling book *The Late, Great Planet Earth*, which describes the alignments between then-current events and biblical scriptures to predict the coming apocalypse, similarly drew from and contributed to the Jesus People movement's eschatology.[21]

Norman expanded on his vision for faith-centered rock and roll with *Only Visiting This Planet* (1972, Verve). The lushly arranged ballad "I've Got to Learn to Live without You" (🎧) provides the template for Christian songs that address the limited temporality of human love and relationships, especially when considered in contrast to the timelessness of God's unconditional love. "Why Should the Devil Have All the Good Music" (🎧) is as much a statement of faith in Christ ("Jesus told the truth and Jesus showed the way") as it is in rock and roll ("There's nothing wrong with playing blues licks"), conflating the two by the end of the song as Norman repeats his mantra: "Jesus is the rock and he rolled my blues away!" "Why Should the Devil" is the sequel to People!'s "We Need a Whole Lot More of Jesus," except in the later song Norman names the Christian anti-rock discourse he finds so antagonizing instead of parodying it: "They say rock and roll is wrong / . . . / They say to cut my hair / . . . / If you got a reason, tell me to my face / Why should the devil have all the good music?"

The song's lyrics point toward multiple interpretations of the question itself. On one hand, Norman questions the devil's apparent monopoly on good music from an aesthetic basis: clearly Norman prefers the sound of rock and roll over that of traditional hymns, and surely there are other Christians who feel similarly, so there is a potential market here for "good" music that is written for Christians. Another interpretation, which foregrounds Norman's resistant identity, is rooted in tying the concept of "good music" to moral reform, instruction, and edification in Christianity. From this perspective, good music is not merely aesthetically pleasing but also capable of communicating and teaching Christian morals; music is not good when it encourages immoral activities. As I discuss further in chapter 3, from a 1960s-era conservative Christian perspective, rock and roll is not good music. Indeed, Anna Nekola writes that Christian critics considered rock and roll to be "a radically and inherently *dangerous music* . . . sonically bad and innately immoral."[22] Norman reminds us that he has a strong moral center ("I know what's right, I know what's wrong / I don't confuse it"), so he is not sliding toward moral relativism when he asks us to consider the aesthetics of music separately from its ethical qualities. The central criticism he makes in "Why Should the Devil"—and the reason why this song and its title became an anthem of the Jesus People movement—is not necessarily that rock and roll *sounds good* (although clearly it does to him), but that it does not *teach bad*. It is okay to dislike music that does not affect you; Norman himself does not like hymns because they lack a strong beat, they do not incite him to dance, they sound funereal. Christian anti-rock critics, on the other hand, dislike rock and roll because they claim it promotes sexual deviance and can hypnotize listeners, ultimately disrupting social norms. "Why Should the Devil" thus embodies Norman's liminality, delivering two messages. For his fellow Jesus People, he wants them to be unashamed of their tastes and to enjoy God-pleasing music no matter what genre. For more conservative Christians, he wants to redefine the concept of "good music" beyond the puritanical obsession with dancing and away from large questions of morality.

FIGURE 1. Album cover for Larry Norman's *So Long Ago the Garden* (1973).

So Long Ago the Garden (1973, MGM), Norman's third studio record, would have been difficult for a Christian label to sell.²³ The controversial cover art features a photo of Norman, from the waist up and shirtless, superimposed over an image of a lion lying in a pasture (figure 1). Instead of straightforward lyrics about loving Jesus, Norman addresses pain, disappointment, and violence on songs like "The Same Old Story" (🎧), "Lonely by Myself," and "Be Careful What You Sign," among others. The album gets its title from the closing lyrics of "Nightmare #71" (🎧), the final track, which provides a more detailed apocalyptic eschatology than "I Wish We'd All Been Ready," referencing in turn natural disasters, the cult of celebrity, urban decay, and declining morals (including the sexual revolution, swinging, and prescription drug abuse).

As Christian music grew in popularity during the late 1970s and '80s, Larry Norman was recognized and revered as a founding father of its market. Even if *Upon This Rock* was not the first Christian rock record, Norman was certainly the first Christian rock star. But as his career progressed, he was marginalized as a difficult artist—both in terms of his ability to navigate the increasingly professional Christian market and its expectations and in terms of the confrontational nature of many of his songs in a milieu that preferred easily understood messages celebrating faith (instead of questioning it). Like Keith Green, Larry Norman had a choice to make in the late 1970s: he could have capitulated to the expectations of the market, tempered his criticism of Christian labels, and let someone like Billy Ray Hearn do the work of releasing and distributing his records while he focused on writing, recording, and performing his music. Instead, Norman chose independence, in part because he distrusted the established labels (as he distrusted Christianity's established denominations and churches). He might have had more stability had he chosen the path of conformity, both in terms of his finances and his health. Yet the independence Norman chose enhanced his persona as a persecuted, troubled, principled, and ultimately resistant Christian artist. By the late 1990s and early 2000s, the concept of resistance in Christian music had changed, as I discuss in chapter 6; Norman's music and his ranting against both the church and the music industry sounded decidedly old-fashioned next to Christian punk and metal artists of the time. In the 2000s he attempted to repair his relationship with the broader Christian market, which recognized his contributions in *CCM* magazine's list of one hundred greatest albums and by inducting him into the Gospel Music Hall of Fame in 2001.[24] After his death in February 2008, he was honored at the Gospel Music Association's Dove Awards and the Grammy Awards ceremonies.

CHRISTIANITY CROSSES OVER: MAINSTREAM POPULARITY AND EXPLO '72

It is tempting to root the Christian market's origin story in the careers of brilliant, convicted, and yet conflicted artists such as Keith Green and Larry Norman. Doing so follows a standard approach that privileges the genius of specific individuals as a catalyst for new genres, such as tying the genesis of rock and roll in the mid-1950s to Elvis Presley's unprecedented ability to translate African American popular music (mainly R&B) for young, white listeners. For Christian music, telling its history through those of individual geniuses is a strategy of highlighting both its uniqueness—look, we have our own foundational figures!—and its similarity to other, better-known genres. These stories, however formulaic, thus grant Christian music a patina of legitimacy because they are comparative.

But individual genius is not the only way to tell the story of the convergence of Christianity and popular music. There were larger social, cultural, and commercial trajectories at play as well, aligned with a period of spiritual awakening in the United States in the 1960s and '70s. In addition to the Jesus People movement, hippies and others found resonance within Buddhist, Hindu, pagan, and Sufi traditions, among others, as well as pan-spiritual practices such as the New Age movement.[25] The general market for popular music in the United States—and the entertainment industries more broadly—increasingly reflected a growing cultural interest in spirituality during this time. Larry Norman and others were focused on rock and roll's acceptance within Christianity, partly through advocating for its legitimacy and relevance among evangelicals and partly through laying the groundwork for a market infrastructure to support the production, distribution, and intermediation of Christian music. At the same time, however, secular companies predicted profit in their consumers' interest in spirituality, resulting in Christianity's increasing presence in rock and roll.

Gospel songs had been frequently heard on Top 40 radio in earlier decades; Don Cusic documents several such examples from the 1950s.[26] For example, Elvis Presley's rendition of Thomas Dorsey's "Peace in the Valley" (🎧), which he performed at the end of his third and final appearance on *The Ed Sullivan Show* on January 6, 1957, peaked at #25 on the *Billboard* Hot 100 later that year; Pat Boone reached #4 with "A Wonderful Time up There" (🎧) in 1958.[27] It should come as no surprise that both Presley and Boone, each of whom built their careers sanitizing Black music for white audiences in the 1950s, also recorded many spirituals and gospel songs for the segregated airwaves. Pop songs from a Christian perspective, however, tapered off and were no longer as common during the beginning of the 1960s. By the mid-'60s, biblical and Christian references in popular music, when they appeared, often reflected a secular perspective more than they did an artist's sincere Christian faith. Appendix 2 lists many examples of singles that reference Christian beliefs charting on Top 40 radio during the 1960s.[28] While several of these singles were spirituals or traditional songs, others were newly composed. As you can see (and hear, on this chapter's companion playlist at the front of the book), the 1960s did not lack for radio singles that either addressed Christian themes or explicitly mentioned Jesus Christ.[29]

One way to think about this deluge of Christianity in popular culture is as a normalizing factor that helped legitimize the Jesus People movement—and, by extension, evangelicalism in general—within U.S. culture and public discourse. Simultaneously, similar forces were moving internally within Christianity, as several ministers and organizations worked to normalize the Jesus People movement and its cultural expressions within existing churches, denominations, and parachurch organizations. While pastors and churches local to the Jesus People movement witnessed the success of street evangelism firsthand, evangelical and mainline Protestant churches nationwide were more hesitant to accept new converts. Churches found it challenging to incorporate Jesus People converts' counterculturalism, embrace of popular culture (especially rock and roll music), individualized spirituality, and rejection of tradition. This apprehension was reciprocal: many Jesus People converts were uneasy about joining existing churches and denominations, which most strongly represented the Christian establishment against which they perceived themselves to be rebelling. As nationally prominent evangelical leaders welcomed the Jesus People movement, however, both sides began to find common ground as disparate groups of Christians overlooked their cultural differences and instead worked toward common goals of ministry and evangelism.[30] For example, Eskridge writes that former Youth for Christ minister Billy Graham's support of the Jesus People movement, after learning of it in early 1971, "had far-reaching implications, particularly for evangelical cognizance and acceptance of the Jesus People"; his public embrace of the movement steadily increased throughout the year.[31] Firsthand accounts from Jesus People participants—including evangelists like Arthur Blessitt, Chuck Smith, Don Williams, and others—also helped normalize the movement for other Christians.[32] Carl Henry (professor at Fuller Theological Seminary and founding editor of *Christianity Today*), David Wilkerson (founder of Teen Challenge), and respected Christian intellectual and theologian Francis Schaeffer encouraged Jesus People converts to seek out the biblical expertise, theological training, and spiritual guidance available at churches.[33]

The Jesus People movement also gained substantial media exposure in the early 1970s. A six-page cover article on "the Jesus revolution" appeared in the June 21, 1971, issue of *Time* magazine accompanied by a six-page color photo spread (see figure 2).[34] Throughout 1971 and '72, coverage also appeared in nationwide publications such as *Life*, *Look*, *Newsweek*, and *U.S. News & World Report* (among others), the major television networks, and many local newspapers and religious publications from a variety of denominational perspectives.[35] Additionally, a number of books about the Jesus People appeared as well, in both the Christian and the general markets. For example, Billy Graham's own *The Jesus Generation* reached evangelicals where his crusade stops could not, giving his stamp of approval.[36] Most of these articles and books demystified the Jesus People, their lifestyles, and their ministries. Others, written from a fundamentalist position, took a moral panic approach, warning readers of the purported dangers of street evangelism, communal living, and popular culture.

FIGURE 2. "The Jesus Revolution," cover of *Time* magazine, June 21, 1971. Collection of the author.

Eskridge notes that this "media blitz" promoting the Jesus People movement was tied to the growing presence of religious themes in popular music (and popular culture in general), as I discussed above.³⁷ Without the successes of "Mrs. Robinson," "Oh Happy Day" (🎧), and "Superstar" (from the concept album and later musical *Jesus Christ Superstar*) (🎧), the Jesus People movement might not have been as relevant a news story. But the story *was* relevant, perhaps more so because it provided a feel-good counterbalance to the era's panicked news stories about countercultural youth rebellion, hippiedom's drug use and free love, the violence at Altamont (in 1969), and Vietnam War protests (the Kent State shootings occurred in 1970). And it became bigger through the recursive nature of the news media, familiar to modern readers of viral news and memes, albeit over a much longer period. Regardless of the media's tone vis-à-vis the Jesus People movement—a hysteria alternating, as Dick Hebdige predicted for "spectacular subcultures," between "dread and fascination, outrage and amusement"[38]—its accelerating exposure ultimately helped mainline Protestants incorporate new converts and normalize their faith practices while simultaneously increasing the visibility of Christianity in the U.S. public sphere. By 1972, then, the Jesus People movement (and, to a lesser degree, evangelical Christianity more broadly, through a transitive relationship) was poised for crossover as a result of these three trajectories: the presence of religious content in (secular) popular music, Protestants' acceptance of Jesus People converts, and the Jesus People movement's visibility in the mainstream news media.

If the Jesus People movement was on the precipice of large-scale acceptance, its tipping point (and broader acceptance by evangelicals) was exemplified by the success of Campus Crusade for Christ's Explo '72 (officially, the International Student Congress on Evangelism), a six-day event (June 12–17, 1972) in which seventy-five thousand to eighty-five thousand participants traveled from around the country to Dallas, Texas, for training in evangelism, ministry, and witnessing.[39] Planning for Explo '72 had started in 1970 and accelerated in '71. As news of the Jesus People movement was cresting in both the mainstream and Christian media, Explo's organizers yoked themselves to this publicity. Eskridge writes that Campus Crusade's founder Bill Bright and Explo '72's director Paul Eshleman "had decided to recast the gathering with the Jesus People in mind and had begun to utilize the publicity surrounding the movement to promote the event."[40] Secondary sources emphasize the scale of Explo '72: two years of planning by three hundred staff with total costs approaching $3 million; attendees from one thousand cities and one hundred countries lodged in all available hotels, church basements, fourteen thousand empty apartments, with private hosts, and at a campsite for two thousand outside the city; workshops at sixty-three locations around the city, necessitating nine hundred fifty buses (both city and chartered) and eleven thousand cars.[41] The emphasis of the conference itself was evangelism training: participants, most of whom were high school and college students, attended seminars and workshops where they learned practical skills to share Christianity's gospel message with strangers, and then they practiced street evangelism and door-to-door witnessing in Dallas. Every evening ended with a rally at the Cotton Bowl, where Billy Graham gave a sermon.

Explo '72 is primarily remembered not for its seminars, however, but rather for its closing, daylong concert that drew as many as two hundred thousand attendees. The concert started around 7:30 a.m. on Saturday, June 17, and featured Jesus People musicians such as Children of the Day, Love Song, Randy Matthews, Barry McGuire, Larry Norman, and others. Celebrity Christians were also present: Kris Kristofferson spoke about his recent conversion to Christianity before singing the hymn "In the Garden" with Rita Coolidge; Miss America 1965, Vonda Kay Van Dyke, also spoke of her faith; Johnny Cash performed a thirty-minute set of gospel songs, including "I See Men as Trees Walking" (🎧) from his forthcoming film and soundtrack *The Gospel Road* (1973), before introducing Billy Graham.[42] Graham's sermon capped the weeklong evangelism training by encouraging attendees to preach the gospel and to trust in Jesus—quoting a #2 *Billboard* single by the general market band Ocean (🎧), to "put your hand in the hand of the man from Galilee."[43] *Life* magazine documented Explo '72 in its June 30, 1972, issue (see figure 3); the Saturday concert was filmed and then broadcast nationwide later that August (along with highlights from the weeknight rallies) on almost two hundred TV stations; and the soundtrack album, *Jesus Sound Explosion*, was mailed free to anyone who requested it.[44] The show and album succeeded where earlier features on the Jesus People movement had fallen short: as Eskridge writes, "the nation could see the Jesus movement in action; hear the new, upbeat gospel music; and see the nation's most prominent evangelicals extol the cause of Christ."[45]

One year prior to Explo '72, *Time* magazine quoted Bill Bright as establishing a "divine timetable" for large-scale evangelism: "Our target date for saturating the U.S. with the gospel of Jesus Christ is 1976—and the world by 1980. Of course, if the Lord wants to work a bit slower, that's O.K."[46] Unstated, of course, is that it would also be okay if the Lord wanted to work more quickly, and Explo '72, Bright's brainchild, was intended to catalyze this mission. Connecting it to the Jesus People movement was both a shrewd strategy meant to capitalize on the movement's popularity and an example of how parachurch organizations like Campus Crusade (and thus, by extension, those denominations and churches whose goals and values aligned with those of Campus Crusade) facilitated its incorporation. Tellingly, as David Stowe notes, although the event was promoted (and is remembered) as the "Christian Woodstock," "there were few recognizable Jesus hippies among the tens of thousands of young people."[47] Already then, and after only a

FIGURE 3. "The Great Jesus Rally in Dallas," cover of *Life* magazine, June 30, 1972. Collection of the author.

year and a half of widespread exposure, the Jesus People movement had transitioned from being a meaningful movement among a small group of participants to being primarily a metonym, or a marker of style or hipness that signified both fashion within Christianity and Christianity's fashionability within popular culture. Casting back to Hebdige again, this period of incorporation into both mainstream Christian culture and U.S. popular culture—not just its debutante ball in Dallas but the entire media frenzy that led up to Explo '72—is the Jesus People movement's moment of crossover.

The Jesus People movement receded from public consciousness when the Watergate scandal became news shortly after Explo '72.[48] As the larger counterculture subsided in the coming months, the street evangelists' target audience dissipated and began to drift away from the concentrated locus on the West Coast. Jesus People converts joined existing churches and started new ones in the wake of the movement. As the Jesus People's focus on everyday spirituality became increasingly common and their relatively unorthodox approach to lifestyle evangelism became normalized, countercultural Christianity itself was no longer niche but increasingly accessible to ever-larger markets, especially in terms of its commodities—due in no small part to the development of a record industry around the Christian music that had arisen in California and elsewhere during the late 1960s and early '70s.

THE MARKET FOR EVANGELISM: BILLY RAY HEARN'S CAREER

If one possible narrative approach to the origin of the Christian market focuses on its founding geniuses, and another addresses the broader sociocultural trajectories that facilitated the Jesus People movement's popularity, then we might split the difference by focusing on individuals conscious of their infrastructural roles in bringing together artists and audiences. In the introduction, I argued that historical and ethnographic insight into the decision-making processes and practices of cultural intermediaries is integral to understanding broader trends in popular music markets. The career of Billy Ray Hearn, whom we met earlier at the moment he released Keith Green from his contract with Sparrow Records in 1979 to pursue a calling outside of the for-profit Christian music industries, demonstrates the intersection of an evangelistic impulse with a talent for identifying undervalued market opportunities. Hearn was a Southern Baptist music and youth minister who catalyzed a movement in the late 1960s to create biblically grounded music for a youth audience before working for Word Records (where he helped launch Myrrh) and later founding Sparrow. Not quite a profiteer, he nevertheless appreciated the role that businesses could play in promoting Christian music, no matter its purpose.

Billy Ray Hearn was an alum of Baylor University (in Waco, Texas) and Southwestern Baptist Theological Seminary (in Fort Worth, Texas) with formal training in classical music.[49] After he graduated from seminary in 1960, he was hired by the Baptist Tabernacle in Atlanta, Georgia, to direct their 150-voice choir. But his passion was for youth ministry, and in Atlanta his attempts to build a strong youth program never gained traction. After two years he joined the staff of the First Baptist Church of Thomasville, Georgia, over two hundred miles south. To hear Hearn tell it, in that small southern town of over eighteen thousand residents, "there wasn't anything else to do. There was one little movie house. There were no game parlors. There was no real big mall where they all gathered. They gathered at church. The church was very important to the community."[50] In Thomasville, Hearn encountered an appetite for new activities at the church. Filling what we might recognize today (outside of church, at least) as an unsated consumer demand, Hearn's youth choirs became incredibly popular. "Every kid in town wanted to be in my youth choir," he told me. "It's that peer pressure, 'This is where it's happening!' . . . I had kids from every church in town."[51] In interviews with Baylor University's Institute for Oral History, Hearn expanded these recollections: he ran eleven choirs for many different age groups, attracting more participants than the church's weekly Sunday School programs. "Everybody would come to my choir program whether they were Methodist, Episcopal or Presbyterian. They'd send their kids to the choir program at the Baptist church."[52]

Hearn started to experiment with combining Christian songs and popular music—particularly the contemporaneous urban folk music revival—for his youth choirs. He explained to me: "You cannot force the Bach chorales on a thirteen-year-old, fifteen-year-old. You have to let him sing with his guitar. And that's what I did. I formed groups with guitars in my little church in Thomasville. You'd take folk songs and make religious words in them, and that's the only music we had. We had to write our own stuff, in a lot of ways. Change the lyrics of secular songs to make them Christian. We'd even take some of the old folk hymns, like 'Amazing Grace,' and put it into that [popular] style."[53] Hearn's goal was evangelism: to attract youth to his church in the hopes of converting them to Christianity. Not only did this work to draw teens to the church—his youth choir had eighty members—but it also provided an opportunity for outreach and ministry outside of the church: "I'd get up groups and we'd perform [hymns as folk music] in the Kiwanis Club and the Lions Club and conventions, and we'd do them for youth fellowships."[54]

Hearn's experience and insight—that popular music succeeded among '60s-era youth where traditional church music failed—proved consequential when he was approached by the Southern Baptist Sunday School Board to produce a youth musical for use throughout the denomination. The result, *Good News!*, featured songs written by Bob Oldenberg; Hearn conducted its debut performance on Saturday, June 10, 1967, at a convention for over two thousand choir directors at Glorieta (a Southern Baptist conference center in New Mexico). But these music ministers initially dismissed it: the following day, Hearn learned that most had thought it awful. Nevertheless, Will Bishop argues in his oral history of the production of *Good News!* that "all pop-styled church choir music written for the evangelical church in the past fifty years can trace its lineage to this first performance."[55] Many other ministers saw the same potential that Hearn himself had experienced: integrating the gospel message with folk and popular music styles was an effective way of engaging and evangelizing youth. Following broader exposure via sheet music, a record, and another performance for the denomination's annual meeting in Houston, Texas, the following year, other ministers started to use *Good News!* within their congregations. According to Hearn, those who performed *Good News!* in their own churches "saw youth choirs of fifteen or twenty people become fifty and sixty people."[56] For local ministers and church leaders, the success of this outreach was undeniable. The youth-oriented gospel-folk musical quickly spread throughout the entire Southern Baptist denomination, eventually selling three hundred thousand copies. "What we were doing was really sweeping the country in churches," recalled Hearn. "They were buying *Good News* hand over fist."[57]

Hearn's success with *Good News!* attracted the attention of Word Records founder Jarrell McCracken and vice president Kurt Kaiser. McCracken was dubious about new styles of popular music, but he was a savvy businessman who recognized that *Good News!* demonstrated the potential market among Christian youth for contemporary music. The way Hearn remembered it, "McCracken and Kaiser came to me and said, 'Why don't you leave the church and come to Word and bring this kind of music and help Kurt [Kaiser] and Ralph [Carmichael] write a musical like *Good News* and *it'll be a commercial thing*, you know, *from a commercial company* instead of a denomination.'"[58] Hearn left full-time ministry to join Word in 1968 as director of music promotion. He oversaw several youth folk musicals in this capacity: Kaiser and Carmichael's *Tell It Like It Is* (1969) and *Natural High* (1970) and Jimmy Owens's *Come Together* (1972). In an interview with Baylor's Institute for Oral History, Kaiser recalled *Tell It Like It Is* to have been a very collaborative experience, with Hearn helping to write dialogue and sequence the songs that he and Carmichael were composing. Kaiser's musical goal was "to say things the way kids like to hear them.... Lyrically, it had to be contemporary and, musically, it had to be contemporary."[59]

Hearn explained to me that in 1972, as he was promoting *Come Together*—the third youth-oriented folk musical that Word produced—he was increasingly becoming aware of a growing demand for contemporary, youth-oriented Christian popular music that accompanied the accelerating Jesus People movement: "There was nobody doing it, making recordings. I was getting a lot of mail and tapes from kids on the street. I met a bunch of the kids and thought, 'Hey, this is the future.' . . . We just built up a whole culture of this street music instead of church music that had the Christian message. . . . They were part of a movement, the Jesus movement. What made their music was the movement."[60] Hearn was not a young Jesus People convert himself; a lifelong Christian, he turned forty-three in 1972. But in the Jesus People he saw an untapped market with few resources for young contemporary Christian artists, one which he felt especially called to serve, and qualified to serve well, unlike the secular labels with little connection to the Christian market. He was able to convince McCracken, however reluctantly, to let him launch Myrrh Records as a subsidiary of Word specifically to release Christian popular music. Myrrh's first releases (🔴), in 1972, were by a couple of Word artists who also performed at Explo '72: Vonda Kay Van Dyke (*Day by Day*) and Randy Matthews (*All I Am Is What You See*). Over the next few years under Hearn, Myrrh's success in the Christian market was driven by recordings from Nancy Honeytree (🎧), Matthews, Barry McGuire, Second Chapter of Acts (🎧), and others.

McCracken was neither the first nor the last record label executive to expand into a new market despite misgivings about its long-term potential, nor is he alone in seeing that gamble pay off: Cusic reports that Word's gross income grew tenfold between 1960 and 1979, to $40 million.[61] During this time, ABC acquired Word. McCracken had been considering options for an influx of capital to sustain the label's growth since 1970 or '71, but he began pursuing opportunities seriously after Myrrh's initial success. In one of a series of interviews with Baylor's Institute for Oral History, he said that he had been close to registering for an initial public stock offering (or IPO) before the stock markets crashed following the 1973 oil crisis. He then looked into financing via banks, insurance companies, and investment firms, but ultimately none were interested. McCracken said that "several [companies] said they just couldn't get excited about a company with religious products. It just didn't seem to them like anything that had any romance to it."[62] He fielded acquisition offers from one or two other companies, but he felt that there was a stronger alignment of business interests and objectives with ABC. He had met ABC's then president, Jay Lasker, through the Recording Industry Association of America (RIAA), where both served on the board of directors. At an RIAA meeting in December 1973, Lasker told McCracken that "[ABC] had recently bought a company that made religious records and that they were interested in getting more into the gospel-type business. . . . He said he was very interested in talking and that if I wanted to pursue discussions to let him know and he'd come to Waco."[63] Lasker visited McCracken the following January, formal negotiations followed, and ABC's acquisition of Word was completed on November 22, 1974. Word, which is currently owned by Curb Records, thus became the first major Christian record label to be bought by a secular entertainment company, in part due to the strength of Billy Ray Hearn's vision and leadership.

COMMODIFYING CHRISTIANITY: RECORD LABELS INVEST IN CHRISTIAN MUSIC

Why would the owner of Word Records—a label born on a college campus (albeit a relatively conservative one: Baylor University) and still headquartered, at the time, nearby in Waco, Texas—only take tentative baby steps into the growing youth market with folk musicals instead of pursuing young Christian artists writing and performing for their peers in contemporary styles? We might expect Word to have had enough knowledge about Christian youth to see at least as much market potential as did Capitol, whose executives gave Larry Norman the artistic freedom to record a Christian album equal parts boogie and psychedelic rock over two years before McCracken and Hearn launched Myrrh. The general market major labels usually do not take such obvious risks; rather, they invest in artists with a clearly defined market—an obvious potential (or demonstrated) pathway toward financial success—or in new markets that are already profitable. As Simon Frith (among others) describes, they leave the risky entrepreneurial work to independent labels, whose lower overhead, smaller scale, and expertise in emerging markets and genres provide a slight upper hand in comprehending, supporting, and—yes—exploiting niche markets whose broader appeal is yet unproven.[64] But in the case of Christian music, we observe a different approach.

In the late 1960s, the Christian record industry consisted primarily of (Black) gospel labels, the Benson Company, and Word Records. Word was founded in 1950 by McCracken, then a student at Baylor University. The label's early successes included recordings by white

Southern gospel artists like Dick Anthony, the Melody Four Quartet, Billy Pearce, the White Sisters, and Baylor's student choirs. Although Benson's pedigree was longer—the company was founded in 1902 as a Christian publishing house—it did not enter the Christian record industry until launching the subsidiaries HeartWarming and Impact in the 1960s. Early successful Benson artists—such as the Bill Gaither Trio, the Rambos, and the Speer Family—similarly defined the label as a home for adult-oriented Southern gospel recordings. Southern gospel's roots lay not in Black gospel music but in white vocal groups singing four-part harmony.[65] On record, Southern gospel artists incorporated piano, drums, and guitars, but would never be confused for rock and roll. Consider, for example, Gaither's "Let's Just Praise the Lord" (🎧), which is driven by a solo voice and moves along at a stately, swinging pace, with lead electric guitar flourishes, horn hits, and a piano accompaniment that gesture toward contemporary styles. "He Touched Me" (🎧) is more traditional, and it has proven to be more consequential: Gaither's 1969 rendition (as the title track of the album that also features "Let's Just Praise the Lord") is firmly a vocal quartet song in triple meter, with organ accompaniment and a slow tempo (around 64 beats per minute [bpm]) that align it with hymn traditions. The Imperials foreground a saccharine string accompaniment in their 1969 version (🎧, it is also a bit faster, starting around 74 bpm and accelerating to 84 by the end of the recording); they later sang backup for Elvis's version (🎧, the title track of his 1972 gospel album, which sits around 78 bpm), in whose hands the piano-accompanied arrangement resembles a featured devotional song one might hear in a Sunday morning church service.

As Hearn laughingly explained to me in an interview, for McCracken, "traditional" Christian music (Black gospel, choral music, hymns, white Southern gospel, and so on) would always be the archetype, and rock and roll was only a peripheral trend: "'This is just a passing fad,' he [McCracken] said. Those were the words from him: 'This is just a fad. The hymns will never go away, but this is a fad.'"[66] This perspective—that rock and roll would only ever be a short-lived fad—was the same opinion that had caused executives at the largest secular record labels to underestimate the potential success of rock and roll in the 1950s.[67] Early hits by Johnny Cash, Jerry Lee Lewis, Roy Orbison, Carl Perkins, Elvis Presley, Gene Vincent, and many others were all released on small, regional, independent record labels in 1955 and '56. One of the immediate effects of this niche market suddenly exploding in popularity was increased competition within the record industry (and a corresponding decrease in its oligopolistic conditions): as Richard Peterson and David Berger illustrate, between 1955 and '59 there was a threefold increase in the number of labels that released a Top 10–charting single, and the market share of the four largest record labels fell from 74 percent to 34 percent.[68]

Having been caught flat-footed by the success of rock and roll among teenagers and young adults in the mid-to-late 1950s, the largest general market record labels with a nationwide presence had been increasingly targeting young consumers in the years since and were well positioned for the successes of British invasion, psychedelic rock, and commercial folk artists (among other styles) in the mid-to-late 1960s. Despite the success of Hearn's youth musicals in the Christian market and the lessons learned in the general market, however, Christian labels like Benson and Word had been slow to adapt a similar youth-marketing emphasis. Given that the Summer of Love, psychedelic rock, and Woodstock demonstrated to the general market labels that the youth market for popular music was still expanding and changing rapidly, perhaps it does make sense that executives at Capitol and elsewhere saw commercial potential in Christian music too.

These competing forces—a lack of interest in youth markets on the part of Christian labels and an overemphasis on those very markets within general market labels—resulted in defying what industry observers might otherwise expect: the largest secular labels shed their conservative approach to risk and took chances on Christian artists that independent Christian labels essentially ignored. Thus, in addition to general market artists drawing from their Christian backgrounds on record (Elvis Presley, Pat Boone), gospel artists on secular labels (The Impressions, The Edwin Hawkins Singers), and popular artists with songs that acknowledge Christianity (The Byrds, Simon and Garfunkel), some of the earliest Christian artists released records on secular record labels: The Crusaders's *Make a Joyful Noise with Drums and Guitars* (1966) on Tower (a Capitol subsidiary), Larry Norman's *Upon This Rock* (1970) on Capitol, and Mylon LeFevre's *Mylon (We Believe)* (1970) on Cotillion (an Atlantic subsidiary).

Profit informs all decisions at the biggest general market record labels. Usually this dynamic works to dissuade executives from making risky choices, but in these examples the potential for profit as an early market entrant persuaded executives to overlook the risks of an unproven, small market with needs and expectations that were relatively unknown. From this perspective, Jarrrell McCracken at Word acted rationally (even if his decision-making process was biased against the youth market) when he chose to invest modestly and slowly by bringing in Hearn to build upon his proven success with *Good News!* and produce more Christian youth musicals. McCracken was able to observe the Christian market's expansion without risking very much. But the secular labels' gamble on Christian music did not pay off during this time, as a result of their overall lack of support for and experience in the Christian market. Record sales failed to meet expectations, and Atlantic, Capitol, and others soon ceded the Christian market to Word, Benson, and others. Waiting and launching Myrrh the same year that the Jesus People movement's popularity crested with Explo '72 proved to have been very good timing for McCracken and Hearn: Eskridge reports that contemporary music accounted for 50 percent of Word's record sales by 1975.[69]

These observations underscore that markets for commercial music, however niche, are capitalist marketplaces nonetheless, susceptible to economic laws of supply and demand, and unable to be sustained by passion (or faith, for that matter) alone. Evangelical Christianity's relationship with capitalism in the United States is multivalent and complicated, problematic yet inextricably symbiotic. Profit, commerce, capital: each of these overlapping forms of money impacts executives' decision-making at record labels (and other music industry institutions) and, ultimately, the overall trajectory of the markets for Christian music as a whole.

ETHICAL OBJECTIONS AND AFFIRMATIONS

Among evangelicals, consumption of Christian commodities became increasingly linked to their Christian identities and lifestyles during the 1970s as the Christian market continued to grow. In no small part thanks to the Jesus People movement, it was increasingly common for self-identifying Christians and churchgoers to purchase Christian goods from Christian producers and retailers. I quoted Hendershot earlier, who argues that Americans "are addressed by mass culture not as citizens but as consumers."[70] It is certainly more complicated than this top-down perspective. Consumers, by definition, are complicit in their acts of consumption: Americans—both individually and collectively—simultaneously encourage and undermine Hendershot's characterization. Regardless, perhaps it should be no surprise that by the end of the 1970s, white evangelical Christianity—like in so many other realms of

U.S. culture—was as much about what you bought, hung on your walls, listened to, read, watched, and wore (both literally and figuratively) as it was about where you worshipped, to whom you prayed, and in which articles of faith you believed.

Eileen Luhr correlates the post–World War II growth of suburbs (and the related rise of isolationism, "family values," meritocracy, and self-sufficiency, among others) with the increasing presence (and consumption) of Christian-themed products and media (such as television shows, movies, straight-to-video series, and so on).[71] One does not necessarily beget the other, but if Christian commodities are partly responsible for legitimizing Christianity within a U.S. middle class increasingly defined by consumption and suburban affluence, then they are also responsible for reinforcing and perpetuating conservative values—economic, political, and social—that have remained an important presence in U.S. political discourse. One way to measure this trajectory is in the expansion of the main retailers of Christian consumer goods: bookstores. The Christian Booksellers Association (CBA), a trade association for the Christian products industry, was established in 1950 to provide a liaison between suppliers (producers and distributors) and retailers (the bookstores themselves). The 219 founding-member retailers in 1950 had increased to 725 in 1965; by 1975 there were 1,850 CBA-affiliated Christian bookstores in the United States.[72]

As these markets expanded, participants struggled to reconcile their commercial goals with their ethics and ideologies, as well as the evangelical mission of Christianity. According to Hearn, Word had started to prioritize commerce over missions soon after he launched Myrrh in 1972: "The label and I both slipped into a more commercial attitude and I sometimes began producing product for the wrong reasons."[73] This shift troubled him, and Hearn recognized that he was complicit in it, telling me in an interview, "I made a lot of mistakes at Myrrh Records. I signed some artists for the wrong reasons, because I got caught up in the commercial side of it."[74] He left Word in late 1975, moved to Southern California, and in early 1976 he launched a new label to support the burgeoning market for Christian rock and contemporary Christian music: Sparrow Records.

With Sparrow, one of Hearn's objectives was to return his focus to Christian music as a ministry over its commodity status. That is, he wanted to reorient his work supporting Christian artists from a commercial to an ideological priority. He told me, "I saw what the real part of the future was. It was the mission- and the ministry-oriented artists that were in it for the ministry. So I left Word and went to California and started Sparrow, and would only sign and release these kinds of artists. [They] just gravitated to me, because that's what they were looking for: a place where [ministry] was the emphasis. I had no problem getting artists; my problem was getting too many!"[75] Early Sparrow releases (◉) by Annie Herring (*Through a Child's Eyes*, 1976) and Barry McGuire (*C'Mon Along*, 1976), both of whom had followed Hearn from Myrrh, put Sparrow on the map.[76] Hearn also signed brothers John Michael Talbot and Terry Talbot shortly after they left their country rock band, Mason Proffit, which had recorded for Warner Bros., and released their joint album, *Reborn*, in 1976, followed by debut solo albums from each of the Talbots in 1977. But Billy Ray Hearn's greatest discovery in the early years of Sparrow was Keith Green, a recent Jesus People convert and a pianist, singer, and songwriter who was extraordinarily passionate about evangelism and ministry.

Hearn first encountered Green at a recording session for *Firewind* (1976), a folk-rock musical (like the ones Hearn had produced for Word) written and produced by Terry Talbot. Talbot had invited Hearn to hear Green, who played him an early version of "Your Love Broke Through" (🎧). On the studio version of this song, Green sings of his conversion to Christianity in a piano ballad accompanied by drums, acoustic guitar, and strings: "Like waking up from the longest dream / How real it seemed / Until your love broke through." Most of his other songs are livelier, such as "You Put This Love in My Heart" (🎧) and "Soften Your Heart" (🎧), the lead-off songs on his first two albums, *For Him Who Has Ears to Hear* (1977) and *No Compromise* (1978). In concert, however, it was usually just Green and his piano; live, "Your Love Broke Through" (🎧) is more immediate, and it functions—like most other Keith Green songs do—very clearly as a sermon and personal testimony uncomplicated by full-band arrangements. Hearn saw Green perform at a church a few days after meeting him and was immediately impressed by his music and personality: "He was so electrifying. You'd just whisper his name and he'd fill up a church. It just spread like wildfire in the Christian youth community." As he recalled in an interview, the church was so crowded—and Green so magnetic—that Hearn literally crawled on the floor to hear him: "I couldn't get in the door, it was so crowded. . . . They were sitting in the aisles on the floor, and I crawled up—and I got right up front. He was playing an old, upright piano with no front on it. It was out of tune . . . and it sounded like an orchestra to me."[77] Melody Green remembers this meeting similarly in her memoir: "Billy Ray slipped in unannounced. He was shocked to find the place packed to overflowing. He even had to crawl over people just to find a place on the floor in an aisle. It was not protocol for record company presidents, but Billy Ray stayed to see what it was about Keith that drew so many people. It was a powerful night of music and ministry."[78] Hearn was so excited about Green's potential that when the two met for breakfast the next morning at a Denny's in Northridge, California, they worked out the details of a recording contract on the back of a napkin.

Green's performances were effective partly because he was so passionate about his faith, having only converted to Christianity in early 1975 after a long spiritual journey led him to Kenn Gulliksen and his Vineyard Christian Fellowship, which was meeting in L.A.'s Coldwater Canyon neighborhood at the time.[79] Following his conversion, Green frequently interrupted songs to pray during concerts, and he ended every performance urging audience members to dedicate their lives to Christ. But his performances were also effective because, like other Christian musicians during this period (such as Barry McGuire, Larry Norman, and the Talbot brothers), Green entered the Christian market already experienced in the music industries as a performer, recording artist, and songwriter (🎵). In early 1965, when he was eleven years old, Green signed a recording contract and released a single on Decca. Decca promoted him as a teen idol in magazines, broadcast appearances, and live concerts, releasing three more singles in '65 and '66, but stardom never fully materialized for the young Green. By 1970 or '71, Decca had abandoned Green to throw its promotional muscle behind Donny Osmond. Green continued writing and performing around L.A., ultimately signing a staff songwriting contract with CBS (with his wife Melody as cowriter) in 1974. Thus, while *For Him Who Has Ears to Hear* (a reference to the Bible verse Revelations 2:7) was his solo debut album, Green's voice is that of an accomplished, experienced, fully formed writer and artist—albeit one strongly committed to his faith.

It is this last characteristic that endeared Green to Hearn, who had hoped and planned for Sparrow to serve as a home for ministry-focused artists. Hearn intentionally limited his artist roster and release schedule to a size and pace he could attend to personally.[80] The financial stability of the label was thus more precarious than at labels with larger rosters and release schedules; essentially, Hearn needed a high success ratio. Signing known quantities (like Second Chapter of Acts and Barry McGuire) and experienced artists (such as the Talbot brothers and

Green) was also a business strategy that minimized his financial risk. But Green's perspective on ministry—that is, his ethical approach to the music industry—became more extreme than Hearn's. By the time he was touring to support *No Compromise*, Green prioritized ministry over commerce so strongly that he refused to charge for his concerts or records; instead, he relied on an optional "love offering" during each performance for payment and did the same with his records. According to Hearn, instead of selling them for a set price at a merchandise table or booth, "all [Green's] records were stacked in the lobbies, you'd just take one, and in the bucket put whatever money you had. He made more money that way than we could have selling them for $10. . . . He knew that God would bless him, and He did."[81] Hearn's last point addresses the strength of Green's faith—knowing that God would bless him if he followed God's calling and did not pursue music for commercial reasons—as well as God's reciprocity. It is this lesson, that God rewards those who follow his will, that led to the conflict I discussed earlier in this chapter (Green asking to be released from his recording contract with Sparrow) and its ultimate resolution (Hearn agreeing, "because when God's telling somebody to do something, I'm not going to stand in the way").

It would be inaccurate to claim that Keith Green walked away from the Christian music industry. He self-distributed his next two albums via his own Pretty Good Records on a pay-what-you-will model that predated Radiohead's *In Rainbows* (2007) experiment by almost twenty-seven years. Much of his attention, however, was focused not on his artistic career but on running Last Days Ministries, which he founded with Melody in L.A. and later moved to East Texas shortly after ending his Sparrow contract. Nonetheless, he remained visible in the Christian market, both critical and supportive of institutions (like Sparrow) and individuals (like Hearn) who struggled to balance the commercial needs of sustaining a business against the ministry obligations of Christian artists like himself.

CCM magazine editor and publisher John Styll interviewed Keith Green in March 1980 before that May's release of his third record, *So You Wanna Go Back to Egypt?* The interview addressed Green's take on the Christian music industries and his own motivations for deprioritizing commercial goals so dramatically. Green's foundation was that he was first and foremost a music minister, not a commercial recording artist:

> If I was doing a disco album or an instrumental album, or even if I was an entertainer who happened to be a Christian, who just happened to do entertaining music, then it would be a *product*. It would be my skill, my trade. But since I'm foremost a minister, my music is just a tool to present the ministry. God has given me His word in the Gospel free. He's given me my talents free. He's given me the opportunities free. I feel that it's wrong for me to put *any* price that would exclude somebody that couldn't afford it.[82]

Here, Green recognized an essential dichotomy between commerce and evangelism as a core conflict in the Christian market. From his perspective, the capitalist foundation of the Christian market necessarily excluded those who would most benefit from his music, such as those in challenging economic circumstances (and cannot afford it) or nonbelievers (who would not choose to purchase a Christian record). Green believed that because his music was primarily a ministry (and not intended to be an entertainment "product"), the ethical thing to do was to make it available to all who seek it out—just as a church with open doors is accessible to its members, seekers, and those in need alike. From this perspective, capitalism itself is antithetical to ministry. In the interview, Styll pointed out to Green that it sounded as if he was "biting the hand" that fed and nurtured his early career. Green replied, "I believe that the Lord used the gospel music industry—and still is—with my records, and I thank Him for using that. But I don't give credit to the industry, I give credit to the Lord."[83] In this response, Green simultaneously articulated a strongly held position of faith—that God used the industry to position Green for success—while eliding (if not erasing) the work of people (including both Billy Ray Hearn and Melody Green) who had been instrumental in his career. Styll later told me that "he [Green] and I fought like crazy because I represented everything he thought was wrong" with the industrialization and commodification of Christian music.[84] Although Green criticized capitalist systems for forcing market scarcity on something he believed should have been freely available (his testimony and the gospel message of salvation), he appears to have internalized capitalism's ability to flourish by alienating workers from the products of their labor. It is perhaps a unique feature of the Christian market that understating the labor of individuals ("I don't give credit to the industry"), all of whom are presumably doing God's work, in favor of spiritual authority ("I give credit to the Lord") is a laudable and unassailable ethical position.

CONCLUSION: AFTER THE JESUS PEOPLE MOVEMENT

Green's ministerial priorities prevailed in this example of negotiating between commerce and ministry. Yet, as the 1980s proceeded and the gulf between the Christian and general markets widened, evangelism receded further from the market's goals. This complicated the tensions between commercial and ideological priorities among participants. Christian artists had difficulty reaching general market listeners: although they were not explicitly prohibited from participating in the general market, neither were they encouraged to do so. Earlier decades' debates over the moral appropriateness of rock and roll still resonated within evangelical culture. As Nekola has pointed out, and as I discuss further in chapter 3, a small but vocal contingent of fundamentalist and conservative Christians continued to warn against the worldly compromise that Christian rock represented.[85] Christian label executives, artists, and cultural intermediaries (such as John Styll) were thus challenged to satisfy the tastes of Christian listeners while simultaneously respecting the boundaries imposed by evangelical gatekeepers, resulting in a type of self-censorship that had five far-reaching effects during the 1980s and '90s.

The first major effect was the market's movement away from the evangelism of Jesus People musicians and early Christian artists such as Keith Green. As the Christian market increasingly defined its target audience as existing Christians, it became harder to justify Christian music as a tool of evangelism. Although many Christian artists often claimed that conversion was a key objective of their music, in reality the nonbelievers who could benefit most from evangelism had no clear access to discover these artists' music: in the general market, music magazines did not feature them, radio stations did not play them, and retail outlets did not sell them. A second effect of self-censorship—the semantic strategy of labeling artists, media outlets, record labels, and other institutions and corporations as "Christian"—both mollified Christian gatekeepers and antagonized secular industry participants, for whom explicitly religious content was generally unwelcome. At best, the general market seemed ambivalent toward Christian music; at worst, Christian artists who publicly identified as such were actively marginalized without regard to the merits of their music. Because of this prejudice, many artists who privately self-identified as Christians preferred to participate in the general market: The Alarm, T-Bone Burnett, The Call, Johnny Cash, Alice Cooper, Bob Dylan, Kansas, Lenny Kravitz, MC

Hammer, Midnight Oil, Mr. Mister, Run-DMC, Donna Summer, U2, and the Violent Femmes, among others, balanced their Christian beliefs against varyingly successful careers in the general market.

As the Christian market grew into a self-contained field of cultural production, participants were increasingly able to avoid the general market altogether, and market segregation (or stratification) largely became a self-perpetuating cycle. Although Christianity in general, and evangelicalism in particular, experienced rising visibility in the U.S. public sphere in the 1970s and '80s, evangelical Christian culture continued to promote separatism from secular culture as an effective guard against moral failure.[86] The simple act of labeling an artist "Christian" contributed to this cycle, as did Christian record labels, retailers, music magazines, and other gatekeepers who offered consumers alternatives to contemporaneous general market artists via record reviews and in-store displays. The third effect of the Christian market's self-censorship was this strategic and explicit derivativeness, which became increasingly necessary as the market attempted to satisfy all possible musical tastes. It functioned proactively as a marketing tactic targeting Christian consumers who shunned secular music entirely: for example, Christian bookstore retail clerks in the 1990s would advise parents to substitute a (Christian) MxPx recording for their teenager who wanted to listen to (secular) pop-punk bands like Green Day or blink-182. Though Christian consumers and retailers may have welcomed these comparisons, in the general market they were often used disparagingly to criticize artists as unoriginal. Thus, from the perspective of the general market, Christian music was clearly derivative of (and inferior to) secular equivalents, yet nonetheless accepted by Christian consumers who lacked a broad basis for critical comparison because of their cultural separatism.

The fourth effect of the Christian market's self-censorship was its creation of a canon and means of legitimation distinct from the general market, increasing the likelihood that the two markets would remain separate in the future, with separate celebrities, foundational figures, genre trajectories, and historical narratives. Though the National Academy of Recording Arts and Sciences (NARAS) has offered Grammy Awards in several religious categories since 1961, the Gospel Music Association's (GMA) Dove Awards, offered since 1969, has far more categories (and thus recognizes more participants). For example, in 2019 there were forty-two different Dove Award categories, compared to only five religious music Grammy Award categories. In addition to promoting Christian artists and recordings otherwise ignored by the general market music press, *CCM* magazine provided sales charts to counter Christian music's underrepresentation in the *Billboard* charts for decades. As a fifth and final effect, the increasing codification and institutionalization of Christian music resulted in the emergence of artists, record labels, and distribution and mediation networks marginal to those of mainstream Christian music, itself already marginal—the margin's margins, or what Andrew Beaujon calls "a subculture within a subculture . . . artists ignored by 'mainstream' Christian music, itself barely noticed by the larger pop culture."[87] The largest Christian record labels pursued archetypal pop music trends, with artists like Amy Grant, Sandi Patty, Michael W. Smith, and others. As Christian music's mainstream stylistic features largely mirrored those of mainstream pop, so did its marginal styles, and vibrant communities emerged to promote and support Christian goth, heavy metal, hip hop, punk rock, and others. These styles, largely youth-oriented, received little attention from the Christian market's mainstream and instead relied on word of mouth and independent networks, including alternative Christian magazines and fanzines such as *Heaven's Metal* (later renamed *HM*), *Radically Saved*, *True Tunes News*, and *White Throne*, among others.[88]

In this chapter, I have presented four themes that are essential to understanding how the boundaries of the Christian market have been both defined and transgressed: ethics, resistance, crossover, and commerce. By tracing historical narratives through the music of the Jesus People movement, we have encountered individuals, institutions, and events that are integral to the origin story of the Christian market: Benson Company, Explo '72, Keith Green, Billy Ray Hearn, Jarrell McCracken, Larry Norman, the Southern Baptist Convention, Sparrow Records, Word Records, and many others. I suggested at the beginning of this chapter that niche markets—including Christian music as well as other genres, styles, and cultures—are best understood not through their formal elements but rather through their priorities and objectives, as articulated and enacted by the individuals and institutions that operate within those markets to produce, distribute, mediate, and consume the music itself. In closing, here I would like to restate the definitional question: not what *is* Christian music, but what is it *for*? In other words, Christian music's functions—whether intended or perceived, imagined or actual—are always already implicated within its ontology. As we move forward through successive chapters in understanding the variety of roles that these four themes have played in the Christian market, we would do well to remember that each intersects with the others within this basic question.

2

The Great Adventure

Commercial Success in the Christian
Record Industry and the Price of Profit

When I first visited the corporate headquarters of EMI Christian Music Group in Brentwood, Tennessee, I was struck by the mission statement prominently displayed in the lobby as I waited for my appointment: "We strive to *create* a challenging and rewarding environment for each other and those we serve—our people as well as our artists, songwriters and business partners. We want to *impact* popular culture and resource the church through music and music-related content and services consistent with a Biblical worldview, and finally, *lead* with excellence and be profitable."[1] Now Capitol Christian Music Group (CCMG), the company is a subsidiary of Universal and one of three major Christian music companies, alongside Provident Music Group (a subsidiary of Sony) and Word Entertainment (until 2016, a subsidiary of Warner, and currently a subsidiary of Curb Records). All three oversee multiple record labels as well as distribution, music publishing, and other divisions (see appendix 3). Following an extended period of record industry corporate consolidation from the 1980s to the early 2000s, these companies represented the investments and interests of the Big Three major labels (Sony, Warner, and Universal) in the Christian market.[2] And, as with their Big Three corporate parents, we can trace the roots of each Christian major to much older labels. Word experienced several ownership changes, ups, and downs since we addressed it in chapter 1 (including parting ways with its founder, Jarrell McCracken, in 1986). Provident's roots lie in Benson (the oldest Christian record label), Brentwood, and

Reunion, which had all been consolidated into a single label group by 1997. CCMG's largest label is Sparrow, which founder Billy Ray Hearn sold to EMI in 1992. EMI launched its Christian Music Group to oversee its Christian subsidiaries in 1994. Universal acquired EMI in 2012.

When EMI purchased Sparrow, its executives committed to keeping Hearn and his leadership team on staff. In contrast to the situation at Word, where McCracken blamed his departure on the label's successive corporate acquisitions, Hearn was able to retain administrative control and institute his preferred plan of succession. His son Bill had worked at Sparrow since he was a teenager, ultimately rising to president and CEO after Billy Ray retired: "He'd come all the way up from sweeping the floor in the warehouse," according to Billy Ray.[3] Billy Ray Hearn passed away in 2015; after Bill Hearn passed away in late 2017, longtime Sparrow executive (and former guitarist for Jesus Music band Second Chapter of Acts) Peter York succeeded him at CCMG.

Although this chain of succession might indicate that CCMG is as much a family business now as it was when Billy Ray Hearn founded Sparrow in 1976, make no mistake: it is thoroughly a modern major music conglomerate, as are Provident and Word. Throughout the 1990s and 2000s, the three Christian majors continually acquired additional record labels and catalogs in a seemingly never-ending quest to expand their market shares. At the same time, all three increased their investments into other sectors of the Christian market: they expanded their music distribution, music publishing, and other artist services businesses (including booking, licensing, management, and merchandising); their repertoire grew to include gospel and contemporary worship music (CWM) alongside their core of contemporary Christian music (CCM); and they were increasingly involved in other entertainment industries, particularly book publishing and film production.

"Be profitable," reads the final two words of CCMG's vision, quoted above. On CCMG's current website this vision is attributed to Bill Hearn, although a nearly identical version was prominently positioned (unattributed) on EMI CMG's website since late 2005.[4] Accompanied by headshots of both Hearns, Billy Ray and Bill, it was bulleted into three main points: create, impact, and lead. As the public-facing vision of CCMG, these three points identified the company's priorities, which could be pursued simultaneously. For example, working toward continuing the company's sales growth would result in its increased profitability, providing a stronger business environment through which artists might promote their ministries, and would ultimately put the company in a more stable financial position from which it might affect popular culture. From the perspective of CCMG's corporate parent, however, profitability was its primary goal. Universal, after all, is a publicly traded company (as a division of the French conglomerate Vivendi) with a legal obligation to maximize the financial return of its shareholders' investments.[5] As a division of a major label, thus, CCMG's executives—for many years Billy Ray and Bill Hearn, and now Peter York—must have contended with their corporate parents' profit expectations.

Thirteen years after Hearn released Keith Green, one of Sparrow's best-selling artists, from his contract to give his records away for free, Sparrow was so successful that it attracted the attention of music executive Jimmy Bowen, president of Capitol Nashville (at the time known as Liberty Records). His label was flush with capital from selling Garth Brooks CDs, and Bowen was looking for a profitable business in which to invest. How did Hearn get from prioritizing his artist's mission in a way that jeopardized his own financial solvency to achieving enough commercial success that his company's purchase was spearheaded by one of the most powerful entertainment executives in Nashville? How did the rest of the Christian market fair during this same period? And what have been the priorities and practices of Christian record labels in the aftermath of these corporate acquisitions, consolidation, and mergers? In the introduction, I argued that aesthetics and ethics are intertwined, mutually constitutive, and inseparable in music markets, an argument that I refine and illustrate further in chapter 5. In this chapter, that argument compels us to ask what commercial success sounds like. In other words, how are the ethics of commerce and capitalism reflected in the evolving sound, style, and substance of Christian music?

Interviews with several current and former Christian record label executives and reporting and editorializing in *CCM* magazine and its sister publications provide insight into the Christian market, in terms of both the market's outward focus (that is, its major labels' relationships to their consumers) and its inward focus (including how executives have understood their objectives and responsibilities as subsidiaries of entertainment conglomerates). Elsewhere I have argued that popular music scholars should assess record labels according to their priorities instead of categorically defining them as either major or independent, and later in this chapter I mobilize that argument to examine how the changing priorities of Christian labels impacted their market's transition following the upheaval of corporate consolidation during and following the 1990s.[6]

For the Christian market, as with the rest of the U.S. record industry, the 1990s was marked by substantial growth. As many have documented, that growth reversed in 2001 as the record industry endured a period characterized by declining sales of recorded music.[7] In 2010, where this chapter's narrative of the Christian record industry ends, labels were still struggling: CD sales continued to decrease, sales of digital downloads had not compensated for that decline (and, ultimately, never would), and streaming was still a relatively small sector. By the end of the 2010s, streaming had come to dominate: the Recording Industry Association of America (RIAA) reported in 2016 that streaming revenue surpassed U.S. record industry revenue from all other sources combined for the first time, including sales of physical media and digital downloads.[8] The International Federation of the Phonographic Industry (IFPI) reported in 2017 that streaming revenue "became the single largest revenue source" globally.[9] Elsewhere I have reported on some of the ways in which the growth of streaming has impacted the Christian market, including the convergence of CWM with CCM and the shift to promoting musical works over recordings to maximize publishing royalties.[10] Here, instead of dwelling on labels' strategies to accommodate the disruptive changes to the circulation of recorded music, I orient my analysis toward understanding the broader effects of an increasing commercial priority at the biggest Christian record labels. First, however, we return to Sparrow Records, as its growth in the 1980s serves as a barometer for the overall success of the Christian market, and (in hindsight) as a predictor of evolving tensions in the 1990s and 2000s.

SPARROW RECORDS: "THE COMPANY THAT JUST WON'T STOP GROWING"

The front page of the August 30, 1993, issue of *The CCM Update* featured a special report written by editor/publisher John Styll:

> This past year has seen the greatest business upheaval in the history of Christian music. Within the past 12 months, the three leading companies in this industry—Word, Sparrow and Benson—came under new ownership. The confidence in the contemporary Christian music market shown by Liberty Records President Jimmy Bowen sparked a flurry of interest from [general market] mainstream labels. . . . More [Christian] industry executives cited the mainstream marketplace as the top growth opportunity than any other. The seemingly greater interest in Christian music from mass merchandisers like Target, Wal-Mart and K-Mart may lead to a major sales opportunity.[11]

  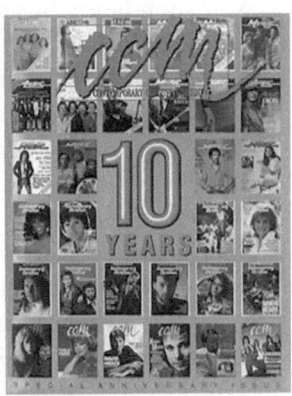

FIGURE 4. *CCM* magazine, March 1983, April 1986, and June 1988. Used with permission, courtesy CCMmagazine.com.

Update was a biweekly trade newsletter for industry professionals in the Christian market. Styll published it for almost twenty years from May 1983 until April 2002 in some form, first as *MusicLine*, then as *The MusicLine Update*, and finally as *The CCM Update*. *Update* was distinct from *CCM* magazine, which Styll had published since 1978. By segregating industry news, rumors, how-to and pedagogical guides for music business topics, gear and equipment reviews, and charts to *Update*, Styll was able to orient *CCM* more directly toward a consumer audience with extensive feature articles, interviews with Christian artists and other celebrities, and album reviews; by the mid-1980s it was more of a lifestyle magazine for Christian music fans (see figure 4). Styll's analysis here in this special report was cold and objective, betraying none of the speculation of *Update*'s front-page headlines in the period leading up to August 1993:

"Is Jimmy Bowen Buying the Christian Music Industry?" (March 9, 1992)

"Nelson Buys Word; EMI Buys Sparrow" (October 5, 1992)

"BMG to Purchase Half of Reunion, Blanton/Harrell" (January 18, 1993)

"Music Entertainment Group Buys Benson" (August 16, 1993)

For readers paying attention to the news Styll and his writers were reporting in *CCM* and *Update*, the acquisition of Sparrow and other

Christian labels by general market companies should not have been a surprise. In July 1992, Styll predicted that "one year from now, every Christian record company with more than $2 million in annual sales will either be under new ownership or reconfigured in some way."[12] This was a bold statement at the time, inasmuch as Styll was predicting dramatic changes that would impact the entire market in a relatively short period of time. But if we focus instead on a single label over a longer timeline, his prediction does not seem as far-fetched and even follows known trajectories of business growth and increasing intersections between the general and Christian markets.

Sparrow's growth had been substantial: the label reported a 31 percent increase in annual sales in 1983, which executives actively limited to 25–30 percent in the following two years, in part because the company lacked the resources to sustain greater success.[13] This growth was partly due to Sparrow entering new markets—Hearn diversified to Spanish-language music, music videos, and computer and video games in the early 1980s.[14] However, it was also partly due to distribution agreements with general market labels. Billy Ray Hearn partnered with MCA for distribution in 1981 after speaking with several labels including Capitol, Columbia, PolyGram, and RCA. He explained the agreement as a way to reach Christian listeners outside of the Christian market: "I think we are going to sell a lot more records to a lot more Christians. The main purpose is not to sell a lot of Christian records to 'secular' people.... There are a lot of Christian people who don't know about our records yet."[15] Bill Hearn expanded his father's justification in a 1985 editorial defending crossover that would be "meaningful in the long run": "First, we must cross our music over to those Christians who for one reason or another don't regularly shop at Christian bookstores. Secondly, we must cross our music over to those Christians who don't regularly listen to Christian radio." The best way to reach those listeners, Hearn argued, was to partner with a "mainstream distributor." The goal was "not primarily to pursue that crossover hit, but to support the entire growth of the Christian music audience."[16] Sparrow renewed the MCA agreement in 1983 before switching to Capitol for general market distribution in 1985. During this period, Sparrow opened its Nashville office, largely because the Christian music scene was no longer centered in California (as it was during the Jesus People movement). As Billy Ray Hearn explained to me, "Kids that were into Christian music and into the new field, they were in Nashville. They weren't in California anymore. There wasn't that movement anymore."[17] By mid-decade, other Christian labels had also contracted for general market distribution, Word with A&M and Benson with Capitol.[18] Notably, these distribution agreements followed the closure of several major label subsidiaries: MCA's Songbird, CBS's Priority, and PolyGram's Lection had all targeted the gospel and Christian markets in the early 1980s with little success. After these setbacks, the general market majors preferred to distribute Christian labels instead of owning them outright, content to let other companies assume the majority of the risk.

By the early 1990s, however, the Christian market was profitable enough to attract Jimmy Bowen's interest in partnerships beyond distribution deals. Bowen broadcast his enthusiasm for the Christian market widely, causing *Update* to ask, "Is Jimmy Bowen buying the Christian music industry? . . . Bowen has held exploratory discussions with almost every major label in the industry."[19] Sparrow had grown even further by that time: the company opened a distribution facility in Jacksonville, Illinois (across the street from a Capitol Records distribution warehouse), in 1989 that ensured better service to retailers in the Midwest, the South, and along the East Coast. In early 1991, Hearn consolidated Sparrow's administrative offices in Nashville, moving forty-seven employees and their families from Southern California in the process.[20] Bowen visited Hearn shortly after this move and immediately offered to buy the label, but Hearn told him it was not for sale. After six months of researching other Christian labels, Bowen returned and offered to buy Sparrow again. He convinced Hearn to meet with EMI Music CEO Jim Fifield in New York City. Hearn told me that Sparrow had many successful recording artists at the time, including Steven Curtis Chapman, but needed additional resources to distribute its recordings to a larger potential audience.

> We didn't have the financing, the resources, the distribution to the Walmarts and everything—I didn't have the money to do that and promote Steven Curtis [Chapman]. He had a new album coming out. So EMI said, "See, what you need is financing. What you need is structure to boom it. If your whole purpose is to get the Gospel to the people, we're the way to do it. We will put you in the Walmarts, the K-Marts, and all these little shops. But we can't do it if we don't own you, if you're not part of our company. . . . If this is what your purpose is, this is the way to go. . . . We just think you can grow, and we want a piece of the growth."[21]

Hearn sought advice from trusted spiritual and business advisors and conferred with his junior executives at Sparrow, but he was unable to find a consensus on whether or not to sell his company. EMI's Bowen and Fifield promised Hearn that they would not seek to change Sparrow's operations or otherwise intervene in its successful business environment beyond funding growth and pursuing new distribution networks. The additional resources available through EMI's ownership would be substantial for Sparrow and might translate into significant opportunities for Sparrow's artists' careers and ministries. For his part, Jimmy Bowen's interest in Christian music was purely a business decision: "Truth was," he writes in his memoir, "I didn't know one Christian record from another. My role was to bring EMI a vision—not of Jesus, but of nineties synergy. To help them see they had the muscle to bring this powerful music to the secular world."[22]

After negotiating for a year, Hearn agreed to sell Sparrow to EMI in late 1992. The Christian market felt the effects of EMI's resources and clout in the marketplace almost immediately. Hearn told me,

> [EMI] took our banks out and poured the money in: here's the money to make new records. Here's the money to buy ForeFront Records, to buy Star Song, buy this, buy the publishing, and get into all the Walmarts and the K-Marts and stuff. They did it. They were having great luck with a big country singer [Garth Brooks]. They would go to Walmart and say, "Do you want one thousand of these [Garth Brooks CDs]? Then you have to take Steven Curtis Chapman." They've got the clout, man! They could go in there. And man, we saw Steven go from four hundred thousand a release to one million a release like that. It was all structure; it was all financing and power in the market.[23]

Peter York had signed Steven Curtis Chapman in the 1980s, shortly after opening Sparrow's Nashville office. After releasing four records on Sparrow (), 1992's *The Great Adventure*—released while Sparrow was undergoing negotiations with EMI—was his first to be certified gold (over half a million copies sold in the United States) by the RIAA, a year after its release. His next album, 1994's *Heaven in the Real World*, went gold within five months of its release and was eventually certified platinum (over one million copies sold) in February 1997. Chapman's albums continued to sell at gold and platinum levels for the next ten years or so. This string of successes did coincide with Garth Brooks's multi-platinum records on Liberty and Capitol Nashville in the 1990s, and you can hear aesthetic similarities between the two artists when you look for them. *The Great Adventure*'s title track, for example, is an up-tempo, danceable southern rock song; Chapman's voice has a noticeable southern accent; and the album's slick production is similar to Brooks's approach to commercial country pop.

Steven Curtis Chapman is not a country artist, but neither is he a pop singer; no doubt the two singers' audiences overlapped somewhat. Yet Chapman's success was not due to his sudden exposure to non-Christian listeners. Each single from these two records—most notably the title tracks, which were each album's lead-off single—delivered clear, unambiguous Christian messages. "The Great Adventure" (🎧), like Christian songs in so many genres and styles, describes God's redemption ("I opened up the Bible / And I read about me / Said I'd been a prisoner / And God's grace had set me free"); his journey of faith is itself the great adventure: "the ride of your life," "discover all the new horizons," "the greatest journey that the human heart will ever see." In "Heaven in the Real World" (🎧) Chapman sings of Jesus healing a broken world: "He is the hope, He is the peace / That will make this life complete / For every man, woman, boy, and girl / Looking for heaven in the real world." In short, these are not songs destined for Top 40 or country pop radio: although both songs topped *CCM* magazine's Christian adult contemporary (AC) charts, neither appeared on *Billboard*'s Hot 100 or Hot AC charts in the general market.[24] These are contemporary Christian music songs through and through, and Chapman's broader exposure through the Walmarts and the K-Marts on Garth Brooks's coattails succeeded not because he became an artist the general market was paying attention to, but rather because—as Bill Hearn predicted in 1985—"Christians who for one reason or another don't regularly shop at Christian bookstores" were now more likely to encounter Chapman where they did shop.

In the pages of *CCM* magazine a decade or more prior, editors (including Styll), writers, and readers (in the "Feedback" letters section) debated the appropriate roles of commerce and profitability within the Christian market. In chapter 1 I discussed Styll's interview with Keith Green, published in the March 1980 issue of *CCM* magazine, as revealing Green's ambivalence about the Christian music industry.[25] During the early '80s there was a lot of anxiety over the intersection of ministry and business throughout the pages of *CCM* magazine, both from the editorial side (explaining, justifying, and hand-wringing over the necessity of making money to pursue ministry) and from readers' responses in the letters section. In an early 1980 editor's note, Styll gave voice to this debate: "Has Christian music become too commercial? . . . Should there even be something called the 'Christian music industry?'"[26] Elsewhere I have examined how these tensions played out in *CCM* magazine in 1985–86 following the release of Amy Grant's album *Unguarded* (1985), her first attempt at crossing over into the general market.[27] As I discuss at length in chapter 4, many readers were concerned that Grant had "sold out" her faith, essentially pitting her earlier music's spirituality against *Unguarded*'s commercial success. Styll ended several months of debate over Grant in his March 1986 editor's note. Titled "Ministry or Industry?," he argued that for Christian music to be a successful ministry it must also be a successful industry: "The actual fact is that Christian music is both a ministry and an industry," he wrote. "Whatever you call it, the important thing is to understand how to have a healthy balance between the two. . . . Without positive income, the capability to minister is impaired."[28] He was blunter in his remarks to me, many years later. "There are still artists that genuinely feel evangelistic about what they do," he said. "That is the artist's platform and motivation. The labels are a mechanism to get it out there. To do the business. The label will try to market the artist because they want to sell records."[29] His utilitarian argument that the two are not incompatible or mutually exclusive—that they actually may be co-constitutive—and his magazines' reporting on the business of Christian music chart a trajectory of normalization in the Christian market.

Billy Ray Hearn explained his decision-making process to me as prioritizing ministry: "Honestly, all of my decisions in the company, in the business, was never 'Was it good for the company?' but 'Was it good for the ministry?' So, the faith determined all of the steps that we took. Not the business. We did very few things because of the business. We look back, we sold to EMI, was that for the business? It was really for the ministry."[30] But claiming to prioritize ministry is not the same as ignoring business concerns, and what we learn in this brief case study of Sparrow Records is that Hearn's decisions for the good of the ministry were largely also good for business. In other words, strategically pursuing ministry—or, at a broader level, prioritizing ideology as a component of one's business plan—can be very profitable under the right circumstances.

Other labels followed suit. When I interviewed Hearn, he claimed that Sparrow's new clout as an EMI subsidiary forced other Christian labels to pursue similar partnerships: "They all had to sell, because they couldn't compete with us. That's the way the [Christian] industry got bought out by the secular. . . . I was the first."[31] Sparrow, however, was not the first major Christian label to be acquired by a general market record company. That distinction belongs to Word, which was purchased by broadcast network ABC in 1976, joining a music division whose other record labels included Blue Thumb, Dot, and Impulse!, among others. Word remained with ABC when MCA bought ABC Records in 1979, and has had four other corporate parents since: Capital Cities (merged with ABC in 1986), Christian book/Bible publishers Thomas Nelson (acquired Word in 1992), Warner (acquired Word in 2001), and most recently Curb, which acquired Word in 2016. Benson followed a similarly complicated path: the Benson family sold the company in 1980, and it became the centerpiece of a joint venture launched by Zondervan (like Thomas Nelson, also a major Christian book/Bible publisher) and Paragon (a Christian label founded by a former Benson executive).[32] But the company struggled throughout the 1980s, undergoing restructuring and leadership changes several times before Zondervan sold it in 1993. Later mergers and acquisitions positioned Benson as a component of Provident, which Sony acquired as part of BMG in 2004. Smaller labels such as Brentwood, ForeFront, Reunion, and Star Song were also acquired during this period.

John Styll summarized the consolidation of Christian labels for the readers of *CCM* magazine in late 1994, reporting that, "during the past two years or so, virtually every major Christian label has experienced significant change in terms of ownership. Large mainstream music companies like EMI have been buying their way into Christian music in anticipation of a major sales upturn." In earlier years, he might have taken the opportunity to debate the intersection of commerce and mission; but here Styll ended his editorial with a punt: "Whether or not this is a good thing will be debated some other time."[33] In his reflections for Baylor University's oral history project, Billy Ray Hearn was unapologetic about how he would respond to that debate: "A lot of people thought it was the devil taking over our industry, but what it was, it was the devil's money giving us money to grow with and really become a tremendous, better witness. We've taken that money and done miracles with it. And none of us are sorry. Not a single executive is sorry we sold this company."[34] In Sparrow Records and in the pages of *CCM* magazine, *MusicLine*, and *The CCM Update*, we see a shifting perspective on the matter of profit, from being (at best) a distraction or (at worst) sinful to being a necessary component of conducting business (including the business of ministry) to, finally, being something to celebrate.

DEFINING THE CHRISTIAN MARKET

Billy Ray Hearn was interviewed in 1980 for a special issue of *CCM* magazine that celebrated Sparrow's first four years. He explained his principle for the label as one rooted in the belief that success follows an artist-centered strategy: "We only sign artists; we don't sign records. . . . I think a lot of our success is due to the fact that we are more dedicated to supporting our artists and making *them* happen than we are to selling records."[35] This strategy clearly worked: Sparrow's first-year sales of around $700,000 grew throughout the 1970s and '80s; by the time he sold the company in 1992, Hearn told me, annual sales were $35–$40 million.[36] The EMI acquisition was profitable for Hearn, netting him enough money that he semi-retired and pursued other interests, including launching a foundation.[37] Some Christian market participants are wary of this level of success, warning that money can have a corrupting influence on other practices and priorities. Charlie Peacock, a musician, producer, and songwriter who has been involved in the Christian market since the 1980s, cautions artists that "signing with a major label and taking on a booking agent, a manager, and a publicist are not neutral choices." The ideologies that inform profit-centered businesses can be used for ministry, he writes, but it is always a balancing act in which Christian artists "risk becoming something entirely different from what we faithfully set out to be . . . and do things we don't want to do, all in the name of ministry."[38] And yet, Peacock argues, "capitalism encourages profit, and profit, when used properly, creates and supports many good things, including the spread of the gospel."[39]

Peacock's warnings and justifications in 1999 followed a period of corporate consolidation in the Christian market. The Christian record industry, in particular, transitioned from relatively independent labels accountable to their own stakeholders, artists, and fans to major label subsidiaries, accountable to executives and shareholders for whom ministry is valuable only when it increases a label's market share or profitability. A stronger emphasis on commercial success and profitability accompanied major label ownership, complicating the already challenging process of balancing artistic, business, and ministerial priorities at Christian record labels. If the mission of a Christian record label is to minister to the spiritual needs of churchgoers (specifically, for CCMG, to "resource the church through music and music-related content and services consistent with a biblical worldview," as quoted earlier) but the mission of its corporate parent is to increase shareholder value, then the former will always be subordinated to the latter.

As in earlier periods, executives at the major Christian record labels pursued dual strategies of consolidation and diversification in the 1990s and 2000s in an effort to increase their profitability. On one hand, they increasingly concentrated on marketing artists to their core audience of Christian music consumers. On the other hand, the labels' corporate parents provided expanded distribution networks through which successful Christian artists could cross over into the general market—an opportunity that some aggressively pursued with varying degrees of success. One result of this stronger commercial priority was the increasing homogenization of mainstream Christian music's aesthetics. The Christian market continued to follow the stylistic trends in general market popular music very closely in the 1990s and 2000s, and its lyrics' theological content was either deliberately ambiguous (appealing to general market consumers) or uncomplicatedly clear and faith affirming (appealing to core Christian music consumers). Media studies scholar Heather Hendershot argues that Christian artists' commercial success is indirectly related to their "evangelical intensity," implying that the least overtly Christian songs would be the most profitable (and vice versa).[40] The success of these strategies is clear in data reported by the Gospel Music Association (GMA), which documented rising sales throughout the end of the 1990s and into the 2000s. For example, the Christian market's annual sales of recorded music increased from $188 million in 1990 to $381 million in '95, and later peaked at almost $1 billion in 2003.[41] For comparison, the RIAA reported overall revenue of $7.5 billion in 1990, $12.3 billion in '95, and $11.9 billion in 2003.[42] As a percentage of the U.S. record industry, Christian music sales thus grew from 2.5 percent in 1990 to 3.1 percent in '95 and 8.4 percent in 2003. Steven Curtis Chapman was not the only artist to regularly reach gold and platinum status following industry consolidation: in 2003 and 2004, the GMA reported twenty-nine gold, thirteen platinum, and six multi-platinum albums.[43]

Christian record label executives have claimed that this success is due, in large part, to their ability to define, segment, and reach a target market of ideal consumers. The relative ease with which Christian labels have defined their core listenership has been extremely attractive to their corporate parents. While their potential audience for Christian music is bounded, it is easily identifiable—an elusive quality in other markets throughout the music industries. Wayne Kusber worked in artist management and A&R (artists and repertoire; i.e., the division of a record company that focuses on scouting and developing new talent) in the early aughts at one of the major Christian record labels. When I interviewed him in 2010, he told me that "every artist is trying to build community. . . . People want to be a part of something. If they feel like they're a part of your thing, and they buy in to what you're about, then they're going to buy stuff. They're going to invest in you as an artist."[44] For Kusber and his label, his target audience is a preexisting "community" that is comparatively easy to find: "A lot of what we do, we already know what community we're going after. If you're just a [general market] pop star, the world is huge. It's overwhelming: 'Where are my people? How do I find my people?' The church, in some ways, for Christian music, there's your group of people. You've got way more defined parameters on who to go after."[45] According to Kusber, strategically marketing to the core Christian audience—however niche—was a more efficient use of resources than pursuing a less definable mass audience. From this perspective, the Christian market was comparable to that of other niche markets, such as country music, electronic dance music, hip hop, Latin music, and others, all of which have had similarly distinct target audiences. The reason why CCMG, Provident, and Word exist as separate subsidiaries for the Christian market, instead of being subsumed by their corporate parents in New York or L.A., is because their employees' specialized contacts, experience, knowledge, and skills (not to mention shared backgrounds as self-identifying Christians) have remained valuable in the increasingly niche-oriented entertainment industries. This would be prohibitively costly (and potentially inefficient) to implement in a more centralized organizational structure. The Christian labels' corporate parents found economic value in this division of labor, partly due to the changing nature of music sales and marketing in the early twenty-first century. In an era of rapid change, the major labels increased their chances of success by diversifying their artist rosters over many niche markets (including the Christian market).

In addition to being easily identifiable, label executives perceived core Christian music consumers to be more loyal than the average music consumer and expected that they would always buy their favorite artists' new recordings. As Kusber explained in an interview, "Once they become fans of that artist and they believe in that artist, that artist has proven themselves to them. [Christian audiences think] 'That's my band. I'm sticking with those guys.' It'll take a long time to lose interest."[46] From a business perspective, this guaranteed audience represented an incredibly valuable resource: because record label executives could expect a relatively large number of repeat customers throughout an artist's recording career, they could more efficiently target their marketing budget and promotional strategies.

Who were all these existing listeners, consumers, and audience members? It was certainly not as broad as all Christians, churchgoers, or evangelicals. As we learned earlier, Christian record label executives have been trying to reach more Christians since at least the 1980s. Obviously they would not have been doing so if all Christians already listened to Christian music. Rather, existing listeners were a subset of self-identifying Christians. The Christian record label executives with whom I spoke identified their ideal listeners as white, middle-class women churchgoers with families. Data provided by the GMA in 2006 bore this out: at the time, Christian music consumers were more likely than the general U.S. population to be female, married, and living in a large household.[47] Christian music consumers were also more likely to live outside of densely populated areas, and more Christian music was sold in the U.S. South and Southeast than in the rest of the country combined. These data are instructive, but only to a point: because the Christian labels' marketing strategies both informed and reflected these audience survey and sales results, they were self-replicating and self-perpetuating. In other words, Wayne Kusber and his counterparts at other Christian record labels used these data to sell their artists to their existing listeners, but in doing so they limited their potential to attract new listeners outside of their market demographics, be they Black, childless, living in the Northeast, male, non-churchgoing Christians, single, or someone else outside of the market's core listenership.

Kusber and his colleagues found that the demographic characteristics of the Christian market were similar to the market for commercial country music—an industry also centered in Nashville, home to the Country Music Hall of Fame and divisions of each of the Big Three major labels.[48] As Kusber explained, this revealed itself in part through the aesthetic expectations of Christian radio, and by extension those of the major Christian labels: "If you listen to core AC [adult contemporary] radio in Christian music, I think you'll hear some stylistic similarities to country. In the style of the singers, you'll hear a little bit of a Southern accent in there every once in a while. . . . Even stylistically, there's a little bit of a country pop to it."[49] Kusber acknowledged that the aesthetics of Christian radio limited the degree of similarity between Christian and country music: "On Christian radio, you can't send them something with too much fiddle or too much mando[lin]. Acoustic guitar is awesome, that's foundational."[50] Eric Weisbard describes catch-all formats like Top 40 and AC as crossover, musically eclectic formats.[51] I would push back against the slightly valorizing tone of his claim by reminding us that these formats, like all commercial radio formats, tend toward a centrism that intentionally incorporates and normalizes otherwise diverse and distinct aesthetics. Top 40 and AC may be eclectic but they are also banal and unthreatening in catering to large listening publics; in these examples we hear the result of radio programming and record label A&R strategies that mix several genres but privilege none.

CONNECTING WITH CHRISTIAN LISTENERS

I have written elsewhere that commercial radio stations, especially those that follow strict formats (such as Christian AC or Christian Contemporary Hit Radio [CHR]), subsist in large part by selling their audience's attention to their advertisers.[52] Radio stations conduct audience surveys and offer potential advertisers very detailed demographic profiles. Success at these stations is measured both by the quantity of listeners (more is better) and by the average amount of time they spend listening (longer is better). The most effective radio programmers and disc jockeys attract lots of listeners and keep them from tuning to a different station by playing a selection of music that is more comfortable, expected, and inoffensive than it is surprising or unfamiliar. The Christian record labels also needed access to this audience, as Kusber told me in 2010: "Radio is still, in our world, the most important way to reach the most people quickly."[53] Because his label was primarily interested in signing artists that fit the requirements of the Christian AC and CHR radio stations, Kusber did not pursue artists who did not fit within these formats' stylistic parameters. One job of Kusber and his counterparts at the other major Christian labels was to supply those radio stations with songs that would keep their listeners' attention. Kusber's advice to the prospective Christian artist or songwriter was simple: listen.

> Go back to what is the musical format of core Christian music, and look at that, "Okay, do I fit within the parameters of that?" If not, go pursue a mainstream pop deal. Go pursue a hip-hop deal.[54]
>
> I told this one guy yesterday, "Go listen to the radio. Whatever format you like. If you don't like any of those artists that are being played on the radio, and you can't hear yourself being played before or after one of those artists, then don't pursue the labels that those artists are on, because that's how those labels function."[55]

As John Styll remarked to me in 2009, the biggest Christian labels were strongly tied to the expectations of radio programmers: "They're signing people that can get on the radio, which is appealing to soccer moms and it results in a pretty homogenous, vanilla output."[56] From Kusber's perspective, some musicians did not understand that the Christian major labels were bound by the expectations of their core audience—confirming tastes rather than disrupting them—as a necessary result of prioritizing commerce over other aspects.

That said, connecting with Christian listeners was not only about sounding a particular way. It was also about having—and living—a faith identity and religious practice in common with Christian listeners and manifesting that faith in observable (and, ideally, marketable) ways. In chapter 5, I discuss this issue of connecting as central to the concept of authenticity within the Christian market: artists who allow themselves to be vulnerable in ways that affirm their faith and belief in God make strong connections with listeners. Being vulnerable humanizes otherwise distant celebrities and artists; it demonstrates that musicians undergo the same challenges and doubts as their listeners; and it also provides a teaching moment, confirming the power of God and the Christian faith to sustain them through difficult seasons in life.

As much as Christian audiences might have wanted to connect with a vulnerable and sincere artist, they also welcomed the opportunity to address larger social and cultural wrongs or problems. Andy Peterson worked at several Christian record labels in the 1990s and early 2000s, ultimately rising to a senior-level position in marketing at Word (in 2002–05). When I interviewed him in 2009 and '10 he was a vice president at Propeller, a marketing and product development consultancy that worked with many Christian and general market entertainment companies. As Peterson explained to me in an interview, a major strategy in the Christian market was to take advantage of Christian listeners' investment in charity by partnering with organizations such as Charity Water, International Justice Mission, Toms, World Vision, and others. Artists, he said, "all have their 'thing' now," but that does not necessarily mean they are cynical about it: "most of them truly believe in these causes that some of them have built from the ground up" and are sincerely involved with nonprofit humanitarian organizations whose missions align with their own ideological and theological values. He continued, "That's distinctive about the Christian music movement, and an important part of it. If you experience a Christian artist in concert, you're going to get hit with an advertising message for one of those organizations."[57]

Other artists, however, were ambivalent about charities, but the up-front financial resources of these organizations were often reason enough to pursue an affiliation, according to Peterson: "Of course, part of it is financial: a lot of these artists maintain their touring business because of, literally, the cash advances they get from World Vision or Compassion." Some saw these partnerships as a way to increase their exposure to new audiences; essentially, partnering with a nonprofit organization was a savvy marketing strategy that exposed the artist to the organization's network (and vice versa) while also authenticating the artist's ethics to their existing audience. As Peterson explained,

> It gives their artists another layer of depth, another dimension that they wouldn't otherwise have.... We need to get ourselves attached to another constituency. Because the defined music-buying public, that box is only so big, and it seems to be getting smaller.... But International Justice Mission has half a million Twitter followers and a million people on their newsletter. That's something that, as a marketer, you can tap into: "Okay, those are real, live bodies who we know, if we can convince them that our artist cares about the same thing that they care about, maybe they'll like our artist."[58]

This then-new facet of marketing Christian music was very prevalent: nearly every artist I saw perform a concert during my fieldwork took time between songs to mention a nonprofit organization or address ways that audience members could contribute to and address humanitarian issues and natural tragedies around the world.

CHANGING PRIORITIES AT CHRISTIAN RECORD LABELS

The strategies I examine above—artists authenticating themselves to listeners, being vulnerable, connecting with nonprofit organizations, and doing so with an aesthetically pleasing (if blandly inoffensive) sound—exist largely to strengthen the relationships between artists and their audiences. Those relationships are key to an artist's overall goal: you cannot achieve results preaching from your pulpit, after all, if no one is listening. The question facing artists and record label executives, then, becomes one of objective: to repeat myself from chapter 1, what is Christian music *for*? Recalling Howard and Streck's division of Christian music into three distinct categories, the greatest impact of the general market's investment in the Christian market has been the overall shift to an integrational approach at the largest Christian record labels in which music is primarily entertainment and, as a result, often prioritizes commerce.[59]

The most turbulent years of corporate consolidation—from 1991 until the middle of the first decade of the 2000s—were also years in which the Christian market expanded quickly, as I discuss above. Andy Peterson described that period of time as one that "changed the trajectory of everything" in the Christian market: "The Christian music business was pretty ministry-focused until EMI, BMG, and Sony came in and bought everything up . . . and that's when all of the [Christian] labels had to behave quite differently in the ways they were making decisions. And there was enough [commercial] success happening that the expectation was that we were going to build on that success. You could never be satisfied with being as successful as you were last year, it was always do more, do more, do more."[60] This increased focus on profitability at the major Christian record labels both settled and complicated earlier discourses on the appropriate goals of Christian music. In one sense, it clarified the position of the largest Christian labels: for CCMG, Provident, and Word, Christian music largely existed as a commodity sold to Christian consumers: what Christian music is *for* is making money. Questions about the market's aesthetic boundaries, evangelistic mission, target audience, ways of measuring success, and so on become easier to answer when we understand that its principal goal is to minimize expenses and maximize revenues. The strategies that I discuss above illustrate this perspective: as Peterson told me, "I've been part of meetings where we've had an artist, and we've gone, 'Okay, they don't have a thing. We need to find them a thing. We need to partner them up with someone.' . . . It's not enough anymore just to go out and sing about Jesus. You have to sing about Jesus and be building wells in Rwanda."[61]

From another perspective, however, this trend toward commodification further aggravated these issues for those participants who preferred to focus on Christian music's potential for evangelism and proselytization. Even if there was no longer debate about what the major Christian labels' priorities were, there remained considerable debate over the appropriateness of their commercial objectives. And although these large questions about the purpose and meaning of Christian music prompted productive and engaging debates in the 1970s and '80s, normalizing profitability as a central goal of the Christian majors effectively marginalized other priorities in the '90s and 2000s. Christian music's theological and/or aesthetic potentials became peripheral to its commercial success. As I discuss in chapters 3 and 5, this shift in priorities has had enormous implications for the ethical orientation of the Christian market and for the ways in which participants articulate their resistance to dogmatic positions (including capitalism and commerce). The danger for Christian label executives has been that the mandate from their corporate parents—to "always do more, do more, do more"—ultimately took precedence over other priorities, objectives, and goals at Christian record labels. Wayne Kusber, in reflecting on his relationships with his general market counterparts and superiors at his label's corporate parent, was very clear about their expectations and yet also hopeful that Christian labels could do more than simply make money: "We are a for-profit company, but there is a ministry emphasis to what we do. The bottom line is, we're owned by [a major label]. They don't really care what we do, as long as it makes money. As long as it's profitable, that's the bottom line for them."[62]

It is simplistic to argue unequivocally that, as the Christian record labels were consolidated within the Big Three entertainment conglomerates, the Christian market transitioned to being purely a profit-making enterprise. The truth is more complicated. On one hand, current and former executives at the Christian majors have told me that profitability is a major concern—perhaps *the* major concern—for their superiors: "As long as it's profitable, that's the bottom line." On the other hand, most have also continued to emphasize the positive work they are able to do while pursuing profit: "There is a ministry emphasis to what we do." The challenge for artists and label executives has been to balance these priorities: to know when to push one's ministry forward, when to compromise in favor of a profitable strategy, what musical styles work best for different market needs and expectations, and how to align each of these sustainably. The danger for observers is in presuming that profitability is the only goal because it is the most visible, and not one of many that can be prioritized concurrently at high levels.

John Mays experienced the profit priority clearly as a record label executive. Mays's career started as a touring and session bassist (for both Christian and general market artists) before transitioning to an A&R position at Word in 1987. In 1995, he moved to EMI CMG where he worked as vice president of A&R at Star Song; in 1999 Provident hired Mays as president of Benson Records. In an interview, Mays described the quarterly process of reporting the financial results of his division to stockholders as a significant measure of his accomplishments as a record label executive: "I was keenly aware that every quarter, there was an accountability for your number. Yeah, you could have a bad quarter, but you can't have two bad quarters. And you sure can't have three bad quarters, something's going to have to change."[63] The quarterly financial reporting required of publicly held companies is meant to protect investors by providing them with a degree of transparency.

Quarterly reports also hold executives accountable for their divisions' profitability on a short-term basis.

Mays had worked at a Christian major since the late '80s, but he had never been responsible for an entire label—let alone a struggling one like Benson. After the Benson family sold the Benson Company in 1980 the company underwent ups and downs in its business throughout the decade. Several presidents came and went; by 1985 a succession of executive turnovers (at Benson and elsewhere) led John Styll to argue in *MusicLine* that such changes "usually force a rethinking of priorities and goals—an especially appropriate exercise for those involved in Christian work. . . . I don't believe they betray a lack of stability or direction. These kinds of changes occur when good businessmen try to optimize their efforts."[64] Less than a year later, Benson had yet another new president with "a new commitment to the bottom line."[65] The bleeding did not stop, however: Benson's corporate parent, the publishing company Zondervan, laid off over sixty Nashville employees, halved its music products and releases, and fired its new president the following year amid a substantial failure to reach profitability.[66] After a couple of corporate acquisitions, Benson became part of Provident in 1997.

When Provident approached Mays to lead Benson in 1999, he knew the label's history and was wary of its difficulties. But he had an emotional attachment to Benson: it was the label for which he had first recorded as a bassist in the '70s, and Mays fondly remembered former owner Bob Benson Sr. as a paternal figure. Having worked in A&R at both Word and EMI CMG earlier in his career, Mays understood that his new job depended on Benson's ability to meet or exceed profit projections: "The whole approach to me was, 'We really want a creative guy, we want an A&R-led label.' That all was very appealing, and of course my concern is that if I'm president, what about the business side of things? 'Well, we got departments that will take care of that for you.' And that is true, they did, but at the end of the day if your quarter doesn't make its number, they're not going to that department. They're coming to you."[67] Mays attempted to rebuild Benson as an artist-oriented label, but—like other executives before him—he had little commercial success. Just as he had feared, as president he was ultimately held accountable for the label's failure. Not only did Provident's executives fire Mays, but in January 2001 they shut down the entire Benson label, fired its staff, and consolidated its assets with two other Provident subsidiaries, Essential and Reunion. Losing his job and failing to revive Benson was a devastating experience for Mays: "That was absolutely the worst, the most stressful; nothing worked, no decision I made either about signings or staff—I was trying to rebuild from scratch and bring in a new team—and in two years they shut it down."[68]

Unfortunately, stories like Mays's are not uncommon in the record industries. Andy Peterson came to Word in 2002 following a series of positions at smaller labels (Rode Dog, Reunion, and Rocketown) with increasing responsibilities. He was eventually promoted to senior director of product marketing—a position high enough to be held accountable for failing to meet or exceed sales targets. Initially in his tenure at Word, Peterson and his colleagues had high spirits: they planned to collaborate tightly with their counterparts at Warner in Burbank (California), promoting artists in the Christian and general markets simultaneously. "That was the idea," he told me in our first interview, "and of course that sounds great! And, of course, the reality of it was, of course, that's not going to happen." Whether Peterson and his colleagues were working with artists they had inherited or with new projects they launched themselves, like Mays's experience at Benson, nothing really worked: "By the end of our run we hadn't really sold any records, and so we all got fired [in 2005]. And for the first time in my career, I was high enough on the ladder to be one of the guys that when they came in to fix things, that I was asked to leave as well."[69] Peterson's superiors at Warner expected their releases to reach gold status regularly: "If you weren't scoring gold records, it wasn't worth staying in business." With hindsight, Peterson realized that the expectations were unrealistic for the Christian market—especially in the early 2000s, when sales were declining at all record labels. "That was really a very wrong mentality," he said, "and that still is the mentality, I think, in a lot of places, in a lot of boardrooms, that the gold record is a moderate success, and if you can't manage that, then you're not going to be doing record deals for very long. It's crazy."[70]

A major entertainment conglomerate's substantial resources can be mobilized to promote an artist heavily: over time, each of the Big Three labels had developed its distribution and marketing networks to target mass audiences as effectively as possible. Peterson and his colleagues expected access to those resources while at Word, but Warner's executives were not interested in facilitating Word's success, despite their shared interests. "Even within the walls of Warner in Burbank," Peterson told me, "as much as they said on paper that they wanted to be supportive, and as nice as they were to us when we would go out there and meet with them and be in the office, I just don't think they ever really thought what we were doing was credible." Word was thus saddled with major label sales expectations but not provided the major label resources that could have enabled them to meet those expectations. As Peterson explained,

> It was a struggle to get any kind of real resources or support to do anything on a large scale. . . . We had a couple of things that were valuable enough that they certainly could have made successful if they wanted to . . . but there was no champion within that system that was going to stand up and say, "We're going to push the big red button on this one." . . . I really believe that that button exists at every label . . . and they push it once a year, and no matter if it's a good reason or not, they push it and say, "We are going to break this artist no matter what."[71]

Minimizing expenses and maximizing revenues is a rational approach to prioritizing profit, but here Peterson revealed the potential for irrational acts—providing unlimited resources to force an artist's commercial success without necessarily needing "a good reason," and withholding resources that would support the commercial success of a different division—thus complicating the idea that for-profit companies consistently make rational choices. If Warner's executives had the freedom to pursue vanity projects or relegate their colleagues at Word to failure (and unemployment), then shouldn't Christian label executives have had the freedom to support artists who had not (yet) sold half a million records? In this case, the answer was no, in part because of power disparities between Christian labels and their general market counterparts in the corporate hierarchy of a Big Three conglomerate. Ultimately, Peterson's criticism of Warner executives was twofold: they held Word to a difficult commercial standard, and they consistently failed to "push the big red button" necessary to meet that standard, ensuring Peterson's (and his colleagues') failure.

If the gold record was the expected minimum, and if achieving that level of sales was increasingly difficult, then label executives must have felt compelled to make decisions that improved their chances to reach that threshold. Wayne Kusber confirmed that the commercial priority sometimes forced labels to make decisions purely for business reasons, without taking into account other factors: "It's not that they want you to change the content or change what you do, where the rub comes is I think you're forced to make decisions quicker based on finances than you would if you were still independently owned." And if sales figures did not improve and short-term revenue did not justify the label's investment, there was increasingly an expectation to focus on a different project: "There's pressure to move on; if it's not working, move on. . . . The bottom line is definitely more intense when you're owned by a major, without a doubt. And that does affect your decisions from time to time, no doubt about it."[72] Like Kusber, Mays repeatedly faced pressure to move on from unprofitable projects and part ways with artists for whom his label might not be the best fit: "I've signed artists that after three records, it was obvious—you know, we tried this and this and this—and we came to a mutual conclusion that nobody liked."[73]

Mays told me that he "never had to drop an artist or make a creative decision based on money alone" at Benson, although he could recall several examples where money played a large part in the decision, or where the decision was out of his hands. Kusber understood that his primary goal was to be profitable within the Christian market, just as other divisions and subsidiaries of the conglomerate that owned his label needed to be profitable within their markets: "The reason they own us is because they want that genre, just like they have jazz and pop and hip hop and rock. . . . They want to be the biggest in that niche. They want to own everything." For Kusber, there was trust on the part of his superiors that he and his colleagues knew best how to profit in the Christian market: "They just want us to be good at what we do. They want us to know our market, be great at it, and be profitable. That's all they care about."[74] Sometimes being profitable takes time to build the committed audience that will yield sustained success for Christian artists: "The bottom line plays into it, but if we feel like there's good things happening, there's momentum, there's a story building, you can feel the touring is growing, there are all these things that are showing positive signs, we try to hang with an artist as long as we can."[75] From Kusber's perspective, his label was attempting to pursue commercial and ministerial goals simultaneously. His superiors may not have understood the Christian market, but they nevertheless held him and his colleagues accountable for "positive signs" documenting their continued success.

CHALLENGES IN THE CORE CHRISTIAN MARKET

New challenges emerged in the first decade of the twenty-first century. From the 2003 peak of $1 billion in Christian music sales, according to data provided by the GMA, revenue halved by the end of 2008.[76] This reflected larger trajectories throughout the entire record industry, according to data provided by the RIAA: sales of CDs peaked in 2000 and then fell for several years as consumers switched to digital formats, both pirated and legitimate.[77] This decline clearly affected the Christian market, though there is no way of knowing the degree to which the downturn in the Christian market was exacerbated by being yoked to the general market. If the Christian major labels were not owned by general market major labels, might they have pursued different strategies and thus avoided (or at least partially alleviated) some of the problems that faced the general market in the early 2000s? We cannot know. Ultimately, the Christian majors faced increasing pressure from their corporate parents to remain profitable.

As a result of these challenges, the Big Three (which were the Big Five of BMG, EMI, Sony, Universal, and Warner when this decline started in 2001) struggled to reorient their business practices, only willing to incorporate small changes and intent on maintaining the status quo.[78] Record labels' overhead costs did not decrease at the same rate as did their average per-release sales figures, and they still needed to hit their overall sales target across all of their releases. Thus, labels started releasing even more records to meet their quarterly targets. Mays explained this counterintuitive strategy to me: "They're selling half as much of those releases; they can't bring that [target] number down by half—that's not acceptable—so what's the only way to try to hit that number is to sign more artists."[79] It is simple math: if Sparrow could count on averaging five hundred thousand copies of twenty releases every year in the mid- to late '90s, and ten years later releases were averaging two hundred fifty thousand copies, but the quarterly targets had not been adjusted downward, then Sparrow would have had to release forty albums to hit their target. The result, according to Peterson, was a higher signal-to-noise ratio in the market, a race to the bottom, a death spiral that alienated listeners further and also complicated relationships with distributors, retailers, and radio programmers: "What [lower per-album sales] forced all the labels to do was create more content, and they flooded the market with mediocre content, which changed the experience for consumers, and overwhelmed the infrastructure; it overwhelmed radio. And so now, all of a sudden there was no room for the good stuff because all of the crummy stuff was there too. Consumers couldn't tell the difference anymore because it was overwhelming."[80] Increasing the quantity of records further saturated an already oversaturated market. Compounding this problem, Christian record label executives found that their core consumers were more open to general market music than in the past. Market research during this period indicated that white U.S. evangelical consumers' media diet had become increasingly diverse, regularly reaching outside the boundaries of the Christian market. Christian labels found themselves in an increasingly competitive landscape of media and entertainment industries, complicating strategies designed for a more strictly defined, less porous niche market.

For example, even though the needs and expectations of Christian radio programmers were important to Wayne Kusber, he knew that listeners did not listen to Christian radio exclusively: "They've got their presets and they're hopping around. There's Christian, there's a country station, there might be a Top 40 station, talk radio, sports."[81] Nick Barre, a former EMI CMG executive who moved to artist management company Proper Management in 2008, suggested that, for younger listeners, tastes were even broader. He remembered using well-defined music tastes to establish identity and community during his own adolescence (in the 1980s)—"the type of music you liked defined what lunch table you sat at," he reminisced.[82] But by the early 2000s, that exclusivity had given way to an eclectic omnivorous inclusivity.[83] He told me, "You'll have kids whose favorite groups are Casting Crowns, they always say Radiohead but they don't know what they're saying, AC/DC, Led Zeppelin, Taylor Swift—that's almost become obligatory, it's everyone's official guilty pleasure—and Tim McGraw."[84] From his perspective, asking kids and teenagers "What kind of music do you like?" was an unproductive question because they like all kinds of music; trying to use musical taste to profile young listeners was a dated strategy: "What's funny is that has become an official old-fart question."

Old farts or not, the labels were slow to catch up to these changes in the market. In the twenty-first century, the Christian majors largely refocused on their core audience in an attempt to maintain their existing consumer base. This was a change from previous strategies: in prior decades, major labels had focused on expanding their consumer base and market share. In the 1990s, for example, Christian labels often pursued crossover hits in the general market (see chapter 7). In the early 2000s, however, when the overall market for recordings appeared to be shrinking, maintaining an existing market was perceived as a success—static profits are preferable to declining profits, especially when increasing profits is an elusive (if not impossible) task. But in prioritizing the core, the Christian market risked alienating peripheral Christian musicians and listeners. This problem was not unique to Christian labels: Simon Frith has characterized descriptions of major labels as "intensely conservative, more concerned with avoiding loss than risking profit, confirming tastes than disrupting them. Records are made according to what the public is known to want already."[85]

But whose public? Certainly not the teenagers who had little affinity or commitment to the Christian market—if we believe Wayne Kusber, those potential listeners were already lost, in part because Christian music's mainstream was so strongly marketed to their moms: "But as her kids get older, when they get in junior high and high school, I think there becomes a little bit of a void of time when those kids ask, 'Okay, what music's there for me?'"[86] John J. Thompson, who was a director of creative and copyright development for EMI CMG's publishing division at the time of our interview, agreed: "By the time they're eighteen, nineteen, and off to college, most high school Christian music fans aren't interested anymore."[87] As I discuss above, Nick Barre believed that things had changed since his adolescence: he argued that young listeners' tastes are decreasingly bound up in stylistic distinctions. The overall perception was that Christian identity was no longer tied to the consumption of Christian commodities (including music) among young listeners. I think this is a difficult argument to sustain, given the strong communities that support more underground and peripheral Christian artists and musicians (see chapter 6). The challenge for Kusber, Barre, Peterson, Thompson, and other Christian record label executives—as if they needed more challenges—was understanding that their niche market had changed while the labels fiddled. Will the labels change as well, or will they neglect the market and let it burn?

3

A Wolf in Sheep's Clothing?
Christian Ethics Encounter Rock

Niche markets for popular music have particular styles and aesthetics: they *sound* and *look* certain ways. But they also have values that are not (or not only) about the music itself. Some niche markets' boundaries reflect their participants' economic, political, religious, or social values; other markets are shaped by the needs and expectations of their geographic locations; still others are defined in relationship to other artforms and creative economies. In popular music, niche market boundaries depend not only on musical characteristics but also on social networks and ethical formations. Analyzing the music itself can reveal much about the sound of a particular market, both in terms of what sounds that market's style clearly includes, what ones it excludes, and what sounds push—and ultimately change or expand—its boundaries. But it is often just as important to consider what market participants expect in terms of appropriate social relationships, networks, and behaviors as well as accepted ways of producing, distributing, and consuming music. These expectations are important to consider because participants often use them to enforce the market's boundaries—to justify both excluding some artists and including others. Musical aesthetics (*sounding* appropriate) and its ethics (*behaving* appropriately) are always co-constitutive, intertwined, and inherently interrelated in niche markets, each informing the other.

In his discussion of Full Gospel Trinidad, Timothy Rommen argues that ethical considerations take precedence over stylistic characteristics:

"In the case of music in Full Gospel Trinidad, ethics is the antecedent of aesthetics. In other words, it would be nice if this or that sounds good, but if it *is* good then that characteristic will override aesthetic concerns."[1] Full Gospel is a loosely defined group of charismatic evangelical Christian denominations in Trinidad that use a variety of popular music styles (dancehall, gospelypso, jamoo, and North American gospel) in their praise and worship music. In Trinidad, as Rommen explains, the term "gospel music" refers to a broader set of musical styles than it does in the United States. Much like the U.S. Christian market's use of terms like "contemporary Christian music" (or CCM) and "Christian music" (or even "gospel" itself, at least in the context of the style-agnostic Gospel Music Association trade organization, or GMA), the category itself "groups rather divergent musical styles under a larger umbrella by virtue of their shared content."[2] Rommen's "ethics of style" explains why some musical styles and characteristics (that *sound* good) are shunned within Full Gospel Trinidad due to their affiliation with unchristian beliefs, behaviors, and lifestyles (that is, they cannot *be* good). There is a clear parallel to anti-rock discourse among U.S. evangelicals in the 1960s and '70s, as I discuss below: when rock and roll emerged, it too was criticized for promoting behavior antithetical to Christian morals and ethics, and thus inappropriate for Christians to listen to or play.

In this chapter and chapter 5, I demonstrate that acts of exclusion and inclusion in the Christian market—in particular, those that weigh its ethical expectations more heavily than they do the music itself—are also moments in which participants prioritize ethics over style. Specifically, the ethics of the Christian market demand that artists adhere to Christian moral behavior in their public and private lives. Consider, for example, Sandi Patty, a prominent and popular Christian singer throughout the 1980s and early '90s whose career nosedived after she revealed that she had had an extramarital affair prior to divorcing her first husband, transgressing the market's ethical and moral expectations. In the Christian market, such transgressions can end artists' careers, although they might carry little consequence (and even be celebrated) in the general market. In addition to setting expectations for artists' behavior or their theology, niche markets often value particular ethics of production, distribution, mediation, and reception. For example, one way to define Christian music is as that which is produced and distributed by Christian record labels. Music outside of these infrastructures has little chance of circulating within the Christian market. These ethics limit niche markets' broader accessibility, keeping them niche, and precede both acceptable and inappropriate musical elements. Ultimately, participants in niche markets consider nonmusical boundaries when deciding which artists (and what music) belong and which do not. In short, ethics shape markets' aesthetics.

These ethical boundaries are not established by fiat from C-level executives in Los Angeles, New York City, or Nashville deciding what the market will bear. Nor are they purely products of grassroots organizing, the inmates running the asylum. Rather, the boundaries of niche markets are discursively defined by negotiation between and among all participants—artists, cultural intermediaries, and consumers—in a perpetual, iterative, and self-replicating process. Here and in chapter 5 I explore ways in which ethics are articulated and implicated within the boundaries of Christian music. Some of these debates are archived in the pages of magazines like *CCM*, present in editorials, interviews, news items, readers' letters, and album reviews. Concertgoers and festival attendees witness justifications made from the stage and participate from the audience and back at the campgrounds. Audiences, artists, and organizers at Christian festivals have particular ethical perspectives and expectations, which a quick glance at the schedule, a stroll past the stages and seminar tents, and conversations at campsites reveal. These are ethics that have been commodified, often in ways eerily similar to the commodification of the music itself: supporting a particular ethical stance, it seems, can be as easy as buying and wearing a T-shirt or donating to a sponsor.

Sandi Patty is not the only Christian artist whose career has relied on her audience's ability to authenticate her within an ethical framework. Many artists have been excluded from the market after ethical transgressions, and in chapter 5 I discuss others who have advocated for inclusion on ethical grounds. Just as the values and theologies of Christian faith vary among believers, so too do the accepted boundaries of Christian music vary among its market participants. Within popular music, niche market ambiguities and sociocultural ambiguities frequently overlap: conflicts over meaning and belongingness in Christian music reflect similar conflicts in Christianity itself. This discourse has been present for several generations: many prominent white U.S. evangelical Christians advocated against rock and roll in the 1950s, warning of its dangers from the pulpit, over the airwaves, and in pamphlets and books. Examining this type of fundamentalism, which is increasingly in the minority, helps to explain broad ethical generalizations, especially those founded on immaterial and baseless assertions, before weighing the ambiguities and nuances of more refined ethical boundaries.

CHRISTIAN RESISTANCE TO ROCK AND ROLL

In the context of Christian popular music, the earliest example of ethical boundaries was the debate over whether rock and roll itself was appropriate within Christian culture. In the United States, this debate—what Anna Nekola calls "conservative Christian anti-rock discourse"[3]— emerged from the moral panic over the growing popularity of rock and roll among white teenagers in the mid-to-late 1950s. Moral panics have accompanied the rise of other styles of popular music, such as big band swing, punk rock, hip hop, and electronic dance music, among others. Many moral panics often scapegoat new forms or genres of media to explain a perceived increase of deviant behavior; most reflect parental anxieties over the *potential* damage to society, not *actual* damage. Mark Sullivan, in an article summarizing religious-led backlash to The Beatles after John Lennon disparaged Christians in 1966, argues that the central concern of moral panics is in protecting children and teenagers—that is, "of saving the young from corruption ... [because] the young consumers are not thought to have sufficient maturity to know what is really good for them."[4] In the 1950s and '60s, the moral panic over rock and roll had very clear racial motives: the corruption from which white youth needed saving was the social and cultural integration of Black youth (not to mention their friendship and romantic partnership). But Randall Stephens has noted that Black religious leaders were also opposed to rock and roll in the 1950s, defending "black respectability against the obscene threats of low culture."[5] Martin Luther King Jr., for example, writing in *Ebony* magazine in 1958, questioned "whether one can be consistent in playing gospel music and rock and roll music simultaneous [sic]." Ultimately, he argued, "the two are totally incompatible."[6]

In later decades, Christian opponents of rock and roll and Christian popular music framed their objectives in broader terms. Some were concerned with insulating traditional hymnody and liturgical music from secular influence, uncomfortable with attempts to reconcile the sacred and secular spheres. Others were concerned with the corrupting potential of the counterculture's more permissive morality via rock and roll. Still other anxieties reflected a lingering McCarthyite fear of the rise of communism and the presence of communist sympathizers within rock and roll. Critics often conflated these concerns, arguing that rock and roll's instrumentation, form, harmonies, and volume were inherently worldly and thus inherently sinful, brainwashing youth who did not yet have the proper moral and ethical framework to enjoy it without succumbing to its nefarious intentions. Rock and roll was evil at its origin, these critics argued, with the power to turn the most clear-headed, model teenager into a juvenile delinquent who rebelled against her parents, church, country, and even God himself.

These debates circulated within individual churches, regional denominational associations, on Christian radio stations, and via published pamphlets and tracts. Some of these survive in archives, such as the eleven-page privately published booklet *Music on the Rocks* by Wendell K. Babcock, a hymn composer, writer, and teacher at Grand Rapids School of Bible and Music (now a part of Cornerstone University).[7] Writing in the 1970s, Babcock discredited rock and roll entirely by arguing that it does not fulfill a "generally accepted definition" of music: "a succession of tones with the components of melody, harmony, rhythm, plus the variable dimension of volume, all pleasing to the ear."[8] He wrote that rock and roll's driving beat, syncopated "erotic" rhythms, distorted timbres, and erratic harmonic progressions deviate from accepted musical norms, in turn producing deviance among listeners. This deviance manifests in physical effects such as hearing impairment, increased sex drive, hysteria, and neurosis; psychological effects such as "attitudes of social and moral permissiveness, . . . indecency, moral degeneracy, escapism, plaintive helplessness, . . . sensuality and anxiety, . . . [mental] imbalance and wrong moral judgment"; and a philosophical reorientation that privileges chaos and confusion.[9] Ultimately, Babcock wrote, "Rather than being a vehicle of uplifting and blessing, this so-called MUSIC of Rock, or even Christian Rock, violates the definition and description of true music and has become rather the vehicle for evil and wickedness, being a means of conditioning the public for all kinds of raucousness and rebellion and removal of restraints."[10]

In addition to Babcock, several prominent white U.S. evangelicals warned that Christian appropriation of popular music was an unnecessary and potentially damaging compromise with worldly values and secular culture. Eileen Luhr and Nekola discuss this discourse in detail, focusing on the work of evangelical leaders in the 1960s and '70s.[11] Frank Garlock, a minister who also taught music at Bob Jones University, had many of the same concerns as Babcock, suggesting that rock and roll's volume and rhythm harmed the physical and mental well-being of listeners.[12] He argued that rock and roll could not be wholesome because it was affiliated with dozens of criminal and deviant behaviors and upset society's status quo. Importantly, as Luhr points out about Garlock's argument, "prominent among rock's associates were signifiers of the antiwar, civil rights, gay rights, and women's movements and the sexual revolution, which were grouped with Satan worshippers, heathens, blasphemers, and other longtime spiritual nemeses of fundamentalists."[13] Bob Larson, a radio and television evangelist, also wrote of rock and roll's dangerous musical elements. He claimed that the music's backbeat and its repetitive harmonic structure could hypnotize listeners and thus expose them to evil influences (intended or not).[14] Like Garlock, Larson blamed the political instability and social unrest of the 1960s on rock and roll, whose power lay in its ability to supplant churches, families, and schools as youths' central affiliation. Rock music, he wrote, had "unified the voice of the teenage bloc and given solidarity to their rebellion."[15] In the 1980s, Bob Larson's concern about occultism, violence, and sexual themes in rock and heavy metal lyrics helped fuel a broader "Satanic panic" among the media and the reactionary attempts at censorship in the United States by the Parents Music Resource Center.[16]

David A. Noebel, a minister affiliated with the anti-communist Christian Crusade and the far-right John Birch Society, contrasted elements of pitch, rhythm, intensity, and atmosphere between rock and roll and "good music" in his book *The Beatles: A Study in Drugs, Sex and Revolution*.[17] Good music, he explained, has a variety of pitches and uses very high pitches for contrast and climaxes, while rock and roll constantly repeats pitches and overuses high pitches "to give wild, screaming sounds." Good music's atmosphere is a "well-ordered system" that "strengthens moral and spiritual principles," while rock and roll's atmosphere is chaotic and "tears away moral principles." Noebel's central criticism of rock and roll, however, was that it promoted a communist agenda. He first launched this attack in the twenty-six-page pamphlet *Communism, Hypnotism and the Beatles* (published in 1965, a year before Lennon's disparaging comments about Christianity prompted broad outcry) and continued in 1974's *The Marxist Minstrels*.[18] He argued that rock and roll was being used deliberately by the Soviet Union to corrupt U.S. youth; he pointed to the banning of rock and roll in the Soviet Union as evidence of protecting Soviet youth from its harm.[19]

Arguments from these and other writers clarified the ethical and moral stakes for Christian parents and churchgoers concerned about disruptive social change and evolving cultural norms. Christian anti-rock discourse reflected common and very real fears about the dangers of political instability (especially the rise of communism, which Noebel and others equated with atheism), drug use, and sexual promiscuity, among other evils. Concerns over the influence of Satan and other religious movements (particularly polytheistic and pantheistic traditions) is understandable, given that Christianity's beliefs in absolute truth and a single path to salvation necessarily invalidate the truth claims and afterlife (including reincarnation) promised in other religions. The world was changing rapidly, leaving many feeling unmoored and grasping for something or someone to blame for their increasing sense of helplessness and loss. Garlock, Babcock, Larson, Noebel, and many others tapped into that anxiety and used it to promote their own ethical stances—which pointedly blamed rock and roll for society's ills—effectively legitimizing fringe beliefs by associating them with more widespread, legitimate concerns. Importantly, these writers conflated several otherwise disparate categories of dangers. For example, criminal behavior, communism, spiritual deviance, and progressive social movements of the era (such as civil rights and second-wave feminism) were often attacked together as being anti-Christian and thus antithetical to U.S. culture. Doing so framed progressivism as being on an equal footing with the moral, political, and spiritual issues of the other three categories, casting aside (or ignoring) any consideration for the relative danger each might pose. Thus, listening to rock and roll was just as likely to lead to drug abuse as it was to Godlessness, Satanism, or miscegenation, all of which were seen to be equally bad and equally sinful.

These criticisms—especially when accompanied by biblical scripture, however specious or circumstantial the connection—were most effective with older generations, who believed that Christianity itself was under attack. In their roles as church elders, parents, and pastors, they fought to keep rock and roll out of their homes, churches, and communities. While the Jesus People movement and the music that accompanied it appealed to many young Christians and converts in the 1960s and '70s (see chapter 1), many older churchgoers found it difficult to reconcile the spirituality of artists like Larry Norman with their very obvious stylistic similarities to rock and roll. "Christian rock" itself became a casualty of this discourse, in part because the term seemed to be an oxymoron to those who believed that rock and roll is inherently (and irredeemably) anti-Christian.

FIGURE 5. Rez Band performing live in 1987. Used with permission, courtesy JPUSA archives.

Such beliefs directly affected Christian artists' ability to perform, tour, and minister. For example, Glenn Kaiser, guitarist and vocalist for the Christian rock group Resurrection Band (figure 5), remembers that live concerts could provoke a confrontation between church elders and youth. Usually, he told me, this confrontation was not directed at his band: "Very few people ever spoke to me directly saying we were playing sinful music as such. Our fans and followers got 99 percent of the harsh comments."[20] He has spoken of one particular church concert when, after "we got several hundred kids going absolutely crazy . . . these two white-haired old deacons with their pink sport-coat thingies on, their faces were red, veins popping out of their necks, and they're literally running to the stage. I yelled over the amps, 'I think we're through!'"[21] Similarly, many Christian bookstores were wary of selling Christian records, affecting Christian record labels' ability to reach new listeners. "That's the only place we could sell anything, Christian bookstores—and the bookstores, they didn't like the music," recalled Billy Ray Hearn, founder of Sparrow Records. Christian bookstores only sold records grudgingly: "They thought it was evil. A lot of preachers were actually preaching against us. . . . One store I know, a big store in Chicago, would put it under the shelves. And if somebody came in and asked for one, they'd give it to you in a brown paper bag."[22] This type of censorship became increasingly problematic as Christian bookstores solidified their positions as the primary retail outlets for Christian commodities (see chapter 1).

As Christian music grew increasingly popular, however, the strength of its critics' positions diminished. As with Hearn's youth musicals in the 1960s (see chapter 1), pastors in the 1970s appreciated the music's ability to attract, retain, teach, and minister to youth. Many Christian artists were zealous evangelists and considered themselves to be primarily ministers (instead of entertainers). Christian music's strong focus on theology and evangelism in the 1970s helped to define it as a lyrically oriented genre distinct from secular rock and roll, as well as to reframe Christian discourse on popular music styles' substantial ministerial potential. Previously hostile churches invited Resurrection Band back to perform, telling Kaiser, "I hate your music but love your preaching."[23] Reflecting on moments like this to me many years later, Kaiser noted the hypocrisy of this ends-means justification, rhetorically asking, "the Bible, sound theology and ethical logic is [sic] okay to jettison if folks come to a commitment to Jesus? . . . So much for spiritual integrity."[24] It dismayed him that church leaders would focus on the number of conversions at their concerts, because highlighting the end product (conversions) framed those concerts as transactional in nature, while Kaiser and his bandmates emphasized a broader ministry and spiritual objective for their music and performances.

When the Jesus People dispersed around the country, their musical tastes gradually influenced the perspectives of church and denominational leaders, effectively normalizing popular music within white U.S. evangelical Christianity. And as Christian consumers' demand for Christian music grew, Christian bookstores ultimately relented and started to carry a wider variety of records. According to Hearn, they could not argue with the results: "It wasn't long till the demand was so high they had to put it out. The market forced the stores to put it out. . . . Mainly, the Christian bookstores were owned by older-mindset people. They would hire kids to run the record department, because they knew records. These young kids would say, 'Listen, we need to put in this youth music.' . . . They'd buy one or two [copies], and they'd sell it. Pretty soon they were selling five, pretty soon they were selling ten.[25] Many Christians and churchgoers remained wary of general market music in the 1980s and '90s, although their anxieties had less to do with any perceived inherent immorality of the music itself and more to do with immoral messages heard in song lyrics, seen on MTV, or learned from celebrity's lifestyles. The Christian market seemed perfectly designed for these listeners: labels like Sparrow sold them contemporary-sounding music with an uplifting, Christ-centered message that provide a wholesome alternative to the moral permissiveness confronted in the general market.

Nevertheless, some continued to criticize Christian music in the 1980s and later as incommensurate with Christian beliefs, despite this being an increasingly unpopular position. Jimmy Swaggart was perhaps the most prominent evangelist to argue against Christian music, well before a prostitution scandal led to his downfall in 1988. John Styll referenced Swaggart's attacks on Christian music in a 1980 issue of *CCM* magazine, drawing many responses from readers.[26] Two months later, Styll reported that his readers largely supported his position over Swaggart's, noting that only "one in six letters opposed our position, and each of those who agreed with Swaggart also seemed to believe that Christian music has only a single application"—namely, worship.[27] But Swaggart's criticisms did not diminish, instead growing stronger as his own reputation grew, ultimately culminating in his 1987 book *Religious Rock'n'roll: A Wolf in Sheep's Clothing*. John Styll interviewed Swaggart in 1985 for *CCM* magazine to confront his views (which were at odds with Styll's own).[28] In the preface to a reprint of the interview, Styll quotes Swaggart's position on Christian music: "The new, so-called contemporary 'Christian' music is incompatible with true biblical Christianity.... I emphatically state that it's impossible to touch anyone's heart with contemporary music."[29] Although Swaggart thought contemporary music sounded "weird, strange, and odd," in the interview he was careful not to base his claims on any particular musical elements he found distasteful, possibly because he did not want to open himself to charges of racism (as did critics in the 1950s), but also because he did not want the discourse to be about different individual musical tastes: "We have to be very careful here that we do not get involved in *taste*.... Taste will vary. That really doesn't have anything to do with spirituality of the particular style or type of music.... So what I want to be very careful we don't do, that *I* don't do, is to get my taste in music, which all of us have, mixed up in our convictions. Those are two different things altogether."[30]

Over the course of the interview Swaggart lodged several arguments against Christian music. He was concerned with "Christian rock" being derived from "rock and roll": "the very idea of labeling oneself after that which is so degrading—that has been a factor that is destroying untold millions of young people—is, number one, in itself wrong."[31] Christian music was too similar to (secular) rock and roll, he said; the former may serve as a gateway to the latter, or as a poor substitute. This might have been acceptable if the music and musicians were successfully ministering to youth, but throughout the interview Swaggart emphasized that he could not believe that Christian music did, in fact, promote Christian beliefs and perspectives. When Styll asked Swaggart about the testimony of believers who felt Christ's presence at a rock concert, Swaggart flatly responded, "I've never heard a single testimony in my life of such, I never have. If they had any type of lasting thing, I've never heard any, period."[32] When pressed about why he doubted the lasting impact of Christian artists, Swaggart fell back on his own experience as an evangelist and the expectation that ministers need to be anointed by the Holy Spirit to be effective: "I have great trouble in my heart believing that many [concert goers] are getting much from the Lord. . . . I know the anointing of the Spirit, and I know how difficult it is to get it there."[33]

Tom Wagner writes of "anointing" as a strategy that "(in)fuses individual, institutional and spiritual authority," and which Christian artists employ to defuse their celebrity.[34] Anointing is a way of claiming that one's music is touched by the Holy Spirit and serves God, especially if the artist in question remains visibly accountable to a religious institution (for example, by regularly attending his home church or conferring with a pastor). For Swaggart, however, anointing was substantiated not by accountability to religious institutions but rather by accountability to him. "One thing about anointing, you can tell when it's there and when it's not there," he told Styll. "It's not a question of making a judgement. You *know*."[35] He never came right out and accused Christian artists of not being anointed, but he was very clear about his doubt: "Knowing what I know about the moving of the Holy Spirit and knowing what I know about music—I'm not saying it's impossible, but I'm saying I have problems with the Holy Spirit working in that type of atmosphere."[36]

Swaggart's response here was revealingly uncharitable at best and obstinately prideful at worst: he claimed to have a better understanding of God's actions and intentions—which biblical scripture teaches are ultimately incomprehensible in their fullness—than those of his fellow Christians, casting doubt on their calling, ministry, and faith.[37] Styll did not call him out on this point, nor on the pride that undergirded Swaggart's strong sense that his theology was truer than that of others. But Swaggart's strategy of anointing clearly differs from that which Wagner discusses. In the latter, anointing manifests as a tool of inclusion through which listeners and audiences authenticate Christian artists and their music, granting them authority to function as a vessel of God and the Holy Spirit. In the former, however, anointing is deployed as a weapon of exclusion, because if the Holy Spirit is absent "in that type of atmosphere" (as Swaggart claimed) then Christian artists are acting on their own authority while claiming spiritual authority—wolves in sheep's clothing—a sacrilege that is dangerous because it leads believers away from God instead of to God. Near the end of the interview, Swaggart admitted that he had never been to a Christian music concert and thus had not had the opportunity to evaluate the legitimacy of concertgoers' spiritual transcendence and see for himself whether or not those artists were anointed. Styll pushed him on this point, suggesting that Swaggart's arguments might be more legitimate if he could speak from the personal experience of attending a concert. Swaggart's response was defensive: "I just couldn't take it, I just couldn't. It has nothing to do with taste. It offends and wounds the Spirit of God within me so much that I couldn't sit there through it."[38]

ETHICAL TRANSGRESSIONS AND MARKET EXCLUSION

Jimmy Swaggart was unwilling to attend a Christian music concert, and he was unwilling to believe the testimony of attendees who encountered God's presence at concerts. For many readers of CCM magazine—at least those whose letters in response were published in later issues—his credibility suffered from this preemptive closed-mindedness.[39] Credibility is important in the Christian market: it is important that listeners believe that artists are being sincere and honest about their faith and beliefs. For many listeners, it is also important that artists are honest and truthful about their personal lives as well, although—and this is crucial—such transparency must reveal a personal life that is ethically and morally unassailable. This is why publicly visible systems of spiritual accountability are prominent: they provide a source of spiritual guidance and mentorship for artists, and they affirm that artists are willing to be held to the same behavioral standards as their fans. In actuality, the Christian market and its listeners hold artists to very high standards, with little room for error (and little appetite for forgiveness). Rejecting the permissiveness of the general market, Christian listeners expect Christian artists to refrain from drug and alcohol abuse, condemn sex outside of a heterosexual marriage, promote antiabortion causes, and avoid using profane language. The justification is that those who identify as Christian, represent Christianity in public culture, or profit from (or because of) their Christian faith should be model Christians. Furthermore, those who are called to minister (whether through their music or some other discipline) are best able to do so from a strong and secure ethical, moral, and spiritual framework. This is also why interviews were so popular in *CCM* magazine: through the interviewer, who acted as a proxy, readers were able to judge the degree to which interviewees met their expectations. And this is also why Swaggart's resistance to attending a Christian music concert fell short: for most fans, concerts are their only opportunity to witness a Christian artist and judge for themselves that artist's sincerity, honesty, and credibility.

There is an obvious orthodoxy at play in the ethical values and expectations of the Christian market, which is complicit in articulating standards of belief and practice as well as stylistic standards. The stylistic standards of the Christian market are largely set by the needs of its commercial infrastructures, and no one with whom I spoke in the Christian market was comfortable aligning its framework of belief with the expectations and effects of its capitalist marketplace. But the two are undoubtedly connected at some level, even if only because capitalism is a tool that many in the Christian market deem necessary for conducting their ministry. In this context, style serves ethics, just as it does in Rommen's discussion of Full Gospel Trinidad.[40] But there are also times when the pendulum swings away from ethical and toward stylistic considerations: when the needs of a radio programmer (and the record label's need to score a radio hit) influence a songwriter's objectives, when a song's lyrics obscure (or minimize) a Christian artist's faith and enable her to "pass" in the general market, or when an artist feels compelled to push musical boundaries without necessarily prioritizing the ministerial potential of his new aesthetic direction. Such negotiations represent compromises that demonstrate a back-and-forth over time. And there are moments when an artist's ethical transgressions are enough to harm her career no matter how strongly she conforms to the market's stylistic norms, a matter of ethics preceding style.

Sandi Patty's career suffered following her marital infidelity. She was and remains the award-winningest Christian singer of all time, including a period when she won the Dove Awards' Female Vocalist of the Year eleven years in a row (1982–92); five times during that period she was also Artist of the Year. Her style, exemplified by early hits like "How Majestic Is Your Name" (♫, written by Michael W. Smith) and "Sing to the Lord" (🎧, written by Robert Sterling), was archetypally that of Christian "inspirational" praise song: saccharine easy-listening production, accompanied by organ, strings, and choirs, with melodic leaps that highlighted her four-octave soprano range and upward modulations for the final chorus or two. Many of the songs she recorded became Sunday morning worship service staples, with prerecorded accompaniment tracks (stripped of Patty's vocals) enabling amateur soloists to attempt their own versions. She maintained her inspirational style with little acquiescence to pop music trends. From a business perspective, this is rational: she was successful and delivered to fans (and her labels, having recorded mostly for Benson subsidiary Impact, followed by Word) comfortable music that did not push stylistic boundaries. Instead of pursuing a more fickle general market audience or younger listeners, she (and her producers) targeted the Christian adult contemporary market. She was successful precisely because she did not push stylistic boundaries, instead setting (and meeting, album after album, song after song, performance after performance) musical standards for Christian inspirational song.

In an interview published in *Christianity Today* in September 1995, Patty admitted to having started an affair with her second husband, Don Peslis (whom she had married earlier that August), about seventeen months before divorcing her first husband, John Helvering, in June 1992.[41] The affair started while they were on tour together: as a member of the vocal trio One, Peslis had been Patty's backup singer during her 1991 tour supporting the album *Another Time . . . Another Place*, and he was also married at the time. Reactions from the Christian market were strong, partly because Patty had celebrated her family in public, at times conspicuously, her husband and children frequently accompanying her on tour and to interviews. *CCM* magazine noted that "Patty, who had carefully cultivated a pro-family image, sent shock waves through the Christian music industry and her fan base when she filed for divorce."[42] In a memoir, Patty explained that the professional repercussions were immediate: canceled concerts, a delayed album release, being dropped from radio station playlists, and having to resign as spokesperson for charitable organizations, among other consequences.[43] In the aftermath of the negative publicity, Patty retreated from public life and focused on seeking forgiveness from her church and ministry partners. She had made mistakes in her personal life that impacted her professional career, and she took steps to account, apologize, and atone for those mistakes. In the 2000s Patty has continued recording and singing, particularly in pops concerts accompanied by symphony orchestras, but her Christian career has never rebounded to its pre-scandal heights.

A year prior, Christian singer Michael English had fared worse. Having risen through the ranks of the white Southern gospel market (including stints with the Gaithers, the market's best-known artists), English transitioned into the larger Christian market with a self-titled album (1991) followed by *Hope* (1993). Also an inspirational singer who, like Patty, fared best in the Christian adult contemporary market, English won an unsurpassed four Dove Awards for his solo work in 1994. The ballad "Holding Out Hope to You" (♫, 1994's Inspirational Song of the Year) is similar in style to Patty's ballads (compare it to "Sing to the Lord"), and he appeared ready to follow in her footsteps. That trajectory came to a sudden halt two weeks after the 1994 Dove Awards ceremony, when he admitted at a press conference that he had had an extramarital affair with Christian singer Marabeth Jordan, who was pregnant with his child.[44] English announced that he was returning his Dove Awards and leaving the Christian market; his label's distributor, Warner, dropped his albums.[45] He has continued working as a record producer, performing for Southern gospel audiences (as a member of the Gaithers and other groups), and has released several other solo records. But, like Sandi Patty, his career in the broader Christian market has never fully recovered.

At *CCM* magazine, John Styll faced a significant ethical decision during this time. As editor and publisher of the main source of news about the Christian market, Styll felt he had an obligation to inform his readers of significant issues impacting artists—particularly issues that affected an artist's ability to minister effectively, both to Christians and to non-Christians. But he was also convicted about the private nature of sin and of the right of every individual—including artists—to repent and seek absolution from God. As he told me later, "We really try to stay out of the gossip realm and people's personal lives because, you know what? Everybody's life has a certain amount of mess to it. . . . We weren't muckrakers."[46] His ethical conflict, then, pitted the public's right to know against individual artists' rights to privacy. Moreover, this was also a decision about business ethics: Styll might sell more copies of *CCM* magazine if he published rumors and gossip more frequently, but at what cost? He might gain readers by doing so, but he would also lose readers for whom trading in gossip was distasteful, against Christian ethics, or both. Would the readers he gained make up for the readers he lost? Would they be the *type* of readers he wanted for *CCM* magazine?

Andy Peterson, a former executive at Word, reflected on this period and on the Christian market's approach to ethical transgressions in an interview. "In the mainstream [general market] world, when someone has to confront one of those major life issues or addictions, they can be—and often are—welcomed back very quickly, and oftentimes celebrated in a way that they never were before," he told me. "In this [Christian market] world, that doesn't happen very much," resulting in a contradiction between Christian talk and the Christian walk:

> That's probably the church in general, that we all talk about accountability, and we all talk about helping people in need, but when something ugly happens, whatever it may be, there's very little tolerance for it. . . . It's the problem that I can't confess out of fear of being ostracized from the same community that says that it wants to reach out and care and shepherd and provide for people in need. It's incredible. It's a very interesting thing about the church; the rhetoric is so strong to being open and loving, kind and generous, patient, but the reality is so far from that. And that has hurt; it has really hurt some people.[47]

The reaction of judgment instead of support, Peterson said, can work against artists being forthcoming with problems. The potential for hurt is unknowable—how many Christian artists have not sought out counseling or addiction treatment, have hidden their sexuality or gender identity, or have stayed in abusive relationships out of fear of the public shame and shunning that might follow?

For those artists who do come forward, sometimes there is indeed a support network that can help them: "The good part of the Christian music industry is that it does provide some safety, some protection that you can't get," Peterson told me. "And of course, Christians mess up bad. . . . But the response to that here is caring, comfort, help, 'Let's get you on a path to restoration, whatever the issue is.'"[48] The path to restoration, if successful, can become part of an artist's testimony to the strength of God to help him through a difficult period of life. But when that process is unsuccessful, or when the sin is too great—Peterson specifically cited an unshakeable intolerance for homosexuality within the Christian market—an artist's Christian music career is effectively over. "One of two things happens," he said. "Either the person immediately is put into a place where there's going to be some sort of intervention and restoration and hopefully resurrection, or they're going to be hidden away and just go away. Whether it's infidelity or drugs and alcohol or whether it's homosexuality, one of those two things happens."⁴⁹

According to Anthony Heilbut, the Black gospel market in the United States tends to overlook musicians' homosexuality without outright accepting it.⁵⁰ But in the Christian market for white U.S. evangelicals, there is no tolerance for homosexuality. Marsha Stevens was the first well-known Christian artist to run afoul of the market's condemnation of homosexuality. As a founding member of Children of the Day, an early Jesus Music band, Stevens played a large role in articulating the aesthetic standards of Christian music with songs such as "For Those Tears I Died" (🎵). But after divorcing bandmate Russ Stevens in 1979, dissolving Children of the Day, and coming out as a lesbian who remained committed to conservative evangelical Christianity, she was ostracized from the market. Her record label (Maranatha! Music) tried to withhold her royalties, and Christian music participants treated her with outright hostility—even celebrating the death of her partner's daughter as "divine judgment."⁵¹ In the twenty-first century, former Christian artists Ray Boltz and Jennifer Knapp have come out as homosexual, although both had left the Christian market prior to coming out. They were not no-name acts but consequential, Dove Award-winning artists who had significant fan bases in the Christian market. Boltz was an inspirational singer, like Patty and English, particularly in the piano ballad "Thank You" (🎵) and the gospel-inflected "I Pledge Allegiance to the Lamb" (🎵). Knapp was a folk-rock singer/songwriter, exemplified in her hit single "Undo Me" (🎵). She had retreated to private life in 2002 after burning out from several years of nonstop recording and touring. As a Christian artist, she had increasingly felt constrained by the ethical expectations of the market. "I wasn't just an ordinary Christian anymore," she wrote in her memoir, "[but] a model example for the Christian life," which included adhering to the "bright line" that renounced homosexuality.⁵² She sacrificed her own identity for her career, and her emotional well-being and faith suffered for it. Once out of the public eye, however, she was able to come to terms with her homosexuality and have a more fulfilling personal life. When she returned to performing in 2010, she knew that her lesbian identity would prevent her from reentering the Christian market. She came out publicly as a lesbian in April 2010, while touring in advance of her comeback album, *Letting Go*. The backlash was immediate, much of it manifesting in comments and messages to Knapp's social media accounts, in addition to admonishing letters from former fans. She has continued to record and perform, however (as do Stevens and Boltz), and she uses her position to advocate for LGBTQIA+ Christians through her organization Inside Out Faith.

CONCLUSION: DISCOURSE AS ETHICS; ETHICS AS DISCOURSE

Each of these artists' music not only fulfilled the stylistic expectations of the Christian market but set the standards against which other artists' music might be judged. Yet, in each of these cases, their careers as Christian artists have been irrevocably damaged by their ethical transgressions. "Certainly, with Michael English, he lost everything, and so did Ray [Boltz]," recalled Andy Peterson. "It's sad. And in the other [general market] world, these guys could have gotten over that."[53] And, well, that is exactly what has happened: each of these artists (Sandi Patty, Michael English, Marsha Stevens, Ray Boltz, and Jennifer Knapp) remain active as artists and performers in different and diverse markets, but with a much lower profile in the Christian market. Transgressions like these in the age of social media can circulate publicly very quickly: when Trey Pearson, the singer of Christian pop-punk band Everyday Sunday (🎧), came out as gay in May 2016, he did so by publishing an open letter to his fans online. Reactions poured in almost immediately via Facebook, Twitter, mainstream media (including the Associated Press newswire, articles in the *New York Times* and the *Washington Post*, and their comments sections), and other media.[54] In the 1990s, however, the pace of news moved more slowly and with more editorial discretion. John Styll faced his own ethical dilemma over the reporting of ethical dilemmas in *CCM* magazine. He considered his responsibility to his readers, to his magazine's financial stability, to the Christian market's artists, to his own understanding of Christian ethics, and ultimately to Christianity itself—responsibilities that did not always align. The seriousness with which he deliberated this dilemma reflected the position of *CCM* magazine itself as the central location for discourse about the Christian market. He understood that the editorial and journalistic discourses in *CCM* magazine's pages, for many readers, indexed the ethical underpinnings of the Christian market. In other words, ethics within Christian music manifested as discourse within *CCM* magazine.

Ultimately, Styll opted to uphold the ideals of caring, shepherding, and providing for artists in need, in part by protecting them from the judgment of Christian audiences. He decided that his values prevented him from publishing unsubstantiated rumors. *CCM* magazine had a responsibility to its readers, but Styll believed that it also had a responsibility to its artists, knowing that moving forward from a crisis is difficult to do in the public eye. He clarified this conflict in early 1994, before Michael English's affair was made public. "It is natural for the personal life of an artist to be of interest to his or her audience," Styll wrote in response to whispered, unpublished rumors. "For Christian artists, this takes on an added dimension because the audience has a right, beyond mere curiousity [sic], to know if they 'walk their talk.' Thus, there is a certain requirement for artists to reveal something of their personal lives." And yet, Styll argued, at times the audience's craving for intimate details of artists' lives itself verged on sinful behavior. He urged his readers to stop gossiping and idolizing artists, because doing so would allow "the [secular/celebrity] culture to take precedence in our lives over our faith."[55] That year, Styll started including a mission and belief statement on *CCM* magazine's masthead. Among several other components, the mission statement's objectives were "to provide news and information about contemporary Christian artists" and "to be a redemptive influence on popular culture."[56] Styll was learning that in order to be a redemptive influence on popular culture he needed to take a strong ethical stance regarding what news and information about Christian artists was appropriate to print. If we expect Christian artists to model Christian ethics within the music industry, then surely we should also expect Christian journalists to model Christian ethics within the journalism industry.

Several months later, in the same issue that reported Michael English's affair, Styll articulated his views on the ethical reporting of moral transgressions within the Christian market. First, he echoed his earlier condemnation of gossip and linked his editorial decision-making process to theology: "In *CCM* magazine, our policy is to avoid gossip and rumor altogether," Styll wrote. "We do not make personal sins public. And when we do learn of such situations (which are rare, fortunately), we look for clear indicators of repentance and behavioral changes before we continue our coverage of the artist." But he also clarified his belief that Christian celebrities are accountable to the market itself: "There is no question that what happened between them [English and Jordan] is a terrible sin which represents a breach of trust not only with their own families, but also with their audience."[57] The following year (1995), in the wake of Sandi Patty's admission of infidelity, Styll wrote again at length of these issues in his strongest statement yet:

> As journalists and Christians, the *CCM* editorial staff faces a delicate situation whenever sin lurks around the spotlight—which is more often than we like to admit. When we learn of less-than-exemplary behavior on the part of our brothers and sisters, we usually don't rush it into print because that would be mere gossip. . . . It has been *CCM*'s policy that sins in the private lives of individuals should remain private. Ideally, confession, repentance and discipline should happen on the church level rather than in the media. Occasionally, however, the consequences of sin become news and public disclosure is unavoidable.[58]

In both editorials, Styll valued private processes of accountability for artists over "breaking" the story first. He could have easily justified the inverse decision as facilitating the ethical boundaries of the Christian market and enabling the constant discourse of authentication. Both acts hinge on trust: trust that all participants agree and adhere to the same ethical and moral standards, and trust that those who have chosen careers in the public eye necessarily carry a larger burden of public accountability as a condition of their successes. Michael English and Sandi Patty had broken that trust; the sooner the Christian market learned this, the healthier it would be overall. Had Styll made this argument, he would have prompted an entirely different conversation: does the welfare of one artist outweigh the welfare of the entire market?

Instead of publishing gossip and rumors of artists' less-than-exemplary behavior, however, *CCM* magazine reported on English's and Patty's affairs only after the consequences of sin had become news. Indeed, in Styll's companion piece to Patty's affair, he walked his readers through a timeline that demonstrated he could have broken the story far earlier than *Christianity Today* did. But, importantly, *CCM* magazine did not publish what Styll and his team knew about Patty's affair earlier because "the potential for damage to the body of Christ outweighed the public's need to know."[59] This was a crucial moment. Styll did not believe that the Christian market would have been made healthier if it constantly judged its artists (and other participants) based solely on rumors, without providing space for private reconciliation and repentance. In fact, reconciling with God is more important than reconciling with one's fans, and the editorial policies and decisions at *CCM* magazine reflected this. Nevertheless, Styll acted from a position of power: he chose what his public needed to know about its artists, and he chose when an artist's repentance and behavioral changes justified covering them again. It is entirely possible that artists vanished from the pages of *CCM* magazine for ethical breaches that Styll did not publicize, returning once he was convinced that they had repented sufficiently.

In addition to Styll's convictions, other examples in this chapter illustrate the ethics of style in the Christian market. Conservative Christian anti-rock discourse during the 1960s, '70s, and '80s laid an ethical foundation for appropriate musical styles and practices. Writers and ministers such as Frank Garlock, Jimmy Swaggart, and others argued that the aesthetics of rock and roll and the ethics of Christianity could never intersect and would forever be in conflict. In the 1990s and 2000s, several Christian artists whose musical styles were entirely consistent with the aesthetics of the Christian market nevertheless suffered professional consequences when audiences learned of ethical and moral transgressions. In each of these cases, participants prioritized ethics over style to exclude artists from the market. There was never a moment in which participants treated style itself with significant, critical attention, arguing over the market's aesthetic boundaries, because the facts of Christian artists' transgressions prohibited any support. In other words, the appropriateness (or lack thereof) of Christian artists like English, Knapp, Patty, and others was not about whether their music *sounded* good, it was about whether their music *was* good, *reflected* and *represented* good, and *taught* good.

4

"Find a Way"

Amy Grant and the Christian Market's Mainstream

The (secular) major record labels' acquisition of Christian record labels during the 1990s marked the beginning of a new phase for the Christian market: a period of growth and prosperity during which Christian record labels' commercial priorities were no longer in question. Neither were label executives and other cultural intermediaries necessarily ashamed or wary of commerce and capitalism; instead, they chose to perceive working with (or for) companies for whom profit and return on investment were central objectives as the necessary cost of achieving their broader ministerial goals for Christian music. John Styll's 1986 proposition in a *CCM* magazine editorial that Christian music was simultaneously both a ministry and a business had become increasingly relevant, as more and more participants agreed with his central assertion that "without positive income, the capability to minister is impaired."[1] Furthermore, the market's ministerial goals had centered unequivocally on the objective of providing music and other forms of entertainment from a Christian perspective for Christian consumers. The market had largely reached a consensus: Christian music was not a tool for evangelizing and converting non-Christians but rather a resource for listeners who already identified as Christians. And, as Bill Hearn had noted in 1985 when explaining Sparrow's general market distribution partnership with MCA to *MusicLine*, many of those listeners did not listen to Christian radio or shop at Christian bookstores. General market distribution was thus key to helping potential listeners discover not just one or two Christian artists but the entire market: "Every time a Christian buys a Christian album anywhere, he becomes a prospective customer of a Christian bookstore where the selection is so much larger. Every time a Christian discovers Christian radio, he becomes much more likely to seek out that larger section."[2]

The Christian market had long relied on infrastructures separate from, but parallel to, those of the general market for its production, distribution, and consumption. This separateness both reflected and reinforced a perceived stratification between white evangelical Christian and non-Christian listeners in the United States. Although general market music publishers and record labels had distributed a variety of religious musics throughout much of the twentieth century, by the mid-1970s most had largely divested from the Christian market. Infrastructurally, this changed, first with the distribution and then with the acquisition and consolidation of Christian labels, which tied the business of producing and selling Christian music to the business of non-Christian music. For audience members otherwise uninterested in the details of the Christian music industry, however, this separateness changed with the career of Amy Grant.

If you listened to Top 40 radio in the United States in early 1991, Amy Grant's single "Baby, Baby" (🎧) was inescapable. Listen to it again, and chances are good that you will recognize the early-'90s-ness of the song's bouncy synthesizer riff, the bass's melodic fills, the processed drums, and Grant's full mezzo-soprano. The track's arrangement and production sit easily alongside those of other pop divas at the time, including Paula Abdul, Mariah Carey, Celine Dion, Whitney Houston, and Janet Jackson. "Baby, Baby" is both recognizable as mainstream pop and clearly at home on Top 40 radio of its era. Radio listeners of the weekly *American Top 40* countdown show the week of April 27, 1991 heard "Baby, Baby" take the coveted #1 slot from vocal trio Wilson Phillips, whose fourth single "You're in Love" had only held onto the top spot for one week. "Baby, Baby" was not Grant's first crossover success in the general market, but it was the first time she broke the top ten as a solo artist, and it marked the apex of her career in the general market. To many listeners and insiders, it indicated that the Christian market, long marginal to the general market, had finally gone mainstream.

If the Christian market's origin story is rooted in its foundational artists' separation from the general market, its industries, and its infrastructures—a clear moment of divergence, as I discuss in chapter 1—then one way to analyze its consolidation within global entertainment conglomerates in the 1990s and early 2000s is as a convergence of markets, industries, and infrastructures. Amy Grant's career is an ideal case study for this analysis. As one of the best-selling and most popular Christian artists of the late 1970s and '80s, her music and career set standards against which other artists were judged and to which they aspired. In a market where an album that sold over one hundred thousand copies was considered a smash hit, by the mid-1980s Grant's albums (🎧) were routinely selling over half a million copies and being certified as gold and platinum. With her attempts to reach listeners in the general market in the 1980s and '90s, she pushed the boundaries of what Christian music could be—sometimes uncomfortably so for many Christian listeners. In focusing on Grant, this chapter ends part 1 of *God Rock, Inc.* by both defining what the Christian market had come to mean for its participants in the 1990s and also demonstrating what potential there was for change and fissure at the turn of the century.

MAINSTREAMING CHRISTIAN MUSIC? AMY GRANT'S EARLY CAREER

Amy Grant debuted as a Christian artist with a self-titled record at the age of sixteen. Her first five studio albums, released on Myrrh Records between 1977 and 1984, explicitly foregrounded her faith and beliefs, placed her vocals high in the mix (a standard technique in Christian music meant to emphasize the lyrical content), and featured mid-tempo arrangements suitable for accessibility and contemplative listening. Early Christian radio singles, such as 1979's "Father's Eyes" (🎧) and 1980's "Look What Has Happened to Me" (🎧) illustrate these features, as well as another characteristic of Christian music: a stylistic derivativeness that is two to three years behind general market Top 40 pop. The earlier single, driven by acoustic guitar, could have been written by Carole King or Rita Coolidge in the early to mid-'70s; the latter is clearly indebted to the popularization of disco by the end of the 1970s. To many Christian radio listeners at the time, these songs might have sounded oddly contemporary; to general market listeners, however, they would have clearly sounded dated, at least a year or two late.

Other Grant singles succeeded on their merits as worshipful, inspirational songs. Consider, for example, her recording of the Michael Card song "El Shaddai" (🎧), released on 1982's *Age to Age* (which takes its title from the song's chorus). It is a piano ballad, suitably slow—around 60 bpm—and forgoes drums until the last two repetitions of the chorus during the final minute of the recording. Grant's vocal melody is accompanied by harp, piano, and strings in a lush arrangement. The song's lyrics attest to the timelessness of God's power, positions humans as unable to comprehend God's plan, and reiterates Christianity's claim to the God of Abraham.[3] The song doubles down on standard popular song strophic form, utilizing the same harmony and melody for both the verses and the chorus. Indeed, the arrangement that Grant sings starts with the chorus—already an unusual form for a single—and the only deviation from the sung melody is a brief instrumental variation as a bridge between the second chorus and second (final) verse. The melody stays squarely within the range of one octave and does not modulate. Grant sings the chorus four times; the (foreign) Hebrew words quickly become familiar to listeners even on first listen. The result is a song that is memorable, easy to learn, hummable, and singable.

The style, production, and content of Grant's recording of "El Shaddai" are consistent with the Christian market's expectations of how inspirational songs should sound and what they should say. Her profile continued to grow during this period as she became a major Christian star. In his article detailing Amy Grant's crossover strategies, William Romanowski writes that her career as a Christian artist was "unprecedented" and "unparalleled."[4] As I detailed in chapter 2, the Christian market itself was expanding as well: although Christian labels like Word/Myrrh, Sparrow, and Benson had long operated on the margins of the music industries, the Christian market's ability to sustain gold- and platinum-selling artists like Grant demonstrated that it was no longer much of a niche. Christian music was big business, complete with its own mainstream, and the general market ultimately came calling. Partnerships between large general market labels and Christian labels started as production and distribution deals, such as the 1984 agreement between Word Records and A&M.[5] Based largely on the demonstrated success and commercial potential of Amy Grant, the partnership enabled A&M to promote and distribute selected releases in the general market while Word served the Christian market.

Romanowski explains these partnerships by contextualizing them within a broader sense that, by the mid-'80s, Christian label executives felt that their market had plateaued. Sure, Grant was doing well, but perhaps she could be doing better—and if so, then other Christian artists could be riding her coattails. The issues were twofold. First, Christian label executives were beginning to recognize that their market's separateness—including retail outlets (Christian bookstores) and radio stations—likely hid Christian music from many potential Christian listeners. And second, reaching those target listeners in the general market required corporate partnerships and financial resources that the Christian labels could not access without help.⁶ For Christian labels, then, working together with (and, later, being acquired by) secular labels was a tacit acknowledgment that fully preserving their market stratification—no matter the theological or ethical justifications—would become a financial liability moving forward. Word's partnership with A&M and the approach they took collaboratively on Grant's next record illustrated both that evangelism via the airwaves was no longer the market's main goal, if it ever was—finding more existing Christians to listen to Christian music is a decidedly lower bar than converting nonbelievers who stumble across a Christian radio station—and that executives at Christian labels were willing to make strategic decisions that aligned their corporate partners' very clear objectives (profiting off of the Christian market) with their own (which included, among other goals, profiting off of the Christian market).

Amy Grant's sixth album, 1985's *Unguarded* (figure 6), was one of the first releases to benefit from this partnership between A&M and Word.⁷ A marketing campaign by A&M (slogan: "You may not know this artist by name. But a million know her music by heart"), placements on significant Top 40 radio stations' playlists, and features in the national press presented Grant to a general market audience. A profile in *Rolling Stone*, relatively tame by that magazine's standards, nonetheless prompted outcry by Grant's Christian fans for her views on sex ("My hormones are just as on key as any other twenty-four-year-old's"), looks ("I'm trying to look sexy to sell a record. . . . I feel that a Christian young woman in the Eighties is *very* sexual"), and an offhand remark about sunbathing nude on a private beach.⁸ *CCM* magazine's response successfully predicted the onslaught of mail that followed: "Will Amy Grant be burned at the stake for her interview in *Rolling Stone*? Possibly so . . . with complaints from fans, ministers, and Christian bookstore owners reaching Amy's management company and Word Records."⁹ Nonetheless, with bigger recording and marketing budgets and A&M's promotional expertise in the general market, *Unguarded* sold faster and charted higher (in the general market) than did any of its predecessors. Its chart positions show crossover success: as expected, the album reached #1 on the Top Contemporary Christian charts, but it also reached #35 on the *Billboard* 200.¹⁰ *Unguarded* also spawned three singles in the general market; the best-performing ("Find a Way," 🎧) was Grant's first to enter the *Billboard* Hot 100 chart, where it peaked at #29.

FIGURE 6. Album cover for Amy Grant's *Unguarded* (1985).

Amy Grant cowrote "Find a Way" with Michael W. Smith, then her keyboardist and a Christian songwriter, later a popular Christian artist in his own right.[11] Including "Find a Way," Grant cowrote seven of *Unguarded*'s ten tracks, more than she had on her prior three albums. Grant's longtime producer, Brown Bannister, helmed this album as well, with the guidance of an executive production team featuring Grant's management (Michael Blanton and Darrell Hall) and her then-husband and songwriting partner (Gary Chapman). In short, Amy Grant and her team contributed as much (if not more) to the recording and production of *Unguarded* as any previous release, so the strategic approaches to the album's songwriting, recording, arranging, production, and mixing to make it more accessible to general market listeners were likely not made without their input.

The arrangement and production in "Find a Way" is Top 40 radio-friendly, pure '80s-era synthpop. Think Huey Lewis and the News from around the same time ("Find a Way" and Lewis's "The Power of Love" were released just a few weeks apart): uptempo (around 128 bpm), standard verse-chorus song form, main accompaniment in the synthesizer, distorted guitar for accent, heavy reverb on the vocals, pristine drum sounds, modulation to the chorus (which is also sung in a higher register). The lyrical content strikes a compromise with Grant's core (Christian) audience and listeners in the general market: although it could be a typical song about the healing potential of love ("I know it's hard to see / The past and still believe / Love is gonna find a way"), the bridge between the second and third iterations of the chorus explicitly calls upon God—not love—as the ultimate healing authority: "If God his Son not sparing / Came to rescue you / Is there any circumstance / That he can't see you through?" Grant's vocals in this section are aurally obscured, both by an echo effect and by reducing her presence in the mix. The result is somewhat of a mixed message: Grant's faith is still present, audible, and articulated here in her first *Billboard*-charting general market single, but the fact that it is easy to miss—her faith is quite literally downplayed, whereas on earlier releases it was foregrounded—called into question Grant's sincerity for many of her Christian listeners. The following year, Amy Grant became the first Christian market artist to chart a #1 *Billboard* single when her duet with Peter Cetera, "The Next Time I Fall" (🎧), reached the top of the Hot 100 on December 6.[12] This song has no obvious biblical message, further prompting Christian listeners to question the costs of general market success for the most celebrated Christian artist of the time.

The September 1988 issue of *CCM* magazine was a special issue devoted to Amy Grant's career. Titled "A Decade of Amy," the lead interview and accompanying articles and reviews were intended, in part, to reintroduce Grant to the Christian market following a two-year break from touring and during the promotional cycle for her new album: 1988's *Lead Me On*.[13] In the interview she came off as sincere and affable; fallible yet faithful; devoted to her religion, family (despite her publicized marital problems), career, and fans. When asked how much her artistic decisions were influenced by commercial priorities, Grant acknowledged that the greater resources freed her from budgetary constraints. "Because of the record company support and of the record buying audience," she said, "we can make decisions with the freedom from money issues," such as hiring a hit-making mixing engineer.[14] At one point, the interviewer asked Grant to respond to criticism that she had sold out, gone secular, and abandoned the Christian world. Her response betrayed the frustration she felt over such accusations:

> I have never sold out. Sold out to who, Satan? Give me a break! That's the worst thing you could ever think or say to anyone who is trying to give their heart to Jesus every day.... I am just trying to figure out what I do well, and do it. What I can do to glorify God, and do it. And what I can do and pay the bills, and do it. I think with a lot of prayer, the three of those can meet.... I don't understand what it means to abandon the Christian world. I feel like as far as having an influence on the world, we are pretty useless if we are all cloistered together.[15]

Her Christian fans perhaps need not have worried at the time: while *Lead Me On* attempted to follow up *Unguarded*'s success with additional singles (such as the album's title track and "Saved by Love," 🎧), its production was decidedly less Top 40 radio-friendly, and the lyrical content was more overtly spiritual. "Word [Records] was very pleased," Grant noted, "and A&M's response was very different.... They said, 'We just want you to know if you get any airplay on this record at all, it's because we worked our tails off.'"[16] There were no obvious Top 40 singles on *Lead Me On*, which made A&M's job of promoting and distributing the album in the general market more difficult. *Lead Me On*'s sales were comparatively disappointing: it took two months longer than *Unguarded* to be certified gold and never reached platinum status. The industry was taking notice, however, and as Grant continued racking up sales and chart positions in both the Christian and general markets, she was also winning awards, including the 1988 Grammy for Best Gospel Performance and the Gospel Music Association's Artist of the Year in 1989.

CROSSING BETWEEN MAINSTREAMS

By the end of the 1980s, Amy Grant was Christian music's biggest superstar, having sung on thirty-two Christian radio hits and won seven Dove Awards and five Grammys.[17] Counting her first (of three) Christmas albums (1983's *A Christmas Album*) and the 1986 greatest hits compilation *The Collection*, four albums had been certified platinum and another three had gone gold—and all this prior to the release of "Baby, Baby." In short, the success that Grant later achieved in the early 1990s was not an unplanned fluke but rather the culmination of a career-long trajectory that reflected a history of achievement and a much broader strategy of the artist, her management, and her record labels. Nor was it much of a traditional crossover from niche to mass market: although Christian music might have been unfamiliar to general market Top 40 listeners, the convergence of its growth as a legitimate mainstream in its own right and Amy Grant's growth as its superstar suggests that she crossed from one mainstream to another. In the process, she opened the door for other artists to cross over from the Christian to the general market while demonstrating Christian music's commercial potential to the major record labels (see chapter 7).

In order to examine Amy Grant as an artist who crossed over from one mainstream to another, we must first accept that there are, indeed, *multiple* mainstreams and not just a single mainstream. Eric Weisbard addresses this issue in his writing on commercial radio formats: the sets of aesthetic characteristics and prerequisites that provide a template, of sorts, for the playlists and programming of individual radio stations.[18] He describes the ways in which commercial radio stakeholders and cultural intermediaries defined and divided the listening public into audiences whose tastes could be predicted, and for whom the predictable qualities of formatted stations (as opposed to freeform stations, which is also a distinct format) became a reliable and tangible connection to a broader taste public.[19] Through radio's format system, Weisbard argues, the music industries saw and exploited commercial potential not only in the pop music that targeted the white cultural mainstream but also in emerging regional musics (such as country and Tejano), Black musics (such as R&B and gospel), and non-pop artforms (such as classical and jazz), among others. From this perspective, the fabric of public musical life is multifaceted indeed, distributed across large geographic spaces and listening demographics while accounting for variation. Discussing *the* mainstream makes little sense when we acknowledge that you and I (and everyone we know) likely listen to several different mainstreams, each with varying degrees of distinction.[20]

Some music markets are more heavily influenced by commercial radio programmers than others. In general, this appears to correlate with stratified demographics: radio has little influence over labels that sign artists who perform music styles that attract listeners who, demographically, make up a relatively small portion of commercial radio audiences. The inverse, of course, is that artists who perform styles of music that attract a relatively large radio audience are more susceptible to being influenced by the needs and expectations of radio programmers, often filtered through their label's A&R representative. These artists' careers rely on their being able to access radio stations' audiences. All artists perform for their market; for mainstream Christian artists, their market and its associated radio formats—Christian Adult Contemporary (AC) and Christian Contemporary Hit Radio (CHR)—are often thought of as one and the same. When speaking with current and former Christian record label executives, many of my interviewees frequently conflated their target audience with that of Christian radio. John Mays, speaking from his experiences at Word, EMI CMG, Benson (a Provident label), and Centricity Music (an independent Christian label), told me that Christian artists "sound and are packaged according to the marketplace, according to their audience, and that's pretty common with the major labels. There's a personification given to the typical CCM [contemporary Christian music] radio listener and music buyer, and her name's Becky. . . . Becky is looking over our shoulders about a song choice, an arrangement, a production, an image."[21]

John Styll gives some demographic details of the average Becky: "a woman, age approximately thirty-four, mother of two, and driving an SUV or minivan."[22] He expanded this factor for me in an interview: "This core is where the money is. And so, today you have safe-for-the-whole-family radio. That's soccer moms. . . . They have the money."[23] Christian music industry professional-turned-academic Dave Perkins provides further context, writing that a Christian radio single promoted to "music directors at adult contemporary Christian stations meets a litmus test: Will Becky like it? . . . She expects her Christian songs to sound as pleasing as pop songs."[24] This is partly because the contemporary Becky has grown up in a more permissive Christian culture, listening to general market music as well as Christian music, in contrast to earlier generations of white evangelical and Protestant Christians who avoided consuming (secular) popular culture. It is also partly because, as Wayne Kusber, who worked in A&R at a major Christian record label, explained to me, market research indicates that Becky is clicking through four or five radio station presets while driving her two kids around town in her SUV: "The core listeners are hitting Christian AC, and they're hitting country would be second, and probably classic rock and oldies would be in the top four. Top 40 would probably be number five."[25] These reflections illustrate that record label executives and artists' managerial teams take into account the norms of the market they are pursuing. Failing to do so can result in lower-than-anticipated sales and stalled careers, artists dropped from their record contracts, and

FIGURE 7. Album cover for Amy Grant's *Heart in Motion* (1991).

out-of-work label professionals.[26] Do so correctly, however, and the sky is the limit. Amy Grant's success in the early 1990s is often held up as a remarkable example of Christian music's potential.

Although Amy Grant came home to her Christian music roots on *Lead Me On*, the singer and her team returned to the crossover strategy of *Unguarded* in a big way on 1991's *Heart in Motion* (figure 7). While she had indeed achieved some crossover success with earlier singles like "Find a Way" (🎧) and "The Next Time I Fall" (🎧), in hindsight that was Grant merely dabbling with the general market. With "Baby, Baby" (🎧) and later singles, her music took a decidedly poppier direction: engaging more polished production elements, prominent synthesizers and keyboard, upbeat and danceable tempos, and—crucially—noticeably downplaying and even absenting her Christian faith. All of these are strategies meant to broaden her accessibility outside of the Christian market. Grant did not cede her authority, either: she wrote or cowrote all but one of the songs on the album and never had a bigger hand in the songwriting responsibilities. She transformed her image, too, visually presenting more as a grownup pop diva than as a sedate choirgirl. (By contrast, the infamous leopard-print jacket of *Unguarded*'s cover seemed downright playful next to the red velvet dress, wispy hair, and clear profile shot of Grant on *Heart in Motion*; compare figures 6 and 7.) "Baby, Baby" was the lead single off the album, and its success seems almost preordained in retrospect. Gone were the allusions to God, unlike in "Find a Way" and "Saved by Love." Instead, "Baby, Baby" was easy to hear as a straight-ahead love song, although Grant wrote in the album's liner notes that the song was inspired by her six-week-old daughter Millie, and not by her husband or a fictional lover. The song briefly breaks from a standard pop arrangement: the pre-chorus that follows the first verse is a tease, leading directly into the second verse; we hear the full chorus for the first time only after the second verse. The song modulates up twice: once heading out of that first chorus and into the third verse, and again after the third (and final) iteration of the chorus into an extended outro, a variation of the verse melody. The piece is danceable but not particularly fast, with a tempo under 100 bpm.

A&M released "Baby, Baby" as *Heart in Motion*'s lead single on January 28, 1991, and it entered the *Billboard* Hot 100 on February 23 at #75. (The album was released on March 5.) A&M followed a singles-driven promotional strategy and released four more songs to radio in overlapping schedules, such that after each song had peaked and was falling down the charts the next single was already climbing.[27] This is the same strategy that the major labels followed with their other pop stars, expecting that the more frequently that listeners heard an artist on their favorite radio stations, the more likely they were to buy that artist's new album. Although "Baby, Baby" was the only single to reach #1 on the *Billboard* Hot 100, three others broke the top ten, spending an average of twenty weeks on that chart: "Every Heartbeat" (🎵), "That's What Love Is For" (🎵), and "Good for Me" (🎵). Grant made a bigger impact on *Billboard*'s (secular) Hot Adult Contemporary chart, where all five singles peaked at #1 or #2 for multiple weeks and averaged over thirty weeks on the chart. Once "Baby, Baby" debuted on these two charts, you could not open *Billboard* without reading about an Amy Grant song charting for another twenty-one months.[28] *Heart in Motion* eventually sold over five million copies—the album was certified triple platinum just one day after the fifth and final general market single was released—and it peaked at #10 on the *Billboard* 200 album chart.

The metrics of singles, charts, and sales are not the only measures of an artist's success, of course. But in the world of Top 40 and contemporary hit radio (CHR) during this time, they were among the most important metrics. Sequential radio singles familiarized artists to radio listeners, who then bought the album because they already liked a third or even half of its songs. Selling the album was of utmost importance: in the wake of vinyl's demise, the U.S. record industry had stopped focusing on selling singles, instead prioritizing full-length cassettes and CDs. Sure, you could still walk into Sam Goody or Tower Records and buy a cassingle or a CD single for less than half the cost of the full cassette or CD, but it did not make economic sense to the record labels. In earlier decades, it was cheaper to press and distribute 45s than 33⅓ LPs: the 45 was a physically smaller medium that used less materials and was more lightweight than the long-player. But it cost almost as much to produce cassingles and CD singles as it did their full-length equivalents. Yes, there is slightly less magnetic tape used in a cassingle, and the labels did try using cheaper packaging (cardboard sleeves for cassingles and slimline plastic cases for CD singles), but the production savings did not justify the significantly lower retail cost. In short, the new singles formats were simply not as profitable as the 45 had been, while the (still) relatively new CD was much more profitable than LPs and cassettes. The labels stood to gain a lot more from pushing full-length CDs than they stood to lose from deprioritizing retail singles. So the single itself, as a purchasable commodity, was becoming increasingly less important: while the major labels shipped 66.7 million CD singles at the format's peak in 1997, according to the RIAA, within three years that number had almost halved and a decade later they shipped fewer than 1 million.[29]

Not only were singles no longer prioritized as a commercial product, they did not even make money for the record labels and recording artists when radio stations played them. In the United States, songwriters and composers earn "public performance" royalties when radio stations report playing their songs; these royalties are administered by the three major performing rights organizations (ASCAP, BMI, and SESAC). But recording artists, who earn royalties in most other situations where their recordings are used in accordance with copyright (such as being sampled, included in a soundtrack, streamed online, and so on) do not earn royalties from radio play.[30] The historical argument for this has been that radio airplay is essentially free promotion for the record labels, which make money from the sale of records (including singles and albums), and thus it is illogical to force radio stations to pay for the privilege of promoting another industry's product.

Thus, in an era of huge album sales expectations, singles were only valuable to the extent that they facilitated album sales. Together with concert tours, singles were part of two- or three-year-long "album cycles" that were strategically planned to maximize public exposure. *Heart in Motion* is not particularly unique for promoting five of its eleven songs to radio; other divas' multi-platinum records from the same period fared similarly, as you can see in appendix 4. Artists like Paula Abdul, Mariah Carey, Celine Dion, Whitney Houston, Janet Jackson, Vanessa Williams, and many others sold millions of copies of their albums, spurred in part by releasing several singles. *Heart in Motion* was a multiplatinum seller, but so were many other records: forty-four other albums released in 1991 were certified platinum by the end of the year, and twenty-nine of them sold multiple millions as well. Of these twenty-nine other multiplatinum albums, twenty-three of them had multiple singles that charted on the *Billboard* Hot 100 or Hot AC charts during their cycles. The degree of success that Amy Grant achieved with *Heart in Motion* would be remarkable if it were not so, well, *un*remarkable when compared to other Top 40 artists of the time.

CROSSOVER OBJECTIVES

Comparatively, Amy Grant's commercial success during the 1980s certainly pales in comparison to what she achieved with *Heart in Motion*. But that album's successes in the early 1990s is not anomalous when considered alongside other mainstream pop artists of the time. In other words, in terms of commercial success, she did not achieve anything that dozens (if not hundreds) of pop artists also achieved. Amy Grant remained in the general market for several years after her breakthrough with "Baby, Baby." Her second Christmas record, *Home for Christmas*, was released in October 1992 as *Heart in Motion*'s final single, "I Will Remember You" (🎧), was falling down *Billboard*'s Hot AC chart. *Home* sold a million copies in two months, peaked at #2 on Billboard's 200 album chart the week of Christmas, and was ultimately certified triple platinum. Grant's true follow-up to *Heart in Motion* was 1994's *House of Love*, which peaked at #13 on the *Billboard* 200 and was certified double platinum. Of that album's five singles, "Lucky One" (🎧)

was the most successful, peaking at #18 on the *Billboard* Hot 100. (Her cover of Joni Mitchell's "Big Yellow Taxi" 🎧 peaked at #67 the following year.) *Behind the Eyes*, released in 1997, sold worse than its two predecessors (it has never reached platinum) but charted higher, peaking at #8 on the *Billboard* 200. The album's lead single, "Takes a Little Time" (🎧), was the only one to chart on the *Billboard* Hot 100, where it peaked at #21. If the decade had started strongly for Grant, it ended ambivalently: unlike other divas of the early 1990s, she was not able to sustain her pop stardom after her initial success. But after pursuing crossover success in the general market and encountering some ethical backlash following her 1999 divorce and remarriage (to country artist Vince Gill in the year 2000), her prospects in the Christian market were not so clear. She ultimately crossed back to Christian music, returning to her roots with a series of albums of hymns and worship songs. Additionally, in the twenty-first century her Christmas collections and greatest hits compilations have been better received than her albums of newly composed Christian pop songs.

Grant's early 1990s success came at a time when the general market major record labels had started to invest heavily in the Christian market. In addition to Grant, other top-selling Christian artists who benefitted from Word's distribution agreement with A&M Records included Carman, Sandi Patty, Petra, Michael W. Smith, Russ Taff, and even Al Green. Grant's successes signaled for many record industry observers and professionals that Christian artists had significant commercial potential in the general market. In other words, from the perspective of the general market and the new (or prospective) owners of Christian record labels, Amy Grant provided the test case for crossover from the Christian to the general market. Whether this test actually worked out is debatable: from one perspective, Grant proved that successful Christian artists could also succeed in the general market under the right conditions; from another perspective, Grant provided the rhetorical exception that proved the rule of the general market not being hospitable to Christian artists. The truth, naturally, lies somewhere in between these two extremes. Many Christian artists have achieved general market success in the years since 1991, and several have had more sustainable, longer-lived general market careers than did Grant.

Some writers who examine Christian crossover artists see this as an encouraging trend. For example, in his history of Christian rock, Mark Joseph notes that dismissive responses to Christian artists within the general market during the 1970s and '80s turned a corner in the '90s, following the crossing over of Grant, Michael W. Smith, DC Talk, Jars of Clay, and other "rebel" artists who, he claims, had themselves dismissed the Christian market.[31] This is perhaps even more true of Christian artists who successfully crossed over to the general market after achieving only moderate success on the fringes of the Christian market, such as Chevelle, Mutemath, MxPx, P.O.D., Sixpence None the Richer, Switchfoot, and others (see chapter 7). Joseph argues that the Christian market's theological and ideological priorities intentionally separate it from the secular general market and are essentially self-imposed and largely self-serving.[32] The Christian industry and its institutions benefit from a well-defined market; participants might perceive attempts to expand the market's boundaries or make them more porous—including individual artists' crossover attempts and broader initiatives to integrate Christian music into the general market—with wariness for disrupting the market's equilibrium. From this perspective, Christian artists who dismiss the Christian market do so because they perceive it as cynically working to preserve its own best interests and not necessarily those of its artists or even the Christian faith's larger objective to evangelize or reach out to lapsed Christians. One objective for crossover, then, is that it demonstrates that Christian artists are good musicians and songwriters, on a par with their general market counterparts, with talent undiminished by their faith, despite what critics might allege.

The introduction of SoundScan in the early 1990s helped buttress this perspective. SoundScan is the computerized system that tracks retail sales of music. It was introduced to most music retailers in 1991 and expanded to Christian bookstores (the Christian market's main retailers) in 1995. Prior to the introduction of SoundScan, sales reports were tabulated and reported manually and were prone to human error (both innocent and intentional). Starting in 1991, however, the SoundScan-automated statistics demonstrated that sales of several musical genres had been previously underreported: suddenly, artists in markets as diverse as hip hop, country, and Christian were appearing on the weekly *Billboard* 200 chart of album sales. These data incentivized general market retailers, especially big box stores like Walmart, to stock more Christian music. They also demonstrated that there was an audience for Christian music outside of the Christian market, which encouraged more investment on the part of the general market major record labels as well as more attention from the general market music press.

Around the time that Hearn was negotiating with EMI about selling Sparrow Records (in 1991), *CCM Update* quoted him describing his market: "I'm not one who wants to produce records for that [general] market. I produce records for the Christian market [that] I know will pay for it, and minister to those who I've been commissioned to make records for."[33] In other words, he was not interested in producing records for non-Christians. Similarly, recall that Becky, whom Simon Frith would call the Christian market's "fantasy consumer," is ideally a Christian already.[34] Regarding Amy Grant's approach to crossover, Romanowski argues that the objective "was not to sing gospel songs to the unsaved, but to use mainstream exposure and distribution channels to reach those evangelicals who did not listen to religious radio or frequent Christian book and record stores."[35] This echoes Sparrow's approach to crossover as far back as the early 1980s, when both Billy Ray Hearn and his son Bill Hearn defended their distribution agreement with MCA as a means to reach Christian listeners outside of the Christian market's standard distribution channels. Taken together, it is clear that the Christian music industry's emphasis shifted from reaching non-Christians to reaching listeners who already identified as Christians. Crossover would satisfy both objectives, so why might it matter that the Christian labels were unconcerned with large-scale evangelism? Partly because crossover marketing and promotional plans are expensive: focusing on general market retailers, radio, magazines, and so on would expand the Christian labels' budgets dramatically, and they would not agree to this investment if it did not align with their overall goals. As Wayne Kusber explained, "It's way more expensive to work a single to mainstream radio than to Christian radio. Your potential payoff is bigger, but you're jumping into competing with everybody else. You're competing with Atlantic, Universal, Interscope, and all these other labels trying to get their rock bands played on the same stations you are."[36]

Despite the expenses of crossover attempts, Christian record label executives became very interested in pursuing crossover once they understood that such strategies would promote their artists to a large body of Christian listeners that had previously remained inaccessible to them. There was an obvious overlap between the Christian and general markets—Christian listeners who did not listen to Christian radio or shop at Christian retailers—that labels like Sparrow and Word needed to pursue if they were going to continue growing. The problem that Hearn encountered at Sparrow was a lack of appropriate resources:

"We didn't have the financing, the resources, the distribution to the Walmarts and everything. . . . I saw that to get the message into the general public, you had to have the power of one of those big companies."[37] For Hearn, this conceptual framework enabled him to consider seriously—and ultimately agree to—an offer to sell Sparrow to EMI: he was not selling out but rather buying in, to reach a larger Christian audience. In doing so, Hearn was consciously expanding the boundaries of the Christian market. Doing so might alleviate similar tensions that ethnomusicologist Jonathan Dueck encountered in the realms of Christian and secular indie rock.[38] The conceptually separate social formations of these two scenes were reinforced by a physical separation of retail and performance places, despite several points of intersection (such as shared musicians, listeners, and distribution infrastructures). Dueck literally had to cross the street from one retailer to another to buy Christian CDs because the music store where he worked did not carry them. Hearn's ideal was for no more street-crossing, literal or otherwise: when Christian music is available at all stores, consumers like Dueck are more likely to discover and buy it.

Despite the Christian market's clarity of purpose that accompanied its consolidation and growth trajectory in the 1990s—or perhaps precisely because of its objectives—contestation over its boundaries did not diminish. If one way to explain the significance of Grant's success is as signifying the overall maturity of the Christian market as a commercial music mainstream in its own right, then the conflicts and disputes over its boundaries and meaning that I discuss in part 2 of *God Rock, Inc.* have much in common with parallel challenges to the popular music mainstream in the general market from its peripheries. The ethics of belonging to the Christian market were enforced to punish artists who engaged unchristian behavior, as I discussed in chapter 3. But these ethics were also deployed by artists who actively claimed to belong to the Christian market, despite not fitting the market's aesthetic or stylistic standards, as I discuss in chapter 5. As the sonic and behavioral expectations of the Christian market became stricter, its fringes became more active. By the end of the 1990s, Christian hardcore, metal, and punk artists were attracting tens of thousands of fans to events like Cornerstone Festival (which I describe in chapter 6), where they embraced and enacted resistance to what they perceived to be the bland homogeneity of Christian music's mainstream. And although no other Christian artist achieved general market success at the scale that Amy Grant did, crossover itself as a strategy was not dead. Indeed, as I discuss in chapter 7, it morphed into a way to have a sustainable career, sometimes straddling multiple niche markets (within both the Christian and general markets), and even at times for artists who crossed back from the general to the Christian market. Amy Grant and "Baby, Baby" might have signified Christian music's highwater mark for some; for others, it demonstrated the need for Christian music to transcend the banal extreme of commercial pop.

PART TWO

Niche Music Markets

Ethics, Profits, and Risk

5

Music to Raise the Dead

Christian Music and the Ethics of Style

The Chicago-based intentional community Jesus People, U.S.A. (JPUSA) is one of the few remaining communes that can trace its origin directly to the Jesus People movement. JPUSA formed as a mobile ministry of the Jesus People Milwaukee community in 1972, traveling as far south as Florida before settling in Chicago the following May.[1] They have lived in their current building in Chicago's Uptown neighborhood since 1990. JPUSA operates a homeless shelter and several other profit-making businesses (such as a roofing supply company and a coffee shop) and has been affiliated with the Evangelical Covenant Church denomination since 1989. Though the community is not without controversy—some observers have compared it to a cult, and former members have accused its elders of facilitating abuse—JPUSA has played an important role in the Christian market as the organizers of Cornerstone Festival (1984–2012) and the home of Resurrection Band (or Rez Band, or sometimes just Rez) for over twenty-five years (see figure 5). Led by singer and guitarist Glenn Kaiser, Rez toured and ministered internationally, earning a strong reputation within the Christian market.

In chapter 3, I introduced Timothy Rommen's "ethics of style" as a means to understand how ethics precede, preclude, and exclude musical styles.[2] Christian anti-rock critics in the 1960s and later used ethical arguments to criticize rock and roll as a musical style unfit for Christians; in the 1990s, several Christian artists faced professional setbacks after transgressing the ethical boundaries of the Christian market, despite setting the market's aesthetic standards with their award-winning music. In this chapter, I consider how participants deploy the ethics of style to justify including music that diverges stylistically from the Christian market's expectations. Ethics can be deployed within niche markets to include just as well as exclude: claiming a biblically consistent Christian message was Rez's response to critics who objected to their bluesy, hard rock style. Their songs often depicted rock and roll excesses, but instead of glorifying them, Glenn Kaiser and his bandmates used destructive lifestyles as teaching moments to promote salvation through belief in Jesus Christ.[3] In "I Think You Know" (🎧), an '80s hair metal song, for example, Kaiser sings: "You used to think you were okay, but now you know it wasn't true / You had the world by the tail, now what you gonna do? / . . . / But what the Savior offers, you can't afford to say no, you can't afford to miss / The light is shining in your eyes, now let Him come and live inside." Other songs are more straightforwardly praiseful, such as 1979's "Midnight Son" (🎧), addressed to God: "You light up the sky / You're the power of the sun / You're the starlight in the darkness / On your laughter, shadows run / You're a mighty wind of glory and the Father all in one / You're the morning star, you're the midnight son."

Like many bands with similarly lengthy careers, Rez's sound on record changed with the era, reflecting in turns blues rock, both first and second waves of British heavy metal, new wave, and pop metal before returning to the blues in the group's later albums (💿). Such stylistic variability might prompt criticism in other markets: Is Rez's music just opportunistically derivative, as some believe all Christian music is, taking advantage of current trends, or did their stylistic flexibility evolve more organically? But their music also consistently provoked derisive responses from conservative Christians who preemptively hated all rock and roll without differentiating between its various styles. Kaiser and his bandmates, however, remained impassioned evangelists, committed as much to preaching biblical salvation as they were to playing rock music. Like Keith Green (see chapter 1), Rez considered their music to be an instrumental component of their ministry, often giving away their first two records at concerts: *Music to Raise the Dead* and the acoustic *All Your Life* (both released in 1974). Many Christian critics relented as they witnessed the impact that Rez was having on their audiences and listeners. Kaiser recalls being invited back to perform at churches where they had felt unwelcome in the past, even though church elders did not quite apologize: "I had so many people come up and say, 'I hate your music but I love your preaching.'"[4]

No statement represents the ethics of style better than this quote: hating the music but loving the message, or overlooking stylistic deviations in favor of ethical convergence. Proponents often use ethical justifications for inclusion in the Christian market as a response to opponents' ethical justification for exclusion. These debates over the ethics of belonging reveal cognitive dissonance and differing theologies: participants base their arguments on scriptures from the same source (the Bible) but often have widely divergent interpretations and applications of those scriptures. Ethics frequently take precedence over other concerns for participants on both sides who stake out and police the boundaries of the Christian market. As I discuss below, the ethics of style are clearly at play in the case of Demon Hunter, a Christian metal band that, like Rez, has often had to justify their appropriateness to (and belongingness within) Christian contexts. First, however, I take us to Cornerstone Festival in 2009—three years before its final summer in 2012—to demonstrate how ethics were visible and audible in organizing Christian festivals and performing Christian metal. In doing so, I expand on Jeffers Engelhardt's "singing the right way" to introduce the theoretical framework "musicking the right way," which articulates, substantiates, and perpetuates ethics through the conditions and acts of musical performance.[5] At Cornerstone, right musicking was everywhere: in the festival's organization, design, programming, and setup, at its campsites, from stages, during Bible studies, and in the model embodied by its former director, John Herrin.

ETHICS AT CORNERSTONE FESTIVAL

John Herrin looks the part of an aging rocker and a former hippie: long hair well past his shoulders, unkempt beard, flannel shirts, year-round cargo shorts. He played drums as a founding member of Rez Band, he cofounded JPUSA in 1972 and served on its leadership council for many years, and he was the director of Cornerstone Festival at its peak and as attendance gradually declined (1999–2011). JPUSA organized the first Cornerstone in 1984, in part because its members felt that the whole Christian market was not being served by existing Christian festivals, which catered to more moderate tastes. As Herrin recalled in an interview, "They always felt a little bit like they were almost apologizing for having a rock band there. You'd have Carman or Sandi Patty or the Gaithers or something do the evening shows, and then you'd have some rock band in the afternoon."[6] For its first seven years, JPUSA held

Cornerstone at the Lake County Fairgrounds in Grayslake, a suburb about forty miles north of Chicago. Then JPUSA purchased a former campsite near the rural western Illinois town of Bushnell, over two hundred miles southwest of Chicago, and held Cornerstone as a camping music festival from 1991 to 2012.

In each of these roles—with Rez Band, JPUSA, and Cornerstone—Herrin witnessed ethical objections to the work that he and his colleagues were doing on behalf of a ministry to which they felt called very strongly. He was able to model and teach both the ethical perspectives that informed his life, relationships, and actions, which were grounded in Christian faith, as well as the social politics of a commune that ministered to the homeless. Herrin stepped away from a public role when two other JPUSA members directed Cornerstone 2012, and he and his wife left JPUSA in 2015, but his work as Cornerstone's director was instrumental in defining and promoting an ethical framework for up to twenty-five thousand attendees during its peak in the late '90s and early aughts.

Christian culture in the United States is heterogeneous, with endlessly varying theologies, scriptural interpretations, accepted degrees of engagement with secular culture, and ethical and moral rules. Herrin was quick to admit to me that JPUSA could be viewed as simultaneously conservative and liberal: "We don't do drugs, we don't even drink, we don't smoke. We're probably pretty conservative in our moral values. But, on the other hand, we're probably pretty liberal. . . . We're really turned off by the Moral Majority, Christians who somehow feel like they have to mandate by law, to legislate morality. We don't believe that. We believe strongly that everybody should be treated equally, and everybody should have the opportunity to live as they see fit. Not necessarily that we think it's the right way to live, but it's your choice."[7] Cornerstone also struck me as a fairly conservative place, at least in contrast to the hedonistic abandon I have experienced at Coachella, Lollapalooza, and other general market festivals. Cornerstone's organizers designed it as a family-friendly, sober event, banned alcohol and drugs outright, requested modest clothing (for example, no bikinis at the beach area), and frowned on sexual contact between unmarried partners. But it nevertheless attracted protests from a fundamentalist Christian group for several years, according to Herrin: "We had this real conservative, right-wing church out of somewhere, Wisconsin, I think. Their mission each year was to come to Cornerstone and stand out front with protest signs." When I asked what, specifically, they were protesting, Herrin was jokingly blunt: "Oh, you know, you can't be a Christian and have long hair."[8]

Herrin's joke here normalized Christian music by placing it in opposition to this unnamed "real conservative, right-wing church," whose members undoubtedly also identified as Christians, although certainly more fundamental and separational than JPUSA and the festivalgoers that came to Cornerstone. The conservative protestors outside of Cornerstone Festival were not really protesting long hair: they were protesting a theology calling itself "Christian" that permits long hair, rock and roll, skateboarding, and tattoos. They were expecting fundamentalist Christian ethics to precede and define style, unable to imagine a more liberal Christianity whose ethics permit styles that so clearly derive from (and thus reference) non-Christian culture. No matter how marginal the niche market for Christian music might be, there are communities and markets that are even more marginal. Cornerstone might have been too liberal for some Christians, but the fact that it existed in the first place is testimony to the demand for festivals more conservative (and more targeted) than those that serve larger, general market audiences (such as Bonnaroo, Coachella, Lollapalooza, Sasquatch!, and so on)—especially those that shy away from Christian music's mainstream in favor of hardcore, heavy metal, and punk.

On Wednesday, July 1, 2009, at 3:30 p.m., Christian metal band The Burial performed in the Sanctuary Tent on the first official day of Cornerstone Festival. The five-piece group from South Bend, Indiana, played rhythmically complex death metal with a prominent bass guitar sound, double kick drum, two independent lead guitars positioned high in the live sound mix, and unintelligible growled vocals. The volume was so loud that the music exerted a physical sensation; coupled with the stage presence of the musicians, the energy close to the stage was palpable, and the tent intensified the unseasonably cool July weather outside. There were at least a hundred audience members watching The Burial perform that afternoon, many of whom appeared to be unfamiliar with their music. Almost all looked like they belonged at a heavy metal concert: the black clothing, T-shirts with dark imagery and gothic lettering (presumably supporting other metal bands), long hair, big beards, tattoos, and piercings contrasted starkly against the more conventionally attired attendees in the prayer tent across the street. The metal fans were both young and old, mostly male, predominantly white, and—judging by their nods of approval and scattered applause—slowly coming around to the band.

The Burial only had thirty minutes to make a first impression at this four-day music festival saturated with metal bands. As they paused in between songs near the end of their set, guitarist Todd Hatfield exhorted the audience to get more physically engaged. "Don't worry about looking foolish while headbanging," he said, "because the only one watching who matters is God, and he doesn't care how you look." Hatfield is a burly guy, about five and a half feet tall, with a shaved head and long beard, and the audience responded with a cheer. As Jamey York, the other guitarist, tuned up, Hatfield continued speaking: he reminded people to fight against letting the devil infiltrate this community, to allow God to be a part of their festival experience, and to talk with and learn from each other. Before launching into their last song and exciting one final circle pit, Hatfield claimed that this music, this concert, this fellowship, "this is our sanctuary, this is our worship."

The following morning at 11:00 a.m., Todd Hatfield led a Bible study at the Impromptu Tent. Although this was early by Cornerstone standards, at least four dozen people were already there when I arrived, sitting on the grass, quietly chatting, and sipping coffee. Hatfield looked exposed and anxious without his guitar and bandmates, and he apologized in advance for the disconnected and jumbled nature of his thoughts. He acknowledged feeling uncomfortable imparting wisdom from the stage, but in the attention of the audience he recognized a divine appointment. As Hatfield shared his ideas on the responsibilities of Christian faith, interspersed with insights from his personal life, he referred often to verses read from his beat-up Bible. Although he appeared not to have much practice in teaching or leading group discussion, Hatfield gained confidence as he continued through his lesson. Everyone appeared to be paying attention: many people followed along in their own Bibles, others took notes, and his main points elicited nods and smiles. Hatfield's style was one of subtly guiding via personal testimony rather than explicit proselytizing. Later that afternoon, I chatted with a group of attendees from St. Louis and Toronto about their Cornerstone experience. Some of them had met at a concert in Philadelphia a few weeks previously and had made plans to reconnect and camp together at Cornerstone. They appreciated the low-key Bible studies, such as the one Hatfield led earlier that morning: "It's there if you want it," said Nick, a thoughtful and talkative eighteen-year old, "but no one expects you to go."

The Burial had another gig the following afternoon at the Anchor Stage, a venue sponsored, programmed, and operated by the Anchor

FIGURE 8. David Marshall of The Burial performing at Cornerstone Festival 2009; his shirt reads "Stay Virgin." Photograph by the author.

Fellowship, a nondenominational evangelical church in Nashville, Tennessee. It was another early afternoon timeslot—around 2 p.m.—but by Cornerstone's third day, attendees were in the festival groove, more willing to sample new artists and musics. There were fewer black T-shirts and more tank tops in the audience, prompting vocalist David Marshall to chastise them for dressing provocatively. He was sincere in his concern, and I found it notable that he directed his disapproval at the boys as well as the girls. His stance against premarital sex was obvious—he wore a T-shirt that read "Stay Virgin" (see figure 8)—and at Cornerstone this perspective was both common and inarguable. But his admonishments, while understandable, were unique: this was (and remains) the only time I have heard an artist at a Christian festival explicitly tell audience members that shorts, swimsuits, tank tops, and other seasonally appropriate clothes are too revealing to be worn in mixed company because they may cause others to have sinfully lustful thoughts.[9] His lesson solicited scattered applause—far less than his band's actual songs—before The Burial launched into the next piece.

Portions of these scenes will be familiar to most music fans who have attended festivals or heavy metal concerts: a relatively unknown band performing to an unenthusiastic crowd in the middle of the day, the aesthetics of heavy metal performance, between-song banter, and even the style of the audience members have much in common with other festivals and performance venues. Yet the religious and ethical dimensions of Cornerstone set it apart from otherwise aesthetically similar general market events. Elements of these scenes will be odd (and maybe even illegible) unless you are familiar with the ethics of performing Christian music: Hatfield's references to God and the devil, explicitly linking a metal concert to collective religious worship, comparing a music venue to a religious sanctuary, and Marshall's admonishments against revealing clothing and his T-shirt promoting sexual abstinence.

Marshall has since explained to me that his zeal in 2009 was partly due to him being a relatively new evangelical Christian after converting from Mormonism only a few months prior. At the time, he was strongly convicted and wanted to share the truth of his beliefs, but ten years later he was embarrassed by the forcefulness of his message. As a more mature Christian, he has come to understand how to explain his ethical positions in a more sensitive manner. But when he was singing for The Burial as a young evangelical, he told me, "I didn't know any better, I didn't have a chance to be discipled."[10] Notably, much of the religious teaching at Cornerstone started from the assumption that audience members were already Christians—religious conversion was not a focus of this Christian event. Instead, much of the testimony was based on individuals' lived experiences, and, like Hatfield's Bible study, emphasized a personal understanding of faith and scripture instead of denominational dogma. Cornerstone was a place where evangelical beliefs intersected with subcultural styles in fruitful and productive—if often incoherent—ways.

"RIGHT MUSICKING" AND ETHICAL JUSTIFICATIONS FOR MARKET INCLUSION

In his book on singing among Orthodox Christians in Estonia, Jeffers Engelhardt writes of "right singing" as music-making that articulates religious belief and musical practice as mutually constructed and, thus, mutually reinforced and perpetuated.[11] For the communities he studies, *singing* the right way is inseparable from *living* the right way: "If the singing was right, then the belief expressed in that singing was right, and if the belief was right, then the musical practices grounded in that belief were right."[12] He writes primarily about singing in congregational and liturgical contexts, but here I extend his ideas to the broader domain of Christian popular music. Clearly, ethics are implicated both in Christian music and in Engelhardt's Estonian communities—ethics that are intertwined with religious belief and practice—and in the Christian market, these ethics are authenticated, communicated, enforced, and taught outside of congregational and liturgical contexts.

If general market metal fans would have found The Burial's aesthetics familiar but their ethics unfamiliar, for many Christians this dissonance may be inverted: while they might have recognized the religious language and priorities of Hatfield and his bandmates, they may have found the aesthetics of heavy metal performance to be unfamiliar. But they would have been comforted by The Burial's religious foundation heard in their lyrics, such as the pleas for salvation in "Demons Never Sleep" (🎧) or the crucifixion narrative in "Reconciliation" (🎧). Thus, right singing is not only that which takes place within a mass or worship service but also at a Christian metal concert. But right singing need not only be about singing, it can also be about music making in all its various capacities, including non-performative ones—what Christopher Small defines as "musicking," or all of the components that result in a successful (and authentic) performance for everyone involved: performers, cultural intermediaries, and listeners.[13] In this expanded framework, *musicking the right way* articulates, substantiates, and perpetuates ethics through performance and production, songwriting and selling, composition and consumption. Many Christians would have been comforted by the Bible studies, sermons and testimonies from the stage, and worship services at Cornerstone, which reflected the spiritual and social tenets of JPUSA and the Christian market in general—even when the growled vocals, distorted guitars, long hair, and tattoos diverged or distracted from the stylistic norms of Christian music's mainstream and white U.S. evangelicalism. This is right musicking in Christian music: when the songs' messages are supplemented by visible, audible, and actionable ethical messages throughout the entire performance context. The Burial and other Christian metal bands provide examples of this market's ethical expectations trumping its stylistic ones: despite their music deviating stylistically from the expectations of the Christian market, their ethics as Christians and their performance of Christianity justify their inclusion.

A word of caution, however: if artists do not understand the market's infrastructure and the various roles of its different corporations and organizations, arguing for ethical inclusion is not always successful. Wayne Kusber, an executive at a major Christian record label, explained to me that many would-be Christian songwriters, artists, and performers expect to find a welcoming environment in Nashville, where the Christian market is centered: "I see a lot of Christian kids that move here [Nashville] that think, 'This is the place that Christian music happens, and I'm a Christian, and I'm a musician, therefore I should move here,' and they have a hard time finding a place, and they get mad about that." Many got frustrated after realizing that the major Christian labels and the commercial Christian radio formats were fairly conservative: "These labels exist because we're doing core Christian music, primarily. And if you're not a part of that, it's fine. . . . But don't get mad at it and say, 'Let me in!'"[14] Kusber believed that these "Christian kids" did not understand that the goals and business needs of executives at major labels like CCMG, Provident, and Word, or radio networks like K-LOVE and The Fish prevented them from being open to all styles and genres of Christian music. John J. Thompson, a writer and former executive with EMI CMG, concurred, explaining to me, "You wouldn't see Sparrow, who specializes in doing music for Christians who listen to Christian radio, signing a Devil Wears Prada [metalcore] band. . . . They need to know what their core competency is, and they want to make sure not to compromise that. . . . You've got to protect your brand."[15]

There is truth in Kusber's advice: even if ethics do precede style, the for-profit corporations that have invested in the Christian market (see chapter 2) have business needs and profit expectations that are not compelled by ethical arguments. Jettisoning standard-bearing artists who have become ethically unsustainable is one thing: they risk hurting business in the Christian market, and it is not too difficult to find other singers who sound like Sandi Patty or Michael English (see chapter 3). But, at a major Christian record label, signing an artist whose music diverges from the market simply because she is a Christian is a risky business choice that Kusber usually could not afford to make. As *CCM* magazine's John Styll remarked to me, labels cannot serve both the "core" Christian market and its margins: "It's almost impossible to please both. If you please the core, then the people outside the core are not going to like it. If you please the people on the outside, this core goes away."¹⁶ In the case of choosing which market segment to serve—as in the case when deciding whether or not to part ways with an artist who no longer fits the market's ethical norms—when the ethics of style confront capitalism in the Christian market, capitalism wins.

Kusber, who worked for one of the major Christian record labels, would have advised artists who did not fit the aesthetic expectations of the Christian market's mainstream to pursue a different label. There are Christian labels that support artists and styles aesthetically tangential to "core Christian music"; Tooth & Nail Records is one of the best known. Founded by Brandon Ebel in 1993, the label (and its sublabels, notably including Solid State Records) built its reputation around "alternative" Christian music genres in the 1990s and early aughts, signing artists who performed Christian hardcore, heavy metal, metalcore, punk, ska, and other aggressive rock subgenres. In the twenty-first century, one of its most consequential artists has been the band Demon Hunter. Demon Hunter has released ten studio albums (💿) between 2002 and 2019 (all on Solid State) with increasing chart success. This has been due in part to Tooth & Nail's strategy of "fringe crossover" (see chapter 7), in which artists conceive of their market as defined more by subgenre or substyle and less by listeners' religious identities. Thus, rather than limiting themselves to the Christian metal market and excluding themselves from the (general) metal market, they pursued the entire metal market.

In earlier decades, Christian artists who attempted to cross over to general market audiences often faced resistance for prioritizing or foregrounding their faith. Simultaneously, many Christian listeners shunned general market music because it did not foreground faith. For example, the Christian metal band Stryper (💿) attempted to straddle both Christian and general markets during glam metal's peak in the 1980s. The lyrics of singles like "Calling on You" (🎧) and the power ballad "Honestly" (🎧) could be read ambivalently: describing romantic love or religious devotion in lyrics like "You make my life complete / You give me all I need / You help me through and through / I'm calling on you" and "Call on me and I'll be there for you / I'm a friend who always will be true / And I love you, can't you see / That I can say I love you honestly." But the members of Stryper were unapologetic Christians and very clear about their mission to bring the gospel to secular audiences; they were also unashamed of their style, both musical and fashion. The former, however, did not fare so well in the general market, while the latter did not fare so well in the Christian market, and Stryper often struggled to be taken seriously in either market.

Demon Hunter and other Tooth & Nail bands fared much differently in the late '90s and early twenty-first century. General market listeners, artists, and cultural intermediaries—especially those active in niche markets—were less likely to dismiss bands who identified as Christians outright. Writing about punk and grindcore, Ibrahim Abraham suggests that this was due to two reasons.[17] First, a growing postsecularity in the public sphere meant that Christian (and other religious) ideals were at least tacitly accepted (if not actively endorsed) as core components of social and cultural norms within nominally secular societies.[18] Second, markets affiliated with "underground" music (such as metal and punk) often emphasized do-it-yourself (or DIY) and anti-corporate ethics of independence and interdependence. Within these scenes and markets, non-Christian participants are willing to overlook a band's Christian identity as long as they affirmed the market's DIY ethics.[19]

During the same time, Christian listeners grew increasingly willing to listen to general market music; this was especially true of fans in niche markets. John J. Thompson explained to me in an interview that fewer Christian listeners perceived a need for a safe alternative to dangerous secular music: "If they were listening to Christian music because they were afraid of secular music and they thought it was going to turn them into rapists, and then they realized, 'Oh, hey, it didn't turn me into a rapist, so I can handle this, listen to secular music and it's not going to destroy me or control my mind and make me do stuff that I'm not prone to doing as a decent human being.' So then they don't really see the need to avoid secular music."[20] These changes in attitude resulted in the overlap (if not outright convergence) of niche markets that might have been separate a generation or two earlier. As I discuss in chapter 7, bands like Demon Hunter have benefitted from these changes: they have performed at both Christian and general market venues and festivals, have Christian and non-Christian fans, and have toured with bands who may or may not be public about their faith identity. Being Christian, for these bands, is often not extraordinary but instead quotidian. Jon Dunn, Demon Hunter's bass guitarist and a Tooth & Nail employee at the time of our interview, claimed that "with those walls [between Christian and general niche markets] being broken down, these Christian bands have become genre-defining bands. . . . There are those key bands that define their genres and happen to be Christians at the same time."[21]

As John Herrin discovered with Cornerstone, however, there was still a sizable and vocal contingent of Christians who perceived any overlap or convergence with non-Christian culture to be sinful. Jeff Carver, who was Demon Hunter's A&R representative at Tooth & Nail at the time of our interview, explained to me, "There definitely is a very conservative side of the Christian music world that might not understand a lot of the releases we put out. Usually it's more appearance-based: tattoos, clothing."[22] Dunn was less diplomatic in his description of these misunderstandings: "There's people out there that hate Demon Hunter. In the Christian world, [some people] absolutely think we're the spawn of Satan and doing anything we can to get their children to hopscotch into hell or whatever."[23] From this imagined fundamentalist perspective, you could not be a Christian and have long hair, tattoos, or piercings and wear leather clothes (see figure 9). Neither could you scream or growl on record instead of sing and be a Christian. This is Christian anti-rock discourse all over again, and as with before, the objections conflate ethics and aesthetics (see chapter 3). Any attempt to separate the two for such critics felt futile to Dunn, who, along with the other members of the band, tried to engage everyone who emailed them with concerns. "The ones that are difficult is where people have already pre-determined that this is what you are, this is what you're about," he told me. "They can't understand what you're saying because it's loud and obnoxious. For all they're concerned, it's evil, period. That's it. There's still people out there that think that any instrument beyond the piano is of the Devil."[24]

But these people are not the Christians with whom Dunn and the other members of Demon Hunter wanted to communicate. Like Jimmy Swaggart, they were closed-minded; to them, Christian metal was a contradiction in terms and not up for debate. Instead of convincing those who will never be convinced, the members of Demon Hunter found it worthwhile to share their faith with fans and parents (or youth pastors) open to learning more about their perspectives. As Carver told me, "Demon Hunter has a very clear outline of exactly what they're doing. Concerned parents ask questions, and they have these very clear responses with scripture and stories to let people know."[25] Dunn agreed: "I feel like Demon Hunter is very clear-cut on where we are spiritually and musically. . . . It's family-friendly. Your mom may not like what Demon Hunter sounds like, but if she pulls out the lyric sheet, she'll think, 'Okay, I guess it's fine.' . . . A concerned parent that emails us says, 'Hey, my son listens to you and says that it's Christian music. What's it all about?' I've no problem writing them a response."[26]

Demon Hunter's musical style is a variation of riff-based melodic death metal (commonly shortened to "melodeath"). Their songs typically

FIGURE 9. Demon Hunter. Photo by Jeff Carpenter, courtesy Demon Hunter.

follow a traditional verse-chorus-verse structure; the vocals alternate between melodically sung and growled or screamed, and often include anthemic backing vocals during the pre-chorus or chorus (ideal for audience sing-alongs at concerts). They have many ballads and slower songs, several of which have string or orchestral accompaniment. The mid-tempo (around 110 bpm) song "I Am a Stone" (🎧) is an outlier that illustrates the band's willingness to expand its stylistic boundaries. Lead singer and songwriter Ryan Clark's vocals (processed and double-tracked) are accompanied only by a full string section, except during the chorus when backing vocal tracks harmonize with his melody. There are no distorted guitars or unrelenting drums—there are no rock instruments whatsoever. "I Am a Stone" is the band's most accessible recording and their most streamed song on Spotify.

Most of Demon Hunter's songs follow melodeath conventions more closely than "I Am a Stone." Clark writes his lyrics, however, from a Christian perspective. In "Not Ready to Die" (🎧), from 2004's *Summer of Darkness*, he addresses an ambivalence about death that he faces as a Christian. On one hand, he believes that his spirit will ascend to heaven when he dies, which is something to celebrate and not mourn: "So when I'm taken to the sky and you're still here / You can clear your mind and dry your tears." Clark alludes to Jesus's age when he was crucified—"If only thirty-three years can save my life"—but he sings of making plans for his own future despite his mortality, feeling like he still has much to accomplish: "I'm burning bridges for the last time / I'm breaking habits for the first time / I saw my future today, it said I'm going away / And I still haven't sung the last line / . . . / I'm not ready to lay / I'm not ready to fade / I'm not ready to die." In "The Last One Alive" (🎧), from 2014's *Extremist*, a more mature Clark describes what it is like to maintain his religious convictions in an increasingly secular world: "Does anyone still try? / Does anyone still hope to set their eyes beyond this place / Where angels fall and darkness reigns / Where time dissolves the brightest flame?" He sings of standing firm in the face of isolation, both the apocalyptic kind he imagines in these lyrics and the daily isolation that Christians feel as they navigate the secular world: "Whether I'm the last one alive / Or ascend before my time / Better I'm the last one alive / Than a soul denied."

There is a hopefulness to these songs that distinguished Demon Hunter (and Clark) from the dystopic themes of many other death metal bands. In their email replies to concerned parents, Dunn, Clark, and their bandmates were able to clarify the lyrical intent of their songs—ministering, in fact (even if they choose not to label it as such), to parents and kids alike. In these moments, Dunn and his bandmates fell back on ethical positions rooted in their Christian faith. They were able to explain with conviction. In doing so, they foregrounded ethics over style to claim legitimate inclusion within the unreceptive and, at times, outright hostile Christian market. In doing so, they were able to change skeptical parents' positions about the appropriateness of Christian metal.

CREDIBILITY, AUTHENTICITY, AND ETHICS

When Christian metal bands like The Burial and Demon Hunter used their musical platforms to preach and teach, they were actively participating in a performative framework that is the norm within the Christian market. Many artists and bands explain or tell stories about their songs; many use their music in service of teachable moments, explicitly promoting ethical values; but Christian artists also use these moments to teach theology or illustrate religious lessons, such as the power of one's faith in God. At times they do so with reflections and testimony drawn from their personal lives. Christian listeners want to feel emotionally connected to artists, and they value both artists' transparency and their ability to teach and minister through music. Wayne Kusber explained his perspective on this to me:

> There's a pastor-like quality—I know that sounds a little heavy—that the core Christian music fan expects and likes in their artists. They want a thoughtful introduction to a song; they want to know the story behind the song. They want to know the heart behind the song. They want to know if there was struggle, if there was joy behind it. They want faith infused in the concert. They want faith messages infused even in the way the songs are introduced, almost like mini-sermons. If you analyze most of the more successful artists in our genre, they have what I call the very pastor-like quality. ... And it's very sincere.[27]

In his reflections, Kusber framed the relationship between artist and audience in the Christian market as one that values authenticity. All of this extra stuff that he claimed fans want—thoughtful introductions, stories, faith-infused concerts, mini-sermons—you cannot hear on record but must experience live. Philip Auslander writes of rock concerts as sites where artists perform authenticity and audiences confirm it: "It is only in live performance that the listener can ascertain that a group that looks authentic in photographs and sounds authentic on recordings really *is* authentic."[28] As Auslander explains, authenticity is not an inherent quality but rather results from a discursive process.

Allan Moore also writes of authenticity, arguing that it "is a matter of interpretation . . . [that] is ascribed, not inscribed," through the process of authentication.[29] Richard Peterson agrees, suggesting that authenticity "does not inhere in the object, person, or performance said to be authentic. Rather, authenticity is a claim that is made by or for someone, thing, or performance and either accepted or rejected by relevant others."[30] Because authenticity is thus linked to social processes, it is necessarily a social construction, particularly because it is so often adjudicated by audiences. When audiences are the ones doing the authenticating, it matters who is in the audience, that audience members agree on shared values, and that artists not only understand the unique expectations of their market but make a point of speaking directly to those expectations. (This is why a Christian artist's language and manner of speaking to a Christian audience is so often incomprehensible from an outsider's perspective.) Individual listeners and entire audiences thus actively engage in authenticating processes that conflate a market's ethics with its authenticity. An artist's authenticity depends on her ability to adhere to the ethical expectations of her market—you cannot be both unethical and authentic. Artists thus perform ethics: they do so on recordings, in interviews, and on television; Auslander argues that they do so in live concerts; and increasingly artists also do so through social media and other forms of communication that feel less mediated. In other words, artists make their ethical appropriateness for a particular market clear: they musick the right way. In this way ethics become yet another venue through which participants define niche markets.

For Moore, authenticity is about speaking truth in three senses: "that artists speak the truth of their own situation; that they speak the truth of the situation of (absent) others; and that they speak the truth of their own culture, thereby representing (present) others," which he distinguishes as authenticity of expression, execution, and experience.[31] The "pastor-like quality" that Kusber described resembles both Moore's authenticity of expression (or what he calls "first person authenticity") and authenticity of experience (or "second person authenticity"). In the former, the audience hears the artist truthfully representing himself; that is, he tells the truth about himself, "conveying the impression that his/her utterance is one of integrity, that it represents an attempt to communicate in an unmediated form with an audience."[32] The latter form of authenticity tells the truth about the listener, "conveying the impression to a listener that that listener's experience of life is being validated, that the music is 'telling it like it is' for them."[33] An important factor is the degree to which artists' true stories resonate with listeners' personal experiences of their faith. In Christian music, authenticity of expression and authenticity of experience resemble the type of theological teaching and spiritual guidance that pastors do on a daily basis in addition to their sermons every Sunday morning. Tom Wagner reminds us that, for Christian artists, "authenticity and identity are always understood in relation to spiritual authority," and this is perhaps even more true for those Christian artists that work (or have worked) as ministers and pastors.[34]

Throughout my conversations with record label executives, the band Casting Crowns repeatedly emerged as an example of a Christian band whose authenticity, sincerity, and "pastor-like quality" played a significant role in their success in the Christian market. Casting Crowns are part of Christian music's mainstream: speaking to me in 2010, Wayne Kusber called them "the biggest band in Christian music right now."[35] The band's chart and sales successes are well documented: seven platinum-selling albums (●) and seven records that have topped *Billboard*'s top Christian albums chart, six of which made the top ten of the *Billboard* 200. Nick Barre is a former EMI CMG executive who had been working at Proper Management for two years when I interviewed him. Proper Management represents Casting Crowns, and Barre explicitly linked the band's commercial success with the connection they (and especially lead singer and songwriter Mark Hall) have forged with their listeners: "There's something in the lyric, the melody, the message that is connecting with people where they're putting their money where their mouth is. They want to experience that. They're getting an experience from that music that they can't get from anything else. . . . Mark Hall is a full-time youth pastor, and his band, they work at this church. . . . All they are is authentic."[36] Consider, for example, Casting Crowns' song "If We've Ever Needed You" (🎧), the second single from *Until the Whole World Hears* (2009). The song is a piano-driven lament addressed to God, with lyrics that reveal the songwriters' vulnerability in a moment of weakness: "You called us out, we turned away, we've turned away / With shipwrecked faith, idols rise / We do what is right in our own eyes / . . . / If we've ever needed you, Lord it's now." This vulnerability is important to the band's appeal, according to Barre: "[Mark Hall] just tells stories. To a lot of kids, that story song of somebody in a moment of doubt, temptation, frustration, and they're engaging their Christianity in the middle of that—even though it's not cool that Joe Public is going through a very challenging time, it's a very compelling thing."[37] But the vulnerability here—that is, the failure to live up to God's standards ("You called us out, we turned away")—is not only

Mark Hall's but also that of the listeners, collectively. As Hall says in his introduction to this song in a live recording (🎧, on 2010's *Until the Whole World Hears Live*), "Our families, our churches, our country, Lord—we need you." In using the first-person plural "our" and "we," Hall sings both *to* and *for* his audience, revealing that his concern is not (only) for his personal salvation but rather for that of everyone.

Listeners have heard the stories that Hall tells about his songs at live performances, on live recordings, and in interviews, talks, and sermons (including several recorded and available on YouTube). For the band's 2016 album, *The Very Next Thing*, Hall recorded brief videos where he provided some insight into the meaning and genesis of five of the album's dozen songs. Many Casting Crowns fans have known that "Oh My Soul" (🎧), the second-most streamed Casting Crowns song on both YouTube and Spotify (behind the 2004 single "Who Am I"), addresses Hall's reactions after receiving a cancer diagnosis (in 2015). But the story video, which has been viewed over three hundred thousand times, is still impactful. In it, Hall discusses speaking with his doctor about the diagnosis over the phone while at a funeral and admits his prideful impulse to shoulder the burden of treatment and surgery with little support: "I'd never been on this side of it, where I realized sometimes when you're hurting, you don't want to hurt around people because you don't want to feel it, and that's pride. . . . [But] God comforts us, through each other."[38] He describes the song originating in Psalm 42–43, where he found comfort in the refrain "Why so downcast, oh my soul? Put your hope in God," sat down at the keyboard, and sang the lyric "Oh my soul / Why are you weary?" According to Hall, "Oh My Soul" addresses his conflict between feeling afraid and helpless while also trusting that his faith will sustain him: "Oh, my soul / You are not alone / There's a place where fear has to face the God you know / One more day, He will make a way / Let Him show you how, you can lay this down."

Judging by YouTube comments on the story video and the song's lyric videos, listeners have found comfort and support both in Hall's lyrics and in his willingness to share his story publicly. His transparency has enabled them to connect intimately with his public persona, and many commenters have described a sense of peace after encountering this song during a particularly difficult and painful periods of their lives:

> Thank you Mark. I am still trying to get through the grief of losing my daughter less than a year ago. . . . With God she survived 20 years after the

doctors said it was impossible. Your beautiful video seems like it was made about her.[39]

When I heard this song, I identified immediately with my grief on losing my only daughter 3 months ago to cancer. . . . Your music has always touched my soul deeply, but this song, it touched and spoke to me. . . . Your music is wonderful testimony to God's amazing love, mercy and grace.[40]

As a fellow cancer survivor, this song resonates very strongly with me. . . . How anyone faces cancer without the Lord, I will never know or understand. . . . That place is where you find healing, both physical, emotional, and spiritual. Thanks for sharing your heart and experience with us, Mark![41]

My husband passed away almost 5 months ago. Since I have felt lost and broken. This song brings me comfort and peace.[42]

According to Barre, "I think people are looking for, 'Are you authentic? I don't care if you're old, I don't care if you're white. I really don't care. Are you authentic, are you real? . . . Can I trust you?'"[43] As he described above, Hall's vulnerability is "a very compelling thing," something to which listeners have connected, and which many have attributed to his work as a youth pastor. His vulnerability and transparency have been important in a market where listeners value authenticity of expression and experience, and this exemplifies right musicking.

ETHICS AND CORNERSTONE FESTIVAL

Even though Mark Hall shares little stylistic similarities with members of The Burial or Demon Hunter, they share the practice of teaching religious lessons through their music and musicking. When Mark Hall confesses weakness in following God ("You called us out, we turned away") and reaffirms God's importance ("If we've ever needed you, Lord it's now") he is singing the right way; when David Marshall promoted sexual purity in between songs at Cornerstone, and when Jon Dunn explained the theological backgrounds of his band's songs to concerned parents over email, each was musicking the right way. The important point here is that the "right" of right singing and right musicking in these different contexts is identical. Casting Crowns' performance of authenticity as one of Christian music's biggest bands articulates the market's ethical values while also providing a template and strategy through which otherwise peripheral bands might lay legitimate claim to the Christian market. At the same time, the stylistic deviations of Christian metal help make those Christian ethics available and accessible to listeners who might not find Casting Crowns (or other core Christian artists) to be musically compelling. Many of these listeners found a supportive community at Cornerstone Festival, which long prioritized the Christian market's margins over its center.

Cornerstone welcomed Christian metal bands like Demon Hunter and their fans, many of whom often felt unwelcome in more conservative church environments at home. When JPUSA launched Cornerstone in 1984, according to former director John Herrin, it was partly in response to other Christian festivals' more conservative approach to programming, which rarely featured niche styles. These were the festivals where, when he was performing in Rez Band, Herrin felt tokenized as a rock band, for which the festivals' organizers had to apologize. He told me that the vision for Cornerstone was to feature niche styles unapologetically: "At that point [1984], there were more and more independent, really creative artists that were Christians. Maybe they were a little too evangelical in who they were and what they stood for to make it in the general market, but a little too wild to really play a part of the fairly conservative Christian music scene at the time. . . . We felt from the very beginning that Cornerstone needed to feature the artistic end of the Christian music world."[44] Herrin's central objective while running the festival was a little self-serving: "I try to do a festival that I think myself, my kids, and the people I know would want to be a part of," he told me.[45] But in trying to please himself, his family, and his friends—and, tacitly, by *not* worrying about pleasing everybody—Herrin's own ethical perspectives shaped Cornerstone. His ethics reflected his experiences performing in Rez Band and living communally in JPUSA. These ethics included promoting an inquisitive (if not wholly critical) approach to theology and faith, encouraging community, and involving and respecting youth.

Cornerstone's organizers booked seminar speakers, some of whom were drawn from JPUSA's community members. As Herrin explained to me, as with the festival's music programming, this was a response to other Christian festivals: "I think one of the things that always turned us off at some of these events was simple, pat answers to tough questions that Christians face, and that all people face." In addition to privileging niche musical styles marginal to Christian music's mainstream, Cornerstone's organizers wanted "to bring thinking Christianity to the table."[46] The seminars grew to be a sizable component of the festival and, for many attendees—especially those who attended the festival despite not being fans of metal or punk—were an important feature of the event. As Herrin explained to me, seminars were another way to distinguish Cornerstone from other Christian festivals: "Most events have a speaker who got up once or twice a day on the main stage and would preach to the crowd. We weren't really so interested in having someone preach there, but we were interested in having smaller groups . . . [and] topics that were relevant to what was going on in the world around us."[47] Cornerstone attendees had the opportunity to learn from scholars, ministers, musicians, writers, and others about varied topics such as homelessness, Marshall McLuhan's media theories, mental illness, poverty, and sexuality, among others.[48]

These seminars were not oriented toward conversion. Despite JPUSA's history with evangelism and their ongoing missions work in Chicago, organizers approached Cornerstone as an event that catered to attendees who already identified as Christians—an approach that Eileen Luhr describes as an "affirmation of Christianity rather than a beacon for society."[49] The writer of a 1984 *Chicago Tribune* article about the first Cornerstone quoted Rez's Glenn Kaiser describing the festival as a place where Christians can let their hair down: "Unbelievers need the encouragement of seeing that you can breathe and have fun even while you are a valid orthodox Christian."[50] In its early years, when the festival took place at the Lake County Fairgrounds in Chicago's suburbs, curious attendees from the surrounding area could easily come for a single day (or more) and return home at night. The region's two largest newspapers (the *Chicago Sun-Times* and the *Tribune*) regularly previewed and covered the event.[51] After JPUSA moved the event to Bushnell, however, attending Cornerstone required a larger commitment from fans, many of whom now had to travel much longer distances. Looking back, Herrin saw this change as instrumental in extending JPUSA's vision of community to festival attendees: "[Moving] created much more of a sense of a community," he claimed. "We build this whole city out here every year, and we have to take care of ourselves." It also reconceptualized the festival as a refuge for Christians, according to Herrin. Part of that was due to the organizers' musical programming, but part was also due to the non-performance events they offered: in addition to the seminars, attendees could participate in arts and crafts workshops, Bible studies, interviews with artists and writers, organized (and disorganized) sports, and worship services both formal and informal.

Herrin described Cornerstone as not just a festival but as

> an annual gathering of people that are either Christians or have some connection to the Christian faith who are more interested in discussion, the arts, I think creative music, fellowship. It's an annual renewal. A lot of these folks live all over the country, and . . . interact everyday with people that are not like-minded. This is a chance [for them] to come together. I'm always surprised at the breath of fresh air that everybody feels. There are so many people that come every year, and this has been part of their lives and significant to them in their walk of faith, their friendships, what they're interested in.[52]

Attendees felt that breath of fresh air while walking Cornerstone's campsites, joining in the community and camaraderie that sprouted in its fields every July. Campers often attended Cornerstone in large groups or arranged to meet each other at the festival. Many told me that they returned every summer and reconnected with their "Cornerstone friends" at the festival, whom they rarely saw during the year. Others explained that the festival was simultaneously a place of social diversity and cohesion, which they appreciated. For example, a group calling themselves "Camp Busted Guitar" told me that they only felt fully understood and accepted at Cornerstone, which they had attended for eight years and acted as their surrogate family. They appreciated that attendees regularly crossed subcultural boundaries that might be less permeable elsewhere. "It's not the Cornerstone Festival," one of them told me, "it's the Cornerstone Experience." Campers shared knowledge and resources, they cooked and prayed for each other, and larger groups of families shared parenting responsibilities. This is not unlike living communally at JPUSA, where members share responsibilities for caring for each other and their dependents, property, ministries, and businesses. Out of context, this is not necessarily unique—families and other groups enjoy similar communal experiences vacationing and camping together at state and national parks and private campgrounds—but when contextualized within Cornerstone's values, the social environment of camping at the festival gains additional significance.

At its inception, Cornerstone's organizers went out of their way to book Christian artists who played a wide variety of rock substyles (including heavy metal, new wave, and punk rock) and advertised the event in underground fanzines and magazines (such as *Burning Bush*, *Gospel Metal*, *HM*, *Lightshine International*, *Ragtime*, *True Tunes News*, and *White Throne*), which frequently reciprocated with previews and reviews of the festival (see figure 10). During the 1980s and '90s, Christian artists benefitted from performing at Cornerstone to fans

FIGURE 10. Fanzine ads for Cornerstone festivals in 1989, 1991, and 1994. Used with permission, from the collection of the Center for Popular Music, Middle Tennessee State University.

who traveled from around the country to attend the festival. John J. Thompson explained in an interview that performing at Cornerstone was significant for artists who might not have otherwise found enough venues for a regional or nationwide tour:

> Cornerstone was the mothership, it was exclusive, you couldn't find those bands anywhere else. Most of those bands didn't ever tour; there wasn't enough places for them to play to do a tour. So, you want to see Adam Again [♫], you went to Cornerstone. You want to see Daniel Amos, or the Lost Dogs, The Choir [♫], the 77s [♫], or Charlie Peacock, or a lot of other of those bands, they played at Cornerstone. That was their tour. They could hit all of the interested people in one week. Those people could go out and tell their story and spread the word.[53]

Because the festival had become strongly associated with marginal styles of Christian music, many niche labels and artists considered Cornerstone to be an important promotional tool. Several record labels sponsored both official and unofficial stages at the festival, including Brave New World, Come&Live!, Grrr Records (JPUSA's in-house label), Raging Storm, Sancrosanct, and others; Cornerstone's Label Showcase Stage featured "up and coming talent" from many labels throughout the week. Tooth & Nail sponsored an entire day of performances at

Music to Raise the Dead | 161

Cornerstone for many years; according to Jeff Carver, Cornerstone's organizers booked and supported the label's artists more than conservative Christian events: "Cornerstone's always been like, 'Come one, come all,' and I think has a similar mentality about the music as probably Tooth & Nail does as a whole. . . . We love it. They have always been really good supporters of us."[54]

When general market "alternative rock" was commercially successful in the '90s and early aughts, several Christian bands experienced crossover success (I discuss the fringe crossover of Tooth & Nail artists in chapter 7). This success trickled down to Cornerstone, where it was a double-edged sword. On one hand, the festival attracted more attendees than ever before, with attendance peaking at around twenty-five thousand festivalgoers in the early 2000s. On the other hand, however, some participants felt that it became increasingly focused on the commodification of Christian music and less on providing theological renewal in a faith-based environment. Joshua Stump, the founding pastor of the Anchor Fellowship, a nondenominational evangelical church in Nashville that sponsored a Cornerstone tent for several years, explained to me that his impression of Cornerstone in the early aughts was that ministry had been superseded by commerce: "It felt more like everybody's there advertising a product. The old days, when it was a huge festival, it was just earthy and sincere, and there was ministry stuff everywhere, prayer tents. You would walk around campsites and people were talking about God at night. It was almost like a little heaven on Earth. . . . There's a legacy of something very sincere that was falling apart."[55] The merchandising at Cornerstone was indeed significant, as it is at most music festivals and concerts in both the Christian and general markets. For touring artists, selling merchandise is an important revenue stream, especially as recorded music sales (and thus royalties) have dropped in the twenty-first century. But other vendors at Cornerstone were there precisely because it was a captive, niche market. Attendees who strolled through the merchandise tents (for many years there were two) passed table after table promoting book publishers, Christian universities, conservative political causes, mission organizations, record labels, T-shirt vendors, visual artists, and more—all of whom had something to sell.

The youth audience was a major target demographic for Cornerstone, as it is for many other festivals. This reflected Cornerstone's status as a destination for church youth group summer trips; it also reflected Cornerstone's ideal as a family-friendly event where there was something for everyone to enjoy. Herrin explained to me that his programming strategy for Cornerstone intentionally articulated this goal, but not without struggle: "There are people that feel like we put way too much emphasis on the kids at Cornerstone. 'What about us—we've been there for twenty, twenty-five years and we want more old-timer bands.' I'm really pretty determined to keep Cornerstone as a youth event. My target audience is that sixteen- to twenty-five-year old [demographic]."[56] Herrin also appealed to youth by designing Cornerstone as a space with comparatively fewer restrictions than other parental or authoritative environments:

> I'm not that put off by kids who are too loud, too rowdy, stay up too late, write on the walls, make a mess. So what, you know? Cornerstone can't be anarchy; on the other hand, I'm not interested in somebody in an orange vest and flashlight every fifty feet telling me to get off the lawn, don't do that, and don't do that. I'm not interested in having an adversarial relationship with the young people that come to the event. I'm not their folks. I'm not telling them when to go to bed. I want to be there to be able to offer them a fresher perspective and look at the Christian faith and what's out there.[57]

Herrin and his staff organized a Christian festival that appealed both to youths' desire for freedom and adults' desire for structure. He was "not telling them when to go to bed," but he did expect them not to drink, do drugs, or have sex.[58] In casting himself as sympathetic with youth—"I'm not their folks"—Herrin recalled his own troubled teenage years as well as JPUSA's identity as a Christian intentional community, long marginal to mainstream churches. The festival's atmosphere, "experience," and sheer breadth of options likewise promoted freedom. In hoping to guide youth toward a "fresher perspective" on Christianity, however, Herrin implicitly took a mentorship role. Similarly, despite the relatively inobtrusive festival security, Cornerstone's rules set moral boundaries for all attendees, prohibiting drugs and alcohol and encouraging modest clothing and swimwear. Herrin and Cornerstone Festival thus exhibited a greater tension, common in the Christian market, between simultaneously encouraging individuality and yet discouraging dissension. In other words, nonconformity was embraced at Cornerstone, but only in certain ways. The ethics of style in this version of subcultural Christianity were not infinitely flexible.

THE STYLES OF ETHICS OF STYLE

As Cornerstone's peak audiences dwindled, alternative rock giving way to other styles in the mass markets, the festival's organizers faced an untenable situation: despite diversifying the event's programming, Cornerstone remained firmly identified with youth-oriented niche markets. As I discussed above, these listeners increasingly had more options. Other audiences remained alienated by the prevalence of niche styles like metalcore and punk or by the commodification of Christianity they had experienced at Cornerstone, despite the work of organizers and partners to reinscribe the festival's theological foundation with worship, Bible study, seminars, and other spiritual components. Herrin, for his part, programmed a Jesus Rally to celebrate the fortieth anniversary of *Time* magazine's Jesus People movement cover story (see figure 2) in 2011, featuring Daniel Amos, Barry McGuire, Petra, Rez Band, Randy Stonehill, and others. But it was too little, too late: faced with decreasing attendance and increasing debt, JPUSA's leadership council decided that 2012 would be Cornerstone's final year. The festival that summer felt like an Irish wake, simultaneously mournful and celebratory, as artists, organizers, and attendees reflected on what Cornerstone had meant to their lives, their music, and their faith.[59] Early the following year, JPUSA announced that it had sold the property where Cornerstone had taken place, confirming for many that the festival was truly over.

The lessons of Cornerstone are many, and several are still being written: in 2020, JPUSA still operates ministries and businesses in Chicago, including Everybody's Coffee and Wilson Abbey, a coffeehouse and concert venue that promote visions of community and the expressive potential of Christian music similar to those found at Cornerstone. As I discuss in chapter 6, AudioFeed Festival—which has taken place in the same week as Cornerstone used to (that of the Fourth of July holiday) every summer since 2013—has explicitly laid claim to Cornerstone's legacy. Its organizers intend to support and promote the same artists and musical communities that called Cornerstone home ("Audiofeed is not Cornerstone," they claim on its website, "but it's the same family, and similar spirit"), and its attendees reminisce about the old days in Bushnell from their new site at the Champaign County Fairgrounds in Urbana, Illinois.[60] Those who cannot (or choose not to) drive to central Illinois continue to memorialize Cornerstone online, particularly in Facebook groups like Cornerstone Memories and The 30th Cornerstone Festival (which would have been in 2013 had it continued). John J. Thompson, who ran a merchandise table representing his former Christian record store and music magazine (both were called True Tunes) at Cornerstone for many years before working on the festival's marketing staff, continues to promote artists he associates with the festival in a variety of capacities as a well-known and respected Christian music industry professional and educator.

For my purposes here, however, the lessons of Cornerstone are those that demonstrate that, in the Christian market, participants can use ethics to advocate for their legitimate inclusion, regardless of their style. For many years, no other event or institution enabled this claim as strongly as Cornerstone did. Even at the festival's peak and during its decline, it provided a physical place where relatively unknown bands like The Burial and comparatively successful bands like Demon Hunter could reach fans in one place (Thompson's "all of the interested people"). This place, coupled with the support of John Herrin and his fellow community members at JPUSA, gave attendees a family and faith community when they felt ostracized from their home churches. It provided a home—albeit one that was physically present for only a few days every year—to a listening community that was otherwise scattered across the continent, with no real geographic center (unlike, say, the Christian music industry, which is centered in Nashville, Tennessee).[61] Because of Cornerstone, Christian rock is dirtier, grittier, louder, noisier, younger, more colorful, more open-minded, more tattooed, and with longer hair than it was before. Cornerstone enabled the legitimation of diverse stylistic expressions and theological orientations within white U.S. evangelicalism, engendering the ethics of style.

6

Lost in the Sound of Separation

Resistance at Christian Music Festivals

The first time you attend AudioFeed Festival, you should find the Radon Lounge soon after you arrive. With café tables, plenty of folding chairs, and the best coffee at the festival, Radon is the most comfortable space to enjoy music there. It is also the only location to buy festival merchandise and has the most eclectic lineup, featuring hip hop, post-rock, rock and roll, singer/songwriter, synth pop, and many other styles. Stage manager Jeff does his best to emulate the quirkiness of his venue in Springfield, Illinois (also called the Radon Lounge), with custom decorations, pinball machines, and homemade baked goods for the artists. If you are into metal, you will spend all day at Sanctuary; punk and hardcore fanatics don't stray too far from the Black Sheep Stage; the goth kids (yes, Christian goth is a thing) hang at the Asylum. Radon Lounge is where you go when you need a break from heavy music, or you need an iced coffee, or you need to buy your annual festival T-shirt, or you just need to sit. Through 2017, Radon occupied a tent very close to the food vendors. But in 2018, organizers moved Radon to the festival's only indoor, air-conditioned venue, so now it is also where you go when you need to avoid the sun, heat, or rain.

AudioFeed has taken place around the Fourth of July holiday since 2013. This is the same time period that Cornerstone Festival was always scheduled, and AudioFeed's organizers launched it to fill the gap left when Cornerstone closed after its 2012 iteration.[1] In my time at AudioFeed in 2017, participants reminisced about Cornerstone in casual conversation, from the stages of its venues, on the T-shirts they wore, in its design (Radon Lounge is a direct homage to Cornerstone's Gallery Stage), and in the festival's booking: AudioFeed books many artists that performed at Cornerstone, and many more newer artists that are of a similar style and ethics who would likely play Cornerstone if it still existed. The two have in common their eclectic programming, casual seating, and on-site coffeeshop, where you can even buy the same ceramic mugs (featuring an illustration by cartoonist Spike, a member of JPUSA and former front man of the Christian punk band Crashdog) for free refills all weekend. Luke Welchel, one of AudioFeed's founders, admitted to me that AudioFeed exists because Cornerstone no longer does: "We've never hid that we did it [AudioFeed] because of Cornerstone. We've been vocal about it. We've been sad that Cornerstone is gone. I think all of us that are working this would much rather go to Cornerstone."[2] AudioFeed is distinct from Cornerstone, but it exists in the older festival's wake, and attendees, bands, and organizers seemingly cannot separate their experiences at the two festivals (perhaps because, in 2017, AudioFeed was still a young event only a few years removed from Cornerstone's closing).

AudioFeed takes place at the Champaign County Fairgrounds in Urbana, Illinois, almost a 150-mile drive from Cornerstone's former location near Bushnell, Illinois. Although AudioFeed is only two miles from the University of Illinois, with plenty of nearby hotel options, the year I attended many attendees chose to camp at the fairgrounds (as they did at Cornerstone). Tents dotted the landscape and hammocks hung in the bleachers. Wandering the festival, like at many other campgrounds, was as much about stumbling into new acquaintances, sharing food with neighboring campers, and commiserating over the state of the bathroom facilities as it was about stumbling across new bands and connecting with new friends over shared musical tastes. At AudioFeed, those tastes tended toward aggressive rock styles and substyles—when I attended the festival in 2017, Black Sheep and Sanctuary were more consistently packed than the other stages—but the organizers have booked a wider variety of music. Welchel, who has directed the festival's programming, told me that this is intentional: "One of our main objectives is having music that everybody likes. If my Grandma comes, which she does, and my son comes, which he does, they would both have a really good time one way or the other. And that's been a very purposeful goal from year one until now."[3] AudioFeed's website promotes the festival as a place to experience "great" music: "That's really our only criteria. We tend toward creative music that is not necessarily 'radio single' type material. From really mellow acoustic to hardcore and everything in between . . . there is something for almost everyone almost all the time."[4] This last claim—that all attendees will find music to suit their tastes—is ambitious at best, but it speaks to a larger concern of the organizers: that they create a welcoming environment for artists and listeners alike. Nonetheless, AudioFeed has definitely catered to subcultural Christians and the niche markets of Christian hardcore, metal, and punk.

The largest Christian festivals provide physical places for what historian Randall Balmer has called the "evangelical subculture" to gather.[5] In doing so, major events (like the annual Creation Festivals) popularize a version of U.S. evangelical culture in which fashion and style, musical tastes, and theology are largely conservative and conforming. Smaller festivals like AudioFeed and Cornerstone, on the other hand, articulate a resistant vision that reflects a divergent approach to Christian music as expansive and diverse. At these festivals, subcultural participation itself becomes a clear and present component of participants' identities, at least for one night (or one week) if not for the entire year. In the prior chapter, I argued that artists often foreground their convergent Christian faith over their divergent musical styles and aesthetics to claim belongingness in the Christian market. Here I take a different approach and instead consider how divergence—framed through the critical lens of subcultural studies—impacts the boundaries, practices, and sounds of Christian music. If we focus on resistance instead of on conformity, for example, how might subcultural studies contribute to our understanding of the Christian market? How might examining the Christian market enhance our understanding of the roles of resistance and boundary-making within subcultural studies? In this chapter, I examine performances at Christian festivals for markers of resistance and subcultural identity. At Cornerstone and AudioFeed we see how resistance informs the intent, organization, and lived experiences of smaller Christian festivals. First, however, I lay the groundwork for considering white U.S. evangelicalism as a subculture, turning to subcultural theory and other studies that address the religious identity and resistance of Christian youth.

RESISTANCE AND SUBCULTURAL CHRISTIANITY

Subculture theory's roots lie in sociology and cultural studies roughly following the middle of the twentieth century. Working within the sociology of deviance and urban sociology (particularly that affiliated with the University of Chicago) in the 1950s and '60s, U.S. scholars such as Howard Becker, Albert K. Cohen, and Milton Gordon situated cultural assimilation and deviation from social norms within particular sociocultural contexts, such as gang life, the immigrant experience, youth culture, and others.[6] Writing around the same time, British cultural studies scholars such as Richard Hoggart, E. P. Thompson, and Raymond Williams emphasized the roles of class and mass media in social life and individual experience.[7] In the 1970s, researchers affiliated with the University of Birmingham's Centre for Contemporary Cultural Studies (the BCCCS, or Birmingham School), including Phil Cohen, Stuart Hall, Dick Hebdige, Angela McRobbie, Paul E. Willis, and others, developed subculture theory to describe acts of resistance and opposition on the part of smaller cultural units (the subcultures) against larger ones (the dominant cultures).[8] Subculture theory emphasizes the roles of leisure activities and friend groups (instead of work and family or ethnic groups, as traditional scholarship often emphasized) in creating meaning around cultural practices, rituals, traditions, and consumption habits that deviate from those of a dominant culture. Subculture theory also tends to focus on the media as a cultural space in which resistance is both enacted (by subcultures) and subdued or subverted (by dominant cultures).

Dick Hebdige's book *Subculture: The Meaning of Style* has become a seminal work that articulates and illustrates these ideas.[9] He lays the groundwork for academic research into oppositional youth cultures, helping bring the term "subculture" fully into both academic and popular discourses, prompting dozens of responses and rebuttals, and influencing a wide range of disciplines and research areas in the social sciences and humanities.[10] In the book, Hebdige discusses several subcultural groups in Britain: beats, hipsters, mods, punks, Rastafarians, and teddy boys serve as his primary subjects. These groups' emergences and practices, together with mainstream British culture's contemporaneous reactions, inform his analyses and conclusions. In Hebdige's reading, members of these groups felt alienated from mainstream culture. Their alienation became the source of their cultural resistance, which they expressed both in their fashion and style and in their ideology as resistant responses to (and breaks from) the mainstream. Youth performed subcultural resistance by "resignifying" existing cultural elements to suit their own purpose or message. This style must be both visible and legible to be effective. For example, think of punks' use of safety pins as jewelry, their repurposing of garbage bags as shirts, pogoing as a break from traditional social dance, and punk rock's aggressive simplicity as a response to the musical complexity of progressive rock.[11]

Hebdige argues that subcultures exist in a dialectic with the mainstream culture. A subculture's resistance to and stylistic break from the mainstream via repurposing and resignification express its opposition. If mainstream assimilation is the problem (or, in a Hegelian dialectic, the "thesis"), then subcultural resistance is a necessary reaction (or "antithesis"). The mainstream reacts with alarmist shock and disgust, often articulated, amplified, and repeated through the mass media. These reactions portray subcultural styles as abnormal, dangerous, extraordinary, and even exotic, and they frequently prompt moral panics (see chapter 3). A "synthesis" resolves the tension between a dialectic's thesis and antithesis. Hebdige describes the mainstream's ultimate incorporation of the subculture into the dominant culture as the synthesis that solves the dialectic. The mainstream's shock eventually subsides as it decodes and "explains" the subculture. Because the mainstream controls the mass media, it also controls this discourse; these explanations are thus conducted in terms defined by and favorable to the mainstream, defusing the subculture's discursive significance. Incorporated into the mainstream, subcultural style becomes fashionable and commodified; subcultural ideology becomes either exoticized or trivialized to insignificance; the subculture itself is defused and eventually ceases to be.

These, then, are a classic subculture's life stages: emergence through resistance, stylistic resignification, and ultimate incorporation back into the mainstream. There are problems with this model, of course. For example, if we focus on subcultures' stylistic resignification only as *re*active, our analyses fail to account for subcultural agency and the degree to which subcultures *pro*actively perform resistance. In other words, resistance becomes only about responding to the dominant culture's faults, and not about articulating a vision forward (to which the mainstream must then respond). If subcultures are always reactive and never proactive, incorporation is thus unavoidable—for how can subcultures be resistant effectively (and perpetually) while utilizing the mainstream's own discourses, infrastructures, institutions, and symbols? Another weakness for which subculture theory has been criticized is a tendency to see resistance everywhere. When we foreground opposition and resistance in everything that members of subcultures do, we risk ascribing intent and ignoring those participants' actual objectives.[12] Sometimes a teenager wears a particular T-shirt to make a statement about her frustrations with the world, but sometimes a teenager wears a particular T-shirt simply because she thinks it looks cool. Nevertheless, Hebdige accurately describes the lifecycles of several classic subcultures, including punk—which many observers have suggested lost its political and cultural significance in the late 1970s after it became fashionable—whose dialectic was repeated over a decade later by the moral panic over, and eventual incorporation of, the underground rave scene, as Sarah Thornton describes.[13]

Randall Balmer suggests that white U.S. evangelicalism can be studied and theorized as a subculture, although he does not explain his concept of the evangelical subculture using Hebdige's language.[14] Rather, he uses "subculture" as a term that describes any minority or non-mainstream culture. His book is comprised of many short ethnographic vignettes exploring white U.S. evangelical communities and events, including a Billy Graham crusade meeting, the Christian Bookseller's Association convention, Chuck Smith's Calvary Chapel, a fundamentalist youth camp, and many others. He illustrates the variety of evangelical beliefs and practices, disabusing the perception of evangelicalism as monolithic and undifferentiated. For insiders, his objectivity and measured insight provide, if not outright sympathy, a contrast to secular writers and journalists who have tended to sensationalize evangelical culture.

Inasmuch as contemporary evangelicalism partly evolved from the Christian fundamentalism that became more visible in the United States following the Scopes Trial in 1925 (see the introduction), there are certainly trajectories of evangelical practice and belief that emerged—and continue to emerge—in response to secular mainstream culture. We should not paint white U.S. evangelicalism in its entirety as one subculture, however, because of the very variability that Balmer illustrates. Furthermore, the fact that some evangelicals may feel ostracized by segments of popular or secular culture does not mean that they are actively performing resistance—minority or marginal cultures are not automatically subcultures. That said, it is not difficult to find evangelicals who (loudly) voice opposition to aspects of mainstream culture that otherwise garner a majority of public support as incommensurate with their sincerely held religious beliefs (consider the opposition of many white U.S. evangelicals to abortion or gay marriage, for example). The Jesus People movement, which I discussed in chapter 1, is a prime example of white evangelical Christians who disrupted accepted modes of religious practice, worship, and ministry, in part because they felt alienated from dominant forms of Christianity. The Jesus People movement's ministers and converts participated in a subculture, and their practices—not to mention their music and other stylistic elements—were ultimately incorporated, to varying degrees, back into mainstream evangelicalism, mainline Protestantism, and post–Vatican II Catholicism.

The Birmingham School scholars (including Hebdige) often deploy subculture theory to analyze and explain opposition and resistance within youth cultures. Christian youth, as objects of study, have not been ignored: several scholars have examined twenty-first-century Christian youth culture from a variety of disciplinary perspectives. Some rely on the extensive quantitative and qualitative data collected by the National Study of Youth and Religion to describe and understand the spiritual and religious lives of U.S. teenagers.[15] Christian Smith and Melinda Lundquist Denton, for example, find that the most religiously committed teenagers (a minority of respondents: about 8 percent) have strong relationships with parents who are also religiously committed, and they also tend to be highly engaged in organized groups through their churches and elsewhere in their communities.[16] Kenda Dean, drawing from the same study, attempts to understand why what she terms "moralistic therapeutic deism" seems to have proliferated among nominally Christian teenagers in the United States.[17] Moralistic therapeutic deism defines a generic moral code without engaging any deeper theological discourse or religious commitment. Dean describes it as a superficial religious identity that "helps people be nice, feel good, and leaves God in the background."[18] She cautions that it acts as something of a "social placeholder" that requires little faith, devotion, or commitment: "Moralistic Theistic Deism is what is left once Christianity has been drained of its missional impulse, once holiness has given way to acculturation, and once cautious self-preservation has supplanted the divine abandon of self-giving love."[19] In contrast to the teens whom Smith and Denton describe as highly committed to religious practice, those who subscribe to moralistic therapeutic deism tend to lack a sufficient grounding in religious education or training. Ultimately, Dean blames not teenagers but those who should be their religious teachers—parents, pastors, ministers, elders—for lacking "robust Christian identities" that leave them unable to express a deeply or sincerely held understanding of the Christian faith. "Maybe teenagers' inability to talk about religion is not because the church inspires a faith too deep for words," she writes, "but because the God-story that we tell is too vapid to merit more than a superficial vocabulary. . . . We reap what we sow. We have received from teenagers exactly what we have asked them for: assent, not conviction; compliance, not faith."[20]

To be fair, most of those whom Dean might describe as moralistic theistic deists would probably self-identify as Christians, despite appearing to lack a robust Christian identity.[21] You can be both. In the eyes of the Christian market, devotion to one's religion is less important than one's own sense of identity. In other words, the question of how you think of yourself—Christian or not?—matters more than that of how scholars like Dean or Smith and Denton might categorize your degree of religious commitment based on how you respond to survey questions. Moralistic theistic deists who self-identify as churchgoing Christians do buy Christian music, attend Christian festivals, and listen to Christian radio. Christian music, after all, helps people be nice, feel good, and often leaves God in the background. Their pastors might be—probably should be—concerned about the watered-down theology that comprises and animates the most popular Christian music. But that question is all but irrelevant to decision-makers in the Christian market; it turns out that vapid and superficial music—whether we label it as Christian or as moralistic theistic deist—often sells better than music that challenges and confronts listeners' faith.

An important outcome of this discussion is that it reveals how, in the United States, a Christian identity or lifestyle does not always indicate a strong commitment to a Christian faith or religious practice. As with other religious identities, one might be culturally (but nonpracticing) Christian, a committed and devoted practicing Christian, or any degree between those two extremes. This is relevant to pastors like Joshua Stump and others at the Anchor Fellowship in Nashville, who encourage young congregants to invest in an "authentic faith" deeper than the fashionable Christian lifestyle that writer Brett McCracken demeans as mere "hipster Christianity."[22] But this question is perhaps less relevant to those actual young hipster Christians whose religious identity and lifestyle marginalize them among their peers. Peter Magolda and Kelsey Ebben Gross, for example, explicitly frame evangelical students' lifestyles at non-Christian colleges as oppositional and resistant to those of their (non-Christian) peers.[23] In their study, Christian students entered college already feeling marginalized due to different moral standards; once at college, they "find themselves on the margins within a dominant campus culture filled with students who demonstrate hedonism, individualism, and materialism—among other 'sinful' secular tendencies."[24]

Socializing with other Christians (instead of with non-Christian peers) serves multiple purposes: it provides a coherent, sympathetic, and distinct peer group; it articulates opposition to campus life norms (sometimes explicitly so); and it deepens their commitment to Christian values.

The Christian teenagers and college students in these studies often claim that their beliefs and lifestyles resist both a normalizing, mainstream culture—which they perceive as ethically permissive and dangerously secular—as well as the cultures of older generations of white U.S. evangelical Christians, whom they perceive as irrelevant and overly concerned with cultural separatism. In doing so, they participate in a longer narrative of countercultural Christianity in the United States, consciously or not, reaching back at least as far as the emergence of the Jesus People movement.[25] Subcultural resistance, in defining contemporary young Christians' liminality, thus describes the ways in which they make sense both of their faiths and of their relationships to organized religion and mainstream culture at large. These examples indicate that Balmer's concept of evangelicalism as subculture has taken root, both in the articulations and self-identifications of the Christian youth in question as well as in the theoretical frames and analyses of their observers.

RESISTANCE AND COMMUNITY AT CHRISTIAN MUSIC FESTIVALS

If navigating young adulthood is, in part, about navigating complicated social situations, hierarchies, and relationships (both romantic and not), then how do we measure the relative successes of young Christians who consciously choose not to participate in that social life? The answer lies in applying a Hebdigian lens—that is, in articulating measures of success that depend not on the norms of dominant (secular) culture but rather on those of marginalized Christians' resistant subculture. I admit that it is often not intuitive to think of white U.S. evangelical Christians as marginalized. (Magolda and Gross christen them "the marginalized majority."[26]) Christianity, after all, is the largest religion in the United States; more Americans self-identify as Christian than any other religious or faith identity; and the sincerely held religious beliefs, ethics, and morals of vocal Christians (particularly conservative evangelicals) have figured prominently in this country's public discourse and modern politics since at least the 1970s.[27] Christianity is conventional in ways that other subcultures are not. But if we look past Christianity's conventionality, we can find strategies in common with other subcultures. And when we do, we gain insight into the intersections of resistance and boundary making that we might otherwise miss precisely because Christianity is so conventional. Christian music may often look and sound normal, but in other ways it is decidedly *not* normal, and the lessons we learn from observing and analyzing it are different from what we learn from other, more obvious, subcultures.

Christian music festivals are ideal places to observe resistance in action within the Christian market (and the evangelical subculture more broadly). The biggest such events are the Creation Festivals, which have drawn over one hundred thousand attendees annually to two locations, one in central Pennsylvania in June and the other in southeastern Washington state in July. Creation started in 1979 and is among the longest-running and largest Christian festivals in the United States. To say that Creation is a known quantity would be an understatement; like the influence of Christian radio stations I discussed in chapter 2, Creation both reflects and generates the theologies and aesthetics of Christian music's mainstream. But I am only interested in the Creation Festivals to the degree that they define a dominant evangelical culture against which relatively niche festivals are reacting. These events may be smaller, but they are no less important to the attendees, the organizers, and the musicians and speakers that grace their stages. Indeed, given their smaller scale and more focused objectives, Cornerstone and AudioFeed are more effective at engendering and promoting cohesion and community among their attendees.

Like the collegiate groups that Magolda and Gross study (see above), Christian festivals allow attendees who might feel marginalized in their daily lives to convene with like-minded individuals and celebrate the things that make them different. Although festivals are ephemeral, occurring over only a few days every year, for many participants they are permanent: accessible as a memory (something in the past to reflect upon), as a destination (something in the future to anticipate), and as co-present, providing a broader context to situate themselves and others year-round outside of the festival.[28] In other words, Christian festivals are both conceptual spaces that far-flung participants project their idealized visions upon (or sentimentalize) and actual places that support musical scenes and subcultures (at minimum, by providing regular performance venues). Festivals are significant to participants in part because they are where imagined communities are made real and where many attendees feel the most accepted.[29]

Festivals are also often homogenous places, particularly when they are held at remote, rural sites whose geographic separateness reinforces the social and cultural boundaries of the festival's attendees and stakeholders.[30] Cornerstone may have welcomed a broadly diverse audience in theory, but in actuality it was difficult to access and often uncomfortable for those unfamiliar with white U.S. evangelical culture. For many of these attendees, however, Christian festivals like Cornerstone supplemented their local churches as the center of face-to-face congregational life. For others, the festival *became* their congregation: they found community and communion in prayer tents, at food courts, on the soccer field, and at the numerous concerts and seminars throughout the program. At times, resistance at the festival was obvious and explicit: confronting and opposing dominant norms about evangelical Christian culture, including issues of style, ethics, commerce, and theology. Festivals also provided sites of renewal, enabling places—however transient or ephemeral or dirty—for worship, transcendence, and reflection.

Congregation and Community at Cornerstone

At Cornerstone Festival, organizers promoted an inclusive, evangelical theology coupled with a resistant ideology—prioritizing, as Shawn David Young describes, "a subcultural aesthetic often absent from gatherings sponsored by the gatekeepers of establishment evangelicalism."[31] These themes were present in the musical and nonmusical official programming, ad hoc performances at attendee-operated "generator stages," formal and informal congregational worship, and branding strategies visible in marketing and social networking. This intentional programming attracted attendees who found that their tastes and styles set them apart from their church communities, while their faith set them apart from the secular music scenes in which they might otherwise have participated. Organizers and attendees alike framed Cornerstone's physical places and social spaces as an imagined community made manifest for a short time every year. To hear Luke Welchel explain Cornerstone is to hear it compared to one's spouse or children: "There's nothing you could love more than this thing. And there's nothing that can frustrate you more than this thing." He attended the festival at least fifteen times. "I loved it and I was extremely frustrated by it," he told me, "because it was really hot, and those showers were awful, and you spent a good half your day miserable. And if it rained you spent the other half of your day miserable. And in the middle, there was this awesome music, and all the bands you love, and just hanging out, and you made tons of friends. And so it was literally the worst and best thing."[32]

Over its twenty-nine years, Cornerstone established a reputation within the Christian market as a destination and a place to see niche Christian artists who often were not booked at the larger festivals and did not tour regularly. Many professionals in the Christian market recall Cornerstone fondly and with respect. Andy Peterson, a former executive at Word Records, told me, "I went to Cornerstone every year I was in college, and for the first six or seven years of my career here in Nashville. I went twelve years in a row."[33] John J. Thompson, a former executive at EMI CMG who used to direct much of Cornerstone's marketing efforts, attended it every single year: "When I first started going to Cornerstone in '84, I was thirteen, about to turn fourteen, and all the way through my teen years Cornerstone was all about The Choir, Altar Boys (🎧), Undercover (🎧), One Bad Pig (🎧). All very much '80s alternative youth punky stuff."[34] This "alternative punky stuff," he explained, was simply not present at other events: "Cornerstone was the mothership, it was exclusive, you couldn't find those bands anywhere else. . . . Cornerstone was just so radical compared to most Christian music back when I was a kid. Not only could you not see those bands at other festivals, but those other festivals wouldn't even think the Cornerstone stuff was Christian. There was no comparison."[35]

Tooth & Nail Records, which has focused on Christian punk, hardcore, and metal artists since its founding in 1993 (see chapters 5 and 7), had a symbiotic relationship with Cornerstone. Jeff Carver worked in A&R at Tooth & Nail when I interviewed him, and he explained the importance of the label's relationship with the festival:

> A lot of these more conservative festivals would never support our heavier bands. And that's still the case. There's Creation, and Spirit West Coast that are always a little hesitant to book in heavier bands. But Cornerstone's always been like, "Come one, come all," and I think has a similar mentality about the music as probably Tooth & Nail does as a whole. They probably just support artists where they're at, and I think [that] leaves a little freedom of interpretation for what exactly Christian art is, or faith-based art is. We love it. They have always been really good supporters of us.[36]

Jon Dunn, who plays bass guitar in Christian metal band Demon Hunter and also worked in A&R at Tooth & Nail, characterized Cornerstone as important to "underground" Christian rock: "Cornerstone used to be the only destination to see this huge Christian community and all this Christian music, [where] you could see your favorite bands all at one time. . . . Cornerstone is still the OG of the underground Christian music fests. Dirty dudes sleeping outside, no tents, sweltering heat, no water. That's all part of the charm."³⁷ Billy Power, who was the singer for Christian punk band Blenderhead and Tooth & Nail's general manager for ten years, recalled Cornerstone as a close community: "Playing at Cornerstone was huge. I remember playing the Underground Stage at Cornerstone; it was packed all the way back; as far as you could see was people. It was fun, the sense of community back in those days. That was the only time we'd see each other; we'd go play Cornerstone."³⁸

For many repeat attendees, the festival crowd was not an impersonal gathering or merely a focused community of fans with similar musical tastes. Rather, Cornerstone was an intimate congregation that was simultaneously ephemeral (in its limited temporality) and permanent (in its annual repetition). This perspective aligns with Gina Arnold's view of "the rock festival crowd [as] often a place, and maybe the only place, where people feel a sense of community with strangers and where they are able to briefly retrieve what industrial society has taken away: that is, a sense of interpersonal intimacy."³⁹ In the three years I attended and volunteered at Cornerstone, many attendees told me that it functioned more like a home church than any other congregation in which they had participated. At Cornerstone they found like-minded Christians with similar tastes and viewpoints. John Herrin, Cornerstone's former director, told me that "a lot of these folks live all over the country, and . . . interact everyday with people that are not like-minded. . . . This [festival] has been part of their lives and significant to them in their walk of faith, their friendships, what they're interested in."⁴⁰ Communal worship, offered every morning at the festival's main stage—complete with a jumbotron and enough space for fifteen or twenty thousand attendees—could feel impersonal at Cornerstone's peak. In the festival's last year (2012), however, only a few hundred congregants gathered under a large circus tent every morning for a worship experience that was more intimate and reminded nostalgic attendees of similarly powerful worship experiences during earlier years of the festival.

Everyone knew, before arriving at the festival grounds in 2012, that it would be the event's final summer. As Cornerstone drew to a close, attitudes of loss, resignation, thankfulness, and hope permeated the grounds, performances, seminars, prayers, and other sessions. Performers, attendees, festival staff, and volunteers mourned Cornerstone even as it was happening. In speaking with festival organizers and attendees during its final two years, I learned that those who did keep returning were longtime attendees. They had built and maintained an emotional attachment to their festival experiences and community over several years and decades. Many experienced a *greater* degree of community as the festival waned because they shared the event with a larger proportion of fellow longtime attendees, relative to the total festival audience; they were mourning not only the passing of the event but the disbursement of their congregation.[41] On the morning of Saturday, July 7, 2012—the final morning of the final Cornerstone, John J. Thompson moderated thirty minutes of reflections and memories, all of which were sincerely touching. He reflected that if Cornerstone could still be meaningful for attendees without fancy Main Stage production and major artists, then it was clearly not only about the music. Thompson later wrote that Cornerstone was his hometown: "These are my people, this is my tribe, my dysfunctional family."[42]

Rebuilding and Resistance at AudioFeed

AudioFeed picked up where Cornerstone left off, launching the following summer (2013). Its genesis lies in a large party that Welchel and others would organize for bands traveling to Cornerstone. After Cornerstone ended, friends asked him if he was going to continue the tradition. Welchel was conflicted: on one hand, he was content to move on from Cornerstone, but he also recognized that this was an opportunity to support a community that had lost its foundation: "Everyone was really upset and then nobody else started anything. . . . By default, we felt like we had to, or else there would be nothing. And I don't think any of us could live with there being nothing, in that sense. So we did it."[43] The timing was difficult: by the time Welchel and AudioFeed's other cofounders decided to move forward in March 2013, many bands and artists had already finalized their summer schedules. But they were ultimately able to put together a lineup featuring Cornerstone favorites (Flatfoot 56, The Choir, Michael Roe of the 77s, and Lost Dog), JPUSA artists (Glenn Kaiser of Rez, Ami Moss and the Unfortunate), and many others.

In the years since AudioFeed's first summer, Welchel and his colleagues have followed a more traditional timeline for booking and organizing the festival, starting as early as August or September to book artists for the following July. They prioritize marginal genres and styles over Christian music's mainstream when booking AudioFeed: like Cornerstone before it, the festival's aesthetic, commercial, ideological, and stylistic elements have more in common with contemporaneous emo, hardcore, metal, and punk rock than with contemporary Christian music (CCM), gospel, or praise and worship music. When I asked Welchel about his objectives for AudioFeed, he talked about his love for the community and its music and about the importance of supporting youth culture:

> I think our objective is to keep a strong place that bands can come and play, people can listen to the music, discover new bands, find the support of other people who are trying to do the same thing. Just to keep the art and the music scene alive, and in some ways maybe rebuilding it.... We want there to still be a place for kids to express themselves. Kids express themselves differently than I did ten years ago. The hardcore music is different than it used to be, hip hop is different, indie stuff is different. It's all different. And we want to give them that chance to do it.[44]

AudioFeed is a Christian event; on the website, a foregrounded belief in Jesus Christ is nevertheless accompanied by other goals: encouraging community, welcoming diversity (including religious diversity), and experiencing "great music and art with others who feel the same way."[45] Similarly, on the festival grounds Christianity is more a backdrop than a foreground: while there were some seminars, Bible studies, and worship services throughout the weekend, they were not the major emphasis of the festival. "There's some speakers, but that's not the goal," Welchel explained to me. "We're not trying to evangelize everybody through some ministry of that sort. We're just—we want people to come together, love each other, and listen to music."[46] Instead of religious conversion, the focus at AudioFeed is on creating a place for musical performance: for artists who identify as Christian or come from faith-centered backgrounds to perform for audiences who also identify as Christian or similarly come from faith-centered backgrounds, many of whom have little access to live music where they live or even face opposition in their home churches or religious communities due to stylistic elements (common in punk and metal) that mark them as different.

I witnessed no religious conversions at AudioFeed 2017, but while walking the festival grounds and attending concerts all weekend I did witness unbridled enthusiasm for music. In almost every impromptu conversation I had, we shared not our faith backgrounds but rather the bands we were excited to see. In 2017, artists such as David Bazan, Living Sacrifice, and Flatfoot 56 were among the most anticipated. Bazan, whom I discuss below, is a singer/songwriter whose lyrics simultaneously express a deep ambivalence about and a deep sincerity for the evangelical Christianity that structured much of his life. Living Sacrifice, an influential Christian metal band, reformed in

2008 after a five-year hiatus; their most recent album, *Ghost Thief*, explores concepts related to death and the afterlife, particularly in the song "Sudden" (🎧). Flatfoot 56, a Celtic punk band, were a highlight of Cornerstone for many Christian punks and are equally at home in general market punk venues.[47]

On one hand, it definitely matters who these artists are: they were AudioFeed's main attractions in 2017, and their musical and lyrical influences and themes bridge the always-porous boundaries between niche Christian music and its general market equivalents. From another perspective, however, it matters little who the actual artists are from year to year. What matters, rather, is that AudioFeed's attendees do not have regular access to this social and musical community outside of one weekend every year. From a classic subculture perspective, then, Audio-Feed functions as a site of resistance for participants who feel alienated from (multiple) dominant cultures: alienated from the dominant musical and stylistic norms of evangelical Christianity; alienated from the secularism of punk, hardcore, and metal scenes outside of Christianity; alienated, perhaps, from the dominant prescriptive worship and ministry emphases of other evangelical festivals and events; or even alienated from polarizing political discourses in the United States that so often appear to pit evangelical Christians against their neighbors.

CHRISTIAN ARTISTS: PROFILES IN RESISTANCE

The organizers of festivals like Cornerstone and AudioFeed intentionally enable and promote congregation (or community), resistance, and renewal at their events. They book artists and speakers whose diverse sounds, aesthetics, and messages challenge accepted norms of Christian music and dogmatic ideologies. They are open to learning more about their faith (and its expectations) from a wide array of voices and perspectives. And their attendees, more often than not, share similar ethics (even if they do not all share a similar taste in music)—they welcome the contradicting voices and confrontational guitars, they find clarity (and not confusion) in the cacophony. In other words, festivalgoers who enjoyed Cornerstone's congregation until its end and those who continue to return to AudioFeed every summer find these events satisfying because of the diversity and open-mindedness, not in spite of it. Many return home renewed in their faith; others return to their daily lives excited about new-to-them artists or even entire genres; still others find the fellowship they experience in the campsites and on the festival grounds to be affirming in ways that they do not experience among their friends, family, and fellow churchgoers at home, sustaining them for another year; several return with a new conviction for a social justice issue or political cause, ready to turn lessons from the seminar tents into actions in their local communities. If the massive Christian music festivals (like Creation) and worship conferences (like Passion) are, in part, about communicating the values of mainline Protestantism and mainstream evangelicalism in the United States—that is, about preaching conviction while teaching conformity—then the smaller niche events (like Cornerstone and AudioFeed) challenge the very notion of complacency without necessarily challenging the foundations of the Christian faith itself.[48] It is an important truth that niche markets and subcultures expand, not limit, the options available to all market participants, be they stylistic or ideological variations. In other words, unless your Christian faith is allergic to ideas or music that sounds divergent or progressive, you will find that these festivals' organizers, performers, and speakers encourage us to think more broadly about Christianity's capabilities, in terms of its aesthetics and ideologies. In the next few pages, I provide short artist profiles and examples of select performances at these festivals to illustrate the ways in which resistance and opposition enable participants to make and remake the boundaries of Christian music to suit their own needs and expectations.

The Chariot and Timbre

I first encountered The Chariot at Cornerstone 2009 when they played a midnight set on the second night of the festival at one of the two Encore stages. As I roamed the campgrounds the previous two days chatting with attendees about their Cornerstone experience, several told me to check out The Chariot—they were a band not to be missed. When I got to Encore 1 around 12:30 a.m. late on Tuesday, July 2, 2009, I understood why: this band was pure spectacle, both in terms of their music and their stage antics. Initially, I did not really know what to make of them. Encore 1 was a huge tent and it was difficult to see and hear what was going on. The band members climbed the stage's lighting rigs, and one of them blew fireballs out of his mouth. I can best describe their sound as experimental metalcore, exemplified in the early song "Dialogue with a Question Mark" (🎧): the murky, muddy, and dark tone; screamed vocals usually in sync with the distorted guitar, bass, and drums (making it difficult to hear any single

FIGURE 11. Josh Scogin of The Chariot performing at Cornerstone Festival 2010. Photograph by the author.

voice separately); and rhythmic discontinuities (a signature element of much metalcore) evidence musical precision and rehearsal—despite the noise and chaos, this was not a sloppy band—but made it hard for listeners to find a beat for dancing or headbanging. In slower, sparser moments, lead singer Josh Scogin (figure 11) makes his ambivalence clear in his vocals. For example, in the opening of "Abandon" (🎧), he asks, "Is this the blessing or a curse? / Should I belong to the trend?" He continues, "At least it's a tragedy / That'll only come once / . . . / The choir of men / They sing sanctuary in faith." From the perspective of a Cornerstone audience, Scogin seemed to describe the challenge of following one's faith in a secular world that is destined for Armageddon ("a tragedy that'll only come once"). And if you could get past the aural aggression, The Chariot's recordings (🎧) reward repeated listening with layers and nuance otherwise unnoticed in the chaos of the band's live performances.

The following summer's Cornerstone set was even more highly anticipated. It was another late-night gig at the Encore tent, scheduled for 12–1:30 a.m. late on Wednesday, June 30, 2010. I volunteered as a stagehand at the Gallery Stage that summer, and after setting up our final act I ran over to Encore with a coworker. Again, The Chariot inspired physical engagement among the audience: their intense moshing, crowd surfing, and climbing fixtures took cues from the bandmembers who threw themselves around the stage and even crowd surfed while still playing. The Encore tent was large enough to accommodate two mosh pits. The harpist and singer/songwriter Timbre (who plays on their song "David De La Hoz" [🎧], named after a fan who won a contest) and some other string players performed an interlude halfway through the set, until some commotion in the rear of the tent distracted us. The Chariot had setup a second line of equipment and instruments behind the sound console, where they played two or three songs on the floor with no lighting. Mosh pits moved, then moved back: the band played the rest of the show from the front stage where several guest vocalists I did not recognize joined Scogin; there was plenty more stage diving; the bassist buzzed off his multiyear beard; and they moved the entire drumkit to the center of the front mosh pit for the final songs. On our way back to the Gallery, my coworker remarked, "That was quite a performance."

Timbre Cierpke seemed to be everywhere at Cornerstone 2010: a 10 p.m. set at the Jesus Village on Tuesday, June 29; mewithoutYou's Main Stage set (7–8 p.m.) on Wednesday, June 30; The Chariot's set later that night; and her own official set at the Gallery on Friday, July 2. At the Gallery she was joined on stage by an accordionist (who doubled on glockenspiel and melodica), a bass guitarist, a drummer (who doubled on flute, guitar, and keyboard), an oboist, and a violinist (who doubled on toy piano) (see figure 12). Shortly after 2 p.m. she opened with a cover of Radiohead's "Like Spinning Plates" (🎧) that impressed me with an expansive arrangement that retained the atmosphere of the original without resorting to synthesized sounds and electronic effects. Her original song "I Will Go Plant Little Flowers" (🎧) was another crowd pleaser that, in its eclectic orchestration (using most of the instruments on stage), recalled the quirkiness of *Illinoise*-era Sufjan Stevens. At one point during her set, Timbre told the audience that her harp had been damaged by a crowd surfer during The Chariot's set the previous night. Repairing a harp is not cheap, and she asked the audience to buy her CDs (💿) and consider donating extra to help her cover the expenses. Timbre said that it was an honor to be playing the Gallery, where she had wanted to perform for as long as she had been coming to Cornerstone. An attentive and appreciative audience crowded the tent for her

FIGURE 12. Timbre performing at Cornerstone Festival 2010. Photograph by the author.

early afternoon set, and they gave her a long standing ovation when she and her band finished performing.

If The Chariot forces you to pay attention by pummeling your senses, Timbre is the opposite: she forces you to pay attention by playing immersive yet restrained songs that feature the interplay of her vocal melodies and harp accompaniment. The stylistic differences between the two are striking. The Chariot's sonic and performative chaos embody the very limits of the heavy, aggressive rock substyles (rooted in hardcore, metal, and punk) that seemed to be omnipresent in Cornerstone's waning years. You would be hard pressed to find a Cornerstone performance that was louder, crazier, or more assaultive. Timbre, on the other hand, approaches songwriting and performance with the ear of a classically trained musician and composer.[49] Her music is subtle and delicate, demanding a different kind of attention from the listener than does The Chariot. Neither artist addresses spirituality directly in their song lyrics, yet both have been comfortable self-identifying publicly as Christian and playing Christian venues (including Cornerstone). No other artist at Cornerstone sounded like either The Chariot or Timbre—both were unique there and in the broader Christian market. By resisting performative and stylistic norms and expectations, The Chariot and Timbre redefined and expanded Christian music's sonic possibilities.

David Bazan

As a founding member, lead singer, and main songwriter of the band Pedro the Lion, David Bazan has candidly discussed and sung about his journey of faith since 1997. His music career started in the Christian market before transitioning to the secular indie and emo markets. Like many other bands who undergo "fringe crossover" in this fashion (crossing from one niche market to another, which I discuss in chapter 7), Bazan has effectively straddled several markets, both Christian and non-Christian. Very early Pedro the Lion releases (🎧) featured songs in which Bazan's religious devotion is clear. For example, in the song "Lullaby" (🎧, on the band's 1997 debut EP *Whole*, released on Tooth & Nail Records), Bazan sings of the comfort and security he finds in God: "I know I'm understood / When I hear Him say: / 'Rest in me, little David and dry all your tears / . . . / And I'm all the strength that you need.'"[50] In other songs, Bazan sings about doubt in one's faith. In "Promise" (🎧), that doubt stems from a lack of apparent evidence: "Jesus said he'd fill my needs / But my heart still bleeds / He's just not physical." Bazan struggles with a core requirement of Christianity—that believers have faith despite a lack of evidence—in the song's chorus: "If I look up and the sky's not there / Is there any reason that I should be scared? / But a promise, is a promise, I know." The song "The Secret of the Easy Yoke" (🎧) is also about doubt, although in this case Bazan is doubtful of his faith in God ("I still have never seen you / And some days I don't love you at all") because his experience differs from the "perfect fire" of other churchgoers. He is critical of them: "The devoted were wearing bracelets / To remind them why they came [to church] / Some concrete motivation / When the abstract could not do the same." Other Christians acting the part, smiling faces and outstretched hands, also inform the later song "Foregone Conclusions" (🎧), in which Bazan sings of his frustrations with believers who are more concerned with being heard than hearing (whether from God or other humans): "You were too busy steering the conversation toward the Lord / To hear the voice of the

Spirit, begging you to shut the fuck up / You thought it must be the devil trying to make you go astray / Besides, it could not have been the Lord because you don't believe he talks that way."

Most Christians experience doubt at some point, and many attendees at Cornerstone and AudioFeed have found that other churchgoers and Christians often lack critical distance, the ability to listen instead of just waiting for their chance to speak, or even basic empathy, similar to the scenes that Bazan dramatizes in "Easy Yoke" and "Foregone Conclusions." In giving voice to that doubt, Bazan expresses a common truth that many often hide out of shame (because a "doubting Thomas" reveals a weak faith). Pedro the Lion was popular in the Christian market because when Bazan sang about these issues, he did so with a knowingness and vulnerability. Christian listeners often hear themselves in Bazan's songs: his experiences as a believer resonate with theirs more strongly than do those of other Christian artists. Thus his appeal, like that of Casting Crowns (which I discussed in chapter 5), can be explained by the authenticity of expression (telling the truth of oneself) and the authenticity of experience (telling the truth of one's listeners).[51] Bazan's appeal was also due to the fact that he was still a believer, even after doubt and temptation, and thus he provided a model of faith that was aspirational but also attainable: experiencing a weakness of faith was only temporary, and ultimately belief in God will sustain you through difficult moments. But all that appeared to change with his first solo album, *Curse Your Branches* (2009), in which Bazan came out as a nonbeliever critical of Christianity. In truth, he had been building toward this moment: he retired Pedro the Lion in early 2006 in part because his faith was already transitioning away from belief and toward agnosticism, and he no longer wanted a performing career saddled with the history of spirituality embodied within Pedro the Lion's identity.

Bazan turned to alcohol during this spiritual transition: in "In Stitches" (🎧), addressed to God, he sings, "All this lethal drinking / Is to hopefully forget / About you." The drinking was not a secret, and he was banned from Cornerstone in 2005 for drunkenness.[52] He returned to the festival in 2009, where I saw him perform at the Gallery Stage on Thursday, July 2, at 10 p.m. While waiting for Bazan to start, I struck up a conversation with a guy named Matt sitting next to me. He told me a story of how Bazan went on a tirade against organized Christianity and closed-mindedness the last time he performed at Cornerstone, and this was the first time he had been invited back in four years. This story is hearsay, Matt promised, but it was believable nonetheless: Bazan had long been a vocal critic of organized religion and church, believing instead that faith ought to be more personal and less didactic. During the set itself, Bazan played a couple of Pedro the Lion songs, a cover of Leonard Cohen's "Hallelujah," and several new songs. He also took questions from the audience. I have seen him perform many times, both before and since this concert, and this Q&A is a regular feature of his sets: he allows the audience to ask him practically anything they want, and he answers as honestly as possible. At Cornerstone he seemed a little reserved, perhaps wary of saying something that could be interpreted as being offensive. Although he has discussed Christianity with disdain elsewhere, it was clear that he was happy being there.

The music critic and journalist (and Bazan's former publicist) Jessica Hopper has written about his return to Cornerstone and her encounter with his Christian fans there who attempted to rationalize his newer songs within a framework of religious belief.[53] But Bazan is very clear about turning away from the God he had believed in for most of his life, after documenting his struggles with doubt and disassociation from organized Christianity in several of his songs: *Curse Your Branches* is very much a breakup record addressed to God. In "Hard to Be" (🎧), he finds the damnation of Eden (in Genesis 3) an unsatisfying explanation for the difficulties that humans (and humankind) encounter: "You expect me to believe / That all this misbehaving / Came from one enchanted tree? / And helpless to fight it / We should all be satisfied / With this magical explanation / For why the living die?" Here and in other songs, God's gift to humans of free will appears to be little more than entrapment, because he sets the conditions that allow for sin and failure. If God was truly all powerful, why would he enable his followers to stray from their faith? Bazan asks as much in the title track (🎧): "Digging up the root of my confusion / If no one planted it, how does it grow?" In the same verse, he is also confused about why God allows some believers to be content in their ignorance while gifting (or damning, as the case may be) others with skepticism that will not be satisfied by biblical arguments alone: "And why are some hellbent upon there being an answer / While some are quite content to answer 'I don't know'?" In "When We Fell" (🎧), he asks God directly about the paradox of being omniscient while granting free will: "When you set the table / And when you chose the scale / Did you write a riddle / That you knew they would fail?"

Even after breaking up with God, however, Bazan has remained welcome in some corners of the Christian market. In addition to his return to Cornerstone in 2009, he also performed at the first Wild Goose Festival in 2011, and I saw him at AudioFeed in 2017.[54] Prior to being banned from Cornerstone, David Bazan played there every year from 1999 to 2004 (a six-year stretch), plus the first three festivals that Cornerstone's staff organized at the Central Florida Fairgrounds in Orlando from 2003 to 2005. John Herrin, Cornerstone's former director, explained to Hopper why they welcomed Bazan back to the festival in 2009: "I know David has a long history of being a seeker and trying to navigate through his faith. . . . We're glad to have him back. We don't give up on people; we don't give up on the kids here who are seeking, trying to figure out what they don't believe and what they do. This festival was built on patience."[55] On one hand, Herrin's position was laudable: clearly he and his staff were willing to forgive Bazan his sins of drunkenness and overlook his sin of apostasy in giving him a stage and a platform to "navigate through his faith." And I do believe that Herrin's patience, at least with respect to one's spirituality, is as infinite as humanly possible: he is not a fire-and-brimstone evangelist, attempting to convert seekers and nonbelievers with a hard sell about salvation through belief in Jesus Christ. Rather, he has promoted a Christianity that welcomes questions and accepts all comers. That said, when Herrin spoke of his patience and of supporting those "trying to figure out what they don't believe and what they do," he was more likely than not rooting for Bazan (and "the kids who are seeking") to return to Christianity. Herrin was glad to have Bazan back at Cornerstone, but he would have been even happier to have Bazan back as a believer.

Given David Bazan's publicly known journey from faith to agnosticism, what do Christians continue to hear in his music? He spent the first phase of his career straining against the boundaries of his belief. The criticisms he lobbed at Christianity ultimately came from a place of love, of wanting Christianity to do better. Now when he criticizes Christianity, he does so from the perspective of one who has turned his back on the church and decided not to believe in God. His criticisms are similarly pointed, but they have a different emphasis: instead of asking Christianity to do better, he seems to be asking Christians to confront the contradictions of their faith, the Bible, and organized religion. Jessica Hopper suggested to Bazan that he performed at Cornerstone "trying to save the Christians," and his response confirmed this: "I am. I am really invested, because I came up in it and I love a lot of evangelical Christians. . . . They were seduced in the most embarrassing and scandalous way into a social, political and economical posture

FIGURE 13. David Bazan performing at AudioFeed Festival 2017. Photograph by the author.

that is the antithesis of Jesus's teaching."[56] And these audiences have seemed to welcome his observations. At AudioFeed 2017, he spent most of his between-song banter talking not about his faith but about white men needing to listen more to women, people of color, and the LGBTQ+ community (see figure 13). Bazan said that white men (and he explicitly included himself) need get out of the way and enable these other constituencies to run the country. When someone from the audience asked, "What really grinds your gears?" Bazan replied, following a lengthy silence, "White supremacy. Any other questions?" The audience laughed nervously, and I wondered then (and now) why they still listen to him. What is it about Bazan that subcultural Christians—those who resist some of the strict expectations of their church communities but still claim a biblically centered faith, which Bazan does not—remain open, willing, and eager to listen and learn from him?

For many who see Bazan perform at secular venues, his crises and criticisms of faith often map onto the journeys we ourselves have also undertaken: from a position of faith and belief through doubt to an articulated atheism or agnosticism based, in part, on a lack of trust in organized Christianity. To these audiences, Bazan speaks a truth grounded in similar experiences. We nod knowingly at concerts, having asked ourselves (and God) the same questions that Bazan sings from stage. For those who continue to identify as Christians, however, Bazan presents a conundrum: he used to speak truth grounded in belief, but now that he professes not to believe in Christ, how seriously should they take him? A broader version of this question is asking what, if anything, can Christians learn about their faith from non-Christians? AudioFeed's Welchel suggested that if "you're looking through that lens [of traditional Christianity], Bazan is just like, 'Hey, this is what I think, you should think for yourself.'"[57] The fact that, as an organizer of a Christian event, Welchel was open to the idea of questioning one's faith and thinking for yourself illustrates a key point of resistance among subcultural Christians, one that resonates with Bazan himself (in "Curse Your Branches"): instead of being content with answering "I don't know"—instead of conforming to the unquestioning obedience that God demands, which many are taught in church—they are willing to question the assumptions of their faith, "hellbent upon there being an answer" or not.

CONCLUSION: RESISTANCE AS IDENTITY, RESISTANCE AS LITURGY

If festival organizers build physical places to resist a normalizing status quo, then musicians often give voice to the space of resistance: they articulate opposition in ways explicit and implicit, legible and illegible, loud and soft, coherent and confused. Christian punk bands like MxPx or Flatfoot 56, both of which played Cornerstone many times, use musical and thematic genre norms that would be easily legible in the general market counterpart of their niche (punk rock) to teach lessons of community, brotherhood, humility, and a faith that can sustain when community cannot. But despite punk rock's commercial success, these bands have remained on the margins of the Christian market. Punk rock may no longer be as subversive as it was at its emergence, but it remains a powerful articulation of resistance, particularly among youth. The Chariot, on the other hand, has charted a stylistic course grounded in metalcore that thrives on abrasiveness and sonic aggression. Singer Josh Scogin's lyrics are abstract, and his musical style is confrontational. In the waning years of Cornerstone, youth attendees flocked to sets by Christian metalcore stalwarts such as Haste the Day, Norma Jean (Scogin's former band), and UnderOath (who was still touring in support of their 2008 album *Lost in the Sound of Separation* when they headlined Cornerstone the following summer, when I first attended); the resistance that The Chariot poses would have been understood by those listeners as expanding that genre's sonic norms, while other attendees would have heard yet another heavy band that merely sounded louder and more chaotic than most. In direct contrast, Timbre's music is easier to listen to: quieter, more melodic, and with intelligible vocals. The years that I attended Cornerstone, many found her sets to be a breath of fresh air among the noise pollution of official and unofficial stages that mostly booked variations on punk, metal, and hardcore. Her resistance is also stylistic, in that she confronts and confounds the expectations of the young listeners that John Herrin courted at Cornerstone—even performing on the same stage as The Chariot—expanding what Christian music might be.

Singer/songwriter David Bazan, whose band Pedro the Lion crossed over from the Christian to the secular indie and emo markets (a transition I discuss in chapter 7 as "fringe crossover") in the late 1990s and early 2000s, has been public about distancing himself from Christianity after the band went on hiatus in early 2006.[58] But despite his spiritual transition, Bazan has kept performing at Cornerstone, AudioFeed, and other Christian venues (in addition to his concerts at general market venues). To these audiences, he speaks and sings as someone who knows white U.S. evangelicalism natively. His message (and the resistance he embodies) is one of clarity, of asking difficult questions, and of validating the act of questioning itself.

The social spaces and physical places of festivals are core components of the subcultures that populate them. The fact that they reemerge and rebuild in the same location at the same time year after year after year cements them as permanent features in participants' lives. Processes of ritual and pilgrimage play very clear roles in festival experiences as well. For longtime, regular Cornerstone attendees, the festival became an annual ritual where they resumed their friendships with their Cornerstone family, saw concerts they could not attend closer to home, and encountered new musicians and friends every year. Even the preparations, road trips, camp showers, porta-potties, and unpredictable weather became familiar, routinized, and tolerated, if not necessarily enjoyed. Many former Cornerstone attendees continue these rituals at AudioFeed, and while the scope and atmosphere may be different, the goal of gathering with music fans of similar tastes and with Christians of similar theologies has remained an annual tradition. In many ways, the communities of festivalgoers that gather at these festivals exemplify a "counterpublic" in enabling what Shawn David Young and others have characterized as the "evangelical left's" response to dominant socially and politically conservative ideals.[59] Inside the festival, a cohesive congregation manifests for a brief time every year in resistance to the dominant norms experienced in attendees' daily lives. When they work—when a critical mass of attendees, organizers, musicians, and speakers find Christian festivals like these to be important and meaningful aspects of their lives and faith practices—resistance becomes an essential component of identity, and community becomes an essential component of lived experience. When subculture is ritualized as faith, resistance itself becomes liturgical.

7

From Margins to Mainstreams and Back

Crossover Cases and Their Markets

In part 1 of this book, I discussed the growth and expansion of the Christian market from a relatively niche market with few resources to a relatively mature market, able to sustain major artists such as Amy Grant, by the 1980s. For a short period in the early 1980s, the Christian market actively pursued general market success for its artists. In 1984, *CCM* magazine's editor, John Styll, reflected on this period as a "crossover mania" that targeted the "secular promised land." Importantly, the stated objective was one of evangelism: "to get gospel product into the secular distribution pipeline and onto the pop radio stations seemed to fulfill both spiritual and financial goals," Styll wrote. "While reaching the lost we could also land the pot of gold at the end of the rainbow."[1] By the middle of the decade, however, the Christian market had largely abandoned the idea of converting nonbelievers; instead of "reaching the lost," Christian labels, radio stations, and artists were providing what Styll later labeled "sanctified entertainment" for listeners who already identified as Christians.[2] This amounted to an admission that non-Christians were not interested in music with an explicitly Christian or conversion message: Styll noted that "music which contrives a message aimed at non-Christians usually fails to attract their attention."[3] It was also an admission that the Christian market's commercial potential was not yet great enough to attract serious attention from general market record labels.

As the 1980s progressed, however, the Christian market changed in three significant ways. First, as I discussed in chapter 2, executives at the three largest Christian labels (Benson, Sparrow, and Word) signed distribution agreements with general market labels, intending not to reach the lost but rather to introduce Christian listeners in the general market to sanctified entertainment. Sparrow's founder and owner, Billy Ray Hearn, admitted as much to *CCM* magazine when he partnered with MCA: "I think we are going to sell a lot more records to a lot more Christians. The main purpose is not to sell a lot of Christian records to 'secular' people. . . . There are a lot of Christian people who don't know about our records yet."[4] Second, Amy Grant's unparalleled success in the Christian market and ability to produce contemporary-sounding pop music made her a prime candidate for a serious crossover attempt on the part of her record label, Word, and its general market distributor, A&M. As I discussed in chapter 4, her 1986 album *Unguarded* yielded her first single to chart on *Billboard*'s Hot 100. Four general market singles from her 1991 album *Heart in Motion* charted in the top ten, and the album itself ultimately sold over five million copies, on a par with other major pop singers of the era, demonstrating that integrational Christian artists could succeed in the general market.[5] And third, apart from Grant's commercial success, general market record executives noticed the Christian market's pace of growth, and each of the three major labels ultimately acquired existing Christian record labels and invested in the Christian market (as I discussed in chapter 3). By the turn of the century, the needs and fortunes of the three major Christian label groups (at the time, EMI's Christian Music Group, Sony's Provident Label Group, and Warner's Word Records) were practically intertwined and indivisible from those of their corporate parents. Following this period of convergence, the Christian market shared resources with the general market. What else did they share? Artists? Audiences? Modes of mediation, production, and consumption?

Crossover is especially suited to questions like these because moments of crossover signify the convergence and intersection of markets otherwise thought to be distinct. "Crossover" typically describes niche music that achieves commercial success in a larger market. Within music industries, this is indicated by an artist moving up the ranks of a niche or genre-specific chart (such as the Christian, classical, country, jazz, Latin, or R&B charts) and then "crossing over" to a more mainstream chart, such as the *Billboard* Hot 100 singles chart. From this perspective, it makes intuitive sense that executives at Sony, Warner, and EMI (and later Universal) would pursue and expect crossover hits from their Christian subsidiaries. Their mandate, after all, is to increase their companies' overall market share and profitability for their investors and shareholders, something that crossover hits and artists are uniquely poised to do, given their successes in multiple markets.

David Brackett dates the term *crossover* in popular music industry discourse to the early 1970s, when it broadly described "movement between musical categories" but frequently meant "attempting to broaden [one's] audience by courting mainstream success."[6] This more specific definition mirrors the standard music industry use of the term, necessarily privileging the needs of major labels and positioning niche markets as tributaries to mainstreams in a hierarchy defined by commercial success. For Brackett, crossover clearly contests the boundaries of musical categories (including markets), although predictions of and reactions to its effects on both niche and mass markets were often met with unease. This unease, Brackett suggests, is often tied to social, economic, and aesthetic concerns. How does crossover impact a niche market's audience, especially when audiences' differences are characterized by demographic distinctions? (What happens, for example, to the relationships between African American listeners and paradigmatic Black musics—funk, gospel, hip hop, soul—when those genres cross over to white markets?) Is a crossover artist better off as a big fish in a small pond or as a little fish in an ocean of choice and competition? How might the expectations of crossover impact artists' aesthetic choices when writing, recording, and performing music?

David Bruenger takes a different approach to crossover, conceiving of it as indicating movement between categories not on the part of an artist, but rather on the part of consumers, who move "from one demographic category to another to buy records."[7] Doing so effectively abandons the problematic practice of assuming homological relationships between musical categories and audience demographics. It also helps us move past the limiting perspective of crossover as a one-way transition from a niche to a mass market—a perspective that echoes (and thus reinforces) the commercial priority of the major labels. I find it productive to define crossover even more broadly, as a gradual or sudden transition from one market (the source) to another (the target). Crossover can certainly be about breakthrough commercial success, of course: about moving from margins to mainstreams, or transitioning from a niche to a mass market. But it can also be about parallel shifts: from one niche market to another, in a process I term "fringe crossover," or from one mass market (or mainstream) to another.[8] And crossover also includes transitions from a mass market to a niche market: a "crossing back" that reverses an earlier crossover from niche to mass.⁹ Although most artists, their management, and their labels might not consider this transition to be a success, it can be a strategy to achieve a sustainable, long-term career in a niche market that offers more stability than a mainstream one.

Crossover impacts the boundaries of music markets in ways both obvious and audible and also in ways less so. In many cases of successful crossover, the most audible impact is the growing sonic diversity of the target market: as listeners are exposed to previously unfamiliar styles, crossover artists gain new audiences. Other artists and producers integrate new musical influences, and the market's aesthetic values change to accommodate these transitions. Crossover successes, especially those that are part of a larger trend, help explain changes in how mainstream pop *sounds*. During the early '90s, for example, Top 40 radio (and, by extension, mainstream pop itself) became noticeably less poppy and more rocking, due in part to the crossover success of grunge artists that resulted in "alternative rock" becoming a dominant commercial radio format for the rest of the decade (recall Nirvana's 1991 album *Nevermind* symbolically dethroning Michael Jackson's *Dangerous* from atop the *Billboard* 200 album chart in January 1992). Crossover often indicates the moment in which an entire niche market starts to draw mainstream attention: consider, for example, the commercial exploitation of rock and roll in the 1950s, of hip hop in the 1980s, and of electronic dance music in the early twenty-first century. Crossover hits of these eras—for example, Elvis Presley's early singles, Run D.M.C.'s collaborative cover of Aerosmith's "Walk This Way," or David Guetta's 2009 singles (off of *One Love*)—are signposts that index the major labels' investments in these (formerly) niche markets. These investments are visible in a bigger marketing campaign, a larger recording budget, promotional appearances on late-night TV shows, bookings at major festivals, and an international tour—all of which are meant to sell more singles, records, concert tickets, and T-shirts to an ever-growing audience. The majors, after all, expect returns on their investments.

This, then, is what we *hear* when we talk about crossover: the mainstream becomes, in turns, grittier, Blacker, slicker, more twangy, worldlier, more electro, sexier, less sexy. But how does crossover sound when it is a parallel transition, from mainstream to mainstream or from niche to niche? If crossover expands the aesthetic boundaries of the target market, what happens to the source market, especially as more and more artists try to achieve crossover? What does reverse crossover sound like, when an artist crosses back from a mainstream to a niche? If crossover largely indicates a commercial imperative—given that markets themselves are locations of commerce, exchange, and trade—then how does it impact the ideological (or theological) values of both the source and the target markets? In the rest of this chapter, I examine several different crossover examples to provide a framework through which we might answer these and similar questions. Later in the chapter, I consider the ways in which crossover is fraught, at least from the perspective of those invested in the source markets, who often deride it as "going mainstream" or "selling out." Insights into the decision-making processes at Christian record labels (both large and small) help illustrate how crossover strategies within music industries changed in the 1990s and early 2000s. The careers of indie stalwart Sufjan Stevens and Christian metalcore bands such as UnderOath provide good examples of "fringe crossover," or the transition from one niche market to another—not exactly a careerist move, but one increasingly important for artists in marginal genres hoping to find more stability.

CROSSOVER OBJECTIVES

Because crossover is so commonly associated with seeking a larger audience for a greater degree of commercial success, Christian record label executives have foregrounded other reasons for pursuing it: sanctified entertainment, for example, for Christian listeners in the general market. But for Christian labels' corporate parents, the objective of crossover has been straightforward and not at all circumspect. From the perspectives of executives at the major labels, successful crossover strategies yield more sales and revenue, and they thus align perfectly well with their need to maximize revenue and prioritize profit. That is, while the Christian labels have justified crossover *despite* its clear commercial potential, the majors have wanted their Christian subsidiaries to cross artists over into the general market *precisely because* doing so can be so profitable. It is important to note that these apparently competing objectives are not mutually exclusive; in fact, they strengthen the argument for institutional support of crossover strategies at Christian labels and in other markets where participants might view commercial success with some distrust. Although the majors and their Christian subsidiaries might have had different objectives, the fact that both sides have seen value in pursuing crossover has made it easier to do so.

This, at least, was still the perspective in 2002 when Andy Peterson started working in marketing for Word following a succession of roles at several independent Christian record labels. Warner had just acquired Word, and as Peterson explained to me, the atmosphere at the time was one that promised collaboration between the major label and its new Christian subsidiary, with access to Warner Bros. staff and resources to promote hit records in the general market. "We were going to be fully integrated," Peterson recalled. "That was the idea, and of course that sounds great! And of course, the reality of it was, of course, that's not going to happen."[10] Peterson's team at Word had inherited successful crossover artists Grant, P.O.D., and Sixpence None the Richer. They had also inherited a major label-scale appetite for record sales, and there was significant pressure to produce crossover hits. Word thought they had one in Mutemath: the band's 2004 debut EP *Reset* did well in both the Christian and general markets, and their song "Control" (🎧) won the 2005 Dove Award for Best Modern Rock Song.[11]

The plan was for Word to work together with Warner and promote Mutemath in both Christian and general markets, with the band's agreement: "They were open to having their product available in Christian retail," said Peterson. "When we put the EP out, we worked it to Christian rock radio, with the full knowledge and support of the band. The band performed at Gospel Music Week here in Nashville, at the Word showcase [in April 2005]. They were there, they agreed to do that." But as Mutemath started to attract media attention, they changed their minds about working with Word. As Peterson recalled, the band "realized that any level of this [Christian] industry 'stink' on them was going to be potentially damaging to who they wanted to be, and the audience they wanted to reach. . . . They realized that they could not be successful if Word was involved in that way."[12] Thinking that they had a better chance at general market success if they were not a "Christian" band, the band members decided that they no longer wanted to be affiliated with Word and sued Warner to be released from their contract.

Peterson was torn. While he understood the band's desire not to be marketed as a Christian band—"I agreed with that philosophy and promoted that philosophy," he told me—he also knew that Mutemath was a key artist for Word: "The guys that I reported to were fighting for their very existence, and needed desperately to claim a hit. And if we couldn't put our name on it, and we couldn't claim it, then they were doomed."[13] After a protracted legal battle, Warner and Mutemath reached an agreement: Warner renegotiated their contract, eliminating

Word's role (and effectively pulling Mutemath from the Christian market), and the band stayed with Warner and ended the lawsuit. This solution, while it benefitted both Mutemath and Warner, left Word without the hit the label's executives needed to sustain crossover as a legitimate strategy. Mutemath was not Word's only failed crossover attempt, but it was a costly failure: after the conflict was resolved, Warner replaced Word's leadership team and reoriented the label away from general market crossover to focus on the Christian market entirely. "And they were right to let us all go, because none of us wanted to do that; none of us had any interest in doing that," Peterson reflected. "We had all been doing that in our careers prior to that. The whole reason we were there was to reach the secular culture."[14]

Wayne Kusber, who started working A&R at a major Christian record label after Peterson's experience at Word, was so focused on the Christian market as the center of his professional objectives that he thought of general market crossover as peripheral. Nonetheless, he and his colleagues still attempted crossover from time to time—what he described as taking "strategic shots at the periphery"—but in doing so, they confronted several issues. The biggest issue was that the general market was more competitive than the Christian market—there were simply more artists vying for cultural intermediaries' and listeners' attention. Furthermore, it was less loyal: Kusber found it easier to build and sustain an artist's audience in the Christian market, where listeners were more likely to stick around. In contrast, in his experience general market audiences were more fickle: "If the hits aren't there, they're not going to go buy a ticket repeatedly to stay connected to the band and go out and see them live."[15] Because the general market was simply larger and less well-defined, it could be more difficult to identify and connect with listeners in the first place. In the Christian market, Kusber noted, "we have a focused audience, a defined audience that we're going after." Whereas, in the general market, "they don't necessarily have that.... We just have a little more defined parameters of the community that we're going after within which to work. It's smaller, but it can be more rabid if they really like what you do."[16] In short, not only was it more difficult and more expensive to establish a crossover hit in the general market, Kusber was not even sure it was worthwhile, given his success establishing sustainable careers in the Christian market. Finally, a remaining tension was the same one that Mutemath was trying to avoid in 2005 and that has afflicted Christian artists trying to appeal to a general market audience: there were "gatekeepers," Kusber said, who dismissed artists preemptively simply for identifying as Christian. "We don't play those kinds of artists," Kusber has heard. "We don't play Christian music; we don't play Christian artists. I don't care how great the song is, I don't want it."[17]

INTEGRATION AND INCORPORATION

If Amy Grant's "Baby, Baby" was the proof of concept for a crossover from Christian to general market, then it was also its high-water mark. The fact that Kusber was still encountering anti-Christian bias in 2010, coupled with Mutemath's wariness of being known as a Christian band in 2005, suggests that not much had changed among general market cultural intermediaries since Amy Grant and her management were strategizing around crossover in the mid-1980s and early 1990s. In contrast, however, the Christian market was changing: the growing involvement of the major labels, their push for crossover, and the period of increased commercial pressures following Grant's success exacerbated tensions over the appropriate role and purpose of Christian music in the first place. Recall, from the introduction, Jay Howard and John Streck's categories of Christian music: separational, integrational, and transformational.[18] These categories help us understand how attitudes of crossover might be linked to ideological and theological priorities in the Christian market. If you believe, for example, that Christian artists have a mission to preach the gospel through their music and that participating in secular culture as a professional artist dilutes and pollutes this mission, then you subscribe to the separational paradigm. Crossover is anathema to you, and indeed can be instructive inasmuch as it informs you which artists to avoid and even criticize: "Success beyond the gospel [sales and airplay] charts, then, is read by some as evidence that an artist has moved outside the realm of God."[19] If you believe, however, that Christian artists can fulfill their calling by providing what Howard and Streck (after Styll) call sanctified entertainment, then the integrational model suits your sensibilities and directs you toward crossover as a way to enact positive change in line with your religious beliefs.[20] This discourse about crossover returns us to some of the longest-lived debates within the Christian market. Artists, listeners, and cultural intermediaries have been arguing about the intent, appropriateness, utility, and boundaries of Christian music since the late 1960s and '70s, as discussed in chapter 1. By the 1990s, the demonstrated potential for reaching a much larger audience (and making a much larger amount of money in the process) through crossover foregrounded these debates again.

These arguments between separational and integrational paradigms are not unique to Christian music. Certainly, few other markets are concerned with evangelism and ministry as a potential core objective. But participants in many other niche markets, music scenes, and subcultures do participate in similar debates. Some participants argue that their shared values are at odds with those of a mainstream and are best served by remaining as separate as possible, while others argue that the best way to impact that mainstream and change its values is by integrating into it. Howard and Streck recognize this, relating R. Serge Denisoff's discussion of the mainstreaming of 1960s-era protest music as a non-Christian example of transition from separational to integrational.[21] Another example is the long-standing debate within do-it-yourself (or DIY) underground rock over "selling out," or compromising one's music and/or ideology (and, by extension, one's music community) in order to achieve commercial success. DIY underground rock participants, almost by definition, are distrustful of mainstream music industries and their infrastructures. Michael Azerrad's history of the "American indie underground" profiles thirteen bands and the networks in which they circulated during the 1980s.[22] He ends each band's narrative either when they broke up or when they signed to a major label, noting that "virtually every band did their best and most influential work during their indie years; and once they went to a major label, an important connection to the underground community was invariably lost."[23] Although bands like Hüsker Dü, The Replacements, Sonic Youth, and others initially recorded for indie labels partly out of necessity—major labels were simply not interested in punk rock, hardcore, and post-punk at the time, despite signing several punk and new wave bands in the 1970s such as Blondie, the Ramones, Talking Heads, and others—doing so came to signify an act of cultural and economic resistance that resonated with the politics and ethics of these artists and their broader communities. For the indie underground, these artists' signing with a major label (Hüsker Dü with Warner Bros., The Replacements with Warner subsidiary Sire, and Sonic Youth with DGC, at the time also a subsidiary of Warner) was interpreted as compromising or abandoning their communities' ethics and politics.

It is tempting to talk about Christian music as if it were subcultural in ways similar to punk, hardcore, and post-punk. As I detailed in chapter 6, subcultural resistance can often be useful in describing the relationships between niche and mass markets in general, between the Christian and general markets specifically, and even within the Christian market: between its margins (Christian punk, metal, and so on) and center (Christian music's "core" or mainstream). Dick Hebdige argues that a key feature of subcultures is that they borrow styles or other cultural elements from the dominant culture but imbue them with new meanings; in a sense, this is also an example of crossing over.[24] In a similar way, the Christian market resignifies cultural elements (that is, popular music styles and infrastructures) to suit its own purposes. Rock and roll is no longer the music of disaffected youth but rather unites believers in a communal act of Christian worship; pop songs about love refer not to carnal lust but to parental love ("Baby, Baby") or the singer's love of God (so-called "Jesus is my boy/girlfriend" songs); the industry itself exists not principally to profit but instead to make the ministry of Christian artists accessible to as broad a public as possible. These new meanings are legible and important to insiders yet often misunderstood or even unseen by outsiders; facility with these (and other) examples of insider knowledge marks participants as belonging to a particular subculture, constituting what Sarah Thornton has termed "subcultural capital."[25] In other words, if you are a subcultural insider, you know things that outsiders do not (and which they may not even value); conspicuously consuming, displaying, and otherwise acting upon this knowledge defines you as an insider to other subcultural insiders.

At least, that is, until outsiders start to learn about and infiltrate your subculture. Hebdige writes that the stylistic innovations of subcultures often attract the attention of the dominant culture.[26] The mass media often erupts in a moral panic over the deviant or antisocial aspects of a subculture (see chapter 3) before its stylistic innovations are incorporated into the mainstream, "codified, made comprehensible, rendered at once public property and profitable merchandise" (see chapter 6).[27] For Hebdige, incorporation is a necessary, final step in a subculture's life cycle. Jason Toynbee describes this process as "mainstreaming," in which larger markets are always shaping themselves in response to their margins. The act of mainstreaming, for Toynbee, is reciprocal: niche markets emerge in response to mainstream hegemony; marginal musics increasingly become centered within larger markets following "a popular urge to find an aesthetic of the centre, or stylistic middle ground."[28] Through mainstreaming and acts of incorporation, Hebdige argues, subcultures are defused, diffused, and made safe for mass consumption.

Consider the incorporation of emo as an instructive tale. Although emo was rooted in the DIY American indie underground in the 1980s and '90s, it began to be incorporated when several bands (and then the niche market itself) achieved commercial success and mainstream recognition in the late '90s and early 2000s. Andy Greenwald's contemporaneous book documents, perhaps unwittingly, the shifts that a niche undergoes as it is incorporated, both via major labels and media publicity: the emo scene's collaborative nature became increasingly precarious as it attracted more and more fans unfamiliar with its participatory ethics.[29] For example, bands such as Jimmy Eat World and Death Cab For Cutie had to learn new ways of interacting with fans whose expectations were shaped by mainstream celebrity culture, following the crossover success of songs like "The Middle" and "Soul Meets Body." Instead of hanging out at a bar with fans or crashing on someone's living room floor after a basement show, artists themselves became commodities: they signed autographs, sold T-shirts, and were segregated from their fans on tour buses, behind security fences, and in well-appointed backstage green rooms. And while later emo bands like Fall Out Boy and My Chemical Romance similarly emerged from DIY scenes, they foregrounded emo's fashion so successfully that detractors criticized the market, its bands, and their fans for promoting style over substance. Indeed, like "punk" in earlier iterations, "emo" became shorthand for a particular form of youth fashion.

The division between a mass market (major record labels, mainstream media) and a niche market (indie labels, DIY scenes) is replicated at the aesthetic level ("their best work," as Azerrad writes) as well as the social level ("an important connection to the underground community"). This relates to the ways in which ethics (see chapter 5) are intertwined within and differ between markets. Crossover, incorporation, and mainstreaming blur these divides, sometimes breaking them down entirely. An artist's successful participation in a niche market is codependent on and co-constitutive with utilizing that niche's infrastructure. In other words, if recording for an indie label marks you as an indie artist and authenticates you to the indie underground, then the parallel is clear: recording for a Christian label similarly marks you as a Christian artist, for better and for worse. When artists in genres like indie, emo, punk, and others cross over, they often make similar justifications—arguing for the benefit of reaching new audiences in mass markets—while facing similar charges of abandoning the values of their original (or source) market (and thus of their original fans). This is, in part, about authenticity within markets, an authenticity related not to one's experience in a particular socioeconomic class (as Hebdige would argue) but instead both to the values of individual markets and to the "affects, actions, and politics" that emerge from these values in a process that Jason Middleton describes as "the production of authenticity."[30] An important characteristic of this type of authenticity is that it is not intrinsic to a given artist, performance, or recording, but rather—as Allan Moore argues—is ascribed or adjudicated by audiences, cultural intermediaries, and other artists through a discursive process of authentication (see chapter 5).[31] Authenticity, seen this way, is not an inherent quality but an ongoing product (and process) of negotiation that involves other participants within music markets. Ultimately, it is not only musical style that links artists to markets, but also all of these other extra-musical elements. Thus, crossover is not only about a musical style becoming newly popular in another market—it is also about artists navigating between the different ethical, social, and ideological expectations as they cross from one market to another.

FRINGE CROSSOVER

At the beginning of this chapter, I argued that crossover need not always be about upward mobility or crossing from a relatively niche to a mass market. If crossover is about crossing between markets, then it also includes parallel and even downward mobility. There are many examples of artists who cross from the Christian to the general market. Amy Grant is the most well-known and successful example. Michael W. Smith similarly crossed from Christian music's mainstream to the Top 40 mainstream in the early '90s. On the other hand, Christian bands Sixpence None the Richer, Chevelle, and P.O.D. had not experienced much success in the Christian market prior to their respective Hot 100 hits—"Kiss Me" (🎧), #2 in 1999; "The Red" (🎧), #56 in 2002; and "Alive" (🎧), #41 in 2002). Pop singer Katy Perry debuted in the Christian market with her 2001 Christian album *Katy Hudson* but ultimately failed; she later emerged as a Top 40 artist with the singles "I Kissed a Girl" and "Hot n Cold" in 2008.[32] These artists provide good examples of crossover from a niche to a mass market.

Other artists transition from one niche to another: Damien Jurado, Pedro the Lion (see chapter 6), Sam Phillips, Starflyer 59, and others all started their careers on the margins of the Christian market before transitioning to the general market, where they have remained relatively niche. Sufjan Stevens, for example, started in the world of Christian indie, performing with freak-folk/fringe Christian artist Daniel Smith and his band Danielson Famile (also known as Danielson Family, or sometimes just Danielson) before transitioning to a solo career as an indie artist in the general market.[33] For his series of Christmas EPs, collected in the compilations *Songs for Christmas* (2006) and *Silver & Gold* (2012), Stevens recorded traditional Christmas carols and original Christmas songs. Several of the recordings are whimsical: one can imagine recording "We Wish You a Merry Christmas" (🎧) during a celebratory sing-along over mugs of mulled wine following a holiday potluck. Many others are explicitly religious, respectful of Christian sacred music: "Come Thou Font of Every Blessing" (🎧) opens with just Stevens's voice over a lightly strummed banjo, expands to a slightly fuller arrangement in successive stanzas, then ends in unaccompanied chorale harmony.

Of course, it is common for both Christian and general market artists to release Christmas albums. Yet Sufjan Stevens is one of only a few indie artists in the general market whose Christmas recordings clearly reflect a sincere engagement with Christian beliefs.[34] Stevens has never been evasive about his faith, elements of which are thematically foregrounded in his 2004 album *Seven Swans* ("The Transfiguration," 🎧) and 2015's *Carrie & Lowell* ("The Only Thing," 🎧), inspired by his estranged mother's death. Indeed, much of the critical reaction to *Carrie & Lowell*, both in the Christian and the general market press, identified and even welcomed Stevens's faith as an integral element of the album. "I still describe myself as a Christian," he told the website *Pitchfork* unequivocally in 2015, "and my love of God and my relationship with God is fundamental."[35]

Tooth & Nail Records has become something of a specialist in fringe crossover. Founded in 1993, the label quickly established itself as a leading Christian independent record label releasing a variety of music styles and substyles marginal to both the Christian and general markets: electropop, grunge, hardcore, punk rock, shoegaze, and thrash metal, among others. Punk and heavy metal artists had been circulating on the margins of the Christian market since the late 1970s, and it should come as no surprise that Christian music's fringe experienced increased visibility (and audibility) around the same time that "alternative rock" was experiencing general market commercial success in the early-to-mid '90s. In particular, the Christian punk band MxPx started to attract fans from the general market in the mid-'90s. A&M Records, at that time a subsidiary of PolyGram, signed a deal with Tooth & Nail to share distribution in both the Christian and the general markets for MxPx. Following a general market reissue of their third album, *Life in General* (1996), MxPx's next two albums were jointly distributed by Tooth & Nail and A&M: *Slowly Going the Way of the Buffalo* (1998) and *The Ever Passing Moment* (2000). Both albums charted on the *Billboard* 200 (#99 and #56, respectively); the single "Responsibility" (🎧), a straight-ahead punk song that addresses well-tread anxieties about adult life, was released in 2000 and charted on *Billboard*'s Modern Rock chart. The band played to larger general market audiences, opened for a dual-headlining tour featuring punk band The Offspring and hip hop group Cyprus Hill, and performed on high-profile stages as part of the Van's Warped Tour in 2000 and 2002 (MxPx first played Warped in 1998).

This partnership strategy, similar to Word's approach with Amy Grant (which had also been in collaboration with A&M), turned out to have been a test balloon for Tooth & Nail. Following the deal with A&M, Tooth & Nail signed a distribution deal with EMI in 1997, gaining general market distribution by EMI-owned Caroline, and Christian market distribution by the EMI Christian Music Group for all their artists. This was followed by a partial-ownership agreement in 2000. In 2013, Tooth & Nail ended its partial-ownership agreement with EMI, thus severing its primary infrastructural connection to the general market, but for over a decade EMI's resources, as a major label in both the Christian and the general markets, enabled Tooth & Nail to straddle niche markets that targeted Christian and non-Christian listeners. This balancing act was tactical and strategic, and the label's bands often moved between markets more fluidly than other crossover artists.

Success for MxPx and other Tooth & Nail bands has been at a different scale than it was for Amy Grant, but artists have nonetheless built sustainable careers playing for niche market audiences both at Christian music festivals such as Agape, Cornerstone, Creation, and Ichthus as well as at general market festivals like Bumbershoot, Lollapalooza, South by Southwest, and Warped. Bands do find chart success: for example, UnderOath's 2006 record, *Define the Great Line*, sold over 98,000 copies in its first week of release, enough to debut at number two on the *Billboard* 200 album chart; it was certified gold four months later. That album's radio single, "Writing on the Walls" (🎧), is a fairly typical UnderOath song: melodic, anthemic vocals alternate with almost unintelligible screaming, undergirded by metal-influenced guitar riffs, electronic elements, and sudden rhythmic shifts—all hallmarks of post-hardcore and metalcore. Many UnderOath songs lack traditional choruses, as does "Writing on the Walls"; the cumulative effect is one of disorienting sonic disruption: you can barely bang your head steadily to this track, let alone dance to it. Even though MxPx's "Responsibility" is more conventional (and thus more accessible), it is hard to imagine either of these songs playing next to Top 40 hits on general market CHR stations like Amy Grant's "Baby, Baby" or even Sixpence's "Kiss Me" did in the 1990s. And yet, UnderOath has become rather popular in the niche market for metalcore and other youth-oriented aggressive rock styles, straddling both the Christian and the general markets. In order to headline the final night of Cornerstone's main stage on Saturday, July 4, 2009, for example, UnderOath took a break from playing amphitheaters on the forty-six-date Van's Warped Tour.

Warped, an annual traveling music festival, was an institution for youth-oriented rock bands and their audiences, and this was true for Tooth & Nail's roster of Christian punk and metalcore artists as well. At least two dozen artists who have played Warped since the mid-'90s have been affiliated with Tooth & Nail or its sublabel Solid State, including Anberlin, Emery, Haste the Day, Norma Jean, and many others. Partly as a result of their general market exposure via Warped, many Tooth & Nail–affiliated bands tour outside of the Christian market infrastructure, regularly performing at medium-sized (general market) clubs instead of (or in addition to) Christian venues. One weekend in 2009, I attended two such metalcore shows on sequential evenings. On Saturday, December 5, Norma Jean headlined Reggie's Rock Club in Chicago's South Loop neighborhood. The Chariot (see chapter 6) opened the show; this was significant not only because both bands recorded for Solid State but also because The Chariot featured Norma Jean's founding vocalist Josh Scogin.[36] Fans of both bands packed the club. The nightclub at Reggie's is a typical rock venue: boxy, painted black, decent bar service, small balcony, and a maximum capacity of four hundred attendees. The next night, a Solid State tour (featuring UnderOath as headliners and supporting acts August Burns Red and Emery) played the Metro. Near Wrigley Field in Chicago's Lakeview neighborhood, the Metro is slightly more ornate than Reggie's and noticeably larger, with a maximum capacity of eleven hundred attendees. The show was sold out—not an easy thing to do on a Sunday evening. I watched the bands from the left of the sound booth near the rear of the main floor and spoke with a woman who had flown to Chicago from Tucson, Arizona, for a conference. We talked about how this music had helped her with her faith and to relate to her friends, both Christian and non-Christian. She was a sincere Christian fan, but we were surrounded by other show-goers swigging beer and heckling the bands (UnderOath in particular) when they spoke about their faith in between songs: "Shut up and rock!"

I had overheard similar comments from a mewithoutYou crowd five months earlier, also at the Metro, where a group of friends groused about "rocking out for Jesus" as they left the club after the show. That concert—also a sold-out Sunday gig—was on July 5, the day after Cornerstone. An eclectic indie band, mewithoutYou was also signed (at the time) with Tooth & Nail, and had just played Cornerstone on Friday, July 3, to the festival's largest Main Stage crowd yet. From speaking with attendees earlier in the week, I knew that this was one of the most anticipated sets of the entire festival: from my vantage point up a hill from the stage I estimated a few thousand kids on the ground with more streaming in throughout the set. I had learned that fans appreciated the singer, Aaron Weiss, for discussing a faith that was ascetic, anti-consumerist, and influenced by the writings and teachings of Shane Claiborne, a founding member of the intentional community The Simple Way.[37] The contrast between reactions from fans at Cornerstone and show-goers just two nights later at the Metro was whiplash-inducing. Audience members at the Metro, near where I was standing in the balcony to the right of the stage, openly laughed when Aaron sang of his chastity in "C-Minor" (🎧): "I'm still technically a virgin / After 27 years / Which never bothered me before / What's maybe 50 more"—lines that had elicited cheers from the Cornerstone audience.

Jeff Carver, who worked in Tooth & Nail's A&R department when I interviewed him, told me that, while they were proud of the label's reputation as a Christian label, they and their artists also intentionally "blurred the lines" between the Christian and general markets. "In a lot of ways, Tooth & Nail has been a pioneer doing that, and really making that an okay thing," he said. "I think we'd like to continue to do that, but I think at the end of the day, we do want to sign bands that we feel are going to go out and represent positivity or faith-based."[38] The label is headquartered in Seattle—far from Nashville, home to the Christian market's major labels—and staffers thought of themselves as having more in common with other Seattle-based indie labels than with Christian labels, according to Carver: "We just operate, image-wise, close[r] to a Barsuk or a Sub Pop than we do to a[n EMI] CMG label, but with the added challenge of having to incorporate this Christian market world into it. . . . I think we probably much [more] closely relate to [those] Seattle-based labels."

Tooth & Nail's strategy for fringe crossover was one of divide and conquer: they had separate sublabels to focus on distinct genre markets as well as separate teams of staff to distribute, market, and promote to the Christian and general markets. Releases on Tooth & Nail and Solid State were handled by a marketing team with prior experience at non-Christian labels such as Crank, Drive-Thru, and Universal; more Christian-centric artists were released by sublabel BEC and handled by a team with prior experience at Compassion International and World Vision (two Christian nonprofit humanitarian organizations). Those releases had additional support from dedicated Nashville-based EMI CMG employees, particularly for radio promotions. "We piece together a team that makes the most sense" for each release, Carver told me, which could also include hiring publicists outside of the label. The resulting structure was an inverted image of how Andy Peterson described Word's relationship with Warner: instead of working with the corporate parent on general market publicity, Tooth & Nail off-loaded the Christian market strategy to EMI CMG's Nashville headquarters and provided the general market expertise in-house: "Our general market marketing department, that's all they know," said Carver. "They exclusively have come from that world, and that's just where they push our bands now."[39]

Carver and his colleagues at Tooth & Nail did their best to support their artists' own goals. "We want to support bands wherever they're at," Carver told me. "We don't want to force a band to go in any direction, we don't want to keep them from going in a direction if that's what they want to do, but they have to define that." But Carver and his colleagues often had to educate bands about how the different markets work, especially because the divide between the Christian and general markets could be so opaque at times:

> We are more than happy to dump money into the general market. But it's not as simple as being on a church tour and then us booking a couple ads in *AP* [*Alternative Press*], or having them make some more rocking songs and all of a sudden, they want to be on these big tours in the general market. It just doesn't work like that.... Touring makes a lot of the decision for them. If you're doing a lot of church tours, that's where your market is. Or if you're doing all general market tours, you are a general market band. It has less to do with your music.[40]

Carver's point about the importance of live performances serving to situate a band within a particular market is especially significant, as the influence of other music industry sectors—including record labels, the music press, and radio—have been evolving dramatically in the twenty-first century. That said, feedback from listeners and critics, often in the form of reviews, illustrates the challenges that face bands who straddle both the Christian and the general markets.

Jon Dunn plays bass guitar in death metal band Demon Hunter and also worked in A&R at Tooth & Nail at the time of our interview; he explained that general market music critics typically prioritized the band's faith over their music: "Read a review and it'll have absolutely nothing to do with the music. It won't reference the music at all.... It's pretty prominent that their first focus is 'Christian metal band,' so they're already viewing through these lenses, whether that's a good thing or bad thing or slightly indifferent."[41] Tooth & Nail staff felt this at the label itself, where—despite a camaraderie with other Seattle-area indie labels—they were ostracized by the local scene, according to Carver: "People that live in Seattle know very little about Tooth & Nail.... Bands will come out on Sub Pop, or Barsuk ... they'll sell like a couple thousand the first week, and it'll be in all the publications in town and on everyone's lips. But then Demon Hunter will come out and sell almost fourteen thousand—it is a metal band from Seattle, from a Seattle label—most people will just have no idea."[42] If people would just give the music itself a chance without these preconceived notions, Dunn explained, they would find that Tooth & Nail bands have transcended the old criticisms—leveled against Amy Grant, Michael W. Smith, and other Christian artists in the 1980s and '90s—of Christian music as derivative. Unlike Christian music in the past, "these Christian bands have become genre-defining bands," he claimed, influencing general market bands in the hardcore, metal, and metalcore markets. "Christian music's not playing catch-up anymore," he argued. "Now, everyone else is following the trail that they're blazing."[43]

MxPx, UnderOath, mewithoutYou, and other Tooth & Nail bands play for punk, metalcore, and indie fans in both the Christian and the general markets. Artists like Sixpence and P.O.D. achieved careers that would have been unattainable had they not crossed over; Amy Grant and Michael W. Smith reached a larger mass audience while crossing over at the peak of their careers. But what do fringe crossover artists achieve, especially those who maintain a strong presence in multiple niche markets (instead of abandoning one for the other)? In the cases of Tooth & Nail artists, the relative security of stable, sustainable audiences in multiple niches has enabled many to treat their identity as "Christian bands" with ambivalence (as the record label itself does):

they could afford to be choosier about fulfilling the Christian market's expectations, knowing that spending another summer on the Warped Tour would net them new, young fans. They also gained credibility for influencing artists outside of the Christian market. No one has ever claimed that Amy Grant was blazing a musical trail in the general market; on the contrary, her crossover success was due to her ability to follow musical trends, not set them. But not only were Christian bands "not playing catch-up anymore," in the early 2000s they were helping establish the sonic and aesthetic standards for their niche markets. Fringe crossover, from this perspective, is dramatically different: it is about finding new audiences but not artificially changing one's style to do so ("selling out"), and it is also about the ways in which changes in taste result in the broader exposure and influence of once-peripheral musical styles.

Markets are not static but culturally determined, bound to social, cultural, economic, and aesthetic changes from within and also influenced by outside forces. These changes affect individual markets—causing a market to grow or shrink—as well as relationships and interactions between distinct markets. The process of crossover, even when considered as mainstreaming (Toynbee) or incorporation (Hebdige), is an audible representation of the values of two formerly distinct markets converging and overlapping. The examples of Tooth & Nail's fringe crossover artists demonstrate the challenges and the benefits of locating or constructing a middle ground between otherwise disparate markets where their peripheries intersect. And Amy Grant's case, which I discussed in chapter 4, shows how specific strategies on the parts of artists, management, record labels, and other cultural intermediaries can broaden one's market and appeal to a wider number of target consumers, facilitating a transition from one mass market to another. Fans, listeners, and others invested in niche markets frequently interpret such shifts—intentional or not—as betraying the ethical values that they understand to form the basis of their market. Thus, the charge of "selling out" can have detrimental effects within one market while an artist attempts to cross to another. Economic changes within music industries clearly play into these tensions, inasmuch as ethical and aesthetic values cannot be isolated from economic value in capitalist markets. Indeed, the popularity of certain musical genres and styles suggests that musical elements can correlate to commercial successes: the largest markets simply sound different from the smallest ones. But we need not reduce the political economy of commercial music to a race to the lowest common denominator of musical middle grounds. Because markets have ethical values as well as aesthetic ones, artists might appeal to their target consumers by adhering to these—in DIY, paying attention to anticapitalist modes of production and distribution; in Christian music, following biblically taught morals.

Conclusion

The Stability of Risk
and the Risk of Stability

In previous chapters I have considered how issues of capital and commerce, ethics, resistance, and crossover impact individual markets' boundaries. We have seen, for example, the roles that differing (and sometimes competing) theological goals have played in solidifying Christian music as a dominant market by the 1980s, and also how ethical, moral, and ideological transgressions complicate an individual artist's ability to participate in that market, given the expectations of its cultural intermediaries and listeners. Resistant aesthetics and ideologies have a place in the Christian market as well, which has proven to be surprisingly flexible and accommodating for a heterogeneous constituency of artists, festival promoters, and listeners who represent a variety of tastes and theological perspectives. Music markets expand and shrink, converge and diverge over time; one way we can hear changes in one market is through crossover songs and artists bridging that market's values with those of another. When markets converge, crossovers increase; when they diverge, artists must make a choice: continue chasing success in the new market, or cross back to the safety and stability of their home.

In this conclusion, I consider stability as a confluence of this book's set of themes. In a way, each thematic trajectory has at its heart the desire to achieve stability. It would be trite to posit merely that markets tend toward equilibrium, but it is nevertheless true that those participants involved in the business of music—artists and cultural intermediators—value predictability, no matter how unattainable. *God Rock, Inc.*'s final case study upends this desire for stability: Chad Johnson intentionally chose the radical instability of quitting his secure job at a well-regarded Christian record label to launch a nonprofit organization and pursue his conviction that what Christian music is for, even in the twenty-first century, should be evangelism and ministry. Johnson's choices and experiences, no matter how ethical or noble, are extraordinary and insightful precisely because they are so far outside the norm for artists and cultural intermediaries who yearn for the stability he abandoned. In the Christian market, stability is both difficult and straightforward. In contrast to the general market, listeners' relative ignorance of earlier decades' Christian music and artists makes it challenging to achieve a stable career without consistently releasing new music. But the Christian market's loyalty rewards those who persevere, even incentivizing some artists to be dishonest lest they be forced to leave behind this niche market's safety.

Amy Grant, whom I discussed in chapter 4, is not the only Christian artist to have returned to her roots later in her career. Christmas albums, greatest hits compilations, live recordings, and worship albums have become something of a victory lap for aging Christian artists. Christmas records have long been welcomed and even expected in the Christian market (Children of the Day's 1975 *Christmas Album* is thought to be the market's first). And although inspirational singers such as Sandi Patty have intentionally recorded and performed hymns and worship music as significant aspects of their careers, more pop-oriented artists like Grant, Steven Curtis Chapman, and Michael W. Smith have recorded far more music for the Christian market's presentational contexts than for the participatory contexts of worship music. But, as I discussed in the introduction, the division between those two contexts—which has always been porous—has been deteriorating even further in the early 2000s and 2010s. For example, both Chapman and Smith have remained present and relevant after the apex of their pop careers in the 1990s, partly by releasing worship albums and performing at worship events. This reflects, in part, the expanding commercial presence and power of the worship music market starting in the 1990s and continuing into the twenty-first century. The success of worship artists such as David Crowder Band, Elevation Worship, Hillsong United (which is tied to an Australia-based Pentecostal megachurch with a growing number of branches worldwide), and Chris Tomlin, and the popularity of events such as the Passion and Urbana worship conferences have been significant trends.¹ Christian artists expanding into worship music to diversify their careers is thus a rational strategy, one that further blurs the boundaries between the pop/rock and worship markets, which increasingly overlap.

Recent trends in the Christian market include the continued growth trajectory of worship music and changes in revenue and listening wrought by streaming. I spoke with a panel of Christian music industry executives in 2018 about the Christian market, and the popularity of worship music stuck out as a significant trend. As I mentioned in the introduction, Christian listeners are increasingly encountering worship music in entertainment contexts that used to be the domain of pop/rock, including playlists at Christian radio stations and on the major streaming services. Chris Hauser, an independent radio promoter, explained that it is easy to pitch a worship song to a commercial radio programmer once that song has already circulated among worship leaders and congregations: "This song is loved everywhere. You can put this song on the air and within three days your audience knows it, or they're already singing along to it in church."² Another trend is intended to capitalize on changing listening habits due to the growth of streaming services: some Christian labels are releasing several different recorded versions of the same song (including both worship and pop/rock songs) to target niche audiences through genre-specific playlists. Dean Diehl, an executive at Provident, labeled this "song-based marketing." The goal, he claimed, is to encourage fans to listen to the same song (or multiple versions of the same song) repeatedly: "I don't care if you listen to the whole album or just one song over and over again. I get the money the same way. So, I'm going to work the songs."³ Both of these trends reflect the continued strength of music publishing revenue and songwriting royalties—income that worship songwriters have long depended on over revenue from recordings, merchandise, or touring. John J. Thompson worried, however, that in the 2010s the Christian market is more risk-averse and less willing to take chances on an artist or songwriter without a record of commercial success: "As the industry has contracted and faced increased financial pressures, the record labels have had to pull in the reins. . . . There really are no creative margins left."⁴

These music executives' insights indicate that Christian record labels are still actively engaging listeners with newly released music. But, in contrast to the general market, in the Christian market there is comparatively little demand for (or even awareness of) older music and artists. For many decades, the general market has relied on back catalog recordings (defined as anything released over eighteen months ago) both to generate revenue and to connect listeners to a shared (if nostalgic or romanticized) past. Keir Keightley has shown that label executives and other cultural intermediaries welcomed catalog albums as relatively stable sources of perennial income that came to account for as much as 50 percent of labels' revenue soon after they became available when the U.S. record industry transitioned to LPs as the dominant recording format in the early 1950s.[5] This was particularly true of those albums marketed to white adult consumers, in contrast to the ephemeral new-release singles markets for youth and Black music.

Commercial radio formats for catalog recordings emerged, including classic country, classic hip hop, classic rock, oldies, urban oldies, and even decade-specific channels on satellite radio (Sirius XM's '50s on 5, '60s on 6, and so on); this programming strategy remains relevant through curated playlists on streaming services. After the CD was introduced in 1982, record labels encouraged consumers to replace their collections of LPs with the new medium. This campaign intensified in the 1990s, supported by an expanded array of catalog products: box sets, compilations, digital remasters, and expanded reissues (often including additional songs, such as B-sides, demos, live versions, and remixes). The labels profited from this format shift as revenue accelerated in the 1990s, as did their artists (although by a smaller degree: recording contracts often stipulated lower royalty rates for catalog and compilation sales), but consumers also benefitted from having a greater degree of choice and access to their favorite music.[6]

SUSTAINABLE CAREERS AND SUSTAINABLE MARKETS

In the general market, the importance of catalog records to the music industries has had four significant impacts. First, as the album gradually gained value as the privileged format in the U.S. record industry, even among youth-oriented popular musics, by the early 1990s singles were largely irrelevant outside of their ability to incentivize radio listeners to purchase full-length albums, cassettes, and CDs (see chapter 4).[7] The emergence of the "album-oriented-rock" (or AOR) commercial radio format in the 1970s and the organization of singles-oriented pop artists' careers around "album cycles" attest to the album's power and status.[8] But not every listener wanted (or could afford) to buy entire albums in order to hear individual songs. The backlash was perhaps inevitable, as consumers began to turn to peer-to-peer file sharing en masse in 1999 to circumvent the record industries' legitimate distribution channels, in part to access single songs. Second, the record industry's reputation as a fickle and unpredictable market grounded in consistent turnover—which continued even during the '90s' boom years of catalog sales discussed above—was, by the mid-1950s or early '60s, no longer an accurate representation. Catalog records were not merely present but important, more readily available (and privileged) as standards against which new artists and musics were judged. Artists were increasingly evaluated against their own past work, as were entire genres and markets; catalogs gradually acquired a cumulative sonic weight whose identity became more difficult to alter. The largest record labels were less and less willing to take aesthetic risks; the sounds of the past constrained the sounds of the future more and more.

Third, as popular music increasingly achieved the temporal transcendence that music scholars had long assumed to define art and classical music—remaining canonical and relevant even as it outlived its composers—it could no longer be dismissed as ephemeral and unworthy of serious critical reflection and study. Cultural elites were less likely to be defined by their cultivated tastes in highbrow art, as Pierre Bourdieu had found in the 1970s, and more likely to be defined by an omnivorous appreciation of various popular musics, as Richard Peterson and Roger Kern found in the early 1990s.[9] Finally, even in the streaming era, back catalogs continue to generate awareness and revenue through the licenses granted to Apple Music, Pandora, Spotify, Tidal, YouTube, and other services. The arrival of some classic artists' catalogs on streaming services—AC/DC and The Beatles in 2015, Neil Young in 2016, and Prince in 2018, among others—have been reported as newsworthy events, contributing to these artists' already substantial reputations. Reissues continue apace, often marking significant anniversaries (twenty or twenty-five years after an album's initial release) and prompting recognition and critical reappraisals.

Reissues and catalog sales have never been a major component of artists' careers and record labels' strategies in the Christian market. There are no classic Christian or Christian oldies radio formats or streaming playlists. Certainly there are passionate connoisseurs of Christian music from the 1960s, '70s, and '80s, but they are outliers in the market: according to John J. Thompson, the average listener is far less aware of Christian music from several decades ago, compared to her equivalent in the general market. "I dare you to go find somebody under forty-five who's ever heard of Second Chapter of Acts," he told me in a 2009 interview. "They were the biggest thing in Christian music twenty years ago. . . . All these bands that blew up in the '90s, they've heard of them. . . . But they don't realize, Second Chapter of Acts is what created that style." Christian music has a rich history, and artists from earlier decades could still be relevant to contemporary audiences. But those audiences, Thompson continued, "have no real concern for their roots at all. . . . I think that we neglect our heritage at our peril. Because we don't have a sense of connection to that stuff, that's why people disconnect from Christian music. . . . If Christian music could find a way to honor its roots, it would be better in the long run, and it would be profitable."[10] In the general market, greater awareness of an artist's substantial back catalog can result in sustainable revenue streams through covers, sampling, streaming, synch licensing (for commercials, movies, television shows, and video games), and touring. But in the Christian market those opportunities are few: there is no history or infrastructure—and thus no existing models or incentives—for celebrating, exploiting, rediscovering, and ultimately honoring classic Christian artists and their music. As a result, the Christian market has not benefited from back catalogs in ways similar to the general market: the market is not normalized along the aesthetic standards of its past, nor does expertise in "classic" Christian music denote any special connoisseurist status. Thompson argued that this is a self-perpetuating cycle: just as promoting back catalogs in the general market results in audience interest and thus new opportunities for artists, in the Christian market the unawareness of back catalogs begets continued ignorance. Back catalogs, key to general market artists' and labels' revenue and business models, are yet another underappreciated niche in the Christian market.

Christian artists' principal strategy to address this challenge has been to keep releasing new recordings on a regular basis, including new studio albums in addition to other records (Christmas, greatest hits, live, and worship, among others) that can then be promoted to cultural intermediaries and fans. Amy Grant remains a major Christian music star, long after her general market success has faded, not because she was a star in the 1980s but because she "crossed back" and has kept releasing Christian music in the 2010s. Others have crossed back as well: the band Switchfoot, for example, launched their career in the Christian market before crossing over to the general market with their fourth album, 2003's *The Beautiful Letdown*, which ultimately sold over 2.7 million copies anchored by Top 40 singles such as "Meant to Live" (🎧) and "Dare You to Move." In media appearances, bandmembers sidestepped questions of their Christian backgrounds, unwilling to be labeled as "Christian music" for fear of how that might contaminate their career in the general market. The band's bassist, Tim Foreman, explained to *Rolling Stone* magazine in 2003 that the band is "Christian by faith, not genre," coining a phrase that others have repeated many times since.[11] Andrew Beaujon interviewed lead singer Jon Foreman at Cornerstone Festival in 2004 and was surprised to find him reticent to articulate his Christian faith, even while preparing to perform at a Christian festival.[12] While pursuing general market success (signed first to Columbia and then to Atlantic Records), Switchfoot nonetheless kept one foot planted firmly in the Christian market, where they were distributed by Sparrow and continued to promote singles to Christian radio stations. *The Beautiful Letdown* proved to be the apex of their general market career, however, and later albums sold subsequently fewer copies and singles charted lower and on less prominent charts. As Switchfoot's general market career has declined, they have seemed more comfortable participating in the Christian market, where they have had more chart success in recent years. Similarly, Christian metal band Stryper had a successful general market career in the 1980s and early '90s but currently perform largely in the Christian market.

Other artists have started in the general market before crossing to the Christian market. Bob Dylan is the best-known example of a general market artist whose conversion to Christianity altered the trajectory of his career. Although his trio of Christian albums (1979's *Slow Train Coming*, 🎧; 1980's *Saved*; and 1981's *Shot of Love*) did not target the Christian market exclusively, their reception in the general market was comparatively lukewarm. Many general market artists have been outspoken about their Christian faith; only a few, however, have actively engaged the Christian market: T Bone Burnett, John Elefante (of Kansas), Joe English (of Wings), Mark Farner (of Grand Funk Railroad), Richie Furay (of Buffalo Springfield and Poco), Kerry Livgren (also of Kansas), Leon Patillo (of Santana), and Brian Head Welch (of Korn) have all cultivated Christian audiences. Members of the band U2, by contrast, have pointedly avoided the Christian market despite publicly identifying as Christian.[13] Niche market artists have also made this transition. Jeremy Enigk's conversion to Christianity in the 1990s was one of several factors that resulted in the breakup of the Seattle-based emo band Sunny Day Real Estate after releasing two records in the early '90s; Enigk recorded a solo album (1996's *Return of the Frog Queen*, ♫) before reforming Sunny Day in 1997. Josh Caterer, of the Chicago-based pop punk band Smoking Popes, wanted to incorporate Christian themes into his music after converting to Christianity in 1998. The Smoking Popes broke up when he quit the following year; he formed Duvall (♫) as a Christian band in 2001. Although the Popes later reunited and continue to record and perform, Caterer has remained active as a worship leader.

SELLING OUT TO REMAIN NICHE

Despite the lack of attention paid to back catalog Christian music, the Christian market does enable many artists to have long, sustainable careers. As I discussed in chapter 2, Wayne Kusber believed that Christian music consumers are very loyal: "Once they become fans of that artist and they believe in that artist, that artist has proven themselves to them. [Christian audiences think,] 'That's my band. I'm sticking with those guys.' It'll take a long time to lose interest."[14] This benefits the likes of Amy Grant and Jon Foreman, for whom remaining active in the Christian market is not such a bad retirement from general market pop stardom. But from a cynical perspective, the audience loyalty that allows for stable careers disincentivizes artists from taking risks. Andy Peterson, the former Word executive, told me that many artists and musicians who were satisfied with making a living in the Christian market did not aspire to reaching larger (or different) audiences or experimenting musically: "They can make it work between the festivals and the worship conferences and all these other things . . . but there's no heart to it. It's just kind of, 'Hey, this is what I do.' And a lot of them don't even really respect what they do. They're just phoning it in. . . . There's no passion in it."[15]

This is problematic for a couple of reasons. For one, artists who were "just phoning it in" were more likely to follow formulas and keep retreading their musical pasts—to repeat and rehash what had already been successful for them—instead of pursuing new aesthetic directions. They became adept at covering themselves, but they sacrificed their creative voice to do so. As Peterson explained, "It's just the fakeness of, 'Okay, we know we need to write certain kinds of songs for Christian radio, we know we need to present ourselves in a certain kind of way, because otherwise they wouldn't let us play at Creation Festival,' . . .

so there aren't very many bands that take chances, that push the envelope creatively, musically."[16] The more Christian artists did this, the more outsiders perceived the Christian market to be an unforgivably banal and derivative refuge for those not good enough to make it in the general market. The stronger this bias, the more difficult it was for Christian artists to cross over to the general market if they chose to do so, and the more understandable it is why a band like Mutemath would not want to be associated with the Christian market in the first place (see chapter 7).

The other reason the promise of a stable career in the Christian market is problematic is that it incentivizes artists to be dishonest about their beliefs, identities, and lifestyles in order to avoid the kinds of ethical transgressions that could irreparably harm their careers (see chapter 3). For example, artists may repress their sexual orientation or gender identity to avoid breaking evangelical Christianity's prohibitions against homosexuality and trans identity. Or they may avoid seeking professional treatment for mental health issues, relationship problems, or substance abuse, choosing to suffer privately (or with the guidance of their pastor or another religious leader) instead of risking the public revealing of what some might condemn as an ethical failure or weakness. Or they may hide a crisis or lack of faith while still performing Christianity, as did *South Park*'s Eric Cartman in the 2003 episode "Christian Rock Hard."[17] Peterson suggested that artists will often remain active in the Christian market, even as their faith falters: "They know that this is a resource for them that will allow them to make a living, and provide for their families, and they're willing to BS their way through it, and fake it for that purpose."[18] Each one of these denials is harmful, whether it is personally damaging for the artist who lives a lie to avoid a larger, more public conflict, or it misleads a trusting audience and takes advantage of their belief in a shared faith and value system.

I understand both these problems as examples of Christian artists prioritizing economic gain or financial stability over aesthetic goals and ideological positions. If "selling out" is about jettisoning one's aesthetics and/or ideologies for commercial success, then artists who choose to phone it in musically or lie about their identities or beliefs to avoid commercial repercussions are certainly selling out. In niche markets, participants are often concerned about artists selling out to reach larger audiences in larger markets—crossing over from the punk or electronic dance music undergrounds, for example, to mainstream Top 40 and top-dollar headlining festival slots. Very rarely, however, do we suspect artists might perform a niche market's ethics or aesthetics strategically. The stakes are usually too low, at least in comparison to the mass market. But the choice facing the artist is not always niche versus mass success. Sometimes it is niche market success versus no career whatsoever; or, put another way, it is a choice between the stable known and the risky unknown. In those cases, the stakes may be high enough to incentivize selling out.

RISKING IT ALL TO COME AND LIVE

I end *God Rock, Inc.* with one final case study, that of Chad Johnson and Come&Live!. Johnson founded Takehold Records in 1997 as a small independent label whose artists played emo, hardcore, metal, screamo, and similar styles from a Christian perspective. Brandon Ebel, the founder and owner of the Christian label Tooth & Nail, noticed Johnson's success with Takehold, bought the label, and hired Johnson in A&R in 2001. At Tooth & Nail, Johnson was eventually promoted to director of A&R. He gained valuable experience working with a successful label and also grew in his faith. In an interview, he told me that he felt a strong calling to help mentor artists at Tooth & Nail, but the pressures of achieving commercial success conflicted with his desire to minister to bands spiritually and teach them to build a sustainable music ministry. Ultimately, Johnson felt that the existing structure of the record industry prevented him from achieving his goals: "I just felt the Lord reawakening my desire for evangelism, my desire to see revival in my own heart and in the hearts of people around me. . . . I was trying to mentor these artists. I was going on the road with some of them, do prayer time, work with them, encourage them. There was good conversation, there were some encouraging moments, but I just felt that I was fighting against a beast that I could not win."[19] Although Tooth & Nail was ostensibly an independent label, when Johnson worked there it was distributed by EMI CMG, which also owned 49 percent of the label. Ebel and his staff had to keep EMI's profit goals in mind, and Johnson came to feel constrained by these priorities. He quit Tooth & Nail in early 2009 to launch Come&Live!, which was originally a nonprofit label that gave away recordings (or made them available for a donation, as Keith Green did in the early 1980s) and trained artists for careers in which ministry and evangelism were major priorities.

In contrast to Tooth & Nail, at Come&Live! there was no profit priority and little overhead. Johnson and his staff worked with artists on developing their skills in ministry and worship and prepared them to face the evolving challenges of the record industry. By giving away music and shifting the label's and artists' focuses to other priorities, in the early 2010s Johnson was preparing his artists for a future record industry where free music will be the norm and not the exception. When he started Come&Live!, he did not know whether any bands would be interested in giving away their music and pursuing full-time music ministry. In the years after founding Come&Live!, however, Johnson had more interest from potential artists than he was able to manage. Artists' ministries were supported through fundraising campaigns—often crowdfunded—that Johnson taught them to conceive and approach as if preparing for overseas missionary work. He had to approach his own life in a similar fashion, and in an update to the Come&Live! email list in late 2018, Johnson wrote of ignoring his family's financial situation during Come&Live!'s early years: "I was too busy focusing on 'ministry' to truly invest my heart into dreaded fundraising."[20] But in 2012 he began to approach fundraising more consistently and intentionally, and he found that his supporters were able to meet more and more of his family's and ministry's financial needs.

This was a humbling experience for Johnson. As director of A&R for Tooth & Nail in the early 2000s, he had a well-paid and -respected job in the Christian market. But he felt unfulfilled, despite being at what he has since called the peak of his music career. In his book *One Thousand Risks* (best described as part memoir, part motivational), Johnson writes of a "spiritual epiphany" through which he came to understand that his career as a "privileged music guy wasn't the path meant for my life," and he set aside his profitable career for his true calling.[21] It would have been safer, easier, less risky, and more financially secure to ignore his convictions and stay at Tooth & Nail, but it also would have been dishonest: "I would have only been a facade."[22] In November 2015, Johnson made another transition, relaunching Come&Live! as an organization only supporting missions work in partnership with Steiger International.[23] He still works with artists, inspiring, resourcing, and training them to prioritize a missions calling in their work, but Come&Live! no longer releases or promotes recorded music.[24] Instead, Johnson and his colleagues produce documentaries and a podcast; they train musicians to fundraise, pastor, and minister; and they evangelize youth worldwide. In many ways, Come&Live!'s vision for Christian music is similar to that of the Jesus People musicians I discussed at the beginning of this book; in their goals for evangelizing and discipleship, they echo Campus Crusade for Christ's goal to train an army of evangelists to preach the gospel.²⁵ Johnson's professional trajectory illustrates a perspective of personal growth and professional success that differs from that promoted at conventional record labels. In deemphasizing profit, he enabled Come&Live! to pursue his (and his artists') missions priorities. Come&Live! reframed financial needs as ministerial and mentoring opportunities, engaged and empowered consumers as active participants, and envisioned a revival in the Christian record industry itself.

In many ways, Amy Grant set the precedent for Christian crossover and commercial success, both in terms of her ascent (strong chart positions, commercial radio airplay, Grammy Awards, and multi-platinum sales, as I discussed in chapter 4) and in terms of her decline. The strategy she and her management team pursued resulted in a string of hits in the early 1990s and the largest exposure the Christian market had experienced up until that point. Grant demonstrated the potential for crossover, and the major Christian record labels applied the lessons her career modeled to other artists on their rosters, almost without prejudice, in a prolonged (and largely unsuccessful) attempt to achieve sustainable, mainstream commercial success outside of the Christian market. Yet, despite several attempts to repeat the success she experienced with "Baby, Baby," Grant was never able to regain the same level of popularity she had achieved in the general market following the end of *Heart in Motion*'s album cycle. Indeed, Grant may only be remembered in the wider public for "Baby, Baby": she made news in 2016 for celebrating the breakout single's twenty-fifth anniversary by rerecording it with singer Tori Kelly (🎧), who is younger than the song. Grant's inability to sustain a crossover career is also instructive, then, as a cautionary tale: for if the biggest artist in the history of the Christian market took a gamble at crossover success and ultimately failed, what different strategies and outcomes might we expect from any other Christian artists' attempts at crossover? From this perspective, Grant's career is yet another persuasive argument to stay within the relatively safe confines of the Christian market, no matter the cost. But if cynics worry that the Christian market is at risk of unscrupulous participants taking advantage of its ethics, even as sincere artists are at risk of being ostracized for ethical transgressions, then the example of Chad Johnson and Come&Live! should restore their faith. He turned his back on a profitable and sustainable career and followed God's calling, committing himself to ministering to artists and supporting their missions to evangelize. His story is a clear echo of Keith Green's biography (see chapter 1), evidence that surrendering one's career to a higher purpose may be unique but not sui generis, and also that there are different pathways to stability within commercial popular music—varying according to individual markets' ethics, values, and objectives.

APPENDIX ONE

Discographies

The following discographies are indicated throughout the book by ●. RIAA certifications connote cumulative U.S. sales: gold = 500,000; platinum = 1 million; 2x platinum = 2 million, and so on.

CASTING CROWNS (2003-18)[1]

Casting Crowns, Reunion. Released October 7, 2003. Certified platinum, February 10, 2005. Certified 2x platinum, August 23, 2012. Peaked on the *Billboard* 200 chart at #59, May 22, 2004.

Live from Atlanta, Reunion. Released September 14, 2004. Certified platinum, October 22, 2004.

Lifesong, Reunion. Released August 30, 2005. Certified platinum, February 14, 2007. Peaked on the *Billboard* 200 chart at #9, September 17, 2005.

Lifesong Live, Reunion. Released October 3, 2006. Certified platinum, May 25, 2007.

The Altar and the Door, Reunion. Released August 28, 2007. Certified platinum, August 20, 2010. Peaked on the *Billboard* 200 chart at #2, September 15, 2007.

---

1. This list includes studio albums, live albums, and EPs. It does not include holiday releases, compilations of previous releases, singles, or the band's two self-released albums before they signed to Reunion Records.

The Altar and the Door Live, Reunion. Released August 19, 2008. Certified gold, December 8, 2008. Peaked on the *Billboard* 200 chart at #114, September 6, 2008.

Until the Whole World Hears, Reunion. Released November 17, 2009. Certified platinum, January 22, 2015. Peaked on the *Billboard* 200 chart at #4, December 5, 2009.

Until the Whole World Hears . . . Live, Reunion. Released August 31, 2010. Certified gold, August 18, 2011. Peaked on the *Billboard* 200 chart at #162, September 18, 2010.

Come to the Well, Reunion. Released October 18, 2011. Certified gold, October 12, 2012. Peaked on the *Billboard* 200 chart at #2, November 5, 2011.

The Acoustic Sessions: Vol. 1, Reunion. Released January 22, 2013. Peaked on the *Billboard* 200 chart at #35, February 9, 2013.

Thrive, Reunion. Released January 28, 2014. Certified gold, March 28, 2016. Peaked on the *Billboard* 200 chart at #6, February 15, 2014.

Glorious Day: Hymns of Faith, self-released in collaboration with the Cracker Barrel restaurant chain. Released March 2, 2015. Peaked on the *Billboard* 200 chart at #52, March 21, 2015.

A Live Worship Experience, Reunion. Released November 13, 2015. Peaked on the *Billboard* 200 chart at #53, December 5, 2015.

The Very Next Thing, Reunion. Released September 16, 2016. Peaked on the *Billboard* 200 chart at #9, October 8, 2016.

Only Jesus, Reunion. Released November 16, 2018. Peaked on the *Billboard* 200 chart at #42, December 1, 2018.

STEVEN CURTIS CHAPMAN (1987–2019)[2]

First Hand, Sparrow. Released June 15, 1987.

Real Life Conversations, Sparrow. Released April 1, 1988.

More to This Life, Sparrow. Released October 5, 1989. Certified gold, May 9, 2002.

For the Sake of the Call, Sparrow. Released December 13, 1990. Certified gold, December 6, 1994.

The Great Adventure, Sparrow. Released June 19, 1992. Certified gold, June 15, 1993.

---

2. This list includes studio albums. It does not include live albums, EPs, holiday releases, compilations of previous releases, or singles.

Heaven in the Real World, Sparrow. Released July 12, 1994. Certified platinum, February 7, 1997. Peaked on the *Billboard* 200 chart at #195, December 9, 1995.

Signs of Life, Sparrow. Released September 3, 1996. Certified gold, January 24, 1997. Peaked on the *Billboard* 200 chart at #20, September 21, 1996.

Speechless, Sparrow. Released June 15, 1999. Certified platinum, November 27, 2000. Peaked on the *Billboard* 200 chart at #31, July 3, 1999.

Declaration, Sparrow. Released September 25, 2001. Certified gold, May 9, 2002. Peaked on the *Billboard* 200 chart at #14, October 13, 2001.

All about Love, Sparrow. Released January 28, 2003. Certified gold, May 14, 2008. Peaked on the *Billboard* 200 chart at #12, February 15, 2003.

All Things New, Sparrow. Released September 21, 2004. Peaked on the *Billboard* 200 chart at #22, October 9, 2004.

This Moment, Sparrow. Released October 23, 2007. Peaked on the *Billboard* 200 chart at #47, November 10, 2007.

Beauty Will Rise, Sparrow. Released November 3, 2009. Peaked on the *Billboard* 200 chart at #27, November 21, 2009.

re:creation, Sparrow. Released August 9, 2011. Peaked on the *Billboard* 200 chart at #45, October 27, 2011.

Deep Roots, self-released in collaboration with the Cracker Barrel restaurant chain. Released March 11, 2013. Peaked on the *Billboard* 200 chart at #68, March 30, 2013.

The Glorious Unfolding, Reunion. Released September 30, 2013. Peaked on the *Billboard* 200 chart at #27, October 19, 2013.

Worship and Believe, Reunion. Released March 4, 2016. Peaked on the *Billboard* 200 chart at #87, March 26, 2016.

Deeper Roots: Where the Bluegrass Grows, self-released in collaboration with the Cracker Barrel restaurant chain. Released March 22, 2019.

THE CHARIOT (2004–12)[3]

Everything Is Alive, Everything Is Breathing, Nothing Is Dead, and Nothing Is Bleeding, Solid State. Released November 16, 2004.

Unsung EP, Solid State. Released December 6, 2005.

The Fiancée, Solid State. Released April 3, 2007.

---

3. This list includes studio albums and EPs. It does not include singles or compilations of previous releases.

Wars and Rumors of Wars, Solid State. Released May 5, 2009.

Long Live, "Good Fight." Released November 23, 2010.

One Wing, "Good Fight." Released August 28, 2012.

DEMON HUNTER (2002–19)[4]

Demon Hunter, Solid State. Released October 22, 2002.

Summer of Darkness, Solid State. Released May 4, 2004.

The Triptych, Solid State. Released October 25, 2005. Peaked on the *Billboard* 200 chart at #136, November 12, 2005.

Storm the Gates of Hell, Solid State. Released November 6, 2007. Peaked on the *Billboard* 200 chart at #85, November 24, 2007.

The World Is a Thorn, Solid State. Released March 9, 2010. Peaked on the *Billboard* 200 chart at #39, March 27, 2010.

True Defiance, Solid State. Released April 10, 2012. Peaked on the *Billboard* 200 chart at #36, April 28, 2012.

Extremist, Solid State. Released March 18, 2014. Peaked on the *Billboard* 200 chart at #16, April 5, 2014.

Outlive, Solid State. Released March 31, 2017. Peaked on the *Billboard* 200 chart at #25, April 22, 2017.

War, Solid State. Released March 1, 2019. Peaked on the *Billboard* 200 chart at #55, March 16, 2019.

Peace, Solid State. Released March 1, 2019. Peaked on the *Billboard* 200 chart at #61, March 16, 2019.

AMY GRANT (1977–2013)[5]

Amy Grant, Myrrh. Released February 3, 1977.

My Father's Eyes, Myrrh. Released April 20, 1979. Certified gold, April 21, 1987.

Never Alone, Myrrh. Released 1980.

Age to Age, Myrrh. Released 1982. Certified platinum, June 24, 1985.

Straight Ahead, Myrrh. Released 1984. Certified gold, May 2, 1985. Peaked on the *Billboard* 200 chart at #133, June 29, 1985.

Unguarded, Myrrh/A&M. Released May 15, 1985. Certified platinum, June 16, 1986. Peaked on the *Billboard* 200 chart at #35, September 7, 1985.

---

4. This list includes studio albums. It does not include live albums, singles, or compilations of previous releases.

5. This list includes studio albums. It does not include live albums, holiday releases, compilations of previous releases, or singles. Exact release dates not available for all albums.

Lead Me On, Myrrh/A&M. Released June 28, 1988. Certified gold, December 22, 1988. Peaked on the *Billboard* 200 chart at #71, August 6, 1988.

Heart in Motion, Myrrh/A&M. Released March 5, 1991. Certified platinum, June 17, 1991. Certified 2x platinum, November 18, 1991. Certified 3x platinum, April 1, 1992. Certified 4x platinum, February 1, 1993. Certified 5x platinum, November 17, 1997. Peaked on the *Billboard* 200 chart at #10, August 31, 1991.

House of Love, Myrrh/A&M. Released August 26, 1994. Certified platinum, December 6, 1994. Certified 2x platinum, March 23, 1995. Peaked on the *Billboard* 200 chart at #13, September 10, 1994.

Behind the Eyes, Myrrh/A&M. Released September 9, 1997. Certified gold, December 11, 1997. Peaked on the *Billboard* 200 chart at #8, September 27, 1997.

Legacy . . . Hymns and Faith, Word/A&M. Released May 21, 2002. Certified gold, June 27, 2007. Peaked on the *Billboard* 200 chart at #21, June 8, 2002.

Simple Things, Word/A&M. Released August 19, 2003. Peaked on the *Billboard* 200 chart at #23, September 6, 2003.

Rock of Ages . . . Hymns and Faith, Word/Warner. Released May 3, 2005. Peaked on the *Billboard* 200 chart at #42, May 21, 2005.

Somewhere Down the Road, Sparrow. Released March 30, 2010. Peaked on the *Billboard* 200 chart at #41, April 17, 2010.

How Mercy Looks from Here, Sparrow. Released May 14, 2013. Peaked on the *Billboard* 200 chart at #12, June 1, 2013.

KEITH GREEN (1965–82)[6]

General Market Singles

"Cheese and Crackers" backed with "I Want to Hurt You," Decca. Released January, 1965.

"A Go-Go Getter" b/w "The Way I Used to Be," Decca. Released May, 1965.

"Girl Don't Tell Me" b/w "How to Be Your Guy," Decca. Released October, 1965.

"You're What's Happening Baby" b/w "Home Town Girls," Decca. Released July, 1966.

"L.A. City Smog Blues" b/w "Fantastic," Era. Released 1969.

---

6. Green had two phases of his career, first as a teen pop star who released singles (no albums) on Decca and Era in the 1960s, and later as a Christian artist with releases on Sparrow and his own Pretty Good Records. Sparrow released several posthumous collections after Green's passing in 1982. Exact release dates not available for singles.

"Sgt. Pepper's Epitaph" b/w "Country Store," Era. Released 1970.

"Pardon Me (Transcript of the 18 Minute Tape Gap)," Rustic. Released 1974.

Christian Market Albums

For Him Who Has Ears to Hear, Sparrow. Released May 20, 1977.

No Compromise, Sparrow. Released November 9, 1978.

So You Wanna Go Back to Egypt, Pretty Good. Released May 7, 1980.

Songs for the Shepherd, Pretty Good. Released April 12, 1982.

MYRRH RECORDS (1972–75)[7]

Vonda Kay Van Dyke, *Day by Day*, MST 6501. Released 1972.

Randy Matthews, *All I Am Is What You See . . .*, MST 6502. Released 1972.

The Crimson Bridge, *The Crimson Bridge*, MST 6503. Released 1972.

Dust, *Dust*, MST 6504. Released 1972.

First Gear, *First Gear*, MST 6505. Released 1972.

The Alethians and The Right Angle, *One Way*, MST 6506. Released 1972.

The Settlers, *Sing a New Song*, MST 6507. Released 1972.

The Spurrlows, *A Slice of the Spurrlows*, MST 6508. Released 1972.

Ray Repp, *Hear the Cryin'*, MST 6509. Released 1972.

Ron Salsbury and The J.C. Power Outlet, *Ron Salsbury and The J.C. Power Outlet*, MST 6511, Released 1972.

Ray Hildebrand, *A Special Kind of Man*, MST 6512. Released 1973.

Anita Bryant, *Naturally*, MST 6513. Released 1972.

The Beautiful Zion Choir, *The Beautiful Zion Missionary Baptist Church Choir*, MST 6514. Released 1973.

Randy Matthews, *Son of Dust*, MST 6515. Released 1973.

First Gear, *Caution! Steep Hill Use . . .*, MST 6516. Released 1974.

Gene Cotton, *In the Gray of the Morning*, MST 6517. Released 1973.

Malcom & Alwyn, *Fool's Wisdom*, MST 6518. Released 1973.

Barry McGuire, *Seeds*, MST 6519. Released 1973.

Danny Thomas, *Tomorrow Belongs to You*, MST 6520. Released 1973.

---

7. The first four years of Myrrh releases are listed here in sequential order by catalog number, with only the year of release provided. This discography is provided by Mike Callahan at *Both Sides Now*, http://www.bsnpubs.com/discog.html, and reproduced here with permission.

Appendix One | 233

The Beautiful Zion Choir, *In the Spirit*, MST 6521. Released 1974.
Danny Thomas, *I'll Still Be Loving You*, MST 6522. Released 1974.
Honeytree, *Honeytree*, MST 6523. Released 1974.
Gene Cotton, *Liberty*, MST 6524. Released 1974.
Ron Salsbury & the J.C. Power Outlet, *Forgiven*, MST 6525. Released 1974.
Second Chapter of Acts, *With Footnotes*, MST 6526. Released 1974.
Petra, *Petra*, MST 6527. Released 1974.
Eddie Robinson, *Reflections of the Man Inside*, MST 6528. Released 1974.
Honeytree, *The Way I Feel*, MST 6530. Released 1974.
Barry McGuire, *Lighten Up*, MSA 6531. Released 1975.
Ray Price, *This Time, Lord*, MSB 6532. Released 1975.
Wanda Jackson, *Now I Have Everything*, MSB 6533. Released 1974.
Malcom & Alwyn, *Wildwall*, MSA 6534, Released 1975.
Henry Jackson Company, *Just Being Alive*, MSA 6535. Released 1974.
Aleksander John, *Days Go By*, MSA 6536. Released 1974.
Marijohn Wilken, *I Have Returned*, MSA 6537. Released 1974.
Ray Price, *Like Old Times Again*, MSB 6538. Released 1974.
Danny Thomas, *Jesus Is My Kind of People*, MSA 6539. Released 1974.
Various artists, *Love Peace Joy*, MYR 6540. Released 1974.
Second Chapter of Acts, *In the Volume of the Book*, MSA 6542. Released 1975.
Water into Wind Band, *Hill Climbing for Beginners*, MSA 6543. Released 1974.
Randy Matthews, *Now I Understand*, MSX 6546. Released 1975.
Randy Matthews, *Eyes to the Sky*, MSA 6547. Released 1975.
Barry McGuire and Second Chapter of Acts, *To the Bride*, MSX 6548. Released 1975.
Marijohn Wilken, *Where I'm Going*, MSA 6549. Released 1975.
The Pat Terry Group, *The Pat Terry Group*, MSA 6550. Released 1975.
Parchment, *Shamblejam*, MSA 6551. Released 1975.
Walt Mills, *Sincerely, Walt Mills*, MSA 6552. Released 1975.
Honeytree, *Evergreen*, MSA 6553. Released 1975.
The SonLight Orchestra, *Love Song & Other Greats*, MSB 6554. Released 1975.
Various artists, *Jubilation!*, MSX 6555. Released 1975.
Wanda Jackson, *Make Me Like a Child Again*, MSB 6556. Released 1975.

LARRY NORMAN (1968-81)[8]

People!, *I Love You*, Capitol. Released 1968.

People!, *Both Sides of People*, Capitol. Released 1969.

Larry Norman, *Upon This Rock*, Capitol. Released 1970.

Larry Norman, *Street Level*, One Way. Released 1970.

Larry Norman, *Bootleg*, One Way. Released 1972.

Larry Norman, *Only Visiting This Planet*, Verve. Released 1972.

Larry Norman, *So Long Ago the Garden*, MGM. Released 1973.

Larry Norman, *In Another Land*, Solid Rock. Released 1976.

Larry Norman, *Streams of White Light into Darkened Corners*, AB. Released 1977.

Larry Norman, *Something New under the Son*, Solid Rock. Released 1981.

PEDRO THE LION / DAVID BAZAN (1997-2019)[9]

Pedro the Lion, *Whole* EP, Tooth & Nail. Released April 8, 1997.

Pedro the Lion, *It's Hard to Find a Friend*, Made In Mexico. Released November 3, 1998.

Pedro the Lion, *The Only Reason I Feel Secure* EP, Made In Mexico. Released May 17, 1999.

Pedro the Lion, *Winners Never Quit*, Jade Tree. Released March 28, 2000.

Pedro the Lion, *Progress* EP, Suicide Squeeze. Released June 27, 2000.

Pedro the Lion, *Control*, Jade Tree. Released April 16, 2002.

Pedro the Lion, *Achilles Heel*, Jade Tree. Released May 25, 2004.

David Bazan, *Fewer Moving Parts* EP, Barsuk. Released June 13, 2006.

David Bazan, *Curse Your Branches*, Barsuk, Released September 1, 2009.

David Bazan, *Strange Negotlations*, Barsuk. Released May 24, 2011.

David Bazan, *Blanco*, Barsuk. Released May 13, 2016.

---

8. This discography is a subset of the comprehensive Norman discography provided by Robert Termorshuizen, http://www.recordconnexion.nl/Norman/Norman.htm, and reproduced with permission. This list includes studio albums released during Norman's classic period only. It does not include live albums, compilations, or post-1981 releases, of which there are many. Only the year of release is provided. Record labels listed are for initial releases only. Most Norman albums were released several times, on different labels, often with different track lists. See Termorshuizen's discography for those details.

9. This list includes studio albums and EPs. It does not include live albums, holiday releases, or singles.

David Bazan, *Care*, Undertow. Released March 7, 2017.

Pedro the Lion, *Phoenix*, Polyvinyl. Released January 18, 2019.

SOLID ROCK RECORDS (1976–81)[10]

Larry Norman, *In Another Land*, SRA 2001. Released 1976.

Randy Stonehill, *Welcome to Paradise*, SRA 2002. Released 1976.

Tom Howard, *View from the Bridge*, SRA 2003. Released 1977.

Randy Stonehill, *The Sky Is Falling*, SRA 2005. Released 1980.

Mark Heard, *Turning to Dust*, SRA 2006. Released 1978.

Larry Norman, *Something New under the Son*, SRA 2007. Released 1981.

Pantano/Salisbury, *Hit the Switch*, SRA 2008. Released 1977.

Mark Heard, *Appalachian Melody*, SRA 2009. Released 1979.

Daniel Amos, *Horrendous Disc*, SRA 2011. Released 1980.

SPARROW RECORDS (1972–75)[11]

Annie Herring, *Through a Child's Eyes*, SPR 1001. Released 1976.

John Michael Talbot, *John Michael Talbot*, SPR 1003. Released 1976.

Various artists, *Firewind*, SPR 1004. Released 1976.

Janny, *Free Indeed*, SPR 1005. Released 1976.

Terry Talbot, *No Longer Alone*, SPR 1006. Released 1976.

Barry McGuire, *C'Mon Along*, SPR 1007. Released 1976.

The Talbot Brothers, *Reborn*, SPR 1008. Released 1976.

Mike and Kathie, *Wings of an Eagle*, SPR 1009. Released 1976.

John Michael Talbot, *The New Earth*, SPR 1010. Released 1977.

Janny, *Covenant Woman*, SPR 1011. Released 1977.

Terry Talbot, *Cradle of Love*, SPR 1012. Released 1977.

Barry McGuire, *Have You Heard*, SPR 1013. Released 1977.

Matthew Ward, *Toward Eternity*, SPR 1014. Released 1979.

---

10. The releases from Solid Rock, the record label that Larry Norman founded and ran, are listed here in sequential order by catalog number, with only the year of release provided. This discography is provided by Mike Callahan at *Both Sides Now*, http://www.bsnpubs.com/discog.html, and reproduced here with permission.

11. The first four years of Sparrow releases are listed here in sequential order by catalog number, with only the year of release provided. This discography is provided by Mike Callahan at *Both Sides Now*, http://www.bsnpubs.com/discog.html, and reproduced here with permission.

Keith Green, *For Him Who Has Ears to Hear*, SPR 1015. Released 1977.

Danniebelle, *Let Me Have a Dream*, SPR 1016. Released 1977.

Children of the Light, *Come on In*, SPR 1017. Released 1977.

Scott Wesley Brown, *I'm Not Religious, I Just Love the Lord*, SPR 1018. Released 1977.

Danniebelle, *Live in Sweden*, SPR 1019. Released 1978.

Second Chapter of Acts, *Mansion Builder*, SPR 1020. Released 1978.

Janny, *He Made Me Worthy*, SPR 1021. Released 1978.

Terry Talbot, *A Time to Laugh, a Time to Sing*, SPR 1022. Released 1978.

Barry McGuire, *Cosmic Cowboy*, SPR 1023. Released 1978.

Keith Green, *No Compromise*, SPR 1024. Released 1978.

Various artists, *Sparrow Spotlight Sampler*, SPR 1025. Released 1978.

Candle, *On the Street*, SPR 1027. Released 1979.

Janny, *Think on These Things*, SPR 1028. Released 1979.

Scott Wesley Brown, *One Step Closer*, SPR 1029. Released 1979.

Barry McGuire, *Inside Out*, SPR 1030. Released 1979.

STRYPER (1984-90)[12]

The Yellow and Black Attack, Enigma. Released July 21, 1984. Peaked on the *Billboard* 200 chart at #103, September 13, 1986.

Soldiers under Command, Enigma. Released May 16, 1985. Certified gold, April 6, 1988. Peaked on the *Billboard* 200 chart at #84, November 30, 1985.

To Hell with the Devil, Enigma. Released October 24, 1986. Certified platinum, January 6, 1988. Peaked on the *Billboard* 200 chart at #32, February 7, 1987.

In God We Trust, Enigma. Released June 28, 1988. Certified gold, September 15, 1988. Peaked on the *Billboard* 200 chart at #32, July 23, 1988.

Against the Law, Enigma. Released August 21, 1990. Peaked on the *Billboard* 200 chart at #39, September 15, 1990.

TIMBRE (2008-15)[13]

Winter Comes to Wake You. Released April 16, 2008.

Little Flowers. Released May 1, 2010.

Sun & Moon. Released April 7, 2015.

---

12. This list includes studio albums released during Stryper's classic period only. It does not include live albums, compilations of previous releases, singles, or post-1990 releases.

13. This list includes studio albums. It does not include holiday releases.

APPENDIX TWO

Pop Singles with Christian References (1957–70)

The entries in the following table are organized chronologically by year and then alphabetically by artist. Several songs appear in chapter 1's accompanying playlist.

Artist	Song Title	Release Year	Label	*Billboard* Chart Peak
Pat Boone	"There's a Gold Mine in the Sky"	1957	Dot	14
Elvis Presley	"Peace in the Valley" (🎧)	1957	RCA Victor	25
Pat Boone	"A Wonderful Time up There" (🎧)	1958	Dot	4
Laurie London	"He's Got the Whole World in His Hands"	1958	Capitol	1
Fats Domino	"When the Saints Go Marching In"	1959	Imperial	50
Wink Martindale	"Deck of Cards"	1959	Dot	7
The Mormon Tabernacle Choir	"Battle Hymn of the Republic"	1959	Columbia	13
The Highwaymen	"Michael"	1960	United Artists	1
Bobby Darin	"Child of God"	1961	Atco	95
Peter, Paul and Mary	"Blowin' in the Wind"	1963	Warner Bros.	2
The Bachelors	"I Believe"	1964	Decca	33
The Impressions	"Amen"	1964	ABC-Paramount	7

Artist	Song Title	Release Year	Label	Billboard Chart Peak
Patti Labelle and Her Blue Belles	"You'll Never Walk Alone"	1964	Parkway	34
Peter, Paul and Mary	"Oh Rock My Soul"	1964	Warner Bros.	93
Peter, Paul and Mary	"Tell It on the Mountain" (🎧)	1964	Warner Bros.	33
The Byrds	"Turn! Turn! Turn!" (🎧)	1965	Columbia	1
The Impressions	"People Get Ready" (🎧)	1965	ABC-Paramount	14
Barry McGuire	"Eve of Destruction"	1965	Dunhill	1
Elvis Presley	"Crying in the Chapel"	1965	RCA Victor	3
Simon and Garfunkel	"Mrs. Robinson" (🎧)	1968	Columbia	1
Norman Greenbaum	"Spirit in the Sky" (🎧)	1969	Reprise	3
The Edwin Hawkins Singers	"Oh Happy Day" (🎧)	1969	Pavilion	3
Tommy James and the Shondells	"Crystal Blue Persuasion"	1969	Roulette	2
Tommy James and the Shondells	"Sweet Cherry Wine"	1969	Roulette	7
Frankie Laine	"Dammit Isn't God's Last Name"	1969	ABC	86
Tommy Leonetti	"Kum Ba Yah"	1969	Decca	54
Billy Preston	"That's the Way God Planned It"	1969	Apple	62
Lawrence Reynolds	"Jesus Is a Soul Man"	1969	Warner Bros.	28
The Youngbloods	"Get Together"	1969	RCA Victor	62
Judy Collins	"Amazing Grace" (🎧)	1970	Elektra	15
Tommy James	"Church Street Soul Revival"	1970	Roulette	62
Paul Kelly	"Stealing in the Name of the Lord"	1970	Happy Tiger	14
Diane Kolby	"Holy Man"	1970	Columbia	67
Pacific Gas & Electric	"Are You Ready"	1970	Columbia	14
Turley Richards	"I Heard the Voice of Jesus"	1970	Warner Bros.	99
James Taylor	"Fire and Rain"	1970	Warner Bros.	82

Source: Cusic, *Saved by Song*, 226, 238–42.

APPENDIX THREE

Major Christian Record Labels and Subsidiaries

Label	Subsidiary	Market
Capitol CMG	Brentwood-Benson Music Publications	Printed Sheet Music
	Capitol Christian Distribution	Distribution
	Capitol CMG Publishing	Publishing
	Credential Recordings	CCM and Christian Rock
	ForeFront Records	CCM and Christian Rock
	Hillsong[1]	Praise and Worship
	Motown Gospel	Gospel
	sixstepsrecords[1]	Praise and Worship
	Sparrow Records	CCM and Christian Rock
	WorshipTogether	Worship Resources
Provident	Beach Street Records	CCM and Christian Rock
	Essential Artist Services	Merchandising
	Essential Music Publishing	Publishing
	Essential Records	CCM and Christian Rock
	Essential Worship	Praise and Worship
	Provident Distribution	Distribution
	Provident Films	Christian Film
	Reunion Records	CCM and Christian Rock
Word	Fervent Records	CCM and Christian Rock
	25 Entertainment	Talent Agency
	Word Distribution	Distribution
	Word Films	Christian Films
	Word Music Publishing	Publishing
	Word Records	CCM and Christian Rock
	Word Worship	Praise and Worship

[1] Hillsong and sixstepsrecords are not wholly owned subsidiaries but rather "partnership imprints."

APPENDIX FOUR

Successful 1990s-Era Pop Singers' Albums

The entries in the following table are organized chronologically by release date.

Artist	Album Title	Release Date	Label(s)	RIAA Certification	Certification Date[1]	Charting Singles[2]
Michael Jackson	Off the Wall	August 10, 1979	Epic	8x Platinum	December 10, 1979	4
Michael Jackson	Thriller	November 30, 1982	Epic	33x Platinum	January 31, 1983	7
Michael Jackson	Bad	August 31, 1987	Epic	10x Platinum	November 9, 1987	7
Janet Jackson	Rhythm Nation 1814	September 19, 1989	A&M	6x Platinum	November 21, 1989	7
Wilson Phillips	Wilson Phillips	May 8, 1990	SBK	5x Platinum	July 10, 1990	5
Mariah Carey	Mariah Carey	June 12, 1990	Columbia	9x Platinum	August 20, 1990	4
Whitney Houston	I'm Your Baby Tonight	November 6, 1990	Arista	4x Platinum	January 15, 1991	4
Madonna	The Immaculate Collection[3]	November 9, 1990	Sire	10x Platinum	January 18, 1991	2
Gloria Estefan	Into the Light	January 25, 1991	Epic	2x Platinum	March 26, 1991	4
Amy Grant	Heart in Motion	March 5, 1991	Myrrh/A&M	5x Platinum	June 17, 1991	5
Michael Bolton	Time, Love and Tenderness	April 23, 1991	Columbia	8x Platinum	June 19, 1991	5
Luther Vandross	Power of Love	April 26, 1991	Epic	2x Platinum	June 20, 1991	4
Paula Abdul	Spellbound	May 14, 1991	Virgin	3x Platinum	June 24, 1991	5
Vanessa Williams	The Comfort Zone	August 20, 1991	PolyGram	3x Platinum	April 30, 1992	5
Mariah Carey	Emotions	September 17, 1991	Columbia	4x Platinum	November 12, 1991	3
Bryan Adams	Waking Up the Neighbours	September 24, 1991	A&M	4x Platinum	December 2, 1991	5
Prince & The New Power Generation	Diamonds and Pearls	October 1, 1991	Warner Bros.	2x Platinum	December 4, 1991	5
Michael Jackson	Dangerous	November 26, 1991	Epic	7x Platinum	January 21, 1992	7
Celine Dion	Celine Dion	March 31, 1992	Epic	2x Platinum	March 12, 1993	5
Whitney Houston	The Bodyguard soundtrack	November 17, 1992	Arista	18x Platinum	January 18, 1993	4

Source: RIAA gold and platinum database, https://www.riaa.com/gold-platinum/.

[1] Certification dates are provided for initial platinum level only (not multi-platinum).

[2] "Charting singles" refers to the number of released singles from each album that charted on *Billboard*'s Hot 100 or Hot AC charts. This category does not include non-charting singles or singles that charted on other charts.

[3] *The Immaculate Collection* was a greatest hits compilation that included two new songs, both of which were released as singles.

Notes

INTRODUCTION

1. Mall, "Concentration, Diversity, and Consequences," 447.
2. Weisbard, *Top 40 Democracy*.
3. Don Cusic addresses nineteenth-century hymns, among other topics, in his history of Christian music, *Saved by Song*. Sandra Graham demonstrates that spirituals circulated as popular entertainment after the Civil War, in *Spirituals and the Birth of a Black Entertainment Industry*. Anthony Heilbut's history of Black gospel music is among the most authoritative: *The Gospel Sound*. For more on Southern gospel, see James Goff, *Close Harmony*.
4. Brackett, *Categorizing Sound*, 1.
5. Brackett, *Categorizing Sound*.
6. Peterson, "Why 1955?"; Keightley, "Long Play."
7. Cavicchi, *Tramps Like Us*.
8. Pruett, "When the Tribe Goes Triple Platinum"; cf. Pruett, *MuzikMafia*.
9. Bourdieu, *Distinction*, 325.
10. Powers, "Intermediaries and Intermediation," 4.
11. Small, *Musicking*, 9.
12. Denisoff, *Solid Gold*; Denisoff, *Tarnished Gold*; Hesmondhalgh, "Post-Punk's Attempt to Democratise the Music Industry"; Negus, *Music Genres and Corporate Cultures*; Ogg, *Independence Days*.
13. Williamson and Cloonan, "Rethinking the Music Industry"; Bruenger, *Making Money, Making Music*; Bruenger, *Create, Produce, Consume*; Frith, *Sound Effects*; Frith, "The Industrialization of Music"; Holt, "The Economy of Live Music in the Digital Age"; Holt, "Rock Clubs and Gentrification in New York City"; Peterson, *Creating Country Music*.
14. Drott, "Music as a Technology of Surveillance"; Marshall, "'Let's Keep Music Special. F—Spotify'"; Morris, *Selling Digital Music*.

15. Garland, "'The Space, the Gear, and Two Big Cans of Beer'"; Taylor, *Music and Capitalism*, 161–76; Whitmore, *World Music and the Black Atlantic*.

16. This claim echoes the genre theory of Franco Fabbri and Simon Frith, who both argue that behavioral, economic, ideological, and social rules play constitutive roles in defining the boundaries of popular music genres. Fabbri, "A Theory of Musical Genres: Two Applications"; Frith, *Performing Rites*.

17. Azerrad, *Our Band Could Be Your Life*.

18. Frith, *Performing Rites*, 86.

19. Howard and Streck, *Apostles of Rock*, 16.

20. Howard and Streck, 16.

21. Howard and Streck, 17.

22. Howard and Streck, 168.

23. Howard and Streck, 173.

24. Howard and Streck, 174.

25. Howard and Streck, 179.

26. Eskridge, *God's Forever Family*, 7.

27. Eskridge, 7.

28. Shires, *Hippies of the Religious Right*, 40–41.

29. Although writers disagree on the terminology, here I follow Shires's practice of referring to "new evangelicalism" (instead of "neoevangelicalism" or "establishment evangelicalism") as the movement that emerged to mediate between fundamentalism and mainline Protestantism in the 1940s—a nondenominational movement later known simply as evangelicalism. Shires, *Hippies of the Religious Right*, 47; also see Hendershot, *Shaking the World for Jesus*, 36; Flowers, *Religion in Strange Times*, 46–47.

30. Hendershot, *Shaking the World for Jesus*, 26.

31. Miller, *Reinventing American Protestantism*.

32. Shires, *Hippies of the Religious Right*, 47.

33. Hendershot, *Shaking the World for Jesus*, 27.

34. Eileen Luhr writes about Christian fanzines' importance to the 1980s' and '90s' Christian punk and metal scenes in *Witnessing Suburbia*, 82–100.

35. Ibrahim Abraham would identify these shared affinities as overlapping consensuses; see "Postsecular Punk."

36. See, for example, Magolda and Gross, *It's All About Jesus!*

37. Kelman, *Shout to the Lord*.

38. Stace, *Secular Music, Sacred Space*; on the worship wars, see Nekola, "Negotiating the Tensions of U.S. Worship Music in the Marketplace."

39. Ingalls, *Singing the Congregation*, 5.

40. Turino, *Music as Social Life*, 26.

41. Ingalls, *Singing the Congregation*, 6; Kelman, *Shout to the Lord*, 23.

42. Miller, *Segregating Sound*.

43. On radio formats, see Weisbard, *Top 40 Democracy*.

44. Coddington, "'Check Out the Hook While My DJ Revolves It': How the Music Industry Made Rap into Pop in the Late 1980s."

45. Lecrae is one of many recent hip hop artists active in the general market to embrace his Christian faith publicly in his music. Others include Chance, Kendrick Lamar, and Kanye West. Christina Zanfagna writes compellingly

about 1990s Christian hip hop in Los Angeles in *Holy Hip Hop in the City of Angels*.

46. Several writers have addressed these and other stakes of scholarly canons within musicology and ethnomusicology in Bergeron and Bohlman, *Disciplining Music*.

47. See, for example, Philip Tagg's early work, such as *Kojak* (originally published in 1979) and *Fernando the Flute* (originally published in 1981).

48. Brooks, "On Being Tasteless," 18.

49. Wald, "How the Smart Kids Study Popular Music, or Why Are There No Papers on Katy Perry?" Will Straw also noted the overwhelming maleness of music connoisseurship in "Sizing Up Record Collectors."

50. Mall, "Concentration, Diversity, and Consequences."

51. Ingalls, Landau, and Wagner, *Christian Congregational Music*; Ingalls and Yong, *The Spirit of Praise*; Nekola and Wagner, *Congregational Music-Making and Community in a Mediated Age*; Riches and Wagner, *The Hillsong Movement Examined*; Ingalls, Swijghuisen-Reigersberg, and Sherinian, *Making Congregational Music Local*; Mall, Engelhardt, and Ingalls, *Studying Congregational Music: Key Issues, Methods, and Theoretical Perspectives*.

52. Engelhardt, *Singing the Right Way*; Porter, *Contemporary Worship Music and Everyday Musical Lives*; Dueck, *Congregational Music, Conflict, and Community*; Stace, *Secular Music, Sacred Space*; Ingalls, *Singing the Congregation*; Kelman, *Shout to the Lord*; Wagner, *Music, Branding and Consumer Culture in Church: Hillsong in Focus*.

53. Marini, *Sacred Song in America*; Stowe, *No Sympathy for the Devil*; Cusic, *Saved by Song*; Eskridge, *God's Forever Family*; Stephens, *The Devil's Music*; Thornbury, *Why Should the Devil*.

54. Luhr, *Witnessing Suburbia*.

55. Moberg, *Christian Metal: History, Ideology, Scene*; Young, *Gray Sabbath*; Abraham, *Evangelical Youth Culture*.

56. I write about Cornerstone in "This Is a Chance to Come Together."

57. I write about the Anchor in "'We Can Be Renewed'"; and "Worship Capital."

58. Rommen, *"Mek Some Noise"*; Engelhardt, *Singing the Right Way*.

59. Hebdige, *Subculture*.

CHAPTER 1: "WHY SHOULD THE DEVIL HAVE ALL THE GOOD MUSIC?"

1. Eskridge, *God's Forever Family*, 170.

2. McDannell, *Material Christianity*, 248; Shires, *Hippies of the Religious Right*, 86–88; also see Di Sabatino, *The Jesus People Movement*; Eskridge, *God's Forever Family*.

3. Tom Wagner addresses the branding of evangelicalism for young audience, paying particular attention to the Australia-based global megachurch Hillsong in the twenty-first century. See Wagner, *Music, Branding and Consumer Culture in Church: Hillsong in Focus*.

4. McDannell, *Material Christianity*, 223–29.

5. Cohen, *A Consumer's Republic*.

6. Stowe, *No Sympathy for the Devil*, 213.
7. Horowitz, *Consuming Pleasures*.
8. McDannell, *Material Christianity*, 223.
9. One example of these tensions is the controversy over "prosperity gospel," a belief that material wealth accompanies or follows (and thus signifies) sincere acts of faith.
10. Hendershot, *Shaking the World for Jesus*, 30, emphasis in original.
11. Moore, "Authenticity as Authentication"; Peterson, "In Search of Authenticity."
12. Green and Hazard, *No Compromise*, 335–36.
13. Green and Hazard, 333.
14. Green and Hazard, 336–37.
15. Interview with the author, March 4, 2010.
16. The broad strokes of Larry Norman's career are well documented in the literature on Christian rock. See, for example, Howard and Streck, *Apostles of Rock*; Joseph, *The Rock & Roll Rebellion*; Thompson, *Raised by Wolves*; Di Sabatino, *Fallen Angel*; Stowe, *No Sympathy for the Devil*; Thornbury, *Why Should the Devil*. It is important to note that *Fallen Angel*'s critical characterization of Norman has been contested by friends and colleagues committed to protecting his legacy, most prominently on the website thetruthaboutlarrynorman.com (retrieved August 14, 2017).
17. Other early artist-directed Christian labels included Ralph Carmichael's Light Records and Pat Boone's Lamb and Lion Records.
18. Thompson, *Raised by Wolves*, 51.
19. A more nuanced explanation of Norman's leaving the band People! is that it resulted from the increasing tension between Norman's Christian identity and his bandmates' adherence to Scientology. See Stowe, *No Sympathy for the Devil*, 35–36.
20. Eskridge, *God's Forever Family*, 85.
21. "I Wish We'd All Been Ready" was not the only song that reflected this preoccupation. Barry McGuire's cover of the apocalyptic song "Eve of Destruction," recorded before McGuire converted to Christianity, served a similar function in the general market where it reached #1 on the *Billboard* Hot 100 on September 25, 1965 (toppling The Beatles' "Help!"). It should be no surprise that Norman considered Lindsey a friend. Lindsey, *The Late Great Planet Earth*.
22. Nekola, "'More Than Just a Music,'" 412, emphasis original. Nekola also includes a table, published in 1969, that directly contrasts musical elements of "good music" with those of rock and roll.
23. Yes, Metro-Goldwyn-Mayer operated a record label. The film studio founded MGM Records in 1946, acquired Verve in 1961, and then sold the whole enterprise to PolyGram in 1972. PolyGram continued issuing new releases via MGM Records through 1976 and soundtracks and reissues through 1982.
24. Norman's *Only Visiting This Planet* was ranked #2, behind Amy Grant's *Lead Me On*. Granger, *CCM Presents*.
25. Goffman and Joy, *Counterculture through the Ages*, 325–27.
26. Cusic, *Saved by Song*, 226, 238–42.

27. Although "A Wonderful Time up There" was written by white Southern gospel artist Lee Roy Abernathy, Pat Boone did not discriminate when it came to recording gospel songs throughout his long career. Among his many gospel albums and compilations is *Pat Boone Sings the New Songs of the Jesus People* (1971, Lamb & Lion; the album closes with a cover of Larry Norman's "I Wish We'd All Been Ready"), demonstrating that he sanitized indiscriminately as well.

28. Thompson, *Raised by Wolves*, 25; Stowe, *No Sympathy for the Devil*, 54–56; Cusic, *Saved by Song*, 238–39.

29. The musical theatre market was similarly impacted: Andrew Lloyd Weber and Tim Rice collaborated on two biblically themed rock operas—*Joseph and the Amazing Technicolor Dreamcoat* (1969) and *Jesus Christ Superstar* (1970)—followed by Stephen Schwartz and John-Michael Tebelak's *Godspell* (1971), all of which have had several stage productions and revivals as well as film versions.

30. Shires, *Hippies of the Religious Right*.

31. Eskridge, *God's Forever Family*, 129.

32. See, for example, Blessitt, *Life's Greatest Trip*; MacDonald, *The House of Acts*; Pederson, *Jesus People*; Blessitt, *Tell the World*; Smith and Steven, *The Reproducers*; Williams, *Call to the Streets*.

33. Shires, *Hippies of the Religious Right*, 129–36; cf. Henry, *Answers for the Now Generation*; Schaeffer, *The Church at the End of the 20th Century*; Wilkerson, *David Wilkerson's Jesus Person Maturity Manual*.

34. "The New Rebel Cry: Jesus Is Coming!," *Time* 97, no. 25 (June 21, 1971), 36–47. This followed a shorter feature ten months prior, "Street Christians: Jesus as the Ultimate Trip," *Time* 96, no. 5 (August 3, 1970), 31–32.

35. "The Jesus Craze," *Life* 71, no. 26 (December 31, 1971), 38; Brian Vachon, "The Jesus Movement Is Upon Us," *Look* (February 9, 1971), 15–21; "The Jesus People," *Newsweek* (March 22, 1971), 97; "The Jesus Movement: Impact on Youth, Church," *U.S. News & World Report* (March 20, 1972), 59–64.

36. Graham, *The Jesus Generation*. David Di Sabatino has exhaustively collected and annotated primary and secondary source materials about the Jesus People. This bibliography includes over 1,260 books, films, and all types of periodicals, and a discography of over 350 recordings; see Di Sabatino, *The Jesus People Movement*.

37. Eskridge, *God's Forever Family*, 125. Eskridge provided a thorough review of this media blitz in chapter 5 ("It Only Takes a Spark"), particularly pp. 128–41.

38. Hebdige, *Subculture*, 92–94.

39. Sources cite different attendance numbers, both for Explo '72's conference and for its final concert. I have chosen to give ranges that capture the various available estimates.

40. Eskridge, *God's Forever Family*, 171.

41. Stowe, *No Sympathy for the Devil*, 60; Eskridge, *God's Forever Family*, 171.

42. Stowe, *No Sympathy for the Devil*, 58–59; Eskridge, *God's Forever Family*, 173–74.

43. Eskridge, *God's Forever Family*, 174.
44. "Rallying for Jesus," *Life* 72, no. 25 (June 30, 1972), 40–45. A note on the album sleeve itself reads: "This album is not for sale. This album was produced for the sole purpose of offering to the EXPLO '72 television audience musical reminders of this historic congress. This album is sent to individuals who let the ministry of Campus Crusade for Christ International know that they are interested in receiving this album."
45. Eskridge, *God's Forever Family*, 177.
46. "The New Rebel Cry," 56.
47. Stowe, *No Sympathy for the Devil*, 62.
48. The Watergate break-in itself was discovered very early on June 17, 1972, the same morning as Explo '72's capstone concert
49. Please see Mall, "Billy Ray Hearn," for a more comprehensive biography.
50. Interview with the author, March 4, 2010.
51. Ibid.
52. Hearn, Oral Memoirs, 34.
53. Interview with the author, March 4, 2010.
54. Hearn, Oral Memoirs, 35.
55. Bishop, "'We're Gonna Change This Land,'" 69.
56. Interview with the author, March 4, 2010.
57. Hearn, Oral Memoirs, 38. Bishop notes that Broadman, the Southern Baptist Convention's publishing company, sold 72,576 copies of the *Good News!* score in 1968—more than the official *Baptist Hymnal*. Bishop, "'We're Gonna Change This Land,'" 72.
58. Hearn, Oral Memoirs, 38, emphasis added.
59. Kaiser, Oral Memoirs, 8.
60. Interview with the author, March 4, 2010.
61. Cusic, *Encyclopedia of Contemporary Christian Music*, 356–57.
62. McCracken, Oral Memoirs, 432–34.
63. McCracken, 443.
64. Frith, *Sound Effects*, 89–90. As I discuss in chapter 2, this is exactly the approach that EMI and other major labels took when reentering the Christian market in the late 1980s and early '90s.
65. See, for example, Goff, *Close Harmony*.
66. Interview with the author, March 4, 2010.
67. Cf. Peterson, "Why 1955?"
68. Peterson and Berger, "Cycles in Symbol Production," 164.
69. Eskridge, *God's Forever Family*, 234.
70. Hendershot, *Shaking the World for Jesus*, 30.
71. Luhr, *Witnessing Suburbia*, 8–11.
72. McDannell, *Material Christianity*, 246.
73. Quoted in Darden and Richardson, *Corporate Giants*, 187.
74. Interview with the author, March 4, 2010.
75. Ibid.
76. Herring was a core member of Second Chapter of Acts, one of Myrrh's best-selling artists. As a group, Second Chapter of Acts released one more record on Myrrh (1977's *How the West Was One*, a live triple LP with guitarist/

songwriter Phil Keaggy and their backing band, David) before their first album on Sparrow, *Mansion Builder* (1978).

77. Interview with the author, March 4, 2010.

78. Green and Hazard, *No Compromise*, 221.

79. Bob Dylan also converted to evangelical Christianity after praying with Vineyard pastors in 1978. Green and Dylan met and became friends through the Vineyard, talking frequently about music and faith. Dylan recorded harmonica for Green's song "Pledge My Head to Heaven" (🎧).

80. Although Hearn released eighteen and fifteen albums in each of his last two years at Myrrh (1974–75), his pace at Sparrow was intentionally slower: he released eight albums in each of the new label's first two years (1976–77).

81. Interview with the author, March 4, 2010.

82. Emphasis original. Printed in *CCM* 2, no. 9 (March 1980), 6–7. Reprinted in Styll, *The Heart of the Matter*, 68.

83. Styll, 70.

84. Interview with the author, December 16, 2009.

85. Nekola, "'More Than Just a Music.'"

86. Preston Shires discusses the rise of the Christian Right in the United States as a legacy of countercultural Christianity, including the Jesus People movement. See Shires, *Hippies of the Religious Right*.

87. Beaujon, *Body Piercing Saved My Life*, 32.

88. Luhr writes about underground Christian fanzines in *Witnessing Suburbia*, 82–100.

CHAPTER 2: THE GREAT ADVENTURE

1. Via http://capitolchristianmusicgroup.com/about/about-ccmg.aspx, accessed June 5, 2018; emphasis added.

2. Dave Laing identifies corporate acquisitions and mergers as a key feature of the record industries overall in the late twentieth century; see "The Recording Industry in the Twentieth Century," 45–47.

3. Hearn, Oral Memoirs, April 14, 1998, 25.

4. The Internet Archive Wayback Machine, https://web.archive.org, has been archiving web pages since 1996. Its archive of the EMI CMG website dates back to late 1998.

5. The same is true of Provident, as its corporate parent Sony is also publicly traded. Word's former corporate parent Warner is a division of a for-profit conglomerate that is privately owned and thus accountable to different legal standards.

6. Mall, "Concentration, Diversity, and Consequences."

7. See, for example, Knopper, *Appetite for Self-Destruction*; Marshall, "The Recording Industry in the Twenty-First Century"; Witt, *How Music Got Free*.

8. RIAA, "News and Notes on 2016 RIAA Shipment and Revenue Statistics," 1.

9. IFPI, "Global Music Report 2018," 10. Both the RIAA's and IFPI's successive annual reports have documented further growth in streaming through 2019.

10. Mall, "As for Me and My House."

11. John Styll, "State of the Industry 1993," *The CCM Update* 7, no. 22 (August 30, 1993), 1.

12. John Styll, "Facing the Future: Will Christian Music Sell More or Just Sell Out?," *The CCM Update* 6, no. 20 (July 27, 1992), 1.

13. "Sparrow Anticipates Banner Year in 1984," *MusicLine* 1, no. 8 (May, 1983), 23; "A MusicLine Salute: Ten Years of Sparrow, the Company That Won't Stop Growing," *MusicLine* 3, no. 12 (April 1986), 55.

14. Vanda Krefft, "Ken Leroy Pennell Brings Spanish to Sparrow," *CCM* 3, no. 5 (November 1980), 23; "Sparrow Anticipates Banner Year in 1984."

15. "Sparrow, MCA Sign Dist. Pact," *CCM* 3, no. 9 (March 1981), 42.

16. Bill Hearn, "Putting Tomorrow's Crossover in a More Timeless Perspective," *MusicLine* 2, no. 10 (February 1985), 59.

17. Interview with the author, March 4, 2010.

18. "Word, A&M Ink Distribution Deal," *MusicLine* 2, no. 9 (January 1985), 1; "Benson Sets Up Mainstream Distribution with Capitol," *The MusicLine Update* 1, no. 1 (October 13, 1986), 1.

19. "Out & About," *The CCM Update* 6, no. 10 (March 9, 1992), 2.

20. Hearn, Oral Memoirs, April 14, 1998, 27–29.

21. Interview with the author, March 4, 2010.

22. Bowen and Jerome, *Rough Mix*, 277.

23. Interview with the author, March 4, 2010.

24. It is easier to hear these songs' roots as country in Steven Curtis Chapman's acoustic re-recordings for his 2011 album *re:creation* (🎧).

25. Printed in *CCM* 2, no. 9 (March 1980), 6–7. Reprinted in Styll, *The Heart of the Matter*.

26. John Styll, "Editor's Corner," *CCM* 2, no. 7 (January 1980), 5.

27. Mall, "Selling Out or Buying In?"

28. John Styll, "Music or Industry?," *CCM* 8, no. 9 (March 1986), 4.

29. Interview with the author, December 16, 2009.

30. Interview with the author, March 4, 2010.

31. Ibid.

32. Zondervan consolidated ownership of Benson in 1983.

33. John Styll, "Editor's Introduction" *CCM* 17, no. 6 (December 1994), 4.

34. Hearn, Oral Memoirs, April 14, 1998, 31.

35. "CCM/Contact," *CCM* 2, no. 11 (May 1980), 32, emphasis original.

36. Interview with the author, March 4, 2010.

37. Hearn, Oral Memoirs, April 14, 1998, 44; Hearn, Oral Memoirs, January 17, 1998, 3.

38. Peacock, *At the Crossroads*, 151.

39. Peacock, 162.

40. Hendershot, *Shaking the World for Jesus*, 52.

41. The GMA's annual *Industry Overviews* present selected statistics compiled by Nielsen SoundScan (which tracks sales of recorded music), the Recording Industry Association of America (which certifies gold- and platinum-level sales in the United States), and various polling companies, and are targeted

toward media outlets reporting on and publicizing the Christian record industry. *Industry Overviews* for the years 2004–09 are available via the Christian Music Trade Association at http://www.cmta.biz/industry2.htm (accessed June 8, 2018).

42. RIAA U.S. Sales Database, https://www.riaa.com/u-s-sales-database/ (accessed May 15, 2019).

43. Gospel Music Association, "Gospel Music Industry Overview 2004"; "Gospel Music Industry Overview 2005."

44. Interview with the author, September 17, 2010. This interviewee's identity has been anonymized.

45. Ibid.

46. Interview with the author, March 5, 2010.

47. Gospel Music Association, "Gospel Music Industry Overview 2006."

48. The Big Three's country music subsidiaries include Sony Music Nashville, UMG Nashville, and Warner Music Nashville, each of which oversees several country music record label subsidiaries.

49. Interview with the author, March 5, 2010.

50. Interview with the author, September 17, 2010.

51. Weisbard, *Top 40 Democracy*, 112–14.

52. Mall, "Tuning In to Locality."

53. Interview with the author, September 17, 2010.

54. Interview with the author, March 5, 2010.

55. Interview with the author, September 17, 2010.

56. Interview with the author, December 16, 2009.

57. Interview with the author, September 13, 2010.

58. Ibid.

59. Howard and Streck, *Apostles of Rock*.

60. Interview with the author, December 11, 2009.

61. Interview with the author, September 13, 2010.

62. Interview with the author, March 5, 2010.

63. Interview with the author, December 17, 2009.

64. John Styll, "Small Change Can Mean Big Pay Off," *MusicLine* 3, no. 5 (September 1985), 5.

65. "Bill Taylor: Benson's New Point Man," *MusicLine* 4, no. 2 (June 1986), 6.

66. "Benson: Bill Taylor Leaving; 1.8M 2nd Qtr. Loss Announced," *The MusicLine Update* 1, no. 21 (August 3, 1987), 1.

67. Ibid.

68. Ibid.

69. Interview with the author, December 11, 2009.

70. Ibid.

71. Ibid.

72. Interview with the author, March 5, 2010.

73. Interview with the author, December 17, 2009.

74. Interview with the author, March 5, 2010.

75. Ibid.

76. Gospel Music Association, "Gospel Music Industry Overview 2009."
77. RIAA U.S. Sales Database, https://www.riaa.com/u-s-sales-database/, accessed February 26, 2020.
78. Lee Marshall documents some of the record industry's biggest transitions and strategies in the first decade of the twenty-first century; see "The Recording Industry in the Twenty-First Century."
79. Interview with the author, December 17, 2009.
80. Interview with the author, December 11, 2009.
81. Interview with the author, September 17, 2010.
82. Interview with the author, March 5, 2010.
83. This observation is consistent with Peterson and Kern's findings in "Changing Highbrow Taste."
84. Interview with the author, March 5, 2010.
85. Frith, *Sound Effects*, 89–90.
86. Interview with the author, March 5, 2010.
87. Interview with the author, December 18, 2009.

CHAPTER 3: *A WOLF IN SHEEP'S CLOTHING?*

1. Rommen, *"Mek Some Noise"*, 37, emphasis original.
2. Rommen, 5.
3. Nekola, "'More Than Just a Music'"; also see Stephens, *The Devil's Music*.
4. Sullivan, "'More Popular Than Jesus,'" 316.
5. Stephens, *The Devil's Music*, 99.
6. Martin Luther King Jr., "Advice for Living," *Ebony* (April 1958), 392. Quoted in Stephens, 99.
7. Babcock, *Music on the Rocks*, Center for Popular Music, Middle Tennessee State University.
8. Babcock, 2.
9. Babcock, 4–9.
10. Babcock, 2–3.
11. Luhr, *Witnessing Suburbia*; Nekola, "'More Than Just a Music.'"
12. Nekola, "'More Than Just a Music,'" 413.
13. Garlock, *The Big Beat: A Rock Blast*, 12–13; Luhr, *Witnessing Suburbia*, 44.
14. Nekola, "'More Than Just a Music,'" 413.
15. Luhr, *Witnessing Suburbia*, 43; cf. Larson, *Hippies, Hindus and Rock & Roll*; Larson, *Rock & Roll*; Larson, *Rock and the Church*. A prolific writer, in the 1980s and later Larson turned his attention to other moral panics with the potential to corrupt Christian youth such as Satanism, cults in general, the new age movement, UFOs, witchcraft, and paganism. See, for example, Larson, *Satanism*; Larson, *Straight Answers on the New Age*; Larson, *Larson's New Book of Cults*; Larson, *UFOs and the Alien Agenda*; Larson, *Larson's Book of Spiritual Warfare*.
16. Larson's outcries were defused somewhat when, after profiling thrash metal band Slayer for *Spin* magazine, he realized that the bandmembers' apparent Satanism was not a set of sincerely held beliefs but rather a performative

stance. Kelefa Sanneh recounted this period in the feature "Record Deal with the Devil" for the podcast and radio show *This American Life* (episode #666, January 18, 2019). See Bob Larson, "Desperately Seeking Satan," *Spin* 5, no. 2 (May 1989), 26–31, 60, 94. On the mid-'80s panic, see Stephens, *The Devil's Music*.

17. Noebel, *The Beatles*, 57; reprinted in Nekola, "'More Than Just a Music,'" 412.

18. Noebel, *Communism, Hypnotism and the Beatles*; Noebel, *The Marxist Minstrels*, Center for Popular Music, Middle Tennessee State University.

19. Luhr, *Witnessing Suburbia*, 40–42; Nekola, "'More Than Just a Music,'" 416–17.

20. Personal communication, September 25, 2019.

21. Quoted in Beaujon, *Body Piercing Saved My Life*, 31.

22. Interview with the author, March 4, 2010. Note the similarity here between the clandestine treatment of Christian records and that of morally fraught consumer goods such as pornographic magazines and alcohol.

23. Quoted in Beaujon, *Body Piercing Saved My Life*, 31.

24. Personal communication, September 4, 2019.

25. Interview with the author, March 4, 2010.

26. John Styll, "Editor's Corner," *CCM* 3, no. 3 (September 1980), 5. Also see Stephens, *The Devil's Music*.

27. John Styll, "Pop and Rock: The Language of the Young," *CCM* 3, no. 5 (October 1980), 5.

28. John Styll, "Christian Rock Wars: Evangelist Jimmy Swaggart Tells Us Why He Hates Today's Christian Rock," *CCM* 7, no. 12 (June 1985), 14–17. Swaggart's criticisms appeared in his organization's magazine *The Evangelist* and his book *Religious Rock'n'roll*.

29. Quoted in Styll, *The Heart of the Matter*, 135.

30. Styll, 137, emphasis original.

31. Styll, 137.

32. Styll, 140.

33. Styll, 142.

34. Wagner, "No Other Name?," 326.

35. Styll, *The Heart of the Matter*, 141–42, emphasis original.

36. Styll, 143.

37. Several Bible verses attest to the incomprehensibility of God, including Job 26:14, Psalm 147:5, Isaiah 55:8–9, and 1 Corinthians 2:10–11, among others.

38. Styll, *The Heart of the Matter*, 144.

39. Styll's interview with Jimmy Swaggart was published in *CCM* magazine's June 1985 issue. Reader's letters in response were published in the August and September issues.

40. Rommen, *"Mek Some Noise."*

41. Doug Jolley and Timothy Morgan, "News: Patty Weds Former Backup Vocalist," *Christianity Today* (September 11, 1995), 72–74.

42. John Styll, Debra Akins, and April Hefner, "Sandi Patty Marries, Admits Affairs," *CCM* 18, no. 4 (October 1995), 18–20.

43. Patty, *Broken on the Back Row*, 136–37.

44. Jordan, as a member of the vocal trio First Call, had toured with English to benefit Mercy Ministries, which counsels women through unplanned pregnancies, among other crises. Both Jordan and English were married at the time of their affair.

45. "Michael English Admits 'Mistakes,' Leaves Christian Music," *CCM* 16, no. 12 (June 1994), 16.

46. Interview with the author, December 16, 2009.

47. Interview with the author, September 13, 2010.

48. Peterson compared this to the sheltered and protective culture of a Christian college (he attended Taylor University, an evangelical Christian college in Upland, Indiana) versus the unstructured freedom at a Big Ten university like Purdue or Indiana University. Interview with the author, September 13, 2010.

49. Interview with the author, September 13, 2010.

50. Heilbut, *The Fan Who Knew Too Much*. Alisha Lola Jones also writes about sexuality and gender in the context of Black gospel in *Flaming?*

51. Stowe, *No Sympathy for the Devil*, 201; Powell, *Encyclopedia of Contemporary Christian Music*, 871.

52. Knapp, *Facing the Music*, 135.

53. Interview with the author, September 13, 2010.

54. See Liam Stack, "Trey Pearson, a Popular Christian Rocker, Tells Fans He's Gay," *New York Times* (June 2, 2016), sec. Arts; Julie Zauzmer, "'I Never Wanted to Be Gay': Christian Musician Comes Out, in Moving Letter to Fans," *Washington Post* (May 31, 2016).

55. John Styll, "Editor's Introduction," *CCM* 16, no. 8 (February 1994), 5.

56. See, "Our Purpose," *CCM* 16, no. 11 (May 1994), 3.

57. John Styll, "Editor's Introduction," *CCM* 16, no. 12 (June 1994), 6.

58. John Styll, "Sin and the Spotlight: An Examination of *CCM*'s Response to the Struggle between the Private Lives of Public People and Your Right to Know," *CCM* 18, no. 4 (October 1995), 49.

59. Styll, 50.

CHAPTER 4: "FIND A WAY"

1. John Styll, "Ministry or Industry?," *CCM* 8, no. 9 (March 1986), 4.

2. Bill Hearn, "Putting Tomorrow's Crossover in a More Timeless Perspective," *MusicLine* 2, no. 10 (February 1985), 59.

3. In addition to the song's title—"El Shaddai" is a Judaic name often translated as "God Almighty"—many of the lyrics are also in Hebrew. Together with the song's allusions to Old Testament acts of God, this explicitly references the shared traditions of Christianity and Judaism.

4. Romanowski, "Move Over Madonna," 47–48.

5. Word subsidiary Myrrh had released Grant's records. Depending on your definition, A&M was technically an independent label distributed by RCA (in the United States; CBS Records handled much of A&M's distribution elsewhere), and not a member of the Big Six record companies at the time. Although Word

was still owned by ABC, the broadcast giant owned no other record labels and thus could not provide the same infrastructural support that A&M could.

6. Romanowski, "Move Over Madonna," 55.

7. Petra's *Beat the System*, released on January 16, 1985—five months earlier than *Unguarded*—was also a joint release between Word and A&M. Petra was signed to Star Song Records, which was distributed by Word between 1983 and '87.

8. Michael Goldberg, "Amy Grant Wants to Put God on the Charts," *Rolling Stone* no. 449 (June 6, 1985), 9–10.

9. Ted Ojarovsky, "Amy Grant: Unguarded Moments?," *CCM* 8, no. 2 (August 1985), 12.

10. I address reactions to *Unguarded* from *CCM* magazine and its readers at more length in "Selling Out or Buying In?"

11. Eric Weisbard incorrectly identifies "the biggest songwriter of the [1980s] era," Diane Warren, as a cowriter of "Find a Way" in *Top 40 Democracy*, 151.

12. "The Next Time I Fall" was recorded shortly after Cetera left the band Chicago in 1985. It appeared on his second solo album, 1986's *Solitude/Solitaire*. (Grant later included it on her *Greatest Hits 1986–2004* collection.)

13. The feature interview was reprinted, unedited, in Styll, *The Heart of the Matter*, 45–63.

14. Styll, 51. *Lead Me On* was mixed by Shelly Yakus, who had worked with some of the most successful artists of the prior three decades, including John Lennon, Blue Öyster Cult, the Raspberries, Chick Corea, Stevie Nicks, Tom Petty, and many others. From 1984 to '95 he was chief engineer and vice president at A&M Studios in Hollywood (currently part of the Jim Henson Company Lot).

15. Styll, 58–59.

16. Styll, 62.

17. Twenty-eight of Grant's radio hits were top ten and higher; seven peaked at #1. Powell, *Encyclopedia of Contemporary Christian Music*, 379.

18. Weisbard, *Top 40 Democracy*.

19. We should not understate formats' commercial utility: following Weisbard, elsewhere I describe radio formats as musical categories that stations use to sell their audiences to advertisers. Mall, "Tuning In to Locality."

20. It is important to note that Weisbard's approach here is a grounded-theory one, constructing a theoretical apparatus with the commercial radio industry's on-the-ground practices as a foundation. By seriously considering the ways in which the concept of radio formats might contribute to broader discourses on popular music, he also argues for the scholarly legitimacy and utility of taxonomies derived from the entertainment and culture industries.

21. Interview with the author, December 17, 2009.

22. Quoted in Perkins, "Music, Culture Industry, and the Shaping of Charismatic Worship," 239.

23. Interview with the author, December 16, 2009.

24. Perkins, "Music, Culture Industry, and the Shaping of Charismatic Worship," 239.

25. Interview with the author, September 17, 2010. This interviewee's identity has been anonymized.

26. Indeed, losing one's job is something of a rite of passage in record industries, given the unpredictable marketplace and frequent corporate acquisitions and realignments. All of the record industry professionals with whom I spoke during my research have been fired at one point, either due to managerial restructuring or to failed artist campaigns.

27. You can see the charting of these singles graphically represented in an illustration on this book's companion website andrewmallphd.com. Word released two additional singles to Christian radio, specifically choosing songs where Grant sang about her Christian faith: "Hope Set High" and "Ask Me."

28. The Hot AC chart only has fifty slots—half as many as the Hot 100—so on one hand there is more competition among singles for chart positions. On the other hand, the Hot 100 has a greater variety of genres represented—and thus a greater number of singles competing for positions—than does the Hot AC.

29. To compare, vinyl single shipments peaked at 228 million in 1973, and cassette singles peaked at 87.4 million units shipped in 1990. See the RIAA U.S. Sales Database, https://www.riaa.com/u-s-sales-database/ (accessed January 29, 2018).

30. This is a quirk of U.S. copyright law; most other countries with modern intellectual property regulations allow for performance royalties from radio airplay to accrue to the rightsholders of recordings.

31. Joseph, *The Rock & Roll Rebellion*; see also Joseph, *Faith, God and Rock & Roll*.

32. Joseph, *The Rock & Roll Rebellion*, 188.

33. Thom Granger, "Sparrow Soaring at Fifteen," *CCM Update* 5, no. 16 (June 3, 1991), 2. Quoted in Joseph, 190.

34. Frith, *Performing Rites*, 85.

35. Romanowski, "Move Over Madonna," 48.

36. Interview with the author, March 5, 2010.

37. Ibid.

38. Dueck, "Crossing the Street."

CHAPTER 5: MUSIC TO RAISE THE DEAD

1. For more on JPUSA, see Young, *Gray Sabbath*.

2. Rommen, *"Mek Some Noise."*

3. Larry Norman similarly used stories of hippie and rock and roll excesses as teachable moments in his songs. For example, *Only Visiting This Planet*'s "Why Don't You Look into Jesus?," a bluesy number reportedly written as a response to Norman's interaction with secular artists (whom he calls out by name later in the album, on "Reader's Digest": The Beatles, David Bowie, Alice Cooper, Jimi Hendrix, Janis Joplin, and The Rolling Stones), suggests that faith in Christ can fill a void that a lifestyle of sex ("gonorrhea on Valentine's Day"), drugs ("shooting junk 'till you're half insane"), and rock and roll ("you'll be deaf before you're thirty-three") will not. See chapter 1 for more on Norman.

4. Quoted in Beaujon, *Body Piercing Saved My Life*, 31.

5. Engelhardt, *Singing the Right Way*; cf. Small, *Musicking*.
6. Interview with the author, March 16, 2010.
7. Ibid.
8. Interview with the author, April 9, 2010.
9. The biblical justification for this and similar ethics is that of keeping fellow Christians from stumbling into sin: "Therefore let us stop passing judgment on one another. Instead, make up your mind not to put any stumbling block or obstacle in the way of a brother or sister," Romans 14:13.
10. Interview with the author, December 11, 2019.
11. Engelhardt, *Singing the Right Way*.
12. Engelhardt, 11.
13. Small, *Musicking*.
14. Interview with the author, March 5, 2010. This interviewee's identity has been anonymized.
15. Interview with the author, September 10, 2010.
16. Interview with the author, December 16, 2009.
17. Abraham, "Postsecular Punk."
18. "Postsecular" refers to the reemergence (or newly recognized presence) of religion and religious ideals in nominally irreligious spaces (cultural, economic, educational, political, social, and so on) long thought to be secular. Abraham, 95; cf. Taylor, *A Secular Age*.
19. Following the political philosopher John Rawls, Abraham uses the framework of "overlapping consensus" to describe situations in which groups with otherwise disparate values and objectives (Christian punks, for example, vs. non-Christian punks) nevertheless find common ground (DIY ethics) that enable them to cohabit the same spaces and places. "Postsecular Punk," 96; see, for example, Rawls, *Justice as Fairness*.
20. Interview with the author, December 18, 2009.
21. Interview with the author, March 23, 2010.
22. Ibid.
23. Ibid.
24. Ibid.
25. Ibid.
26. Ibid.
27. Interview with the author, March 5, 2010.
28. Auslander, "Seeing Is Believing," 12, emphasis original.
29. Moore, "Authenticity as Authentication," 210.
30. Peterson, "In Search of Authenticity," 1086.
31. Moore, "Authenticity as Authentication," 209.
32. Moore, 214.
33. Moore, 220.
34. Wagner, "No Other Name?," 325.
35. Interview with the author, March 5, 2010.
36. Interview with the author, March 5, 2010.
37. Ibid.
38. "'Oh My Soul' Story behind the Song with Mark Hall," https://www.youtube.com/watch?v=_BPNLi1TPXE.

39. needlenut, comment on "'Oh My Soul' Story Behind the Song with Mark Hall," 2017.
40. isa Sanchez, comment on "'Oh My Soul' Story Behind the Song with Mark Hall," 2017.
41. Amanda H, comment on "Casting Crowns - Oh My Soul (Official Lyric Video)," 2017.
42. Christine M_Believe70, comment on "Casting Crowns - Oh My Soul (Official Lyric Video)," 2018.
43. Interview with the author, March 5, 2010.
44. Interview with the author, March 16, 2010.
45. Ibid.
46. Ibid.
47. Ibid.
48. See, for example, McLuhan, *Understanding Media*.
49. Luhr, *Witnessing Suburbia*, 87.
50. Bruce Buursma, "Festival Celebrates Rock 'n' Religion," *Chicago Tribune* (July 1, 1984), B3.
51. See, for example, Buursma; Tom Popson, "A Rock 'n' Roll 'n' Religion Festival," *Chicago Tribune* (June 21, 1985), sec. Friday, 1; Gary Wisby, "Festival Rocks to a Divine Beat," *Chicago Sun-Times* (July 3, 1986), sec. News, 5; Gary Wisby, "Rock Fest Has a Pro-Life Beat," *Chicago Sun-Times* (July 1, 1988), sec. News, 3.
52. Interview with the author, March 16, 2010.
53. Interview with the author, September 10, 2010. See also Thompson, *Raised by Wolves*, 150.
54. Interview with the author, March 23, 2010.
55. Interview with the author, September 16, 2010.
56. Interview with the author, March 16, 2010.
57. Ibid.
58. Consuming alcohol was prohibited at Cornerstone and was the main reason that attendees were ejected from the event.
59. I analyze Cornerstone's closure further in "This Is a Chance to Come Together."
60. See https://audiofeedfestival.com/info#about, accessed May 27, 2019.
61. I describe the production of space and place at Cornerstone and its significance to attendees as a scene in "Music Festivals, Ephemeral Places, and Scenes."

CHAPTER 6: *LOST IN THE SOUND OF SEPARATION*

1. For more on Cornerstone's ending, see Mall, "This Is a Chance to Come Together."
2. Interview with the author, July 2, 2017.
3. Ibid.
4. See http://audiofeedfestival.com/about, accessed December 19, 2018.
5. Balmer, *Mine Eyes Have Seen the Glory*.
6. See, for example, Cohen, *Delinquent Boys*; Becker, *Outsiders*; Gordon, *Assimilation in American Life*.

7. See, for example, Hoggart, *The Uses of Literacy*; Williams, *Culture and Society, 1780–1950*; Thompson, *The Making of the English Working Class*.

8. See, for example, Willis, *Profane Culture*; Hall and Jefferson, *Resistance through Rituals*.

9. Hebdige, *Subculture*.

10. I describe subcultural theory and its legacy more fully in "Subculture."

11. Bernard Gendron, drawing from music critic Lester Bangs's 1970s writing, cites aggressiveness and minimalism as two defining characteristics of punk. Gendron, *Between Montmartre and the Mudd Club*, 233–34; cf. Bangs, *Psychotic Reactions and Carburetor Dung*.

12. At a larger level, this problem is not unique to subculture studies—academics and scholars from a wide variety of theoretical and disciplinary backgrounds (including myself) are guilty of social and cultural analyses that ignore real people's opinions and perspectives. This is why, in my own research, I value grounding my observations in the lived experiences of myself (as a participant) and in those of others involved in Christian music.

13. Thornton, *Club Cultures*.

14. Balmer, *Mine Eyes Have Seen the Glory*.

15. For information on the National Study of Youth and Religion, see https://youthandreligion.nd.edu/.

16. Among other characteristics, the most religiously devoted teens also tend to be evangelical or Mormon, while mainline Protestant and Catholic youth tend to be less religious. Smith and Denton, *Soul Searching*, 111–12.

17. Dean, *Almost Christian*. Christian Smith, the director and principal investigator of the National Study of Youth and Religion since 2001, writes about moralistic therapeutic deism in an earlier article. See Smith, "Is Moralistic Therapeutic Deism the New Religion of American Youth? Implications for the Challenge of Religious Socialization and Reproduction"; cf. Smith, "On 'Moralistic Therapeutic Deism' as U.S. Teenagers' Actual, Tacit, De Facto Religious Faith."

18. Dean, *Almost Christian*, 21.

19. Dean, 39–40.

20. Dean, 36–37.

21. Dean herself cites Jesus Christ's caution against criticizing the faults of others before addressing our own, Matthew 7:5. Dean, 38.

22. McCracken, *Hipster Christianity*; see Mall, "Worship Capital."

23. Magolda and Gross, *It's All About Jesus!*

24. Magolda and Gross, 72.

25. See, for example, chapter 1 in this book; Shires, *Hippies of the Religious Right*; Eskridge, *God's Forever Family*.

26. Magolda and Gross, *It's All About Jesus!*, 280.

27. Shires, *Hippies of the Religious Right*.

28. For example, Cornerstone attendees often spoke fondly of their "Cornerstone friends," with whom they stayed in touch year-round, and "Cornerstone bands," whom they often listened to but rarely had an opportunity to see perform live outside of the festival. Many festival organizers worked on behalf of the event year-round; for these professionals, their festivals were constantly present.

29. On the concept of "imagined communities," see Anderson, *Imagined Communities*. Elsewhere I argue that festivals, as scenes, value and promote interdependence; see Mall, "Music Festivals, Ephemeral Places, and Scenes."

30. Arnold, *Half a Million Strong*, 84–86.

31. Young, *Gray Sabbath*, 184.

32. Interview with the author, July 2, 2017.

33. Interview with the author, December 11, 2009.

34. Interview with the author, December 18, 2009.

35. Interview with the author, September 10, 2010.

36. Interview with the author, March 23, 2010.

37. Interview with the author, March 23, 2010.

38. Interview with the author, September 15, 2010.

39. Arnold, *Half a Million Strong*, 3.

40. Interview with the author, March 16, 2010.

41. I discuss Cornerstone's final year and its closing further in "This Is a Chance to Come Together."

42. John J. Thompson, "Goodnight, Cornerstone," *ChristianityToday.com* (July 3, 2012), http://www.christianitytoday.com/ct/2012/julyweb-only/goodnight-cornerstone.html (accessed September 14, 2014).

43. Interview with the author, July 2, 2017.

44. Ibid.

45. See http://audiofeedfestival.com/about, accessed December 19, 2018.

46. Interview with the author, July 2, 2017.

47. I discuss Flatfoot 56's festival performances further in "'Lift Each Other Up': Punk, Politics, and Secularization at Christian Festivals."

48. On Passion, see Busman, "(Re)Sounding Passion"; Ingalls, *Singing the Congregation*.

49. Timbre's father, Dr. Timothy Cierpke, was a professor of music and ensemble director at Trevecca Nazarene University in Nashville, Tennessee, from 1988 to 2016.

50. In "Diamond Ring" (🎧), Bazan sings from the perspective of God pursuing a wayward follower. Other early songs are inspired by scripture: "Of Minor Prophets and Their Prostitute Wives" dramatizes the story of Hosea, and "The Well" speaks of the Samaritan woman at the well in John 4:4–26.

51. Moore, "Authenticity as Authentication."

52. Cornerstone was officially a dry event, and John Herrin explained to me that most of their security problems and ejections were related to alcohol consumption.

53. Jessica Hopper, "The Passion of David Bazan," *Chicago Reader* (July 30, 2009), 15–18; reprinted in Hopper, *The First Collection*, 115–22.

54. In addition to these Christian festival appearances, I have seen Bazan perform several times in secular venues, both under his own name and with Pedro the Lion: at the Fox Theatre in Boulder, Colorado, on Sunday, June 30, 2002; at Lincoln Hall in Chicago, Illinois, on October 24, 2009; in an empty storefront in Chicago's Pilsen neighborhood on Tuesday, March 29, 2011; at the Metro in Chicago on Thursday, November 8, 2011; and at the Brighton Music Hall in Boston, Massachusetts, on Friday, August 10, 2017.

55. Quoted in Hopper, *The First Collection*, 118.
56. Quoted in Hopper, 118.
57. Interview with the author, July 2, 2017.
58. Pedro the Lion reformed and started performing publicly again in late 2017.
59. Warner, *Publics and Counterpublics*; Young, *Gray Sabbath*.

CHAPTER 7: FROM MARGINS TO MAINSTREAMS AND BACK

1. John Styll, "Let's Stick to the Knitting," *MusicLine* 2, no. 1 (May 1984), 4. *MusicLine* was a spinoff publication of *CCM* magazine; see Mall, "Selling Out or Buying In?"
2. John Styll, "Amy Grant's Sanctified Entertainment," *CCM* 9, nos. 1–2 (July–August 1986), 4; cf. Howard and Streck, *Apostles of Rock*, 82, 97.
3. Styll, "Let's Stick to the Knitting."
4. Quoted in "Sparrow, MCA Sign Dist. Pact," *CCM* 3, no. 9 (March 1981), 42.
5. Amy Grant is a key example of Howard and Streck's "integrational" category of Christian music in *Apostles of Rock*, 75–77.
6. Brackett, *Categorizing Sound*, 280–81.
7. Bruenger, *Making Money, Making Music*, 106.
8. One way to analyze Amy Grant's success is as an example of mainstream-to-mainstream crossover, an approach that dovetails with Eric Weisbard's argument that categories of popular music, including commercial radio formats, constitute "multiple mainstreams" that often converge, in *Top 40 Democracy*, 2.
9. Brackett has called this kind of transition "reverse crossover" in *Categorizing Sound*, 240.
10. Interview with the author, December 11, 2009.
11. "Control" was later included on Mutemath's 2008 self-titled album and released as a radio single that year.
12. Interview with the author, December 11, 2009.
13. Ibid.
14. Ibid.
15. Interview with the author, March 5, 2010. This interviewee's identity has been anonymized.
16. Ibid.
17. Ibid.
18. Howard and Streck, *Apostles of Rock*.
19. Howard and Streck, 90.
20. Howard and Streck, 97.
21. Howard and Streck, 94; Denisoff, *Sing a Song of Social Significance*.
22. Azerrad, *Our Band Could Be Your Life*.
23. Azerrad, 5.
24. Hebdige, *Subculture*, 100–102.
25. Thornton, *Club Cultures*.
26. Hebdige, *Subculture*, 93.
27. Hebdige, 96.

28. Toynbee, "Mainstreaming," 150.
29. Greenwald, *Nothing Feels Good*.
30. Middleton, "D.C. Punk and the Production of Authenticity," 338.
31. Moore, "Authenticity as Authentication."
32. Katy Perry was an early client of Alabaster Arts, the artist management firm that Jennifer Knapp cofounded, and she accompanied Knapp on a 2001 Christian market tour. Knapp, *Facing the Music*, 157–60. Incidentally, Perry recorded backing vocals and appeared in the music video for P.O.D.'s 2006 single "Goodbye for Now."
33. One storyline in the 2006 documentary *Danielson: A Family Movie* follows these two artists' divergent paths: we see Stevens performing for successively larger crowds in the wake of *Illinoise* (2005), while Smith is shown recording music in his basement and playing for small or uncaring audiences.
34. Two other examples include Low's *Christmas* EP (1999), the band's two main members identify as Mormon; David Bazan, whom I discussed in chapter 6, compiled his series of Christmas seven-inch singles on *Dark Sacred Night* (2016).
35. Ryan Dombal, "True Myth: A Conversation with Sufjan Stevens," *Pitchfork* (February 16, 2015), https://pitchfork.com/features/interview/9595-true-myth-a-conversation-with-sufjan-stevens/ (accessed May 11, 2017).
36. This show also featured Horse the Band, a non-Christian band signed to general market indie label Vagrant Records.
37. See Claiborne, *The Irresistible Revolution*.
38. Interview with the author, March 23, 2010.
39. Ibid.
40. Ibid.
41. Interview with the author, March 23, 2010.
42. Interview with the author, March 23, 2010.
43. Interview with the author, March 23, 2010.

CONCLUSION

1. Ingalls, *Singing the Congregation*; Kelman, *Shout to the Lord*.
2. Quoted in Mall, "As for Me and My House," 18.
3. Quoted in Mall, 22.
4. Quoted in Mall, 15–16.
5. Keightley, "Long Play," 382–85.
6. Lee Marshall argues that the record industry's revenue boom in the 1990s due to the CD replacement cycle was an anomaly that should prompt a reevaluation of the subsequent drop in revenue in the 2000s, which has largely been blamed on peer-to-peer digital music piracy. See Marshall, "The Recording Industry in the Twenty-First Century."
7. Quantitative data provided by the Recording Industry Association of America (RIAA) support this claim. In 1973, singles accounted for 9.5 percent of U.S. record industry revenue; by 1983, that share had dropped to 7.1 percent; and in 1993 it dropped further, to 3.9 percent. See RIAA U.S. Sales Database, https://www.riaa.com/u-s-sales-database/, accessed May 31, 2019.

8. On AOR, see Weisbard, *Top 40 Democracy*.
9. Bourdieu, *Distinction*; Peterson and Kern, "Changing Highbrow Taste."
10. Interview with the author, December 18, 2009.
11. Kirk Miller, "Switchfoot: How God, Surfing and Bono Inspired This San Diego Band," *Rolling Stone* no. 933 (September 24, 2003), 36.
12. Beaujon, *Body Piercing Saved My Life*, 12–13.
13. Only three of U2's four members (Bono, The Edge, and Larry Mullen Jr.) publicly identify as Christian. Similarly, the band Creed intentionally distanced themselves from the Christian market despite the biblical imagery in their lyrics and singer Scott Stapp speaking publicly about his Christian faith.
14. Interview with the author, March 5, 2010. This interviewee's identity has been anonymized.
15. Interview with the author, September 13, 2010.
16. Ibid.
17. *South Park*, season 7, episode 9, "Christian Rock Hard," directed and written by Trey Parker, aired October 29, 2003 on Comedy Central. As far as I can tell, no major Christian artist has been publicly accused of faking their faith to be successful like Cartman did. The closest case is that of Mike Warnke, a Christian comedian who was alleged to have built his career on a fabricated biography as a reformed Satanist. This was uncovered by an investigation published in JPUSA's *Cornerstone* magazine in 1992 and expanded into a book, Hertenstein and Trott, *Selling Satan*.
18. Interview with the author, December 11, 2009.
19. Interview with the author, September 15, 2010.
20. Chad Johnson, "The Fun in Fundraising," Come&Live! Newsletter, November 27, 2018.
21. Johnson, *One Thousand Risks*, xxxiii.
22. Johnson, xxxv.
23. Steiger is a worldwide organization that sponsors missionaries and missions teams to minister to urban youth. See https://steiger.org, accessed February 27, 2020.
24. Come&Live!'s website articulates this very clearly: "Come&Live! is not a record label. We do not distribute music nor do we serve as management/booking agents for our artists. Come&Live! Artists have no contractual obligations to us." http://www.comeandlive.com/aboutus/whoweare, accessed June 3, 2019.
25. Eskridge, *God's Forever Family*, 170.

Bibliography

INTERVIEWS
Nick Barre
Jeff Carver
Jon Dunn
Billy Ray Hearn
John Herrin
Chad Johnson
Glenn Kaiser
Wayne Kusber (pseudonym)
David Marshall
John Mays
Andy Peterson
Billy Power
Joshua Stump
John Styll
John J. Thompson
Luke Welchel

NEWSPAPERS AND MAGAZINES

Billboard

CCM

The CCM Update

Chicago Reader

Chicago Sun-Times

Chicago Tribune

Christianity Today

Ebony

The Evangelist

Life

Look

MusicLine

The MusicLine Update

New York Times

Newsweek

Radio & Records

Rolling Stone

Spin

Time

U.S. News & World Report

USA Today

Washington Post

BOOKS AND ACADEMIC JOURNALS

Abraham, Ibrahim. *Evangelical Youth Culture: Alternative Music and Extreme Sports Subcultures*. New York: Bloomsbury Academic, 2017.

———. "Postsecular Punk: Evangelical Christianity and the Overlapping Consensus of the Underground." *Punk & Post Punk* 4, no. 1 (2015): 91–105.

Anderson, Benedict R. *Imagined Communities: Reflections on the Origin and Spread of Nationalism*. 1983. Rev. and Extended ed. London: Verso, 1991.

Arnold, Gina. *Half a Million Strong: Crowds and Power from Woodstock to Coachella*. Iowa City: University of Iowa Press, 2018.

Auslander, Philip. "Seeing Is Believing: Live Performance and the Discourse of Authenticity in Rock Culture." *Literature and Psychology* 44, no. 4 (1998): 1–26.

Azerrad, Michael. *Our Band Could Be Your Life: Scenes from the American Indie Underground 1981–1991*. Boston: Little, Brown, 2001.

Babcock, Wendell K. *Music on the Rocks*. Grand Rapids, MI: privately published, 1975.
Balmer, Randall Herbert. *Mine Eyes Have Seen the Glory: A Journey into the Evangelical Subculture in America*. 1989. 25th anniversary ed. New York: Oxford University Press, 2014.
Bangs, Lester. *Psychotic Reactions and Carburetor Dung*. New York: Vintage Books, 1988.
Beaujon, Andrew. *Body Piercing Saved My Life: Inside the Phenomenon of Christian Rock*. Cambridge, MA: Da Capo Press, 2006.
Becker, Howard S. *Outsiders: Studies in the Sociology of Deviance*. Glencoe, IL: Free Press, 1963.
Bergeron, Katherine, and Philip V. Bohlman, eds. *Disciplining Music: Musicology and Its Canons*. Chicago: University of Chicago Press, 1992.
Bishop, Will. "'We're Gonna Change This Land': An Oral History Commemorating the Fiftieth Anniversary of Good News: A Christian Folk-Musical." *Artistic Theologian* 5 (2017): 58–81.
Blessitt, Arthur. *Life's Greatest Trip*. Waco, TX: Word Books, 1970.
———. *Tell the World: A Jesus People Manual*. Old Tappan, NJ: Revell, 1972.
Bourdieu, Pierre. *Distinction: A Social Critique of the Judgement of Taste*. 1979. Translated by Richard Nice. Cambridge, MA: Harvard University Press, 1984.
Bowen, Jimmy, and Jim Jerome. *Rough Mix: An Unapologetic Look at the Music Business and How It Got That Way*. New York: Simon & Schuster, 1997.
Brackett, David. *Categorizing Sound: Genre and Twentieth-Century Popular Music*. Oakland: University of California Press, 2016.
Brooks, William. "On Being Tasteless." *Popular Music* 2 (1982): 9–18.
Bruenger, David. *Create, Produce, Consume: New Models for Understanding Music Business*. Oakland, CA: University of California Press, 2019.
———. *Making Money, Making Music: History and Core Concepts*. Oakland: University of California Press, 2016.
Busman, Joshua Kalin. "(Re)Sounding Passion: Listening to American Evangelical Worship Music, 1997–2015." PhD diss., University of North Carolina at Chapel Hill, 2015.
Cavicchi, Daniel. *Tramps Like Us: Music and Meaning among Springsteen Fans*. New York: Oxford University Press, 1998.
Claiborne, Shane. *The Irresistible Revolution: Living as an Ordinary Radical*. Grand Rapids, MI: Zondervan, 2006.
Coddington, Amy. "'Check Out the Hook While My DJ Revolves It': How the Music Industry Made Rap into Pop in the Late 1980s." In *The Oxford Handbook of Hip Hop Studies*, edited by Justin D. Burton and Jason Lee Oakes. Oxford University Press, 2018. https://doi.org/10.1093/oxfordhb/9780190281090.013.35.
Cohen, Albert K. *Delinquent Boys: The Culture of the Gang*. Glencoe, IL: Free Press, 1955.
Cohen, Lizabeth. *A Consumer's Republic: The Politics of Mass Consumption in Postwar America*. New York: Alfred A. Knopf, 2003.

Cusic, Don, ed. *Encyclopedia of Contemporary Christian Music: Pop, Rock, and Worship*. Santa Barbara, CA: Greenwood Press, 2010.
———. *Saved by Song: A History of Gospel and Christian Music*. Jackson: University Press of Mississippi, 2012.
Darden, Bob, and P. J. Richardson. *Corporate Giants: Personal Stories of Faith and Finance*. Grand Rapids, MI: Fleming H. Revell, 2002.
Dean, Kenda Creasy. *Almost Christian: What the Faith of Our Teenagers Is Telling the American Church*. Oxford: Oxford University Press, 2010.
Denisoff, R. Serge. *Sing a Song of Social Significance*. Bowling Green, OH: Bowling Green University Popular Press, 1972.
———. *Solid Gold: The Popular Record Industry*. New Brunswick, NJ: Transaction Books, 1975.
———. *Tarnished Gold: The Record Industry Revisited*. New Brunswick, NJ: Transaction Books, 1986.
Di Sabatino, David, dir. *Fallen Angel: The Outlaw Larry Norman*. Film. Jester Media, 2011.
———. *The Jesus People Movement: An Annotated Bibliography and General Resource*. Westport, CT: Greenwood Press, 1999.
Drott, Eric A. "Music as a Technology of Surveillance." *Journal of the Society for American Music* 12, no. 3 (2018): 233–67.
Dueck, Jonathan M. *Congregational Music, Conflict, and Community*. New York: Routledge, 2017.
———. "Crossing the Street: Velour 100 and Christian Rock." *Popular Music and Society* 24, no. 2 (2000): 127–48.
Engelhardt, Jeffers. *Singing the Right Way: Orthodox Christians and Secular Enchantment in Estonia*. New York: Oxford University Press, 2015.
Eskridge, Larry. *God's Forever Family: The Jesus People Movement in America*. New York: Oxford University Press, 2013.
Fabbri, Franco. "A Theory of Musical Genres: Two Applications." In *Popular Music Perspectives: Papers from the First International Conference on Popular Music Research, Amsterdam, June 1981*, edited by David Horn and Philip Tagg, 52–81. Göteborg, Sweden: International Association for the Study of Popular Music, 1982.
Flowers, Ronald B. *Religion in Strange Times: The 1960s and 1970s*. Macon, GA: Mercer University Press, 1984.
Frith, Simon. "The Industrialization of Music." In *Music for Pleasure: Essays in the Sociology of Pop*, 11–23. New York: Routledge, 1988.
———. *Performing Rites: On the Value of Popular Music*. Cambridge, MA: Harvard University Press, 1996.
———. *Sound Effects: Youth, Leisure, and the Politics of Rock'n'roll*. New York: Pantheon Books, 1981.
Garland, Shannon. "'The Space, the Gear, and Two Big Cans of Beer': Fora Do Eixo and the Debate over Circulation, Remuneration, and Aesthetics in the Brazilian Alternative Market." *Journal of Popular Music Studies* 24, no. 4 (2012): 509–31.
Garlock, Frank. *The Big Beat: A Rock Blast*. Greenville, SC: Bob Jones University Press, 1971.

Gendron, Bernard. *Between Montmartre and the Mudd Club: Popular Music and the Avant-Garde.* Chicago: University of Chicago Press, 2002.
Goff, James R. *Close Harmony: A History of Southern Gospel.* Chapel Hill: University of North Carolina Press, 2002.
Goffman, Ken, and Dan Joy. *Counterculture through the Ages: From Abraham to Acid House.* New York: Villard, 2004.
Gordon, Milton M. *Assimilation in American Life: The Role of Race, Religion, and National Origins.* New York: Oxford University Press, 1964.
Gospel Music Association. "Gospel Music Industry Overview 2004," 2004. http://www.cmta.biz/industry2.htm.
———. "Gospel Music Industry Overview 2005," 2005. http://www.cmta.biz/industry2.htm.
———. "Gospel Music Industry Overview 2006," 2006. http://www.cmta.biz/industry2.htm.
———. "Gospel Music Industry Overview 2009," 2009. http://www.cmta.biz/industry2.htm.
Graham, Billy. *The Jesus Generation.* Grand Rapids, MI: Zondervan, 1971.
Graham, Sandra J. *Spirituals and the Birth of a Black Entertainment Industry.* Music in American Life. Urbana: University of Illinois Press, 2018.
Granger, Thom. *CCM Presents: The 100 Greatest Albums in Christian Music.* Eugene, OR: Harvest House Publishers, 2001.
Green, Melody, and David Hazard. *No Compromise: The Life Story of Keith Green.* 1989. Legacy ed. Nashville: Thomas Nelson, 2008.
Greenwald, Andy. *Nothing Feels Good: Punk Rock, Teenagers, and Emo.* New York: St. Martin's Griffin, 2003.
Hall, Stuart, and Tony Jefferson, eds. *Resistance through Rituals: Youth Subcultures in Post-War Britain.* 1975. 2nd ed. London: Routledge, 2006.
Hearn, Billy Ray. Oral Memoirs of Billy Ray Hearn, First Session. Interview by Ray F. Luper, January 17, 1998. Baylor University Institute for Oral History.
———. Oral Memoirs of Billy Ray Hearn, Third Session. Interview by Ray F. Luper, April 14, 1998. Baylor University Institute for Oral History.
Hebdige, Dick. *Subculture: The Meaning of Style.* London: Methuen, 1979.
Heilbut, Anthony. *The Fan Who Knew Too Much: Aretha Franklin, the Rise of the Soap Opera, Children of the Gospel Church, and Other Meditations.* New York: Alfred A. Knopf, 2012.
———. *The Gospel Sound: Good News and Bad Times.* 1971. 6th Limelight ed. New York: Limelight Editions, 2002.
Hendershot, Heather. *Shaking the World for Jesus: Media and Conservative Evangelical Culture.* Chicago: University of Chicago Press, 2004.
Henry, Carl F. H. *Answers for the Now Generation.* 1949. Moody Press ed. Chicago: Moody Press, 1969.
Hertenstein, Michael, and Jon Trott. *Selling Satan: The Tragic History of Mike Warnke.* Chicago: Cornerstone Press, 1993.
Hesmondhalgh, David. "Post-Punk's Attempt to Democratise the Music Industry: The Success and Failure of Rough Trade." *Popular Music* 16, no. 3 (1997): 255–74.

Hoggart, Richard. *The Uses of Literacy: Aspects of Working Class Life with Special References to Publications and Entertainments.* London: Chatto and Windus, 1957.
Holt, Fabian. "The Economy of Live Music in the Digital Age." *European Journal of Cultural Studies* 13, no. 2 (2010): 243–61.
———. "Rock Clubs and Gentrification in New York City: The Case of The Bowery Presents." *IASPM@Journal* 4, no. 1 (2014): 21–41.
Hopper, Jessica. *The First Collection of Criticism by a Living Female Rock Critic.* Chicago: Featherproof Books, 2015.
Horowitz, Daniel. *Consuming Pleasures: Intellectuals and Popular Culture in the Postwar World.* Philadelphia: University of Pennsylvania Press, 2012.
Howard, Jay R., and John M. Streck. *Apostles of Rock: The Splintered World of Contemporary Christian Music.* Lexington: University Press of Kentucky, 1999.
IFPI. "Global Music Report 2018." International Federation of the Phonographic Industry, 2018. https://www.ifpi.org/downloads/GMR2018.pdf.
Ingalls, Monique M. *Singing the Congregation: How Contemporary Worship Music Forms Evangelical Community.* New York: Oxford University Press, 2018.
Ingalls, Monique M., Carolyn Landau, and Thomas Wagner, eds. *Christian Congregational Music: Performance, Identity and Experience.* Surrey, UK: Ashgate, 2013.
Ingalls, Monique M., Muriel Swijghuisen-Reigersberg, and Zoe C. Sherinian, eds. *Making Congregational Music Local in Christian Communities Worldwide.* New York: Routledge, 2018.
Ingalls, Monique M., and Amos Yong, eds. *The Spirit of Praise: Music and Worship in Global Pentecostal-Charismatic Christianity.* University Park: The Pennsylvania State University Press, 2015.
Johnson, Chad. *One Thousand Risks: Fighting Fear for an Awkward, Awesome Life with Jesus.* Nashville: Everett Brave Books, 2017.
Jones, Alisha Lola. *Flaming? The Peculiar Theopolitics of Fire and Desire in Black Male Gospel Performance.* New York: Oxford University Press, 2020.
Joseph, Mark. *Faith, God and Rock & Roll: How People of Faith Are Transforming American Popular Music.* Grand Rapids, MI: Baker Books, 2003.
———. *The Rock & Roll Rebellion: Why People of Faith Abandoned Rock Music and Why They're Coming Back.* Nashville: Broadman & Holman Publishers, 1999.
Kaiser, Kurt. Oral Memoirs of Kurt Frederic Kaiser. Interview by David Bruce Stricklin, July 11, 1988. Baylor University Institute for Oral History.
Keightley, Keir. "Long Play: Adult-Oriented Popular Music and the Temporal Logics of the Post-War Sound Recording Industry in the USA." *Media, Culture & Society* 26, no. 3 (2004): 375–91.
Kelman, Ari Y. *Shout to the Lord: Making Worship Music in Evangelical America.* New York: New York University Press, 2018.
Knapp, Jennifer. *Facing the Music: My Story.* New York: Howard Books, 2014.
Knopper, Steve. *Appetite for Self-Destruction: The Spectacular Crash of the Record Industry in the Digital Age.* New York: Free Press, 2009.

Laing, Dave. "The Recording Industry in the Twentieth Century." In *The International Recording Industries*, edited by Lee Marshall, 31–52. New York: Routledge, 2013.
Larson, Bob. *Hippies, Hindus and Rock & Roll*. McCook, NE: privately published, 1969.
———. *Larson's Book of Spiritual Warfare*. Nashville: Thomas Nelson, 1999.
———. *Larson's New Book of Cults*. Wheaton, IL: Tyndale House, 1989.
———. *Rock & Roll: The Devil's Diversion*. Rev. ed. McCook, NE: privately published, 1970.
———. *Rock and the Church*. Carol Stream, IL: Creation House, 1971.
———. *Satanism: The Seduction of America's Youth*. Nashville: Thomas Nelson, 1989.
———. *Straight Answers on the New Age*. Nashville: Thomas Nelson, 1989.
———. *UFOs and the Alien Agenda*. Nashville: Thomas Nelson, 1997.
Lindsey, Hal. *The Late, Great Planet Earth*. Grand Rapids, MI: Zondervan, 1970.
Luhr, Eileen. *Witnessing Suburbia: Conservatives and Christian Youth Culture*. Berkeley: University of California Press, 2009.
MacDonald, John Allan. *The House of Acts*. Carol Stream, IL: Creation House, 1970.
Magolda, Peter, and Kelsey Ebben Gross. *It's All about Jesus! Faith as an Oppositional Collegiate Subculture*. Sterling, VA: Stylus, 2009.
Mall, Andrew. "'As for Me and My House': Christian Music Executives Roundtable." *Journal of Popular Music Studies* 32, no. 1 (2020): 10–25.
———. "Billy Ray Hearn." In *The Canterbury Dictionary of Hymnology*, edited by J. R. Watson, Carlton R. Young, Colin Gibson, Margaret Leask, and Jeremy Dibble. London: Canterbury Press, 2013.
———. "Concentration, Diversity, and Consequences: Privileging Independent over Major Record Labels." *Popular Music* 37, no. 3 (2018): 444–65.
———. "'Lift Each Other Up': Punk, Politics, and Secularization at Christian Festivals." In *Christian Punk: Identity and Performance*, edited by Ibrahim Abraham, 137–73. London: Bloomsbury Academic, 2020.
———. "Music Festivals, Ephemeral Places, and Scenes: Interdependence at Cornerstone Festival." *Journal of the Society for American Music* 14, no. 1 (2020): 51–69.
———. "Selling Out or Buying In? CCM Magazine and Anxieties over Commercial Priorities in Christian Music, 1980s–1990s." *Journal of Religion, Media and Digital Culture* (2020).
———. "Subculture." In *The SAGE International Encyclopedia of Music and Culture*, edited by Janet Sturman, 2088–92. Thousand Oaks, CA: SAGE, 2019.
———. "'This Is a Chance to Come Together': Subcultural Resistance and Community at Cornerstone Festival." In *Congregational Music-Making and Community in a Mediated Age*, edited by Anna E. Nekola and Tom Wagner, 101–21. Burlington, VT: Ashgate, 2015.
———. "Tuning In to Locality: Participatory Musicking at a Community Radio Station." In *The Routledge Companion to the Study of Local Musicking*,

edited by Suzel Ana Reily and Katherine Brucher, 139–53. New York: Routledge, 2018.

———. "'We Can Be Renewed': Resistance, Renewal, and Worship at the Anchor Fellowship." In *The Spirit of Praise: Music and Worship in Global Pentecostal-Charismatic Christianity*, edited by Monique M. Ingalls and Amos Yong, 163–78. University Park: The Pennsylvania State University Press, 2015.

———. "Worship Capital: On the Political Economy of Worship Music." *American Music* 36, no. 3 (2018): 303–26.

Mall, Andrew, Jeffers Engelhardt, and Monique M. Ingalls, eds. *Studying Congregational Music: Key Issues, Methods, and Theoretical Perspectives*. New York: Routledge, 2021.

Marini, Stephen A. *Sacred Song in America: Religion, Music, and Public Culture*. Urbana: University of Illinois Press, 2003.

Marshall, Lee. "'Let's Keep Music Special. F—Spotify': On-Demand Streaming and the Controversy over Artist Royalties." *Creative Industries Journal* 8, no. 2 (July 3, 2015): 177–89.

———. "The Recording Industry in the Twenty-First Century." In *The International Recording Industries*, edited by Lee Marshall, 53–74. New York: Routledge, 2013.

McCracken, Brett. *Hipster Christianity: When Church and Cool Collide*. Grand Rapids, MI: Baker Books, 2010.

McCracken, Jarrell. Oral Memoirs of Jarrell McCracken. Interview by Thomas L. Charlton, August 11, 1976. Baylor University Institute for Oral History.

McDannell, Colleen. *Material Christianity: Religion and Popular Culture in America*. New Haven, CT: Yale University Press, 1995.

McLuhan, Marshall. *Understanding Media: The Extensions of Man*. 1964. Reprint, Cambridge, MA: MIT Press, 1994.

Middleton, Jason. "D.C. Punk and the Production of Authenticity." In *Rock Over the Edge: Transformations in Popular Music Culture*, edited by Roger Beebe, Denise Fulbrook, and Ben Saunders, 335–56. Durham, NC: Duke University Press, 2002.

Miller, Donald E. *Reinventing American Protestantism: Christianity in the New Millennium*. Berkeley: University of California Press, 1997.

Miller, Karl Hagstrom. *Segregating Sound: Inventing Folk and Pop Music in the Age of Jim Crow*. Durham, NC: Duke University Press, 2010.

Moberg, Marcus. *Christian Metal: History, Ideology, Scene*. New York: Bloomsbury Academic, 2015.

Moore, Allan F. "Authenticity as Authentication." *Popular Music* 21, no. 2 (May 2002): 209–23.

Morris, Jeremy Wade. *Selling Digital Music, Formatting Culture*. Oakland: University of California Press, 2015.

Negus, Keith. *Music Genres and Corporate Cultures*. London: Routledge, 1999.

Nekola, Anna E. "'More Than Just a Music': Conservative Christian Anti-Rock Discourse and the U.S. Culture Wars." *Popular Music* 32, no. 3 (2013): 407–26.

———. "Negotiating the Tensions of U.S. Worship Music in the Marketplace." In *The Oxford Handbook of Music and World Christianities*, edited by Suzel Ana Reily and Jonathan M. Dueck. New York: Oxford University Press, 2016.

Nekola, Anna E., and Tom Wagner, eds. *Congregational Music-Making and Community in a Mediated Age*. Burlington, VT: Ashgate, 2015.

Noebel, David A. *The Beatles: A Study in Drugs, Sex and Revolution*. Tulsa, OK: Christian Crusade Publications, 1969.

———. *Communism, Hypnotism and the Beatles: An Analysis of the Communist Use of Music, the Communist Master Music Plan*. Tulsa, OK: Christian Crusade Publications, 1965.

———. *The Marxist Minstrels: A Handbook on Communist Subversion of Music*. Tulsa, OK: American Christian College Press, 1974.

Ogg, Alex. *Independence Days: The Story of UK Independent Record Labels*. London: Cherry Red Books, 2009.

Patty, Sandi. *Broken on the Back Row: A Journey through Grace and Forgiveness*. West Monroe, LA: Howard Publishing Co., 2005.

Peacock, Charlie. *At the Crossroads: An Insider's Look at the Past, Present, and Future of Contemporary Christian Music*. Nashville: Broadman & Holman Publishers, 1999.

Pederson, Duane. *Jesus People*. Glendale, CA: G/L Regal Books, 1971.

Perkins, Dave. "Music, Culture Industry, and the Shaping of Charismatic Worship: An Autobiographical/Conversational Engagement." In *The Spirit of Praise: Music and Worship in Global Pentecostal-Charismatic Christianity*, edited by Monique M. Ingalls and Amos Yong, 230–46. University Park: The Pennsylvania State University Press, 2015.

Peterson, Richard A. *Creating Country Music: Fabricating Authenticity*. Chicago: University of Chicago Press, 1997.

———. "In Search of Authenticity." *Journal of Management Studies* 42, no. 5 (2005): 1083–98.

———. "Why 1955? Explaining the Advent of Rock Music." *Popular Music* 9, no. 1 (1990): 97–116.

Peterson, Richard A., and David G. Berger. "Cycles in Symbol Production: The Case of Popular Music." *American Sociological Review* 40, no. 2 (1975): 158–73.

Peterson, Richard A., and Roger M. Kern. "Changing Highbrow Taste: From Snob to Omnivore." *American Sociological Review* 61, no. 5 (1996): 900–907.

Porter, Mark. *Contemporary Worship Music and Everyday Musical Lives*. New York: Routledge, 2016.

Powell, Mark Allan. *Encyclopedia of Contemporary Christian Music*. Peabody, MA: Hendrickson Publishers, 2002.

Powers, Devon. "Intermediaries and Intermediation." In *The SAGE Handbook of Popular Music*, edited by Andy Bennett and Steve Waksman, 120–34. Thousand Oaks, CA: SAGE, 2015.

Pruett, David B. *MuzikMafia: From the Local Nashville Scene to the National Mainstream*. Jackson: University Press of Mississippi, 2010.

———. "When the Tribe Goes Triple Platinum: A Case Study Toward an Ethnomusicology of Mainstream Popular Music in the U.S." *Ethnomusicology* 55, no. 1 (2011): 1–28.
Rawls, John. *Justice as Fairness: A Restatement*. Cambridge, MA: Harvard University Press, 2001.
RIAA. "News and Notes on 2016 RIAA Shipment and Revenue Statistics." Recording Industry Association of America, 2017. https://www.riaa.com/reports/news-notes-2016-riaa-shipment-revenue-statistics/.
Riches, Tanya, and Thomas Wagner, eds. *The Hillsong Movement Examined: You Call Me Out upon the Waters*. Cham, Switzerland: Palgrave Macmillan, 2017.
Romanowski, William D. "Move Over Madonna: The Crossover Career of Gospel Artist Amy Grant." *Popular Music and Society* 17, no. 2 (1993): 47–67.
Rommen, Timothy. *"Mek Some Noise": Gospel Music and the Ethics of Style in Trinidad*. Berkeley: University of California Press, 2007.
Schaeffer, Francis A. *The Church at the End of the 20th Century*. Downers Grove, IL: Inter-Varsity Press, 1970.
Shires, Preston. *Hippies of the Religious Right: From the Countercultures of Jerry Garcia to the Subculture of Jerry Falwell*. Waco, TX: Baylor University Press, 2007.
Small, Christopher. *Musicking: The Meanings of Performing and Listening*. Hanover, NH: Wesleyan University Press, 1998.
Smith, Christian. "Is Moralistic Therapeutic Deism the New Religion of American Youth? Implications for the Challenge of Religious Socialization and Reproduction." In *Passing on the Faith: Transforming Traditions for the Next Generation of Jews, Christians, and Muslims*, edited by James L. Heft, 55–74. New York: Fordham University Press, 2006.
———. "On 'Moralistic Therapeutic Deism' as U.S. Teenagers' Actual, Tacit, De Facto Religious Faith." In *Religion and Youth*, edited by Sylvia Collins-Mayo and Pink Dandelion, 41–46. Aldershot, UK: Ashgate, 2010.
Smith, Christian, and Melinda Lundquist Denton. *Soul Searching: The Religious and Spiritual Lives of American Teenagers*. Oxford: Oxford University Press, 2005.
Smith, Chuck, and Hugh Steven. *The Reproducers: New Life for Thousands*. Glendale, CA: G/L Regal Books, 1972.
Stace, April. *Secular Music, Sacred Space: Evangelical Worship and Popular Music*. Lanham, MD: Lexington Books, 2017.
Stephens, Randall J. *The Devil's Music: How Christians Inspired, Condemned, and Embraced Rock 'n' Roll*. Cambridge, MA: Harvard University Press, 2018.
Stowe, David W. *No Sympathy for the Devil: Christian Pop Music and the Transformation of American Evangelicalism*. Chapel Hill: University of North Carolina Press, 2011.
Straw, Will. "Sizing Up Record Collectors: Gender and Connoisseurship in Rock Music Culture." In *Sexing the Groove: Popular Music and Gender*, edited by Sheila Whiteley, 3–16. London: Routledge, 1997.

Styll, John, ed. *The Heart of the Matter: The CCM Interviews*. Nashville: Star Song Communications, 1991.

Sullivan, Mark. "'More Popular Than Jesus': The Beatles and the Religious Far Right." *Popular Music* 6, no. 3 (1987): 313–26.

Swaggart, Jimmy, and Robert Paul Lamb. *Religious Rock'n'roll: A Wolf in Sheep's Clothing*. Baton Rouge, LA: Jimmy Swaggart Ministries, 1987.

Tagg, Philip. *Fernando the Flute: Analysis of Musical Meaning in an Abba Mega-Hit*. 1992. 3rd ed. New York: Mass Media Music Scholars' Press, 2000.

———. *Kojak—Fifty Seconds of Television Music: Toward the Analysis of Affect in Popular Music*. 1979. Reprint. New York: Mass Media Music Scholars' Press, 2000.

Taylor, Charles. *A Secular Age*. Cambridge, MA: Belknap Press of Harvard University Press, 2007.

Taylor, Timothy D. *Music and Capitalism: A History of the Present*. Chicago: University of Chicago Press, 2016.

Thompson, E. P. *The Making of the English Working Class*. New York: Vintage Books, 1966.

Thompson, John J. *Raised by Wolves: The Story of Christian Rock & Roll*. Toronto: ECW Press, 2000.

Thornbury, Gregory Alan. *Why Should the Devil Have All the Good Music? Larry Norman and the Rise of Christian Rock*. New York: Convergent, 2018.

Thornton, Sarah. *Club Cultures: Music, Media, and Subcultural Capital*. Hanover, NH: University Press of New England, 1996.

Toynbee, Jason. "Mainstreaming, from Hegemonic Centre to Global Networks." In *Popular Music Studies*, edited by David Hesmondhalgh and Keith Negus, 149–63. London: Arnold, 2002.

Turino, Thomas. *Music as Social Life: The Politics of Participation*. Chicago: University of Chicago Press, 2008.

Wagner, Tom. *Music, Branding and Consumer Culture in Church: Hillsong in Focus*. Oxford: Routledge, 2020.

———. "No Other Name? Authenticity, Authority, and Anointing in Christian Popular Music." *Journal of World Popular Music* 1, no. 2 (2014): 324–42.

Wald, Elijah. "How the Smart Kids Study Popular Music, or Why Are There No Papers on Katy Perry?" Popular Music Section keynote lecture at the annual meeting of the Society for Ethnomusicology, Indianapolis, Indiana, November 15, 2013.

Warner, Michael. *Publics and Counterpublics*. New York: Zone Books, 2002.

Weisbard, Eric. *Top 40 Democracy: The Rival Mainstreams of American Music*. Chicago: University of Chicago Press, 2014.

Whitmore, Aleysia K. *World Music and the Black Atlantic: Producing and Consuming African-Cuban Musics on World Music Stages*. New York: Oxford University Press, 2020.

Wilkerson, David R. *David Wilkerson's Jesus Person Maturity Manual*. Glendale, CA: G/L Regal Books, 1971.

Williams, Don. *Call to the Streets*. Minneapolis: Augsburg Publishing House, 1972.

Williams, Raymond. *Culture and Society, 1780–1950*. New York: Columbia University Press, 1958.
Williamson, John, and Martin Cloonan. "Rethinking the Music Industry." *Popular Music* 26, no. 2 (2007): 305–22.
Willis, Paul E. *Profane Culture*. London: Routledge & K. Paul, 1978.
Witt, Stephen. *How Music Got Free: The End of an Industry, the Turn of the Century, and the Patient Zero of Piracy*. New York: Viking, 2015.
Young, Shawn David. *Gray Sabbath: Jesus People USA, the Evangelical Left, and the Evolution of Christian Rock*. New York: Columbia University Press, 2015.
Zanfagna, Christina. *Holy Hip Hop in the City of Angels*. Oakland: University of California Press, 2017.

Index

Page references followed by an italicized *fig.* indicate illustrations or material contained in their captions.

A&M Records, 73, 118, 119, 126, 129, 206–7, 254n5, 255n14
ABC, 54–55, 76–77, 255n5
ABC Records, 77
Abdul, Paula, 116, 128
Abernathy, Lee Roy, 247n27
abortion, 105–6, 171
Abraham, Ibrahim, 148, 257n19
AC/DC, 92, 218
addiction treatment, 109
Adult Contemporary (AC) radio, 81–82. *See also* Christian Adult Contemporary (AC)
Aerosmith, 197
aesthetics: anti-rock discourse and, 145; CCM vs. CWM, 19–20; Christianity and, 182; of Christian music, 79, 110, 117, 175; at Christian music festivals, 144, 181; of Christian radio, 81–82; ethics vs., 8–9, 42, 69, 94–96, 106, 114, 149; heavy metal, 144, 145; interrelationships of, 11; of niche markets, 94; race and, 21; resistant, 214; of rock and roll, 114; "selling out" and, 222–23. *See also* "ethics of style"; style
African Americans, 44, 97. *See also* Black gospel music
Agape Music Festival (Greenville, IL), 34, 207
Age to Age (album; Grant), 117–18
Alabaster Arts, 262n32

Alarm, The, 64–65
album-oriented rock (AOR), 217–18
alcohol abuse, 2, 105, 187, 253n22, 258n58
"Alive" (song; P.O.D.), 205
All I Am Is What You See (album; Matthews), 54
All Your Life (album; Rez Band), 138
Altamont Speedway Free Festival (CA, 1969), 47
Altar Boys, 177
alternative rock, 12, 161, 163, 177, 197, 206
Ami Moss and the Unfortunate, 179
Anberlin, 208
Anchor Fellowship (Nashville, TN), 24, 142–43, 161, 173
anointing, 104–5
Another Time . . . Another Place (album; Patty), 107
Anthony, Dick, 56
antiabortion causes, 105–6
anti-Christian bias, 200–201, 220
anticommunism, 97–98, 99
anti-rock discourse: anticommunism and, 97–98, 99–100; Christian metal and, 148–49; "ethics of style" and, 114, 137; sacred/secular dichotomy and, 97–99; use of term, 97
Apostles of Rock (Howard and Streck), 9–11, 14, 261n5
Apple Music, 218

277

Arnold, Gina, 178
artist services businesses, 68
ASCAP, 127
As I Lay Dying, 17
"Ask Me" (song; Grant), 256n27
Associated Press, 111
atheism, 100
Atlantic Records, 57, 58, 131, 220
AudioFeed Festival (Urbana, IL): author's fieldwork at, 24; community at, 175; as Cornerstone successor, 164, 166–67; launching of, 179; musical styles appearing at, 167–68, 179–80; musicians appearing at, 180–81, 189, 190, 190 fig., 192; objectives of, 180; organizers of, 181; resistance at, 27, 181–82
August Burns Red, 208–9
Auslander, Philip, 152
Australia, 215, 245n3
authenticity, 36, 152–56, 187, 204–5
Azerrad, Michael, 202, 204

Babcock, Wendell K., 98, 100
"Baby, Baby" (song; Grant): Christian music and, 133, 201; crossover strategies in, 203; as crossover success, 116, 125–26, 128, 201; release of, 122, 126; Top 40 radio airplay of, 116, 125–26, 208; 25th anniversary re-recording of, 225
Balmer, Randall, 168
Band Called David, A, 249n76
Bangs, Lester, 259n11
Bannister, Brown, 120
Baptist Hymnal, 248n57
Baptist Tabernacle (Atlanta, GA), 51
Barre, Nick, 92, 154–55, 156
Barsuk Records, 211
Baylor University (Waco, TX), 51, 52, 55, 56, 77
Bazan, David: author's interview with, 186; at Christian music festivals, 188, 189, 190 fig., 192; Christmas singles of, 262n34; as crossover artist, 192; discography, 234–35; doubt expressed in music of, 186–88, 190–91, 260n50; resistant identity of, 27, 180; at secular venues, 190–91, 260n54
Beatles, The, 97, 218, 256n3
Beatles, The (Noebel), 99
Beat the System (album; Petra), 255n7
Beaujon, Andrew, 66, 220
Beautiful Letdown, The (album; Switchfoot), 219–20
BEC Records, 210
"Be Careful What You Sign" (song; Norman), 43
Becker, Howard, 169

"Becky" (typical CCM consumer), 124, 131
Behind the Eyes (album; Grant), 129
Benson, Bob, Sr., 87
Benson Company, 58; changing priorities at, 90; Christian music as commercial domain of, 36–37, 55; Christian music market and, 118; distribution agreements of, 73, 195; Mays as president of, 86–88, 124; musicians recording with, 56, 107; as oldest Christian record label, 56, 67; ownership changes at, 67, 70, 77, 86–88, 124, 250n32; subsidiaries of, 107; youth-marketing strategies at, 57
Berger, David, 57
Bethlehem (PA), 12
Beyond Belief (album; Petra), 2
Bible, 139, 142, 257n9. See also specific book of the Bible
big band music, 97
Big Five entertainment conglomerates, 91
Big Three entertainment conglomerates: challenges facing, 91; Christian recording industry consolidated within, 67–69, 86–90, 116–17; country music subsidiaries of, 81, 251n48; defined, 67; distribution/marketing networks of, 88–89. See also Sony; Universal; Warner Brothers
"Big Yellow Taxi" (song; Mitchell), 129
Billboard magazine, 16, 49, 121; album charts, 126–27, 130, 154, 207; Hot AC list of, 75, 126, 256n28; Modern Rock charts, 207. See also Hot 100 list (*Billboard*)
Bill Gaither Trio, 56
Birmingham Centre for Contemporary Cultural Studies (BCCCS, or Birmingham School), 169, 172
Bishop, Will, 53, 248n57
Black gospel music, 16, 45, 55, 110, 123, 254n50; scholarship on, 243n3
Blanton, Michael, 120
Blenderhead, 178
Blessitt, Arthur, 46
blink-182, 65
Blondie, 202
blues rock, 138
Blue Thumb Records, 76
BMG, 77, 85, 91
BMI, 127
Bob Jones University (Greenville, SC), 98
Boltz, Ray, 110, 111
Bono (U2 singer), 263n13
Boone, Pat, 45, 57, 246n17, 247n27
boundaries, 7–9
Bourdieu, Pierre, 6–7, 218
Bowen, Jimmy, 69, 73–74

Bowie, David, 256n3
Brackett, David, 4, 5, 196, 261n9
branding, 32, 245n3
Brave New World, 160
Brentwood (TN), 67–68
Brentwood Records, 77
Bright, Bill, 31, 48, 49
British invasion, 57
Broadman (publisher), 248n57
Brooks, Garth, 69, 74–75
Brooks, William, 23
Bruenger, David, 7, 196
Bryan, William Jennings, 13–14
Buddhism, 44
Buffalo Springfield, 220
Bumbershoot music festival (Seattle, WA), 207
Burial, The, 141–44, 143 fig., 152, 164
Burnett, T-Bone, 64–65, 220
Burning Bush fanzine, 159
Bushnell (IL), 140, 158, 164, 167
Butler Act, 14
Byrds, The, 57

California, 72
Call, The, 64–65
"Calling on You" (song; Stryper), 147
Calvary Chapel (Costa Mesa, CA), 171
Campus Crusade for Christ, 15, 31, 48, 49, 225, 248n44
Capital Cities, 77
capitalism: changing priorities regarding, 115; Christian music market and, 63, 106, 146–47; DIY ethics vs., 213; ethics of, and Christian music, 69; "ethics of style" vs., 147; ministry vs., 63, 78; popular music markets and, 5–6, 8, 36, 58, 212–13; resistance to, 85, 213; white U.S. evangelicals and, 33–34, 58. *See also* commerce
Capitol Christian Music Group (CCMG): changing priorities at, 85; Christian music market and, 80, 239; mission statement of, 67, 68–69, 78; subsidiaries of, 16, 239. *See also* EMI Christian Music Group
Capitol Nashville, 69, 74
Capitol Records, 39, 40, 57, 58, 72, 73
Card, Michael, 117
Carey, Mariah, 116, 128
Carman, 129, 139
Carmichael, Ralph, 53, 246n17
Carrie & Lowell (album; Stevens), 206
Carter, Jimmy, 15, 33
Carver, Jeff, 149, 161, 177, 209, 210–11
Cash, Johnny, 49, 56, 64–65
cassettes, 127, 217

Casting Crowns, 92, 154–56, 187, 227–28
catalog albums, 217–19
Categorizing Sound (Brackett), 261n9
Caterer, Josh, 221
Catholic Church, 14, 34, 172, 259n16
Cavicchi, Daniel, 6
CBS, 61, 73
CBS Records, 254n5
CCM magazine: AC charts in, 75; author's research using, 26; *CCM Update* vs., 71; on Christian music as ministry and business, 115; Christian music market and, 69; on crossover, 194, 195; founding of, 16; on Grant, 119, 121–22; Green interview in, 62–63, 75; Hearn interview in, 77–78; interview popularity in, 106; ministry/profitability debate in, 75–76; musicians' ethical transgressions and, 108–9, 111–14; readership of, 71; on record label vs. Christian market needs, 146–47; sales charts in, 66; secular music press vs., 65–66; Styll as editor of, 108; Swaggart interview in, 103–5, 253n39. *See also* Styll, John
CCM Update magazine, 26, 70–72, 73, 77, 131
CD replacement, 262n6
CD sales, 70, 90–91, 127, 217
celebrity lifestyles, 103
Celtic punk, 181
censorship, 99, 101–2, 253n22
Center for Popular Music (Murfreesboro, TN), 24
Central Florida Fairgrounds (Orlando, FL), 189
Centricity Music, 124
Centrifuge (Southern Baptist summer camp), 2
Cetera, Peter, 121, 255n12
Champaign County Fairgrounds (Urbana, IL), 164, 167
Change Your World (album; Smith), 2
Chapman, Gary, 120
Chapman, Steven Curtis, 2, 73, 74–75, 215, 228–29, 250n24
Chariot, The: at Cornerstone Festival, 182–86, 183 fig.; discography, 229–30; musical style of, 191; at Reggie's Rock Club (Chicago, IL), 208; resistance by, 27, 186, 191–92
charismatic practices, 14
charities, 83–84, 210
Charity Water, 83
Chevelle, 130, 205
Chicago (IL), 24, 137, 140, 158, 164, 208–9
Chicago Sun-Times, 158
Chicago Tribune, 158
Children of the Day, 18, 49, 110, 215
Choir, The, 177, 179

280 | Index

Christian Adult Contemporary (AC), 124
Christian Booksellers Association (CBA), 59, 171
Christian bookstores: censorship at, 101–2, 253n22; Christian music market and, 65, 72, 75, 115–16, 118–19; as Christian music retail outlet, 118–19, 130; Christian music sold at, 2, 16; crossover and, 72; numbers of, in U.S., 59; ownership of, 102; "recommended if you like" signage at, 2, 12, 16, 65
Christian colleges, 254n48
Christian Congregational Music Conference (Ripon College Cuddesdon, England), 23
Christian Contemporary Hit Radio (CHR), 82, 124
Christian Crusade, 99
Christian emo, 17
Christian goth, 16, 66, 166
Christian hardcore: author's experience, 17, 18, 22; at Christian music festivals, 132, 168, 179; Christian music market and, 27; Christian record labels recording, 147, 177; at Cornerstone Festival, 185, 192; incorporation of, in progressive worship services, 20; non-Christian hardcore vs., 17–18
Christian heavy metal, 147
Christian hip hop, 16, 244n45
Christian indie rock, 206
Christianity: author's experience, 12–13, 24–25; commodification of, 15–16, 32–34; countercultural, 51, 174, 249n86 (see also Jesus People movement); as diverse, 35; evangelical, 13–16, 17, 33, 34, 40, 58–59; faith as requirement in, 186; faking faith in, 263n17; hipster, 173; Jesus People reframing of, 31–32, 33, 34; legitimization of, 59, 65; material, 32–33; musicians as converts to, 220–21, 249n79; musicians critical of, 189–91; Orthodox, 144–45; pop singles with references to (1957–1970), 237–38; popularity of, 33, 50; rock and roll as viewed in, 45; subcultural, and resistance, 171–74, 190
Christianity Today magazine, 46, 107, 113
Christian metal: anti-rock discourse and, 148–49; at AudioFeed Festival, 180–81; author's experience, 22; at Christian music festivals, 132, 168, 179; Christian music market and, 16, 18, 27; Christian record labels recording, 177; at Cornerstone Festival, 141–44, 143 fig., 157, 185, 192; crossover and, 220; emergence of, 16; incorporation of, in progressive worship services, 20; Norman and, 44. *See also* Burial, The; Demon Hunter; *specific metal band*

Christian metalcore, 17, 147, 191–92, 198, 208, 211. *See also* Chariot, The; UnderOath
Christian morality, 42. *See also* ethics
Christian music: aesthetic standards of, 79, 110, 117, 175; authenticity in, 153–54; author's experience, 1–2, 11, 12–13, 16–17, 22; author's research on, 24–27; back catalog, 221; boundaries of, 7–9, 16, 182; commercial potential of, 123, 125, 129, 194; commodification of, 36–37, 75–76, 161; concerts, 105–6; defining, 17–22, 95; dismissal of, 148; as diverse, 35; ethical objections to, 26; evangelism as focus of, 102; highwater mark of, 201; historical narrative of, 25–26; listenership of, 218–19; mainstream, 16, 66, 132, 154, 203, 205; meaning/purpose of, 9, 35–36, 38, 85; old recordings of, 218–19; origins of, 15–16; resignified, 203; sales statistics, 79, 90–91; scholarship on, 243n3; subcategories of, 4, 84, 201, 261n5; typical consumers of, 124, 131; use of term, 4
Christian music festivals: authenticity and audience at, 187; author's experience, 208–9; author's research at, 5, 24; hecklers at, 209; as homogenous sites, 175–76; Jesus People movement and, 13; mainstream, 182; merchandizing at, 162; organizers of, 181; resistance/community at, 27, 174–76, 181–82, 186, 191–93; rock musicians performing at, 18–19; seminars at, 157–58; Tooth & Nail artists appearing at, 207. *See also* AudioFeed Festival; Cornerstone Festival
Christian music market: artist/audience relationship in, 152–54; authenticity and, 152–56; back catalog awareness in, 218–19; boundaries of, 8, 18–22, 25–27, 95–97, 118; capitalist foundation of, 63, 106; challenges of, 194, 195; changes in, 90–93, 194–95; competitiveness of, 200; core vs. margins, 146–47; corporate consolidation of, 25–26, 84–85, 116–17, 146–47, 194–95; dismissal of, 129–30; ethical transgressions and exclusion from, 105–11; ethics and, 85, 95–97, 102–3, 106, 137–38, 139; evangelism and, 64–66; growth of, 115, 118, 194, 195; as homogenous, 11; infrastructures promoting, 16, 116; loyalty of, 80, 215, 221; mainstreaming of, 116; Nashville as center of, 146, 165; origins of, 3–4, 13, 19, 25, 31, 44, 51, 116 (see also Jesus People movement); performativity

in, 152; profitability of, 73, 85, 86–90; radio and, 124; record label connection with, 82–84; record label identification of, 79–82, 239; religious devotion vs. Christian identity in, 173, 259n16; risk tolerance of, 216–17; secular, 130; secular music and, 148; self-censorship by, 64–66; stability in, 214–15; subcategories of, 9–11

Christian Music Trade Association (CMTA), 251n41

Christian punk, 167; author's experience, 12, 17; at Christian music festivals, 132, 168, 179; Christian music market and, 16, 27; Christian record labels recording, 147, 177, 208; at Cornerstone Festival, 185, 192; crossover and, 206–7; DIY ethics and, 257n19; emergence of, 16; ethical transgressions within, 111; non-Christian punk vs., 17–18, 257n19; Norman and, 44. *See also* Flatfoot 56; MxPx; *specific punk band*

Christian radio: AC, 124; aesthetic expectations of, 81–82; boundary enforcement by, 18; CHR, 82, 124; Christian music mainstream and, 175; Christian music market and, 18–19, 34, 72, 115–16, 118–19; Christian record industry and, 124–25, 131–32; Christian rock on, 18–19; conservative formats of, 146; crossover and, 72, 220; early singles on, 117; "ethics of style" and, 106; Grant songs appearing on, 117, 122, 256n27; listenership of, 92, 117, 119, 131, 146, 173; "sanctified entertainment" provided by, 194; "selling out" to appear on, 221–22; worship music on, 216

Christian record industry: artist-directed labels, 246n17; challenges facing, 90–93, 101–2, 249n9; changing priorities in, 69, 77, 84–90, 115; Christian music definition and, 95; commodification of, 75–76, 106; conservatism of, 146; consolidation/diversification strategies used by, 78–79; Cornerstone sponsorships of, 160–61; corporate consolidation of, 67–68, 69, 73, 76–77, 86–90, 115, 195, 249n5; crossover attempts by, 131–32; crossover strategies in, 198–201; development of, 51; Green's disillusionment with, 75; growth in, 70, 115; listenership identified by, 79–82; marketing strategies, 82–84; Nashville as center of, 165, 209; nonprofit labels, 223–26; racial segregation in, 21–22; "sanctified entertainment" provided by, 194; secular market partnerships of, 118–19; as support network, 109; worship music and, 216–17. *See also* Benson Company; Sparrow Records; Word Records; *specific record label*

Christian Right, 249n86

Christian rock: aggressive subgenres, 18, 147, 185; Christian music market and, 18–19; as Christian music subcategory, 4; Christian resistance to, 98, 100–102, 103–5; infrastructures promoting, 16, 59; Norman as "father" of, 36, 246n16; scholarship on, 246n16; "underground," 177–78. *See also specific Christian rock type*

Christian ska, 17, 147

Christian worship conferences, 182

Christian youth, 162–63, 173–74

Christmas (EP; Low), 262n34

Christmas Album (album; Children of the Day), 215

Christmas Album, A (album; Grant), 122

Christmas albums, 122, 206, 215, 219, 262n34

civil rights movement, 100

Claiborne, Shane, 209

Clark, Ryan, 151

classical music, 123

classic rock stations, 217

Cloonan, Martin, 7

clothing, suggestive, 143–44, 257n9

"C-Minor" (song; mewithoutYou), 209

C'Mon Along (album; McGuire), 60

Coachella Valley Music and Arts Festival (Indio, CA), 140

Coddington, Amy, 21

coffeehouses, 32

Cohen, Albert K., 169

Cohen, Leonard, 188

Cohen, Lizabeth, 33

Cohen, Phil, 169

Collection, The (album; Grant), 122

Columbia Records, 72, 220

Come&Live!, 160, 223–26, 263n24

"Come Thou Font of Every Blessing" (song; Stevens), 206

Come Together (youth folk musical; Owens), 53–54

commerce: author's research on, 9; case studies illustrating, 36; changing priorities regarding, 25–26, 115; Christian media debate over, 75–76, 77; Christian music market boundaries and, 9, 25, 66, 214; Christian record industry and, 58, 59, 83, 84, 115; Cornerstone Festival and, 161–62; corrupting influence of, 38; crossover and, 198; crossovers and, 198; ethics of, and Christian music, 69; "ethics of style" vs., 146–47; Green and, 38, 62–63, 64;

commerce (*continued*)
  interrelationships of, 25, 26, 27; Jesus
    People movement and, 36; ministry vs., 9,
    59, 62–63, 64, 75–76, 78, 115, 161–62;
    niche markets and, 11; Norman and, 40;
    prosperity gospel and, 246n9; resistance to,
    85, 176. *See also* capitalism
communes, 32, 46, 137, 157
communism, 97–98, 99
Communism, Hypnotism and the Beatles
  (pamphlet; Noebel), 99
community, 175
Compassion International, 84, 210
concerts, 210–11
conformity, 17
conservatism, 59, 140–41, 148–49, 249n86
consumer culture, 33, 34, 58–59
consumers, 96
contemporary Christian music (CCM): Christian music market and, 18–19; as Christian music subcategory, 4, 18; Christian resistance to, 103–5; CWM vs., 19–21; infrastructures promoting, 16; record labels supporting, 59, 68; typical consumers of, 124; use of term, 95
contemporary hit radio (CHR). *See* Top 40 radio
contemporary worship music (CWM): CCM vs., 19–21; Christian music market and, 19; as Christian music subcategory, 4; defined, 20; record labels supporting, 68
"Control" (song; Mutemath), 199
Coolidge, Rita, 49
Cooper, Alice, 64–65, 256n3
Cornerstone Festival (IL), 17, 24, 132; advertising for, 159, 160–61 *fig.*; attendance at, 161; Bible study at, 142, 145; Christian metal performances at, 141–44, 143 *fig.*, 157; commodification of, 161–62; community at, 175, 176–79, 181, 259n28; conservative protesters at, 140–41; crossover successes performing at, 161; ejections from, 187, 189, 258n58, 260n52; end of, 163–64, 166, 178–79; ethics and, 157–63, 164, 165; launching of, 157; legacy of, 164–65, 166–67, 179; musicians appearing at, 182–86, 183 *fig.*, 185 *fig.*, 187, 188–89, 191–92, 209, 220; niche styles welcome at, 157, 177; organizers of, 137, 181; record label sponsorships at, 160–61; resistance at, 27, 182, 185 *fig.*; "right musicking" at, 139, 145–46; seminars at, 157–58; Tooth & Nail artists appearing at, 207; youth as target demographic for, 162–63
Cornerstone magazine, 263n17

Cornerstone University (Grand Rapids, MI), 98
Cotillion Records, 57
Cotton Bowl (Dallas, TX), 48
counterculture, 13, 32, 46, 47, 50–51, 174, 249n86
counterpublic, 192–93
country music, 81, 123, 130, 217, 250n24, 251n48
Crank Records, 210
Crashdog, 167
Creation Festivals, 168, 175, 182, 207
credibility, 105
Creed, 263n13
crossovers: author's research on, 9; case studies illustrating, 36; Christian music market boundaries and, 25, 66, 214; Christian music market success and, 16; in Christian record industry, 72; commerce and, 198; cultural resignification and, 203; decision-making process for, 214; defined, 27, 195–98; ethics and, 26–27; evangelism as objective of, 194; Grant inability to sustain, 225; interrelationships of, 25, 26, 27; Jesus People movement and, 48–50, 50 *fig.*; mainstream-to-mainstream, 261n8; markets and, 204; objectives/strategies of, 128–33, 198–201; parallel, 197, 205; reverse, 196–98, 205, 219–20, 261n9; "selling out" and, 212–13; stability and, 219–21; use of term, 196. *See also* fringe crossover; Grant, Amy; Smith, Michael W.; *under specific musician/group*
Crowder, David, 19, 215
Cru, 15. *See also* Campus Crusade for Christ
Crusaders, The, 57
cults, 252n15
cultural elites, 218
cultural intermediaries, 20, 219; authenticity and, 205; author's interviews with, 25; Christian-identified artists and, 148; Christian music market and, 96, 200, 212; Christian record industry racial divide and, 21–22; corporate consolidation and, 25–26, 115; crossover and, 201–2; ethical expectations of, 212, 214, 215; ethics and, 9; historical/ethnographic insight into, 51; listening public defined by, 123; niche markets and, 96; popular music markets and, 3, 5–7; "right musicking" and, 145; scholarship on, 6, 7; self-censorship and, 64
Curb Records, 55, 67, 77
Curse Your Branches (album; Bazan), 187, 188
"Curse Your Branches" (song; Bazan), 188, 191
Cusic, Don, 45, 243n3

Daigle, Lauren, 19
Dallas (TX), 48–50
Danielson: A Family Movie (film; 2006), 262n33
Danielson Famile, 206
"Dare You to Move" (song; Switchfoot), 220
Dark Sacred Night (album; Bazan), 262n34
Darwinism, 14
David Crowder Band, 19, 215
"David De La Hoz" (song; The Chariot), 184
Day by Day (album; Van Dyke), 54
Dayton (TN), 13–14
DC Talk, 2, 11, 12, 16, 130
Dean, Kendra, 172–73, 259n17, 259n21
Death Cab for Cutie, 204
death metal, 149–50
Decca Records, 61
Dees, Rick, 1
Define the Great Line (album; UnderOath), 207–8
DeGarmo & Key, 2
deism, moralistic therapeutic. *See* moralistic therapeutic deism
Demon Hunter, 150 *fig.*, 177; chart success of, 147, 211; Christian/secular market venues of, 148; conservative Christian resistance to, 148–49; at Cornerstone Festival, 164; discography, 230; "ethics of style," 151–52; musical style of, 149–51
"Demons Never Sleep" (song; The Burial), 145
Denisoff, R. Serge, 7, 202
Denton, Melinda Lundquist, 172, 173
Devil Wears Prada, The, 146
DGC Records, 202
"Dialogue with a Question Mark" (song; The Chariot), 182–83
"Diamond Ring" (song; Bazan), 260n50
digital downloads, 70, 90–91, 262n6
Dion, Celine, 116, 128
Di Sabatino, David, 246n16, 247n36
discographies, 227–36
disco music, 117
divergence, 168
diversification, 72, 80
diversity, 180, 181
divorce, 107, 129
DIY ethics: artist adherence to, 213; author's experience, 11–12; Christian vs. non-Christian, 17, 257n19; emo rooted in, 204; in punk/hardcore subcultures, 8–9, 11–12; "selling out" debate and, 202; "underground" markets promoting, 148
Dorsey, Thomas, 45
Dot Records, 76
doubt, 186–87

Dove Awards, 22, 44, 65, 106, 108, 122, 199
Drive-Thru Records, 210
Drott, Eric, 7
drug abuse, 2, 100, 105
Dueck, Jonathan, 23, 132
Dunn, Jon, 148, 149, 151, 156, 177–78, 211
Duvall, 221
Dylan, Bob, 41, 64–65, 220, 249n79

Ebel, Brandon, 147, 223
Ebony magazine, 97
Edge, The (U2 guitarist), 263n13
Ed Sullivan Show, The (TV show), 45
Edwin Hawkins Singers, 47, 57
electronic dance music, 97
electropop, 206
Elefante, John, 220
Elevation Worship, 19, 215
"El Shaddai" (song; Card), 117–18, 254n3
Emery, 208
EMI Christian Music Group (EMI CMG): corporate consolidation and, 195; distribution agreements of, 207, 223; executives at, 86, 87, 92, 93, 124, 146, 154, 177, 210; fringe crossover and, 210; HQs of, 67; launching of, 68; mission statement of, 67; subsidiaries of, 16, 210; website of, 68, 249n4
EMI Music, 85, 91, 195; Sparrow acquired by, 68, 73–74, 77, 131, 132
emo, 204, 220–21
Engelhardt, Jeffers, 23, 27, 139, 144–45
English, Joe, 220
English, Michael, 108, 110, 111, 112, 113, 114, 254n44
Enigk, Jeremy, 220–21
Episcopal Church, 14
Eshleman, Paul, 48
Eskridge, Larry, 13, 31, 41, 46, 47, 49
Essential Records, 87
Estonia, 144–45
ethical transgressions, 95, 105–11, 132
ethics: aesthetics vs., 8–9, 42, 69, 94–95, 94–96, 106, 114, 149; anti-rock discourse and, 145; authenticity and, 153; author's research on, 9; biblical justifications for, 257n9; case studies illustrating, 36; charities and authentication of, 84; Christian music market and, 95–97, 106, 137–38, 139; Christian music market boundaries and, 25, 66, 214; of commerce/capitalism, 69; commodification of, 96; Cornerstone Festival and, 157–63, 164; as discourse, 111–14; Green's, 37–39; interrelationships of, 11, 25, 26, 27; journalistic, 111–14; markets and, 204; ministry and, 106;

284 | Index

ethics (*continued*)
  musical styles and, 137; niche markets defined by, 26–27, 138. *See also* DIY ethics
"ethics of style," 27; anti-rock discourse and, 95, 114, 137; capitalism vs., 146–47; at Cornerstone Festival, 163, 165; defined, 139
ethnographic studies, 6, 7
ethnography, 24
ethnomusicology, 7, 22–24
Evangelical Covenant Church (ECC), 137
evangelicalism, 222; anti-rock discourse of, 95; branding, for young audiences, 245n3; converts to, 249n79; development of, 171; mainstream Christian music festivals and, 182; media sensationalization of, 171; use of term, 244n29
evangelical left, 192–93
evangelical subculture, 168
evangelism, 25; as activism, 31–32; airwave, 119; Christian music and, 85, 102; Christian music market and, 64–66; Come&Live! and, 224–25; commerce vs., 62–63; crossovers and, 194; history of, 13–16; JPUSA and, 158; legitimization of, 45; lifestyle, 51; street, 31, 46, 48, 50–51; training in, 48, 49, 225. *See also* ministry
"Eve of Destruction" (song; McGuire), 246n21
Ever Passing Moment, The (album; MxPx), 207
Everybody's Coffee (Chicago, IL), 164
Everyday Sunday, 111
evolutionary theory, 14
Explo '72 convention (Dallas, TX; 1972), 48–50; attendance at, 48, 247n39; evangelism training as focus of, 48; Jesus People movement and, 36, 48, 49–50; media coverage of, 50 *fig.*; musicians appearing at, 49, 54; soundtrack album from, 49, 248n44; Watergate scandal and, 248n48
Extremist (album; Demon Hunter), 151

Fabbri, Franco, 244n16
Facebook, 111, 164
Facedown Records, 17
Fallen Angel (film; Di Sabatino), 246n16
Fall Out Boy, 204
Falwell, Jerry, 15
Family Bookstores, 2
"family values," 59
fanzines, 17, 159
Farner, Mark, 220
"Father's Eyes" (song; Grant), 117
feminism, 100
Fifield, Jim, 73–74
file sharing, 218, 262n6

"Find a Way" (song; Grant and Smith), 119–21, 125, 126, 255n11
Fireside Bowl, 18
Firewind (folk musical; T. Talbot), 60
First Baptist Church (Thomasville, GA), 51–52
Fish, The (radio network), 146
Flaming? (Jones), 254n50
Flatfoot 56, 179, 180, 181, 191
"Flood" (song; Jars of Clay), 12
folk music, 57
ForeFront Records, 74, 77
"Foregone Conclusions" (song; Pedro the Lion), 186–87
Foreman, Tim, 220, 221
For Him Who Has Ears to Hear (album; Green), 37, 60, 61
"For Those Tears I Died" (song; Stevens), 110
Free at Last (album; DC Talk), 2
"Friends" (song; Smith), 2
fringe crossover: Bazan and, 186, 192; benefits of, 27; challenges of, 27; Christian metalcore bands and, 198; defined, 147, 196; Stevens (Sufjan) and, 204–5; as Tooth & Nail strategy, 27, 147, 206–12
Frith, Simon, 7, 9, 55, 92–93, 131, 244n16
Fuller Theological Seminary (Pasadena, CA), 46
Full Gospel Trinidad, 94–95, 106
fundamentalism, 96–97, 171, 244n29
Furay, Rich, 220

Gaither, Bill, 56
Gaither family, 108, 139
Garden State Arts Center (NJ), 11
Garland, Shannon, 7
Garlock, Frank, 98–99, 100, 114
Garofolo, Reebee, 7
gay marriage, 171
gender, 254n50
gender identity, 109, 222
Gendron, Bernard, 259n11
general market. *See* popular music markets
genre, 4–5
genre studies, 5, 244n16
geography, 4–5
Ghost Thief (album; Living Sacrifice), 181
Glass Harp, 34
Glorieta conference center (NM), 52–53
Godspell (rock opera; Schwartz and Tebelak), 247n29
"Goodbye for Now" (song; P.O.D.), 262n32
Good News! (youth musical), 52–53, 58, 248n57
Gordon, Milton, 169
Gospel Metal fanzine, 159
gospel music: author's experience, 2; Black, 110; Black vs. white, 21–22; Christian

music market and, 16, 21–22; Christian record labels recording, 55–56, 68; at Explo '72 convention (1972), 49; popular music markets and, 3; rock and roll vs., 97; on Top 40 radio, 45; use of term, 95; white Southern, 55–56, 108, 247n27
Gospel Music Association (GMA), 24; Artist of the Year, 122; Christian music market as profiled by, 81; Christian music sales documented by, 79, 90; Dove Awards, 22, 44, 65, 106, 108, 122; *Industry Overviews*, 250n41; style and, 95
Gospel Music Hall of Fame, 44
Gospel Music Week (Nashville, TN), 199
Gospel Road, The (film; 1973), 49
Gospel Sound, The (Heilbut), 243n3
gossip, 108–9, 112
Graham, Billy, 46, 48, 49, 171
Graham, Sandra, 243n3
Grammy Awards, 44, 65, 122
Grand Funk Railroad, 220
Grand Rapids School of Bible and Music (MI), 98
Grant, Amy, 2, 208; Christian music market and, 194, 221; criticism directed at, 122; as crossover artist, 16, 27, 75–76, 116, 125–27, 125 fig., 130, 195, 199, 201, 205, 211, 212, 219, 225, 256n27, 261n8; crossover strategies of, 118, 125–26, 132–33, 201, 207, 212; discography, 230–31; early career of, 117–22, 120 fig., 254n3, 255n12,14; ethical transgressions of, 129; as integrational artist, 261n5; late career of, 215, 219, 225; musical style of, 66, 212; as pop-oriented artist, 215; as "sellout," 74–75, 122; success of, 25, 26, 117, 118, 122–23, 128, 129, 195, 212, 225, 246n24, 255n17. *See also* "Baby, Baby" (song; Grant); *Unguarded* (album; Grant)
Great Adventure, The (album; Chapman), 2, 74–75
"Great Adventure, The" (song; Chapman), 74, 75
Greatest Hits 1986–2004 (album; Grant), 255n12
greatest hits compilations, 215
Green, Al, 129
Green, Keith: career surrender of, 51, 62, 69, 226; *CCM* interview of, 62–63, 75; Christian music market and, 44; Christian record industry as viewed by, 75; discography, 231–32; double marginalization of, 16; Dylan and, 249n79; ethics of, 37–39, 223; ministry focus of, 62, 138; musical career of, 60–63; musical style of, 18
Green, Melody, 37, 60–61

Green Day, 12, 65
Gross, Kelsey Ebben, 173–74, 175
grounded-theory approach, 255n20
Grrr Records, 160
grunge music, 197, 206
Guetta, David, 197
Gulliksen, Kenn, 61

Hall, Darrell, 120
Hall, Mark, 154–56
Hall, Stuart, 169
"Hallelujah" (song; Cohen), 188
Hammer, MC, 64–65
hardcore music, 202, 206. *See also* Christian hardcore
hardcore subculture, 8–9, 11–12, 17–18
"Hard to Be" (song; Bazan), 188
Haste the Day, 17, 191, 208
Hatfield, Todd, 142, 144, 145
Hauser, Chris, 216
Head, Murray, 47
Heard, Mark, 39
Hearn, Bill (son), 68, 69, 72, 115
Hearn, Billy Ray: albums released by, 249n80; author's interview with, 56; career of, 51–55; *CCM* interview of, 77–78; on Christian bookstore censorship, 101–2; on Christian music market, 131; on crossover, 195; death of, 68; decision-making process of, 76; diversification efforts of, 72; Explo '72 convention and, 58; Green released from contract by, 37–39, 69; ministry prioritized by, 59–60, 76; musicians recording with, 60; as Myrrh founder, 51, 59; retirement of, 68, 78; as Sparrow Records founder, 37, 68, 101; Sparrow sold to EMI by, 68, 73–74, 77, 131, 132; youth musicals of, 52–54, 57, 102
Heart in Motion (album; Grant), 2, 125–27, 125 fig., 195, 225. *See also* "Baby, Baby" (song; Grant)
HeartWarming Records, 56
Heaven in the Real World (album; Chapman), 74
"Heaven in the Real World" (song; Chapman), 75
Heavens Metal magazine, 17, 159
heavy metal, 138
Hebdige, Dick, 27, 48, 169–71, 172, 174, 203, 205, 212
hecklers, 209
Hegelian dialectic, 170
Heilbut, Anthony, 110, 243n3
Helvering, John, 107
Hendershot, Heather, 15, 34, 58, 79
Hendrix, Jimi, 256n3
Henry, Carl, 46

Herrin, John, 139–41, 157, 158–59, 162–63, 178, 189, 260n52
Herring, Annie, 60, 248n76
Hesmondhalgh, David, 7
"He Touched Me" (song; Gaither), 56
Hillsong United, 19, 215, 245n3
Hinduism, 44
hip hop, 97, 130, 217, 244n45
hippies, 31, 44
HM Magazine, 17, 159
Hoggart, Richard, 169
"Holding Out Hope to You" (song; English), 108
Hollywood Free Paper, 32
Holt, Fabian, 7
Holy Hip Hop in the City of Angels (Zanfagna), 244–45n45
Home for Christmas (album; Grant), 128
Home Mission Board (Southern Baptist Convention), 1
homogenization, 79
homosexuality, 105, 109–11, 171, 222
"Honestly" (song; Stryper), 147
Honeytree, Nancy, 54
Hope (album; English), 108
"Hope Set High" (song; Grant), 256n27
Hopper, Jessica, 188, 189–90
Horowitz, Daniel, 33
Hot 100 list (*Billboard*): CCM and, 75; competition on, 256n28; crossovers and, 195; gospel music appearing on, 45; Grant songs appearing on, 119, 121, 126, 129, 195; Jars of Clay songs appearing on, 12; McGuire song appearing on, 246n21; multiplatinum albums and, 128
"Hot n Cold" (song; Perry), 205
House of Love (album; Grant), 128–29
Houston, Whitney, 116, 128
Howard, Jay, 9–11, 14, 84, 201, 202, 261n5
Howard, Tom, 39
"How Majestic Is Your Name" (song; Smith), 106
How the West Was One (album; Second Chapter of Acts), 248–49n76
Huey Lewis and the News, 121
Hüsker Dü, 202
hymns, 13, 20, 129, 215, 243n3, 248n57
hymn writers, 3

"I Am a Stone" (song; Demon Hunter), 151
"I Am on the Rock" (song; Petra), 2
Ichthus Music Festival (KY), 207
"If We've Ever Needed You" (song; Casting Crowns), 154
"I Kissed a Girl" (song; Perry), 205

Illinoise (album; Stevens), 262n33
"I Love You" (song; Zombies), 39
Impact Records, 56, 107
Imperials, The, 56
Impressions, The, 57
Impulse! Records, 76
In Another Land (album; Norman), 39
incorporation, 203–4
indie labels, 262n36
indie rock, 8, 9, 132, 202, 204, 206
indulgences, selling of, 34
industrialization, 33, 178
Industry Overviews (GMA), 250–51n41
Ingalls, Monique, 20, 23
In Rainbows (album; Radiohead), 62
Inside Out Faith (advocacy organization), 111
inspirational praise songs, 107, 110, 117–18
"In Stitches" (song; Bazan), 187
Institute for Oral History (Baylor University, Waco, TX), 52
integration, racial, 21–22
integrational artists, 9–11, 14, 22, 84, 195, 201–2, 261n5
intentional communities. *See* communes; Jesus People, U.S.A. (JPUSA)
International Federation of the Phonographic Industry (IFPI), 70, 249n9
International Justice Mission, 83
International Student Congress on Evangelism. *See* Explo '72 convention (Dallas, TX; 1972)
Interscope Records, 131
Inter-Varsity Christian Fellowship, 15
"In the Garden" (hymn), 49
"I Pledge Allegiance to the Lamb" (song; Knapp), 110
"I See Men as Trees Walking" (song; Cash), 49
isolationism, 59
"I Think You Know" (song; Rez Band), 138
"I've Got to Learn to Live without You" (song; Norman), 41
"I Will Go Plant Little Flowers" (song; Timbre), 184
"I Will Remember You" (song; Grant), 128
"I Wish We'd All Been Ready" (song; Norman), 43, 246n21, 247n27

Jackson, Janet, 116, 128
Jacksonville (IL), 73
Jars of Clay, 12, 16, 130
jazz, 123
Jesus Christ, 31, 259n21
Jesus Christ Superstar (rock opera; Weber and Rice), 47, 247n29

Jesus music, 4, 36, 110, 247n27
Jesus People, U.S.A. (JPUSA; Chicago, IL), 167; author's fieldwork at, 24; as Christian intentional community, 163; Cornerstone Festival ended by, 163–64; Cornerstone Festival organized by, 137, 139–40, 157, 158; current ministries of, 137, 164; formation of, 137; magazine published by, 263n17; record label of, 160; spiritual/social tenets of, 141, 145. *See also* Cornerstone Festival
Jesus People movement: anti-rock discourse and, 100; Christianity reframed by, 31–32, 33, 34; Christian music market based in, 3–4, 13, 19, 25, 31, 44; commodification of, 15, 32, 33–34, 58; converts of, 38, 41, 45–46, 50–51; crossover moment of, 36, 48–50, 50 fig.; decline of, 50–51, 72; dispersal of, from California, 102; evangelism of, 31, 224; legacy of, 34, 102, 137, 249n86; legitimization of, 45–48, 47 fig.; musicians in, 34, 38, 39, 49, 60; popularity of, 33; predecessors of, 15; resistant ideals/theologies of, 41, 171–72; scholarship on, 247n36. *See also* Explo '72 convention (Dallas, TX; 1972); Jesus People, U.S.A. (JPUSA)
Jesus Sound Explosion (Explo '72 soundtrack), 49, 248n44
Jimmy Eat World, 204
John, Gospel of, 260n50
John Birch Society, 99
Johnson, Chad, 27, 215, 223–26
Jones, Alisha Lola, 254n50
Joplin, Janis, 256n3
Jordan, Marabeth, 108, 254n44
Joseph, Mark, 129–30
Joseph and the Amazing Technicolor Dreamcoat (rock opera; Weber and Rice), 247n29
journalism, 111–14
Jurado, Damien, 205–6

Kaiser, Glenn, 101, 102, 137, 138, 179
Kaiser, Kurt, 53
Kansas, 64–65, 220
Katy Hudson (album; Perry), 205
Keaggy, Phil, 34, 249n76
Keightley, Keir, 5, 217
Kelly, Tori, 225
Kelman, Ari, 19–21, 23
Kent State shootings (OH, 1970), 47
Kern, Roger, 218
King, Martin Luther, Jr., 21, 97
"Kiss Me" (song; Sixpence None the Richer), 205, 208
K-LOVE (radio network), 146

K-Mart, 70, 74, 75
Knapp, Jennifer, 110–11, 114, 262n32
Korn, 220
Kravitz, Lenny, 64–65
Kristofferson, Kris, 49
Kusber, Wayne: A&R experience of, 79, 124, 200; on authenticity, 152, 153; author's interview with, 79–80; on Casting Crowns, 154; on Christian music market loyalty, 221; on Christian record industry marketing strategies, 79–81; on commerce and Christian music market, 86, 89–90; on crossover, 200–201; on ethics vs. aesthetics, 146–47; on radio and Christian record industry, 82–83, 92, 131; on typical Christian music consumers, 124–25; on youth market, 93

Laing, Dave, 249n2
Lamb and Lion Records, 34, 246n17
Langguth, Esther, 17, 18
Larson, Bob, 99, 100, 252nn15–16
Lasker, Jay, 54–55
Last Days Ministries, 62
"Last One Alive, The" (song; Demon Hunter), 151
Late, Great Planet Earth, The (Lindsey), 41
Lead Me On (album; Grant), 121–22, 125, 246n24, 255n14
"Lead Me On" (song; Grant), 122
Lection Records, 73
Led Zeppelin, 92
LeFevre, Mylon, 57
Lehigh University (Bethlehem, PA), 12
Lennon, John, 97, 99
lesbianism, 110–11
"Let's Just Praise the Lord" (song; Gaither), 56
Letting Go (album; Knapp), 110
Lewis, Huey, 121
Lewis, Jerry Lee, 56
LGBTQIA+ Christians, 111
Liberty Records, 69, 70, 74
Life in General (album; MxPx), 207
Life magazine, 46, 49, 50 fig.
Light Records, 246n17
Lightshine International newsletter, 159
"Like Spinning Plates" (song; Radiohead), 184
Lindsey, Hal, 41, 246n21
live recordings, 215, 219
Livgren, Kerry, 220
Living Sacrifice, 180–81
Lollapalooza music festival, 11, 12, 140, 207
"Lonely by Myself" (song; Norman), 43
"Look What Has Happened to Me" (song; Grant), 117

Los Angeles (CA), 61, 62
Lost Dog, 179
Lost in the Sound of Separation (album; UnderOath), 191–92
Love Song, 34, 49
Low, 262n34
LPs, 217
"Lucky One" (song; Grant), 128–29
Luhr, Eileen, 59, 98, 99, 158
"Lullaby" (song; Pedro the Lion), 186
Luther, Martin, 34

Madison Square Garden (New York, NY), 11
Magolda, Peter, 173–74, 175
mainstreaming, 202, 203, 204
mainstream(s), 123
Make a Joyful Noise with Drums and Guitars (album; Crusaders), 57
Mansion Builder (album; Second Chapter of Acts), 249n76
Maranatha! Music, 34, 110
Marshall, David, 143–44, 143 fig.
Marshall, Lee, 7, 252n78, 262n6
Marxist Minstrels, The (Noebel), 99
Mason Proffit, 60
mass culture, 33, 58
Matthew, Gospel of, 259n21
Matthews, Randy, 49, 54
Mays, John, 86–88, 90, 91, 124
MCA Records, 72, 73, 77, 115, 131, 195
McCarthyism, 97–98
McCracken, Brett, 173
McCracken, Jarrell, 34, 53, 54–55, 56, 57–58, 67, 68
McDannell, Colleen, 32–33
McGraw, Tim, 92
McGuire, Barry, 16, 49, 54, 60, 61, 246n21
McLuhan, Marshall, 158
McRobbie, Angela, 169
Meadowlands (East Rutherford, NJ), 11
"Meant to Live" (song; Switchfoot), 220
media, 46–48, 47 fig., 49, 111, 210–11, 250n41
megachurches, 215, 245n3
melodeath, 149–50
Melody Four Quartet, 56
merchandizing, 162
MercyMe, 18–19
Mercy Ministries, 254n44
meritocracy, 59
metal, 145, 147, 206. *See also* Christian metal
metalcore, 146, 163, 182–83, 208, 211. *See also* Christian metalcore
Metro (rock club; Chicago, IL), 208–9
Metro-Goldwyn-Mayer, 246n23
mewithoutYou, 209, 211

MGM Records, 246n23
Michael English (album; English), 108
"Middle, The" (song; Death Cab for Cutie), 204
middle class, 33, 59
Middle Tennessee State University (Murfreesboro, TN), 24
Middleton, Jason, 205
Midnight Oil, 65
"Midnight Son" (song; Rez Band), 138
Miller, Donald, 15
Miller, Karl Hagstrom, 21
Milwaukee (WI), 137
ministry: as business plan component, 76; Christian media debate over, 75–76, 77; Christian music focus on, 102; commerce vs., 9–11, 37–39, 59, 62–63, 64, 161–62; corporate consolidation and, 85; ethics and, 106, 140; Green and, 37–39, 64; Hearn and, 59–60, 76; profitability vs., 75–76, 78, 115; prosperity gospel and, 246n9; Rez Band and, 138; secular culture and, 10–11; training in, 48. *See also* evangelism
miscegenation, 100
Mitchell, Joni, 129
mixed-methods ethnographic approach, 24
modernism, 14
Moore, Allan, 152, 205
moralistic therapeutic deism, 172–73, 259n17
Moral Majority, 15, 140
moral panics, 97, 252n15
Mormonism, 259n16, 262n34
Morris, Jeremy Wade, 7
Moss, Ami, 179
Mr. Mister, 65
"Mrs. Robinson" (song; Simon and Garfunkel), 47
MTV, 103
Mullen, Larry, Jr. (U2 drummer), 263n13
Murfreesboro (TN), 24
music, commodification of, 5–6
musical theatre, 102, 247n29
music critics, 211
music distribution, 68, 72–73, 79, 115–16, 195, 218
music festivals, 140, 162, 178, 260n29. *See also* Christian music festivals
musicians: audience connection strategies, 84; Christian music market and, 96; Christian view of, 2; ethics of, 84, 95; Jesus People, 34, 38, 39, 49, 55, 60; ministry to, 223–26; popular music markets and, 3
music industry: challenges facing, 262n6; Christian record industry partnerships with, 118–19; corporate consolidation of, 26, 249n2; growth in, 70; objectives of, 36;

radio and, 123–24; recording format shifts in, 217, 262n6; revenues in, 262nn6–7; risk aversion of, 217–19; scholarship on, 7, 252n78. *See also* Christian music market; Christian record industry; popular music; popular music markets; record labels
music industry studies, 7
musicking, 7, 145
MusicLine magazine, 26, 77, 87, 115. See also *CCM Update* magazine
music piracy, 262n6
music publishing, 68
Music to Raise the Dead (album; Rez Band), 138
Mutemath, 130, 199–201, 222
MxPx, 12, 65, 130, 191, 206–7, 211
My Chemical Romance, 204
Mylon (album; LeFevre), 57
Myrrh Records: album releases at, 54, 249n80; Christian music market and, 16, 118; Christian popular music released by, 34; commerce vs. ministry at, 59; discography, 232–33; Explo '72 convention and, 58; founding of, 34, 51, 54, 55; musicians recording with, 54, 59, 117, 248n76, 254n5

Nashville (TN), 24, 72, 74, 81, 146, 165, 209
National Academy of Recording Arts and Sciences (NARAS), 65
nationalism, 33
National Study of Youth and Religion, 259n17
Natural High (youth folk musical; Carmichael and Kaiser), 53
Negus, Keith, 7
Nekola, Anne, 42, 64, 97, 98
Nevermind (album; Nirvana), 197
New Age movement, 44, 252n15
new evangelicalism, 14–16
New Jersey, 11–12
newspapers, 32
Newsweek magazine, 46
new wave, 138
New York (NY), 11
New York Times, 111
"Next Time I Fall, The" (song; Grant and Cetera), 121, 125, 255n12
niche markets: anti-Christian bias and, 148; artist success in, 204–5; AudioFeed Festival and, 168; for Christian music, 141, 219; Christian music market and, 80, 194; Christian record industry and, 92, 93; Cornerstone Festival and, 162, 163; crossover and, 132–33, 186, 196–98 (*see also* fringe crossover); defined, 3; defining conflicts in, 9, 11; emergence of, 203; ethics and definition of, 26–27, 95–97, 138, 153, 202,

222–23; genre-specific playlists targeting, 216; mainstreaming of, 203–4; mainstream success and, 196; mass market vs., 204; options expanded by, 182; overlapping, 148; priorities/objectives of, 66; record labels and exploitation of, 55, 56–57, 80; relevance of, 27; "right musicking" and, 153; rock and roll as, 56–57; style/aesthetics of, 94–95; youth-oriented, 163. *See also* Christian music market; *specific niche market*
Nielsen SoundScan, 250n41
"Nightmare #71" (song; Norman), 43
Nirvana (band), 197
No Compromise (album; Green), 37, 60, 62
Noebel, David A., 99, 100
nonconformity, 163
Norma Jean, 191, 208
Norman, Larry: anti-rock discourse and, 100; apocalyptic themes in music of, 41, 246n21; Christian identity of, 246n19; Christian music industry and, 55; Christian music market and, 16, 44; death of, 44; discography, 234; double marginalization of, 16; as Jesus People musician, 34, 39–44, 43 *fig.*, 49, 55; ministry focus of, 256n3; musical style of, 18; psychedelic rock career of, 39, 61, 246n19; resistant identity of, 36, 42, 43–44; sanitized covers of music of, 247n27; scholarship on, 246n16; secular record label releases by, 57; success of, 246n24
North American Mission Board (Southern Baptist Convention), 1
"Not Ready to Die" (song; Demon Hunter), 151
Nu Thang (album; DC Talk), 2

objectivity, 24
Ocean, 49
Offspring, The, 207
"Of Minor Prophets and Their Prostitute Wives" (song; Bazan), 260n50
Ogg, Alex, 7
"Oh Happy Day!" (song; Edwin Hawkins Singers), 47
"Oh My Soul" (song; Casting Crowns), 155
oil crisis (1973), 54
Oldenberg, Bob, 52
oldies stations, 217, 218
One Bad Pig, 12, 177
One Love (album; Guetta), 197
One Thousand Risks (Johnson), 224
online bulletin boards, 17
"Only Thing, The" (song; Stevens), 206
Only Visiting This Planet (album; Norman), 41–42, 246n24, 256n3
Orbison, Roy, 56

Orthodox Christianity, 144–45
Osmond, Donny, 61
Owens, Jimmy, 53

paganism, 44, 252n15
parachurch organizations, 49
Paragon, 77
Parents Music Resource Center, 99
Parker, Trey, 263n17
Passion worship conferences, 215–16
Pat Boone Sings the New Songs of the Jesus People (album; Boone), 247n27
Patillo, Leon, 220
Patty, Sandi, 96; Christian media view of, 112–13; at Christian music festivals, 139; Christian record industry and, 66; comeback of, 107–8, 111; ethical transgressions of, 95, 106, 107, 112–13; "ethics of style" and, 114; musical style of, 66, 107, 110; success of, 106–7; Word/A&M partnership and, 129; worship music of, 215
"Peace in the Valley" (song; Dorsey), 45
Peacock, Charlie, 78
Pearce, Billy, 56
Pearson, Trey, 111
Pederson, Duane, 32
Pedro the Lion, 186–88, 192, 205–6, 234–35
Pentecostalism, 14
People!, 39, 40–41, 42, 246n19
performance contexts, 20–21, 23–24
performing rights organizations, 127
Perkins, Carl, 56
Perkins, Dave, 124
Perry, Katy, 24, 205, 262n32
Peslis, Don, 107
Peterson, Andy, 254n48; author's interview with, 83; on Christian music market strategies, 83; on Christian record industry consolidation, 85, 88–89, 91, 210; on Cornerstone Festival, 177; crossover artists recording with, 199; on ethical transgressions and Christian music market, 109–10, 111; record industry career of, 83, 88; on "selling out," 221; as Word Records executive, 83, 88, 109, 177, 199, 200
Peterson, Richard, 5, 7, 57, 83–84, 152–53, 218
Petra, 2, 129, 255n7
Phillips, Sam, 205–6
pilgrimage, 192
Pitchfork (website), 206
"Place in This World" (song; Smith), 2
"Pledge My Head to Heaven" (song; Green), 249n79
Pluto Records, 17
PNC Bank Arts Center (Holmdel, NJ), 11

Poco, 220
P.O.D., 130, 199, 205, 211, 262n32
political instability, 100
PolyGram, 72, 73, 207, 246n23
pop metal, 138
pop-punk bands, 65
popular culture, 32, 46, 50
popular music: author's experience, 1–2, 11–12; boundaries of, 23, 244n16; Christian appropriation of, 98; Christian wariness of, 102–3; multiple mainstreams in, 261n8; normalization of, among evangelicals, 102; resignified, 203; scholarship on, 22–24, 69, 255n20; singles with Christian references (1957–1970), 237–38; successful albums (1990s), 242; temporal transcendence achieved by, 218
popular music markets: authenticity within, 204–5; back catalog awareness in, 219; boundaries of, 8–9, 20, 94, 197; catalog albums and, 217–19; competitiveness of, 200; crossovers in, 27, 197–98, 214; defined, 3; mass vs. niche, 3, 27, 80, 204–5; scholarship on, 4–7; spirituality and, 44–45. *See also* niche markets
popular music studies, 22–24
pornography, 253n22
Porter, Mark, 23
post-hardcore, 208
post-punk, 202
postsecularity, 148, 257n18
Power, Billy, 178
"Power of Love, The" (song; H. Lewis), 121
Powers, Devon, 7
Presley, Elvis, 44, 45, 56, 57, 197
Pretty Good Records, 62
Prince, 218
print fanzines, 17
Priority Records, 73
privilege, 23
profane language, 106
progressive social movements, 100
Project 86, 17
"Promise" (song; Pedro the Lion), 186
Proper Management, 92, 154
prosperity gospel, 246n9
Protestantism: Christian fundamentalism and, 13, 14, 244n29; Christian music festivals and, 182; evangelicalism and, 14–15; Jesus People converts to, 45–46, 48, 172; popular culture and, 124; youth and religious devotion in, 259n16. *See also* evangelicalism; white U.S. evangelical Christians
Protestant Reformation, 34
protest music, mainstreaming of, 202

Provident Label Group, 16, 195
Provident Music Group: Christian music market and, 80, 85, 239; conservatism of, 146; corporate consolidation of, 67–68; executives at, 87, 216; as Sony subsidiary, 67, 249n5; subsidiaries of, 77, 87–88, 124, 239
Pruett, David, 6
Psalms, Book of, 155
psychedelic rock, 40–41, 57
punk rock/subculture: Christian converts in, 221; Christian vs. non-Christian, 17–18, 65, 181, 191; crossover and, 204–5; defining characteristics of, 259n11; DIY ethics of, 8–9, 11–12; lifecycle of, 171; moral panics over, 97; as niche style, 163, 206; record industry disinterest in, 202; subcultural resistance in, 169–70. *See also* Christian punk

quarterly financial reports, 86–87

R&B, 44, 123
race, 21–22, 33, 45, 97
racism, 21
Radically Saved fanzine, 17
radio: audience and programming on, 123–24; Christian music market and, 16; commercial formats, 81–82, 216, 217, 218, 255nn19–20, 261n8; crossover and, 210–11; as cultural intermediary, 6–7; performance royalties from, 256n30; racial segregation in, 21; royalties and, 127–28; satellite, 217; worship music and, 216. *See also* Christian radio; Top 40 radio
Radiohead, 62, 92, 184
Radon Lounge (AudioFeed Festival), 166, 167
Raging Storm Records, 160
Ragtime fanzine, 159
Rambos, The, 56
Ramones, 202
Raney, Wayne, 40
rave scene, 171
Rawls, John, 257n19
RCA Records, 72, 254n5
"Reader's Digest" (song; Norman), 256n3
Reagan, Ronald, 15
rebelliousness, 2
Reborn (album; Talbot Brothers), 60
Recon, 2
"Reconciliation" (song; The Burial), 145
Recording Industry Association of America (RIAA), 24, 55, 70, 79, 90–91, 127, 249n9, 250–51n41, 262n7
record labels: Christian music and, 17; Christian record industry partnerships with, 118–19; Christian record labels acquired by, 115; corporate acquisitions/mergers in, 25–26, 249n2, 256n26; crossover and, 210–11; independent, 17; job losses in, 256n26; radio and, 123–24, 127–28; scholarship on, 7, 252n78. *See also* Christian record industry; music industry
re:creation (album; Chapman), 250n24
Red, 18–19
"Red, The" (song; Chevelle), 205
Reggie's Rock Club (Chicago, IL), 208, 262n36
regional musics, 123
reissues, 218
Religious Rock'n'roll (Swaggart), 103
Replacements, The, 202
Reset (EP; Mutemath), 199
resignification, 169–70, 203
resistance, 132; author's research on, 9; case studies illustrating, 36; at Christian music festivals, 174–76, 181–82, 186; Christian music market boundaries and, 25, 26–27, 66, 214; interrelationships of, 25, 26, 27; Jesus People movement as, 41; to secular culture, 36; subcultural, 169–70, 202–3; subcultural Christianity and, 171–74; subculture theory and, 168–71, 172–73; white U.S. evangelicals and, 17; in youth cultures, 172–73
"Responsibility" (song; MxPx), 207, 208
Resurrection Band: anti-rock discourse and, 102; at Cornerstone Festival, 157; "ethics of style" and, 138, 140; founding members of, 139, 140; JPUSA and, 137; live concerts of, 101, 101 fig.; musical style of, 18, 138
Return of the Frog Queen (album; Enigk), 221
Reunion Records, 68, 77, 87, 88
reviews, 211
Rez Band. *See* Resurrection Band
Rice, Tim, 247n29
"right musicking," 139, 145–46
"right singing," 27, 139, 144–45
Ripon College Cuddesdon (England), 23
ritual, 192, 193
rock and roll, 16; aesthetics of, vs. Christian ethics, 114; Christian view of, 45, 95, 96–97, 246n22; emergence of, 95; "good music" vs., 99, 246n22; gospel music vs., 97; Jesus People movement and, 32, 34; moral panic over, 97; Norman and, 45; popularization of, 5, 57. *See also* anti-rock discourse
rock concerts, 152
Rocketown Records, 88
rock operas, 247n29
Rode Dog Records, 88
Roe, Michael, 179

Rolling Stone magazine, 16, 119
Rolling Stones, The, 41, 256n3
Romanowski, William, 118–19, 131
Romans, Book of, 257n9
Rommen, Timothy, 27, 94–95, 106, 137
royalties, 127–28, 256n30
rumors, 108–9, 112
Run-DMC, 65, 197

salvation, 33–34
"Same Old Story, The" (song; Norman), 43
Sancrosanct Records, 160
"sanctified entertainment," 194, 195, 198
sanitization, 247n27
San Jose (CA), 39
Sanneh, Kelefa, 253n16
Santana, 220
Satanism, 99, 100, 252–53nn15–16, 263n17
Saved (album; Dylan), 220
"Saved by Love" (song; Grant), 126
Saved by Song (Cusic), 243n3
Schaeffer, Francis, 46
Schwartz, Stephen, 247n29
Scientology, 246n19
Scogin, Josh, 183, 183 fig., 191, 208
Scopes Trial (TN, 1925), 13–14, 171
Seattle (WA), 24, 209, 211
Second Chapter of Acts, 18, 54, 61, 219, 248–49n76
"Secret of the Easy Yoke, The" (song; Pedro the Lion), 186, 187
secular culture: anti-rock discourse and, 97–99; evangelicalism and, 13–15; evangelicalism as response to, 171; ministry and, 10–11; postsecularity and, 148, 257n18; separatism from, 65
secular music, 1–2, 148. *See also* popular music
segregation, racial, 21–22, 45
self-censorship, 64–66
self-sufficiency, 59
"selling out": crossover and, 212–13; defined, 212; DIY underground debate over, 202; examples of, 222; Grant and, 74–75, 122
Selling Satan (Hertenstein and Trott), 263n17
separational artists, 9–11, 141, 201–2
separationism, 14–15
SESAC, 127
Seven Swans (album; Stevens), 206
77s, 179
sex, extramarital, 2, 95, 105, 107, 143, 254n44
sexual abstinence, 143, 144, 209
sexual identity, 109, 222
sexuality, 254n50
sexual promiscuity, 100
shadow infrastructures, 9

Shires, Preston, 14, 244n29, 249n86
shoegaze, 206
Shot of Love (album; Dylan), 220
Silver & Gold (album; Stevens), 206
Simon and Garfunkel, 47, 57
Simple Way, The (intentional community; Philadelphia, PA), 209
singles, 126, 127, 217, 256nn28–29, 262n7
"Sing to the Lord" (song; Sterling), 106–7, 108
Sire Records, 202
Sirius XM, 217
Sixpence None the Richer, 16, 130, 199, 205, 208, 211
Skillet, 18–19
Slayer, 252–53n16
Slowly Going the Way of the Buffalo (album; MxPx), 207
Slow Train Coming (album; Dylan), 220
Small, Christopher, 7, 145
Smith, Christian, 172, 173, 259n17
Smith, Chuck, 46, 171
Smith, Daniel, 206, 262n33
Smith, Michael W.: author's experience, 2, 11, 12, 13, 16; Christian music market and, 19; as crossover artist, 16, 129, 130, 205, 211; Grant and, 120; musical style of, 66; as pop-oriented artist, 215; songs written by, 106; worship music of, 215
Smoking Popes, 221
soccer moms, 124
social media, 110, 111, 164, 218
social networks, 94
Society for Ethnomusicology, The (SEM), 23
Solid Rock Records, 39–40, 235
Solid State Records, 147, 208, 210
Solitude/Solitaire (album; Cetera), 255n12
So Long Ago the Garden (album; Norman), 43, 43 fig.
Songbird Records, 73
song lyrics, 102–3
Songs for Christmas (album; Stevens), 206
Sonic Youth, 202
Sony, 16, 67, 77, 85, 91, 195, 249n5. *See also* Provident Music Group
Sony Music Nashville, 251n48
Souled Out (Christian youth club, IL), 17, 18
"Soul Meets Body" (song; Death Cab for Cutie), 204
SoundScan (music sales tracker), 130
South Bend (IN), 141
South by Southwest music festival (Austin, TX), 207
Southern Baptist Convention (SBC), 1, 2, 25, 51, 52–53, 248n57
South Park (TV cartoon series), 222, 263n17

Southwestern Baptist Theological Seminary (Fort Worth, TX), 1, 51
So You Wanna Go Back to Egypt? (album; Green), 62
Sparrow Records: album releases at, 249n80; CCM promoted by, 16; challenges facing, 91; changing priorities at, 77; Christian music as commercial domain of, 36–37; Christian music market and, 34, 118; corporate consolidation of, 70, 71–72; discography, 235–36; distribution agreements of, 195; founding of, 51, 59–60, 68, 101; Green released from contract at, 37–39, 51, 69; growth of, 72–73, 78–79; ministry focus of, 76; musicians recording with, 60, 73, 249n76; ownership changes at, 68, 73–74, 76, 131, 132, 239; secular market partnerships of, 115
Speer Family, 56
Spike (cartoonist), 167
spirituality, 32, 44–45, 185–86
spirituals, 243n3
Spirituals and the Birth of a Black Entertainment Industry (Graham), 243n3
Spotify, 19, 155, 218
stability: back catalog sales and, 216–19; benefits of, 214–15; crossover and, 219–21; nonprofit labels and, 223–26; "selling out" and, 221–23
Stace, April, 20, 23
Stapp, Scott, 263n13
Starflyer 59, 205–6
Star Song Records, 34, 74, 77, 86, 255n7
Steiger International, 224
Stephens, Randall, 97
Sterling, Robert, 106–7
Stevens, Marsha, 110, 111
Stevens, Russ, 110
Stevens, Shadoe, 1
Stevens, Sufjan, 184, 198, 206, 262n33
Still Remains, 17
Stonehill, Randy, 39
Stowe, David, 49
streaming, 7, 19, 70, 218, 249n9
Streck, John, 9–11, 14, 84, 201, 202, 261n5
Stryper, 147, 220, 236
Stump, Joshua, 161–62, 173
style: of Christian music, 117; ethics vs., 94–95, 106, 114; resignified, 169–70; variations in, 138. *See also* aesthetics; "ethics of style"
Styll, John: on Benson leadership changes, 87; as *CCM* editor, 71, 108; on CCM typical consumer, 124; on Christian music as ministry and business, 115; on Christian record industry consolidation, 70–72, 77;

on commerce and Christian music market, 75–76; on crossover, 194; as cultural intermediary, 64; Green interviewed by, 62–63, 75; musicians' ethical transgressions and, 26, 108–9, 111–14; on radio and Christian record industry, 82–83; on record label vs. Christian market needs, 146–47; Swaggart interviewed by, 26, 103–5, 253n39. *See also CCM* magazine
subcultural capital, 203
subculture, 4–5, 192–93, 202–3
Subculture: The Meaning of Style (Hebdige), 169–71
subculture theory, 168–71, 172
Sub Pop, 211
suburbanization, 59
"Sudden" (song; Living Sacrifice), 181
Sufism, 44
Sullivan, Mark, 97
Summer, Donna, 65
Summer of Darkness (album; Demon Hunter), 151
Summer of Love (1967), 57
Sunny Day Real Estate, 220–21
"Superstar" (song; Head), 47
Swaggart, Jimmy, 26, 103–5, 114, 149
Swift, Taylor, 20, 92
swing music, 97
Switchfoot, 130, 219–20

Taff, Russ, 129
Takehold Records, 17, 223
"Takes a Little Time" (song; Grant), 129
Talbot, John Michael, 60
Talbot, Terry, 60
Talbot Brothers, 60, 61–62
Talking Heads, 202
Target, 70
Taylor, Timothy, 7
Taylor University (Upland, IN), 254n48
Tebelak, John-Michael, 247n29
Teen Challenge, 46
Tejano music, 123
televangelists, 26, 103–5
television, 49, 103, 248n44
Tell It Like It Is (youth folk musical; Carmichael and Kaiser), 53
"Thank You" (song; Knapp), 110
This American Life (podcast/radio show), 253n16
Thomas Nelson (publisher), 77
Thomasville (GA), 51–52
Thompson, E. P., 169
Thompson, John J.: on Christian market risk tolerance, 216; on Christian music back

Thompson, John J. (*continued*)
  catalog awareness, 218–19; on Christian vs. secular music, 148; Cornerstone Festival and, 160, 164, 177, 179; as EMI CMG executive, 93, 146; on Norman, 39–40; on radio and Christian record industry, 146; on youth market, 93
Thornton, Sarah, 171, 203
thrash metal, 206
Through a Child's Eyes (album; Herring), 60
Tidal, 218
Timbre, 27, 184–86, 185 fig., 236
Time magazine, 46, 47 fig., 49
Tomlin, Chris, 19, 215
Toms, 83
Tooth & Nail Records: A&R representative at, 149, 223, 224; Carver employed at, 209; Cornerstone Festival and, 160–61, 177–78; crossover artists recording with, 27; crossover strategies of, 27, 147, 206–12; distribution agreements of, 207, 223; founding of, 147, 177, 206, 223; HQs of, 24, 209; musical styles released by, 17, 206; musicians recording with, 148, 177, 186, 206–7; ownership changes at, 207; sublabels of, 208, 210, 223
Top 40 radio, 128; alternative rock and, 197; as artist success metric, 127; author's experience, 1–2; Christian crossover artists on, 16, 205, 219–20; Christian music vs. pop on, 117, 123; crossover and, 222–23; as crossover format, 81–82; gospel music on, 45; Grant songs appearing on, 116, 119, 121, 255n17; Grant songs not appearing on, 122; mass markets and, 3; popular music studies and, 23; racial segregation in, 21; singles referencing Christian beliefs on, 45; typical consumers of, 124. *See also* Christian Contemporary Hit Radio (CHR)
Top Contemporary Christian charts, 119
Tower Records, 57
Toynbee, Jason, 203, 212
"Transfiguration, The" (song; Stevens), 206
transformational artists, 9–11, 201–2
transgender identity, 222
Trinidad, 94–95, 106
True Times News magazine, 66, 159, 164
Turino, Thomas, 20
Twitter, 111

UFOs, 252n15
UMG Nashville, 251n48
Undercover, 177
UnderOath, 17, 191–92, 198, 207–9, 211
"Undo Me" (song; Knapp), 110

Unguarded (album; Grant), 255n7; album cover of, 120 fig., 126; as crossover album, 75–76; hit singles on, 119–21, 195; reactions to, 255n10; success of, 119, 122; Word/A&M partnership and, 119
United States: anti-rock discourse in, 97; Christian bookstores in, 59; Christian culture in, 140; Christian fundamentalism in, 171; Christian identity in, 172, 173–74; Christian music festivals in, 175; Christian music variety in, 35; Christian Right in, 249n86; Christian vs. non-Christian listenerships in, 116; copyright law in, 127–28, 256n30; countercultural Christianity in, 13, 174; evangelicalism and capitalism in, 58; gospel music as indigenous to, 3, 95; homophobia in, 110; material Christianity in, 32–33; music censorship in, 99; political discourse in, 181; racial divide in, 21, 110; recorded music sales as tracked in, 74, 250–51n41; spiritual awakening in, 44–45; Top 40 radio in, 116. *See also* white U.S. evangelical Christians
Universal Music, 67, 68, 69, 91, 131, 195, 210, 251n48
University of Birmingham (England), 169, 172
University of Chicago (IL), 169
Until the Whole World Hears (album; Casting Crowns), 154
Until the Whole World Hears Live (album; Casting Crowns), 155
Upon This Rock (album; Norman), 39, 40–41, 43, 57
Urbana worship conference, 215–16
urbanization, 33
urban oldies stations, 217
U.S. News & World Report magazine, 46
U2, 65, 220, 265n13

Vagrant Records, 262n36
Van Dyke, Vonda Kay, 49, 54
Verve Records, 246n23
Very Next Thing, The (album; Casting Crowns), 155
Victorian aesthetic, 33
Vietnam War protests, 47
Vincent, Gene, 56
Vineyard Christian Fellowship (Los Angeles, CA), 61, 249n79
Violent Femmes, 65
vulnerability, 154–56

Waco (TX), 55
Wagner, Tom, 23, 104–5, 154, 245n3
Wald, Elijah, 23, 24

"Walk This Way" (song; Aerosmith), 197
Wal-Mart, 70, 74, 75, 130
War & Remembrance (album; Petra), 2
Warner Bros.: Christian subsidiaries of, 16, 67, 77, 88–89, 199, 210; corporate consolidation by, 67, 91; crossover and, 195–96, 199–200; indie underground artists recording with, 202; musician ethical transgressions and, 108; musicians recording with, 60. *See also* Word Records
Warner Music Nashville, 251n48
Warnke, Mike, 263n17
Warped Tour, 207, 208, 262n36
Warren, Diane, 255n11
Washington Post, 111
Watergate scandal (1972), 50, 248n48
Weber, Andrew Lloyd, 247n29
Weisbard, Eric, 3, 81–82, 123, 255n11, 255nn19–20, 261n8
Weiss, Aaron, 209
Welch, Brian Head, 220
Welchel, Luke, 167, 176, 179–80, 191
"Well, The" (song; Bazan), 260n50
"We Need a Whole Lot More of Jesus (And a Lot Less Rock and Roll)" (song; Norman), 40, 42
"We Wish You a Merry Christmas" (song; Stevens), 206
"When We Fell" (song; Bazan), 188
White Heart, 2
White Sisters, 56
white Southern gospel music, 16, 108
white supremacy, 190
White Throne magazine, 17, 159
white U.S. evangelical Christians: anti-rock discourse of, 96–97; Bazan and, 192; capitalism and, 33–34, 58–59; Christian metal and, 145–46; conformity demanded by, 17; conservatism of, 192–93; Cornerstone Festival and, 165, 176; counterpublic response to, 192–93; Jesus music and, 40, 102; as "marginalized," 174; media diet of, 91–92; musicians critical of, 189–91; musicians' ethical transgressions and, 110; older generations of, 174; popular music normalized among, 102; as subculture, 168, 171–72
Whitmore, Aleysia, 7
Whole (EP; Pedro the Lion), 186
"Why Don't You Look into Jesus?" (song; Norman), 256n3
"Why Should the Devil Have All the Good Music" (song; Norman), 41–42
Wild Goose Festival (NC), 189
Wilkerson, David, 46
Williams, Don, 46

Williams, Raymond, 169
Williams, Vanessa, 128
Williamson, John, 7
Willis, Paul E., 169
Wilson, Woodrow, 13–14
Wilson Abbey (Chicago, IL), 164
Wilson Phillips (vocal trio), 116
Wings, 220
witchcraft, 252n15
witnessing, 48
"Wonderful Time up There, A" (song; Boone), 45
Woodstock (1969), 57
Word Entertainment, 16, 67, 239
word-of-mouth, 17
Word Records: changing priorities at, 85, 88–89; Christian music as commercial domain of, 36–37; Christian music market and, 80; conservatism of, 146; crossover attempts by, 131, 195, 199–201, 207; distribution agreements of, 195; founding of, 55, 67; Mays employed at, 86, 87, 124; musicians recording with, 55–56, 107, 118, 195, 256n27; ownership changes at, 67, 70, 76–77, 88–89, 199, 210, 249n5, 254n5; Peterson employed at, 109, 177, 199; secular market partnerships of, 118, 119, 129; subsidiaries of, 34, 199, 255n7; youth-marketing strategies at, 51, 53–54, 57–58
working class, 33
World Vision (humanitarian organization), 83, 84, 210
World War I, 33
World War II, 14, 33, 59
worship music, 215–16
worship wars, 20
"Writing on the Walls" (song; UnderOath), 207–8

Yakus, Shelly, 255n14
York, Peter, 68, 74
Young, Neil, 41, 218
Young, Shawn David, 176, 192–93
"You're in Love" (song; Wilson Phillips), 116
"Your Love Broke Through" (song; Green), 60
youth, 162–63
youth camps, 171
youth cultures, 172–73, 180
Youth for Christ International, 15, 46
youth musicals, 102
YouTube, 155–56, 218

Z100 (radio station; New York, NY), 1–2
Zanfagna, Christina, 244n45
Zombies, The, 39
Zondervan (publisher), 77, 87, 250n32

Founded in 1893,
UNIVERSITY OF CALIFORNIA PRESS
publishes bold, progressive books and journals
on topics in the arts, humanities, social sciences,
and natural sciences—with a focus on social
justice issues—that inspire thought and action
among readers worldwide.

The UC PRESS FOUNDATION
raises funds to uphold the press's vital role
as an independent, nonprofit publisher, and
receives philanthropic support from a wide
range of individuals and institutions—and from
committed readers like you. To learn more, visit
ucpress.edu/supportus.

www.ingramcontent.com/pod-product-compliance
Lightning Source LLC
Chambersburg PA
CBHW021337230426
43666CB00006B/320